CONSTRUCTION LAW

PRINCIPLES AND PRACTICE

McGraw-Hill Series in Construction Engineering and Project Management

Consulting Editor: Raymond E. Levitt (Stanford University)

Barrie and Paulson: Professional Construction Management
Douglas: Construction Equipment Policy
Jervis and Levin: Construction Law: Principles and Practice
Koerner: Construction and Geotechnical Methods in Foundation Engineering
Levitt and Samelson: Construction Safety Management
Parker and Oglesby: Methods Improvement for Construction Managers
Peurifoy and Ledbetter: Construction Planning, Equipment, and Methods
Shuttleworth: Mechanical and Electrical Systems for Construction

CONSTRUCTION LAW

PRINCIPLES AND PRACTICE

Bruce M. Jervis
Amerling & Burns, P. A.

Paul Levin
WPL Associates, Inc.

McGraw-Hill Book Company

New York   St. Louis   San Francisco   Auckland   Bogotá
Hamburg   London   Madrid   Mexico   Milan   Montreal   New Delhi
Panama   Paris   São Paulo   Singapore   Sydney   Tokyo   Toronto

This book was set in Times Roman
by the College Composition Unit
in cooperation with Black Dot, Inc.
The editor was B. J. Clark;
the production supervisor was Denise L. Puryear.
Project supervision was done by The Total Book.
R. R. Donnelley & Sons Company was printer and binder.

CONSTRUCTION LAW: PRINCIPLES AND PRACTICE

1 2 3 4 5 6 7 8 9 0   DOCDOC   8 9 2 1 0 9 8 7

ISBN 0-07-037442-2

Library of Congress Cataloging-in-Publication Data

Jervis, Bruce M.
    Construction law, principles and practice.

    Bibliography: p.
    Includes index.
    1. Building—Contracts and specifications—United
States. 2. Construction industry—Law and legislation—
United States. 3. Liability (Law)—United States.
I. Levin, Paul, (date). II. Title.
KF902.J47 1988   343.73'07869   87-22812
ISBN 0-07-037442-2 347.3037869

ABOUT THE AUTHORS

Bruce M. Jervis received his B.A. (1972) from Hobart College in Geneva, New York, and his J.D. (1977) from the University of Maine School of Law in Portland, Maine. He served as staff attorney for a large engineering firm prior to joining the Portland, Maine, law firm of Amerling & Burns, P.A. in 1980. The firm's practice concentrates on construction contract negotiation and litigation on behalf of contractors, project owners, and design professionals throughout the New England region.

Mr. Jervis is the founding editor of the widely accepted newsletter *Construction Claims Monthly*, published by Business Publishers, Inc. of Silver Spring, Maryland. He has edited the publication since its formation in 1979. He also edits *Federal Contract Disputes*, published by Business Publishers, Inc., and the *Construction Claims Citator*, published by Construction Industry Press of San Rafael, California.

Mr. Jervis is a member of the Maine State Bar Association, the American Bar Association, the ABA Forum Committee on the Construction Industry, and the ABA Section of Public Contract Law.

Paul Levin received his B.S. in civil engineering (1969) from the University of Maryland in College Park, Maryland, and his masters of engineering administration in construction management (1977) from George Washington University in Washington, D.C.

From 1969 to 1978, Mr. Levin served in technical and management positions for several major construction companies and engineering firms. Since 1978, he has engaged in extensive lecturing, consulting, and publishing for the construction industry, with an emphasis on the application of computers to construction administration.

Mr. Levin is the author of the widely used construction handbook *Claims and Changes*, published by WPL Associates, Inc. of Silver Spring, Maryland. He is also the founding editor of *Construction Computer Applications Newsletter* and *Construction Computer Applications Directory*, both published by Construction Industry Press of San Rafael, California.

CONTENTS

PREFACE

It is hard to imagine a more challenging undertaking than a construction project. The process is physically complex. It must be designed in such a way that thousands of separate pieces can be fabricated, installed, and connected to create a complete, functioning structure.

The construction process defies standardization. Unlike the manufacturing process, it is difficult to benefit from rote repetition. Every site is different and every structure, to some extent, is unique. The process is one of ongoing adaptation and innovation. Even the most carefully detailed design can be affected by an unanticipated ledge, the bankruptcy of a key supplier, or changes in the financial markets.

A successful construction project requires a vast array of disparate skills possessed by individuals with very different roles and backgrounds. Yet these individuals don't work for a single company. They work for a network of design professionals, contractors, subcontractors, suppliers, lenders, bonding companies, and consultants. Each makes a commitment through a contract with one particular party, but has no agreement with numerous other parties with whom the work must be coordinated.

It is not surprising, then, that the construction industry has gained a reputation for being contentious and prone to litigation. The potential for honest misunderstanding is enormous. In order to function professionally on today's construction project, one must be able to recognize and diagnose problems as they evolve and apply the appropriate principles in order to avoid or resolve the problems.

This book is designed to provide the reader with a fundamental professional skill: an understanding of the principles and applications of construction law. An attentive reader should come away having achieved four basic objectives:

1. An understanding of the numerous contractual relationships that exist on a construction project.

2. A recognition of the basic varieties of claims and disputes that may arise.

3. An understanding of the basic legal principles which are used to avoid or resolve construction disputes.

4. An appreciation of the practical considerations involved in addressing relationships on a construction project. There is nothing worse than one who is learned in the letter of the law, but oblivious to the ultimate goal: a successfully completed construction project.

This book is not a legal treatise for attorneys. Nor is it a claims manual for people in the field. It is a presentation of basic legal principles within the context of the actual situations in which they are applied. It is dedicated to the enhanced professionalism of the participants in tomorrow's construction projects.

We would like to express our thanks for the many useful comments and suggestions provided by colleagues who reviewed this text during the course of its development, especially to James Diekmann, University of Colorado; Raymond Levitt, Stanford University, and Dohn A. Mehlenbacher, Illinois Institute of Technology.

Bruce M. Jervis
Paul Levin

CONSTRUCTION
LAW
PRINCIPLES AND PRACTICE

CHAPTER 1

CONTRACT PRINCIPLES AND THE CONSTRUCTION PROJECT

CONTRACT FORMATION

Mutual Consent

There is nothing mysterious about how contracts are created. When two parties mutually agree to a transaction, a contract is formed.

This mutual agreement must apply to all significant, or "material," aspects of the arrangement. For instance, if a developer and a contractor agree that the contractor will perform certain construction work and be paid by the developer, but they fail to establish a price, a contract has not yet been created. But once the basic ingredients of the transaction have been agreed upon, a "contract" exists.

It is important to note that although the written document is commonly referred to as "the contract," it is really nothing more than evidence of the mutual intentions of the parties. It is the mutual consent that creates a contract, not the signatures on a piece of paper. The written document is very powerful evidence of the terms of the agreement, however, as the law limits the use of subsequent oral testimony or explanation to establish the terms of the agreement.

If a written contract is clear and unambiguous in its terms, those terms cannot be challenged by one party's explanation of what it thought the contract meant or what it had been led to believe the contract meant. The express written terms of the contract will govern the relationship regardless of any misunderstanding on the part of one of the parties.

If a provision of the contract is ambiguous, however, courts will allow the use of oral testimony to try to establish the mutual intent of the parties. In this situation, it will be permissible for one or both of the parties to explain what they thought the contract meant and why the contract was written the way it was. Obviously, it is preferable to use clear, explicit language which is not subject to differing interpretations. The primary purpose of reducing agreements to writing is to avoid misunderstanding and avoid the need for parties to explain what they thought the agreement was.

When faced with ambiguous provisions in a contract, courts also look to the conduct of the parties. Actual conduct on the project is far more persuasive evidence of a party's intent and understanding than any self-serving statements of understanding. For instance, if contractors proceed to perform work in a certain manner without objection, it is difficult for them to later argue that this work was over and beyond what was required by the contract.

There is another aspect of contract formation which is particularly important in the construction industry. This is the doctrine of incorporation by reference. Documents outside the body of the written contract may be made a part of the contract simply by reference. The most common device is to refer to a document which is "attached hereto and made a part hereof." The terms of that document are then just as binding as any of the terms and conditions contained in the body of the contract.

Although it is preferred practice to physically attach any documents incorporated by reference into a contract, it is not necessary. The mere explicit reference, without any physical attachment, is sufficient to make an external document a binding part of the agreement. On public contracts, it is common to reference a number of regulations and standard specifications which are not attached to the contract. It is also common for contractors to ignore these provisions. Nonetheless, they are just as much a part of the contract as the provisions printed out in full.

Offer and Acceptance

In order to reach the point where the parties have mutually agreed to the terms of a contract, it is necessary for one party to make an offer and the other to accept. While this sounds rather straightforward, it is not always easy to identify an offer and an acceptance and establish that point at which agreement has been reached.

The challenge is to distinguish negotiations from a firm offer which is subject to acceptance. If an offeror states all the basic elements of a contract such as price, schedule, and scope of work, it is subject to a binding acceptance. If it lacks one or more of the essential elements, it will be considered mere negotiations and will not be subject to acceptance.

Acceptance is accomplished simply by stating, "I accept your offer." A contract has then been formed, and it is too late for the offeror to change its mind.

It is important to note at this point that oral agreements are binding. Each state has a so-called statute of frauds which requires certain types of contracts to be in writing. These statutes generally pertain to things such as the sale of real estate or contracts which cannot possibly be performed in less than 2 years. Generally speaking, they do not apply to construction contracts. The case books are full of court decisions holding that oral construction contracts are enforceable against both parties.

As a practical matter, only agreements for very small projects are likely to be oral, and it is a bad practice even then. The type of project a professional architect or engineer is likely to be involved with will almost certainly be documented in writing.

The concepts of offer and acceptance become somewhat confusing in the context of the competitive bidding process, however. The competitive bidding system will be covered in detail in Chapter 3, but it is important to consider it now in terms of offer and acceptance.

When a project owner, public or private, solicits bids on a contract, this is not considered an offer to award a contract. It is simply an invitation to contractors to submit offers. Once the bids, or offers, are received, the owner may elect to accept one.

Another question that frequently arises regarding construction contracts is the duration of the offer. On competitively bid jobs, the bid solicitation frequently states that all bids must be firm and irrevocable for a stated period of time, usually 60 days. During that period the bidder may not withdraw or alter its bid. The bid is an offer which is subject to acceptance at any time until the offer expires.

On negotiated projects, the terms of the offer and the time and method of acceptance are less clear than with competitively bid work. Private project owners sometimes do put a contract out to bid in a manner similar to that used in the public sector. More commonly, however, the private project owner simply asks two or three contractors to price the work. If the prices come in too high, the scope of work is reduced. There is considerable give and take in arriving at terms that are mutually acceptable.

The informality of contract negotiation sometimes leads to the problem that was mentioned earlier. Was the contractor's proposal sufficiently specific on the basic, material aspects of the project to constitute an offer which was subject to acceptance? Did the owner accept the offer or simply make a counter-proposal? How long did the contractor's offer stay open?

Private project owners can avoid these uncertainties by establishing more formal procedures for awarding contracts. Private project owners sometimes avoid anything that looks like formal competitive bidding because they fear they will become subject to the rigid rules that apply to public project owners. These rules will be discussed in Chapter 3.

Actually, private project owners may solicit bids while maintaining as much flexibility as they want to reject bids, refuse to award the contract to the low bidder, or change the scope of work. By establishing a formal structure for bid submittal, however, they will avoid the confusion and uncertainty that arise when contracts are negotiated on a very informal basis.

Consideration

In addition to offer and acceptance, the third necessary ingredient for a binding contract is "consideration." Consideration is simply something of value that each party furnishes. Without mutual consideration, there can be no enforceable contract.

Fifty years ago, the issue of consideration frequently came up when addressing the enforceability of contracts. Was the consideration sufficient? Did consideration flow each way?

Today, consideration is seldom addressed and there is little reason to be concerned about it. It is well recognized that mutual promises are sufficient to form a binding contract. No money need change hands. There is no need for recitations such as "for one dollar and other valuable consideration."

In the context of construction contracting, consideration is almost always provided in the form of reciprocal promises. The contractor promises to furnish the labor and materials necessary to construct a well-defined structure. In return, the project owner promises to pay the contractor a certain amount of money. Period. It is not even necessary to recite that the agreement is executed "in consideration of the mutual promises contained herein." That is self-evident.

In the absence of some form of fraud, courts will not get involved in examining the sufficiency of the consideration or the "fairness" of the transaction. Commercial enterprises are presumed to be familiar with the terms of the agreements they sign, and they will be held to those agreements. If hindsight proves the agreement to be foolhardy, that is the risk the party assumed when signing the agreement.

BREACH OF CONTRACT

Material versus Immaterial Breach

A breach of contract is of course a violation of one or more of the terms and conditions of that contract. The concept of "material" versus "immaterial" breach becomes important because it determines what the nonbreaching party may or may not do.

A breach is material if it involves one of the vital aspects of the agreement. A breach is immaterial if it involves a less important aspect of the agreement. A contractor's failure to show up at the job site for week after week would almost surely be considered a material breach. The contractor's failure to clean up the job site at the end of the day would be considered immaterial.

The significance of this distinction is that a material breach of contract will justify a default termination of the contract and a suit for damages. An immaterial breach will not justify a termination but will simply entitle the nonbreaching party to some form of financial compensation.

For instance, if the project owner is forced to clean the job site with its own forces, it will be entitled to set off this cost against the money owed the contractor for performance of the construction work. It is unlikely, however, that a court would allow the owner to simply kick the contractor off the job for failure to clean at the end of the day.

The application of this material versus immaterial distinction is one of the more difficult aspects of construction contracting. Everyone agrees that the owner's obligation to make payment is material to the contract. But if the owner is a week late in making a monthly progress payment, is this a material breach which would entitle the contractor to walk off the job? Probably not. If the owner consistently fails to make progress payments, however, it probably would be a material breach.

From the owner's standpoint, if a contractor falls a week behind schedule on a 6-month project, is this a material breach? Despite the fact that "time is of the essence" on a construction contract, it probably is not. If 90 percent of the performance period had elapsed and the contractor had completed only 50 percent of the work, however, it probably would be a material breach.

These issues will be discussed in greater detail in future chapters. No black letter rules will be stated, however, for it is always a judgment call as to

---

CASE STUDY 1-1

Contractor awarded subcontract calling for monthly progress payments. Contractor then refused to pay Subcontractor until Subcontractor's work was complete.

Subcontractor refused to perform any more work on the grounds that it was not being paid. Contractor claimed the refusal to work was a breach of the subcontract.

The Appellate Court of Connecticut ruled that Contractor's failure to make progress payments was a material breach of the subcontract, as payment was fundamental to the purpose of the agreement. Contractor's material breach justified Subcontractor's refusal to perform. Subcontractor was not liable for breach of the subcontract.

Silliman Company v. S. Ippolito & Sons, Inc., 467 A.2d 1249 (Conn.App. 1983).

whether or not a breach is material. For now, it is sufficient to understand the practical ramifications of this distinction.

If a contractor treats an owner's breach as material and walks off the job, and if it is subsequently determined that the owner's breach was not material, then it will be the contractor, not the owner, who is the breaching party liable for damages. Conversely, if an owner treats a contractor's breach as material and orders the contractor off the job, and if it is subsequently determined that the contractor's breach was not material, it is the owner who will have breached the contract.

Termination of the Contract

In an effort to impose some order and predictability on the breach of contract issue, most construction contracts contain a termination clause. This clause typically attempts to define those shortcomings of the owner which would justify the contractor's work stoppage. The clause also requires that the owner be given written notice of the alleged breach and a certain period of time to "cure" the breach. In this way, the damaging effects of a sudden work stoppage may be avoided.

A termination clause also defines the owner's right to terminate the contract. This right will be discussed in detail in Chapter 5. For now, it is sufficient to understand the distinction between an owner's termination of a contractor for default and a termination for convenience.

A termination for default is based on a contractor's material breach of contract, as defined in the termination clause. It basically allows the owner to terminate the contractor with little or no notice and hold the contractor liable for any increased cost of completing the project.

A termination for convenience is a contractual right the owner can exercise

---

CASE STUDY 1-2

Owner was dissatisfied with the quality of Contractor's workmanship. Owner took the position that the poor workmanship was a material breach of contract which justified a change in the payment terms of the contract.

The Court of Appeals of Indiana disagreed. Given the complexity of a construction project, it would be unfair to treat every defect in the workmanship as a material breach of contract. Contractor was entitled to notice of the problem and a reasonable opportunity to correct it.

Defective workmanship is an immaterial breach of contract unless and until Contractor fails to correct the problem after a reasonable opportunity to do so. At that point it becomes a material breach of contract.

Burras v. Canal Construction and Design Co., 470 N.E.2d 1362 (Ind.App. 1984).

to terminate a contractor even though the contractor is in full compliance with the contract requirements. As the name implies, this right can be exercised for any reason or none at all. Most commonly, it is exercised because of problems the owner encounters with project financing.

Unlike a default termination, a termination for convenience obligates the owner to compensate the contractor. Contracts vary in terms of the costs a terminated contractor may recover. At a minimum, however, the contractor is usually entitled to be paid for the labor and materials furnished prior to the effective date of the termination. Additionally, the owner is usually required to provide advance written notice of a termination for convenience.

Termination clauses will be discussed in greater detail later. These clauses do not provide all the answers in determining when a material breach has occurred and what may be done about it, but they do furnish some order and predictability to what is one of the most difficult issues in construction contracting.

Remedies for Breach of Contract

A nonbreaching party has three basic choices when faced with a breach of contract. It may excuse the breach, elect to rescind the contract, or terminate the contract for default and sue for damages.

If a party overlooks, or excuses, a breach, that party runs the risk of having waived that particular contract requirement. For instance, if a project owner consistently ignores a contractor's slow performance and makes no effort to enforce the contractual schedule, it may be ruled that the owner waived the right to enforce the schedule.

A nonbreaching party may protect itself when excusing a breach by stating in writing that it is excusing this one limited breach for this one time only and it is not its intent to waive any requirement of the contract. Any time a party elects to overlook a breach, it should exercise forethought and document the particular instance in writing.

Rescission is more a trap for the unwary than an actual remedy for breach of contract. If the nonbreaching party elects to rescind the contract, it is basically saying that, owing to the other party's material breach, the nonbreaching party now considers the contract to be of no legal force or effect.

If a contract is rescinded, it no longer exists; so the nonbreaching party loses the right to sue for damages under the contract. This is seldom a desirable result.

If a nonbreaching party wishes to express its displeasure with the other party's performance, it is important to state that it considers the other party to be in breach of the contract. It is dangerous to state that one considers the contract "null and void" or, worse yet, "rescinded."

The most common remedy for a nonbreaching party is to elect to terminate the contract for default and sue for damages. The measure of damages for breach of contract is discussed in the next section.

DAMAGES FOR BREACH OF CONTRACT

Compensatory Damages

The purpose of awarding damages for breach of contract is to put the non-breaching party in the same position it would have been in but for the breach. With this principle in mind, most of the rules regarding damages for breach are simply common sense.

As the name indicates, compensatory damages compensate the nonbreaching party for the losses caused by the breach. For a project owner whose contractor has breached, there are two basic methods of computing compensatory damages.

The most common method is "cost of completion." If the contractor is terminated for failing to complete the project in accordance with the terms of the contract, the project owner will be forced to bring in a new contractor to complete the work. If the new contractor charges a higher price, the breaching contractor will be liable for the difference.

Expressed as a formula, the owner's damages would be the amount paid to the original contractor prior to breach plus the amount paid to the replacement contractor for completing the work minus the original contract price. For example, if the original contract price was $100,000 and the contractor was paid $30,000 prior to its breach and the replacement contractor charged $80,000 to complete the project, the breaching contractor would owe the project owner $10,000. This would leave the owner with the benefit of the bargain it made with the original contractor: a completed project that cost $100,000.

If the work is being performed on a cost-plus basis rather than a lump-sum basis, the computation of compensatory damages becomes more difficult. The same principle applies. An amount must be computed that leaves the owner with the benefit of its original bargain.

Sometimes, however, it is not appropriate to apply the cost of completion method of computing damages, particularly when the breach results from defective rather than incomplete work. If the cost of ripping out and replacing defective work amounts to a large percentage of the cost of the entire project, courts will refuse to use the cost of completion method. If this procedure would amount to "economic waste," courts will instead measure damages according to the "diminution of fair market value."

Under this method, the fair market value of what was actually built will be subtracted from the fair market value of the project as originally contracted for. Again, the principle is to give the owner the benefit of its bargain. While the owner won't end up with what it originally contracted for, the contract price will be reduced to reflect the lower value of what was actually provided.

When the owner breaches a contract, the measure of the contractor's damages is somewhat more complex, although the same principle governs. The contractor is awarded the contract price for all work performed prior to the owner's breach plus the profit the contractor reasonably anticipated on the remainder of the work which it was denied the opportunity to perform. Once again, the purpose is to put the contractor in the position it would have been in but for the breach by the owner.

Computation of the contractor's damages becomes more complex when the owner's breach causes the contractor to perform work which was outside the scope of the original contract or causes the contractor to remain on the job longer than originally planned.

As described earlier, these problems are usually handled under the terms of the contract itself as claims against the contract rather than an action for breach of contract. In that case, the price adjustment for the contractor will be established by the terms of the contract. As subsequent chapters address different types of claims, the method of establishing the price adjustment will also be discussed.

Foreseeability

When compensating the nonbreaching party for the loss of its bargain, it is sometimes difficult to determine the extent of the benefits bargained for. For instance, if a contractor fails to complete a project, it is easy to see that the owner should be awarded the additional cost of completion.

If the contractor's breach causes the owner's project to be completed later than it otherwise would have been, it seems logical to award the owner the increased cost of its construction loan. If the late completion causes the owner to lose rental income it otherwise would have received, it seems logical to award the owner its lost rent.

But if the late completion causes the owner to lose credibility in the business community and damages the owner's future business prospects, should the contractor pay for this as well? It is not always easy to determine the point at which damages should be cut off.

This is where the doctrine of "foreseeability" comes in. The rule is that damages for breach of contract will be limited to the cost of the consequences

---

CASE STUDY 1-3

Subcontractor performed work on a commercial building project. Contractor refused to pay. Subcontractor sued to recover compensatory damages.

The Appeals Court of Massachusetts ruled that there are two ways of measuring compensatory damages for a builder who has not been paid as promised.

The unpaid builder may recover the contract price less the cost of completion that would have been incurred if the builder had completed its work.

Alternatively, the builder may recover the fair market value, not to exceed the contract price, of the work performed prior to the builder's justified cessation of work.

Jeremiah Sullivan & Sons, Inc. v. Kay-Locke, Inc., 458 N.E.2d 837 (Mass.App. 1984).

that were reasonably foreseeable at the time the contract was signed. Applying this rule to the example above, lost rent would be recoverable, but lost business prospects would not.

Although the foreseeability rule is quite easy to state, its application varies widely from case to case and state to state. At a minimum, however, it places some limitation on the damages for which a breaching party can be held liable.

It should also be mentioned at this point that punitive damages generally do not apply to breach of contract. While civil law may seek to deter dangerous driving by assessing punitive damages against someone who is grossly or outrageously irresponsible in the operation of a motor vehicle, this doctrine has no place in construction contracting. The law will only seek to make the nonbreaching party whole, and this is accomplished through the award of compensable damages.

Liquidated Damages

There is one form of damages that is more widely used in construction contracts than other types of agreements. This is "liquidated damages."

Liquidated damages will be discussed in greater detail in Chapter 7, but should be mentioned at this point. Liquidated damages apply to the contractor's late completion of the project. As discussed earlier, it is frequently hard to measure the actual damages that flow from a contractor's late completion. In order to avoid this problem, the parties stipulate in the contract a liquidated sum, usually expressed on a per diem basis, that will be assessed against the contractor for late completion.

The general rule is that liquidated damages are enforceable if it would be difficult to measure the actual damages and if the liquidated damage amount reflects a reasonable, good faith effort to estimate the actual damages that might result from late completion. The fact that the actual damages turn out to be more or less than the liquidated amount does not affect the enforceability of the liquidated damages clause.

If the liquidated damage amount is set with no regard for what the actual

---

CASE STUDY 1-4

Owner awarded highway construction contract to Contractor. Owner made irregular progress payments, violating the terms of the contract.

Contractor experienced severe cash-flow problems and went out of business.

Contractor sued Owner for the destruction of the business.

The Commonwealth Court of Pennsylvania denied the claim, saying that the destruction of an entire business is simply not a foreseeable result of the failure to make timely progress payments. Therefore, these were not recoverable consequential damages.

Commonwealth, Dept. of Transportation v. Cumberland Construction Co.,
494 A.2d 520 (Pa.Cmwlth. 1985).

damages might be, however, the provision will be subject to attack as a penalty. If the liquidated damage amount is unreasonably large and serves only to intimidate the contractor and punish the contractor for late completion, it will not be enforceable.

Finally, it should be noted that if a contract contains a liquidated damages clause, that will serve as the owner's sole remedy for the contractor's late completion. The owner cannot waive the liquidated damages clause and attempt to recover its actual damages. However, liquidated damages apply only to late completion. The owner will still be entitled to recover its actual damages for breaches other than late completion; for instance, faulty workmanship.

CONTRACTUAL RELATIONSHIPS ON THE CONSTRUCTION PROJECT

Figure 1-1 indicates the contractual relationships that customarily exist on a traditional construction project. The solid lines reflect a direct contractual relationship. The dotted lines reflect obligations that exist between parties who do not have a direct contractual relationship. The diagram should be referred to during the following discussion of the roles of the various parties on a traditional construction project.

General (or Prime) Contractor

On a traditional construction project, there is only one construction contractor who has a direct, or "prime," contract with the project owner. Customarily, this contractor is referred to as the "general contractor."

FIGURE 1-1
Contractual relationships on a traditional construction project.

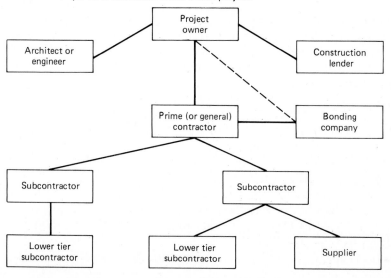

The role of the general contractor is easy to state and hard to accomplish. The general contractor is responsible for completing the entire project in strict accordance with the plans and specifications and terms and conditions of the construction contract.

The general contractor need not perform all the construction work with its own forces, of course. It is customary to subcontract out much of the work. On certain types of projects the general contractor must perform most of the work itself in order to offer a competitive price. On other types of projects, the general contractor functions almost as a broker and administrator. Sometimes the terms of the prime contract require the general contractor to perform a certain percentage of the work with its own forces.

Regardless of how the general contractor elects to accomplish the work, the general contractor is fully responsible to the owner for the sufficiency of the work. If a subcontractor or supplier fails to adhere to the specifications or schedule, the project owner does not need to deal with that sub or supplier. The general contractor is the sole source of responsibility. This is part of what the project owner pays for.

The general contractor's responsibilities also include the scheduling and coordination of all purchasing and all construction work. Slow performance or slow delivery by a sub or supplier will not serve as an excuse in the general contractor's dealings with the owner.

Another important, and risky, aspect of the general contractor's duties is responsibility for overall job site safety. While contracts and subcontracts address this issue in various ways, courts have generally ruled that the degree of control over the job site that is granted to the general contractor carries a commensurate degree of responsibility to maintain safe working conditions.

Subcontractors and Suppliers

The role of the subcontractor is to perform certain aspects of the construction work pursuant to a contract with the prime contractor. Typically, subcontracts are awarded according to certain traditional trades within the construction industry such as plumbing; heating, ventilation, and air conditioning (HVAC); earthwork; and foundation.

The specialized nature of subcontractors' work, combined with the fact that they have no direct agreement with the project owner, gives rise to some difficult legal issues and some challenging considerations. These will be addressed in Chapter 10.

Sometimes subcontractors in turn subcontract out a portion of their work. The recipients of these contracts are commonly referred to in the industry as sub-subcontractors, although they may be more artfully referred to as "lower tier subcontractors." As with the general contractor, a subcontractor who assigns a portion of its duties to another retains full responsibility for the sufficiency of the other's work.

Suppliers furnish materials and equipment, as opposed to labor and construction services, to the project. Most suppliers have a contract with a sub-contractor. Many suppliers contract directly with the general contractor, however, particularly if they are furnishing a major item of equipment or material.

Agreements with suppliers are typically in the form of purchase orders rather than construction contracts. A number of important legal ramifications stem from this distinction, as will be discussed in Chapter 10.

Architect/Engineer

Of all the parties on a construction project, the architect or engineer (commonly referred to as A/E) has the longest span of involvement next to the project owner.

Typically, the A/E is retained by the owner when the project is nothing more than an idea or concept. The A/E may assist the owner in evaluating the feasibility of the project and in establishing a realistic budget. The planning phase may also include evaluation of potential sites and preparation of materials to be presented to construction lenders and investors.

The design phase of the project is usually the sole responsibility of the A/E. With the assistance of specialized consultants such as structural engineers and soils and foundation engineers, the A/E develops the plans and specifications which define the structure that is to be constructed. This process evolves from preliminary or schematic drawings to actual working drawings which are sufficiently detailed to guide the contractor in the performance of its work.

When the design is complete, the A/E assists the project owner with selection of a contractor or the conducting of a competitive bidding procedure. If bids exceed the budget, the A/E may redesign portions of the project to make it feasible.

Once construction work begins, the A/E is frequently the owner's representative who monitors the contractor's progress, examines the work for compliance with the plans and specifications, and authorizes the release of payments. The A/E also may have administrative responsibilities on the owner's behalf during the construction phase. When the project is complete, it is the A/E who observes the work, certifies completion, and authorizes release of final payment to the contractor.

It should be noted that the A/E does not always have responsibilities during every phase of the project. For instance, an owner may hire an A/E strictly for planning and budget purposes. It is common, however, for the same A/E to work on a project from initial planning to completion of construction. A good argument can be made that it is desirable for the same A/E who designed a project to monitor the construction of that project. As will be discussed in Chapter 4, however, there are also countervailing arguments.

Chapter 4 will go into detail regarding the legal rights and responsibilities of design professionals. There is one point that needs to be stressed at the outset, however.

The schematic drawing shown earlier indicates that the A/E has a contract solely with the project owner. A generation ago, this meant that the A/E answered only to the owner and could be held accountable only to the owner. Changing legal doctrine now subjects the A/E to potential liability to contractors, subcontractors, bonding companies, and construction lenders, as well as the A/E's client, the owner. No party on the construction project walks as much of a tightrope as the A/E.

This new legal climate has changed the way A/Es must practice their profession. It poses new challenges and new demands. Technical excellence is no longer sufficient. A familiarity with the administrative and legal aspects of the design and construction process is now essential.

Bonding Company

The bonding company, or "surety," enters into contracts with the contractor. These contracts, called "bonds," run to the benefit of the project owner and the subcontractors and suppliers. The bonds do not benefit the contractor but are usually required by the project owner as one of the terms of the construction contract.

There are two basic types of bonds. Performance bonds, which will be discussed in Chapter 5, guarantee that the contractor will complete the project in accordance with the terms and conditions of the contract. If the prime contractor fails to perform its work, the project owner is entitled to call upon the bonding company to have the work completed. If the total cost exceeds the original contract price, the bonding company is responsible for the difference.

Prime contractors frequently require that their key subcontractors furnish performance bonds. These bonds run to the benefit of the prime contractor and offer the same kind of protection that the project owner derives from the prime contractor's performance bond.

Payment bonds, which are covered in Chapter 9, also provide contractual protection for which the prime contractor pays the bonding company. As with performance bonds, the protection of the payment bond runs to the benefit of other parties. In this case, the benefit is derived by the subcontractors and suppliers, as well as the project owner.

A payment bond guarantees that if the prime contractor fails to pay its subcontractors or suppliers, those subs and suppliers can call upon the bonding company to make payment. This obviously benefits the subs and suppliers. It also benefits the project owner, who is protected against double payment and the assertion of liens against its property. It is for this reason that owners customarily require the prime contractor to furnish a payment bond.

Construction Lender

The least visible member of the construction team provides an indispensable ingredient: capital. The construction lender enters into an agreement with the project owner to provide the financing necessary to build the project. Once construction is complete, the financing is converted to a conventional long-term mortgage.

Although the construction lender contracts only with the project owner, its presence is felt by every other party on the project. The flow of funds from owner to prime contractor to subcontractors and suppliers is dependent on the disbursement of loan proceeds by the lender.

As the loan is secured by a mortgage on the project itself, the lender is careful not to release funds in an amount that exceeds the value of the work in place. This gives rise to a good deal of tension, as the lender's evaluation of the work in place tends to be more conservative than that of the contractor. The A/E is one of the parties who is in the middle of these disputes. These issues will be discussed in greater detail in Chapter 4.

Other Forms of Project Organization

The schematic diagram shown earlier is based on the traditional method of organizing a construction project. In recent years, new methods of organizing projects have evolved.

Sometimes the prime contractor offers the owner a complete "design/build" package and then hires the A/E as a subcontractor. Sometimes the project owner awards as many as six or eight prime contracts and hires the A/E to coordinate the work and administer the project.

These evolving forms of construction contracting will be discussed in Chapter 11. While it is important to keep in mind that these alternative methods exist, the traditional structure reflected in the schematic diagram is still far and away the prevalent one. The discussions in this book assume the existence of traditional relationships among the parties. And the legal principles are just as applicable to the novel forms of contracting that are covered in Chapter 11.

KEY TERMS AND CONCEPTS

offer   Promise to do something in exchange for a price.

acceptance   Assent to the exact terms of the offer, thereby creating a contract.

consideration   Something of value. Some form of consideration must be furnished by each party to the contract. Consideration may be a promise to perform in the future or a promise to pay.

competitive bidding   A process whereby a project owner requests offers, known as bids, from contractors and, at its discretion, accepts an offer.

breach of contract   A failure to honor one's obligations under a contract.

material breach   A breach which relates to a fundamental purpose of the contract and entitles the other party to cease performance and recover damages.

immaterial breach   A breach which is not sufficiently serious to warrant cessation of performance by the other party but does entitle the other party to damages.

termination   The contractually established right to end the contractual relationship under certain specified circumstances.

compensatory damages   The cost of completing or correcting improperly performed work or the diminished value of the project resulting from improperly performed work.

consequential damages   Indirect losses caused by breach of the contract. These damages are recoverable if they were reasonably foreseeable at the time the contract was formed.

liquidated damages   A contractually stipulated amount to be paid for a particular breach of contract.

THE CONTRACT DOCUMENTS

THE AGREEMENT

There is no particular form of agreement which is required to create a construction contract. As discussed in Chapter 1, a binding agreement can even be created by an oral offer and acceptance.

Despite the lack of any rigid requirements for a particular format, the custom of the construction industry has evolved to the point where most contracts follow a fairly predictable format and consist of certain standard parts.

The "agreement" itself is usually the shortest document of all the contract documents. It establishes the essential elements of the contract which vary from project to project. These elements are price, payment, and schedule.

Price

There are several methods of establishing the price that the project owner will pay the prime contractor for the work. The most common is a so-called lump-sum price. As its name implies, this is just a stated fixed amount, for instance, "$1,368,400."

In order for the parties to intelligently agree on a fixed price, it is necessary that the scope of work be very well defined. A contractor will be unable to accurately estimate its cost of performance if the owner, through its A/E, has failed to depict the work in detail and specify the materials and equipment that will be required. A poorly defined scope of work on a fixed-price contract will surely result in disputes and claims by the contractor for additional compensation.

It should be noted that many publicly bid contracts are required by law to be fixed-price. This places a premium on both a detailed scope of work and a reasonable change order process for these contracts.

Some construction contracts are priced on the basis of the contractor's cost of the work plus a fixed fee. These so-called cost-plus contracts call for the contractor to be paid its direct and indirect costs of performing the work, plus a fixed fee which serves as the contractor's profit. While the total cost of the project may be more or less than the original estimate, the owner will bear this cost and the contractor will receive the same fee originally negotiated.

One of the real challenges in drafting a cost-plus contract is to come up with a comprehensive definition of the contractor's "cost" of performance. Direct costs, such as labor and materials, are usually not much of a problem. Indirect costs, such as insurance and office overhead, are a problem, as these costs must be allocated among all the projects being performed by the contractor. On cost-plus contracts, it is not unusual for the definition of "cost" to cover several pages. This is necessary if misunderstandings and disputes are to be avoided.

A cost-plus contract enables the parties to work with a somewhat less precise definition of the work. This is true only to a limited extent, however, as it is unlikely the project owner will give the contractor a blank check to incur all the costs it wants.

Most cost-plus contracts include a guaranteed maximum price, cost plus fee, which is not to be exceeded without the written consent of the owner. A contractor obviously cannot commit itself to a guaranteed maximum price unless it has an accurate idea of what it will be required to construct.

Sometimes cost-plus contracts include a "shared savings" provision. In addition to establishing a guaranteed maximum price, the contract states a target amount of costs to be incurred in constructing the project. If the contractor is able to complete the work for less than the target cost, the contractor and the owner share the savings according to a formula established in the contract. Any payment the contractor receives under the shared savings provision is in addition to the contractor's fixed fee.

The purpose of the shared savings provision is to give the contractor an incentive to minimize costs. In the absence of such a clause, the contractor has no incentive to do so as long as the total cost plus fixed fee stays within the guaranteed maximum price.

A third method of pricing construction work is the "unit-price" method. Under this method, the project is divided into certain elements which can be quantified, such as linear feet of pipe or cubic yards of earth. The owner and the contractor agree on a price per unit of each element of the work. Payment is made on the basis of the actual quantities of work performed.

Typically, the contract documents for a unit-price contract will state estimated quantities for the various elements of the work. These quantities are not binding on the owner and are used primarily for purposes of bid comparison. Total bid amounts are computed by applying the bid unit prices to the estimated quantities of work. On publicly bid jobs, contract award must be made to the low bidder. It is understood, however, that actual payment will be made on the basis of the actual quantities. The total price is not fixed.

Unit-price contracts are widely used on projects such as excavation, highways, and sewer or water pipe. The routinized nature of this work lends itself to unit-price measurement. The contractor knows it will be paid for all work performed and the owner knows that it will pay for no more than the actual volume of work performed. The unit-price payment method is not generally applicable to building construction, because the project breaks down into too many diverse elements and defies any workable formula.

A fourth method of pricing construction work is "time and materials." A fixed price is placed on each hour of labor the contractor furnishes. The owner also agrees to pay the direct costs of the material and equipment used on the project. Typically, no payment is made for any indirect costs. The parties agree as to who will receive the benefit of any trade discounts on materials that the contractor receives from its suppliers.

The time and materials method provides very little certainty for project owners and is not used on large projects. It is a useful method for small volumes of work where the parties want to avoid the time and expense of a detailed scope of work and detailed cost estimates. It is also widely used as a method of pricing extra work on change orders.

Method of Payment

The construction agreement also establishes the method of payment to be used by the owner. The method of payment refers to the issue of how much will be paid to the contractor and when. Payment issues will be discussed in detail in Chapter 9. At this point, however, it is useful to mention the basic elements that are commonly covered in the agreement.

Most construction projects are performed over a period of months or even years. It would be not only inequitable but probably not feasible to ask the contractor to wait until completion to receive payment. The contractor's financing costs would add greatly to the bid price of the work.

For these reasons, construction contracts commonly call for progress payments. These payments, usually made monthly, are based on the value of the work performed during the preceding payment period.

On a unit-price contract, the value is easy to measure, as the unit prices are simply applied to the actual quantities of work performed. On a fixed-price contract, it is necessary to measure the value of the work in place by determining the percentage of completion. The A/E plays a crucial role in determining this amount. Frequently, a "schedule of values" is established under the contract whereby various phases or portions of the work are assigned particular values for progress payment purposes.

The agreement usually calls for the project owner to withhold "retainage" from the contractor's progress payment. The retainage, which usually is 5 to 10 percent of the progress payment, is withheld to protect the owner against defects in the work or other losses caused by the contractor which are not discovered until after the progress payment has been released. The retained funds have already been earned by the contractor, but they will not be released until completion of the project. Payment of the retainage will be subject to setoffs for defects or other problems which are discovered later.

Frequently the agreement will call for a reduction of retainage as the contractor makes progress toward completion. For instance, once the contractor completes 50 percent of the project, retainage may be reduced from 10 percent of each progress payment to 5 percent of each payment. The rationale is that the owner already has a large pool of retained funds to protect itself with. And as the contractor gets closer to completion, there is somewhat less risk to the owner.

The construction agreement also establishes the timing of final payment to the contractor. Final payment consists of the last monthly progress payment plus the accumulated retainage. As discussed in Chapter 13, there are a number of important legal consequences attached to release of final payment. The agreement itself does not address these issues, but it does establish the timing of the release of final payment.

Usually, the agreement will state that once the contractor finishes all but the "punch list," or touch-up items, the contractor will be entitled to the contract balance less 1½ or 2 times the estimated cost of completing the punch list items. In other words, the retainage will be reduced to leave only enough to assure the owner of proper completion of those items.

Once the punch list has been completed, the work will be inspected again by the A/E. If everything is in order, the owner will release final payment. The agreement will establish whether final payment is due immediately upon final acceptance, 30 days after final acceptance, or some longer period of time after final acceptance.

If there are still incomplete or improperly performed items of work, the owner may continue to withhold a setoff from final payment sufficient to cover these items. This may be done by agreement with the contractor. It may also be done despite the contractor's protest, in which case it would be treated as a dispute or claim.

Schedule

The third essential ingredient of the construction documents which is addressed in the agreement itself is the project schedule.

The agreement establishes the period within which the contractor must complete its work. This may be expressed as a specific calendar date. More frequently, it is expressed as a stated number of calendar days.

When the performance period is expressed in calendar days, the period starts to run upon the owner's issuance of a formal, written notice to proceed. The formal notice is desirable because it avoids any confusion as to when the performance period started to run. Sometimes the contract documents will state that the notice to proceed will be issued within so many days of contract signing. The computation of the performance period is crucial because it will determine when liquidated damages can be assessed against the contractor for late completion.

Although the agreement establishes the total performance period, it does not establish the specific interim schedule which the contractor must meet while performing the work. Frequently, the general conditions of the contract require that after contract award, the contractor submit a proposed progress schedule to the owner or A/E for review and approval. As discussed in Chapter 7, this process has a number of legal consequences.

Documents Incorporated by Reference

As discussed in Chapter 1, it is possible to incorporate a number of separate documents into an agreement by reference. This device is widely used in the construction industry.

The construction agreement itself is frequently quite short, simply naming the parties, stating the name and location of the project, and establishing the terms of price, payment, and schedule. The actual terms and conditions of the contract, as well as the definition of the work, are contained in separate documents which are listed in the agreement and (at least ideally) physically attached to the agreement.

The incorporated documents, which will be discussed in greater detail below, commonly consist of: (1) the "general conditions," which are usually pre-printed, so-called boilerplate provisions under which the work must be performed;

CASE STUDY 2-1

Owner awarded Contractor a contract for construction of an apartment building. The contract stated that Contractor would comply with the provisions of the "Manual of Accident Prevention in Construction" of the Associated General Contractors of America (AGC).

An employee of a subcontractor was injured when he fell from an upper floor.

Contractor said it was not responsible for the safety of subcontractors' employees.

The Court of Appeals of Iowa ruled that the AGC manual had been incorporated by reference into Contractor's agreement. The manual gave Contractor overall responsibility for job site safety and required Contractor to erect and maintain proper barricades. Contractor had failed to do this, so Contractor was liable for the injury.

Farris v. General Growth Development Corp., 354 N.W.2d 251 (Iowa App. 1984).

---

(2) the "supplementary general conditions," which are usually customized provisions developed by the parties to address particular concerns which have arisen with regard to the project; (3) the plans, or drawings, depicting the work, usually listed in the agreement by number; (4) the specifications which define the standards which the work, material, and equipment must meet; and (5) the various government regulations which the contractor will be required to conform to during performance of the work.

Although the agreement itself is a very concise document, it incorporates all the documents which will determine the rights and obligations of the project owner and the prime contractor during the performance of the work.

Execution of the Contract

Last, but certainly not least, the agreement provides for the signing, or "execution," of the contract documents. Usually, it is the only document which is actually signed by the parties. As all the other documents are incorporated by reference into the agreement, it is not necessary that they be signed in order to become binding on the parties.

There is little to be said about the execution of a contract. The two issues that may arise, however, are authority of the individual who signs and last-minute changes.

It is important that the agreement be signed by an individual who is authorized by his or her organization to bind that organization to the agreement. For instance, an agreement should be signed by a duly authorized officer of a corporation or the general partner of a limited partnership. Below the signature line, it should indicate the name and title of the signing individual and recite the fact that the individual is duly authorized to do so by its organization.

Ideally, each signing individual should produce documentation of their authority, i.e., a corporate resolution or a copy of a partnership agreement. This should be attached to and incorporated into the agreement. As a practical matter, this procedure is seldom followed.

It is common for the parties to make last-minute changes to the contract documents, frequently just prior to execution. Changes should be handwritten and in ink. Every change should then be initialed in the adjacent margin by the parties executing the agreement. This way, there will be no confusion regarding the parties' intent to include these changes in the agreement.

THE GENERAL CONDITIONS

Function

As described above, the construction agreement itself usually covers only the basic business terms of the transaction. The function of the general conditions is to establish the legal terms and conditions that will govern the construction of the project. They include a number of provisions that are crucial in determining the respective rights and responsibilities of the owner and contractor.

With most preprinted contract forms, the general conditions comprise a separate document which is attached to the agreement. Sometimes, however, the general conditions are simply a section of a single integrated document. It makes no difference from a legal standpoint, of course.

From a practical standpoint, it is advantageous to keep the two documents separate. The agreement necessarily requires extensive customization and may be altered right up to the time of execution. The bulky general conditions tend to be less extensively modified. By keeping the documents separate, the parties can make last-minute changes with greater ease and clarity.

Contents of the General Conditions

The general conditions address everything from the mundane (such as site cleanup or maintaining order among the crew) to the crucial (such as change order procedures or compensation for unanticipated subsurface conditions).

A list of the important issues addressed in the general conditions basically describes the content of the remainder of this book: insurance requirements, change order procedures, time extensions for excusable delay, compensation for differing site conditions, the resolution of disputes, etc. This is the document where the respective rights and responsibilities are established.

Supplementary General Conditions

Considering the legal significance of the general conditions, it is not surprising that one or both of the parties may want changes made in the preprinted terms. Although this is not possible on publicly bid work, it is common on private projects.

If the changes are not extensive, it is easy to simply make them with a pen and initial them upon contract execution. If the changes are extensive, however, it is preferable for the parties to draft specific provisions to supersede particular provisions of the preprinted general conditions. These provisions are usually contained in a document labeled "Supplementary General Conditions."

The supplementary general conditions are really a "catch-all" document covering any aspect of the arrangement which is peculiar to that project and therefore not addressed in standard, preprinted forms. For instance, the owner's on-site representative may be designated. Certain limitations on site access may be established. Local ordinances affecting the work may be referred to. And, as mentioned above, if the parties have rewritten the indemnification clause contained in the preprinted general conditions, this is the place for the new clause.

The supplementary general conditions take precedence over the general conditions. It is a good practice to include a written statement to that effect in the supplementary general conditions in order to avoid any ambiguity.

DEFINING THE SCOPE OF WORK

The Drawings

Drawings are the documents most commonly associated with the design of a building. They are frequently referred to as "plans," although technically the plans are only those drawings depicting the total project. This overview of the project is not sufficiently detailed to enable a contractor to bid or construct the building, so a number of other drawings are typically found in the contract documents.

One or more drawings will depict the elevations of the structure. This indicates the height above sea level of the footings, foundation, sills, etc. Additionally, a number of sectional drawings will depict the various sections of the building in greater detail than that shown on the plans.

The drawings described above are typically prepared by the architect who is serving as the prime design contractor. On an "engineered" project such as a bridge or highway, an engineer usually serves as the prime design contractor and prepares the plans, elevations, and sectional drawings.

Regardless of who serves as the prime design contractor, it is customary to retain the services of design consultants from various specialized disciplines. The drawings prepared by these consultants also become part of the contract drawings. It is common to find structural drawings depicting the conformation and connection of structural members of the structure. Another set of commonly found trade drawings depicts the building's mechanical system. Foundation drawings prepared by a soils and foundation engineer are also common.

Many drawings, regardless of their nature, contain "details." As the name implies, these drawings depict a certain small portion of the structure in greater detail and smaller scale than that shown on the drawing itself. This is usually done because of the complexity or sensitivity of that particular portion of the work. The details are set off to the side of a larger drawing. They are seldom found on separate sheets.

Another traditional aspect of drawings is "schedules" of materials to be used. Generally, the selection of materials is mandated in the specifications. It is customary, however, to list the selection of certain items such as wall and floor finishes and hardware in schedules written on the side of a drawing. This practice probably stems from the fact that the drawings sometimes take precedence over the specifications and cautious designers have wanted to make sure that their selection of materials was followed.

The Specifications

The specifications are a volume of written material which defines the equipment and materials to be used on the project and, to a lesser extent, the method of applying, installing, or assembling this equipment and material.

The importance of the specifications has grown in recent years owing to the complexity of construction and the larger number of choices available with regard to equipment and material. Forty years ago, it was common for buildings to be constructed simply from a set of drawings.

The growing importance of specifications also reflects the reluctance of project owners and A/Es to rely simply on "trade practice" to define the method of application or installation. The specifications give the owner and designer greater control over these methods.

With regard to the selection of equipment or materials, there are two basic types of specifications: proprietary and performance.

Proprietary specifications call for a particular brand and model to be used. On private construction contracts, the contractor is required to use that specific product.

On public contracts, a proprietary specification is usually stated as "brand name or equal." In order to foster competition, public laws and regulations prohibit specifying a single product. If the contractor can convince the A/E that a different product is "equal," it must be allowed to use that product.

If a proposed alternate product possesses all the "salient characteristics" of the specified brand, it is considered equal. The salient characteristics are the physical properties and performance capabilities that reasonably meet the public project owner's minimum needs for the project. Obviously, opinions frequently differ as to whether or not a proposed alternate product is equal to the proprietary product listed in the specifications.

Performance specifications do not refer to any particular brand or product. Instead, the specification states certain performance capabilities which the equipment or material must meet. For instance, a pump might be required to be capable of moving a specified number of gallons per minute, or roofing material might be required to be guaranteed for a certain number of years. The selection of a particular product is left up to the contractor.

Performance specifications are not as widely used as proprietary specifications because the project owner and A/E do not have the same degree of control over the contractor's work. As will be seen in Chapter 11, however, some of the emerging forms of construction contracting make it necessary to use performance rather than proprietary specifications.

The specifications are usually organized according to the 16 standard sections of the Uniform Construction Index, originally developed by the Construction Specifications Institute. The sections generally reflect the customary building trades and are listed below.

1 General requirements
2 Site work
3 Concrete
4 Masonry
5 Metals
6 Carpentry
7 Moisture protection
8 Doors, windows, and glass
9 Finishes
10 Specialties
11 Equipment
12 Furnishings
13 Special construction
14 Conveying systems
15 Mechanical
16 Electrical

In recent years, certain standard, computerized master specifications have been developed to assist the designer in defining the work. The most widely used is a system called Masterspec. While these standard specifications can be a useful tool in getting started in defining the work, they are not a substitute for the careful individual attention of an experienced specification writer.

Owner's Implied Warranty

When discussing plans and specifications, there is one legal principle which is of crucial importance to the A/E.

Courts have long held that when a project owner provides a set of plans and specifications to a construction contractor, the owner extends an implied warranty that the documents are accurate, complete, and suitable for their intended purpose. If they are not, the contractor will be entitled to recover its increased cost of performance caused by the defective design documents.

This warranty is implied; so it need not be stated in the contract documents themselves. It applies regardless of whether the project is public or private and regardless of whether the contract is competitively bid or negotiated.

This doctrine is of great significance to the A/E because the project owner

---

CASE STUDY 2-2

Owner awarded a contract for construction of a water pumping station. The drawings indicated the presence of an electrical pole 50 feet from the structure but failed to indicate that no telephone service could be made available from that pole.

In order to bring in a telephone cable, Contractor was forced to dig an 11,000-foot trench. Contractor sought additional compensation. Owner relied on contract language stating that utility locations were only approximate.

The Appeals Court of Massachusetts ruled that Owner extended an implied warranty that the plans and specifications were accurate and complete. The failure to indicate that no telephone service was available from the pole rendered the contract documents incomplete. Therefore, Owner breached the implied warranty.

Richardson Electrical Co., Inc. v. Peter Franchese & Son, Inc., 484 N.E.2d 108 (Mass.App. 1985)

---

relies on the professional expertise of the A/E in developing a set of complete, accurate plans and specifications. If the plans and specifications are defective and the owner pays the contractor additional sums as a result, the owner will probably seek reimbursement from the A/E. Given the scope of the A/E's professional responsibilities, the owner will in all likelihood succeed in this quest.

The A/E's liability to the owner and contractor for defective design documents will be discussed in greater detail in Chapter 4.

INTERPRETING THE CONTRACT

Considering the complexity of the contract documents described above, it is not surprising that the various parties on the project sometimes have differing interpretations of what is required. Over the years, courts have developed cer-

---

CASE STUDY 2-3

Owner awarded a contract for highway construction. Elevations indicated in the drawings were higher than the actual elevations in the field. This forced Contractor to bring in additional fill.

Contractor brought a claim for additional compensation. Owner argued that contract stated that elevations were for informational purposes only and could not be relied on without independent verification.

The Appellate Division of the Superior Court of New Jersey held that notwithstanding the contractual disclaimer, Owner extended an implied warranty of the accuracy of all affirmative representations in the contract documents. The elevations were inaccurate, and this was a breach of the implied warranty.

Golomore Associates v. New Jersey State Highway Authority, 413 A.2d 361 (N.J.App. 1980).

---

tain basic rules of interpretation which should be kept in mind when dealing with these disagreements. The most significant rules of interpretation are described below.

Construed against the Drafter

If any provision of a contract is ambiguous, that provision will be construed, or interpreted, against the party who prepared the agreement. This rule of law is sometimes referred to by the Latin phrase *contra proferentem.*

A contract provision is considered ambiguous if it is subject to two different interpretations and each interpretation is reasonable. In that event, the reasonable interpretation of the party that did not draft the agreement will prevail.

As agreements are usually prepared by project owners, this rule of interpretation is more frequently applied against owners to the benefit of contractors. This is particularly true on publicly bid projects where the complete set of contract documents is presented to prospective bidders on a "take it or leave it" basis. If a bidder's interpretation of the contract requirements was reasonable and the bidder relied on that interpretation when pricing its bid, then that interpretation will prevail.

On private projects, there tends to be more negotiation, more give and take, in arriving at the terms of the contract. The more negotiation there is, the less likely that a court will characterize the owner as the drafter of the agreement.

Even on private projects, however, it is common for the owner to present the contractor with a complete set of contract documents. Negotiation is usually limited to matters such as price or schedule. In this situation, courts will not hesitate to apply the rule of *contra proferentem* against the project owner when interpreting an ambiguous provision in the specifications or general conditions.

CASE STUDY 2-4

Contractor awarded subcontract using Contractor's standard, preprinted subcontract form. Subcontract stated that payment to Subcontractor would be due 10 days after Contractor received payment from Owner.

Owner didn't pay Contractor, so Contractor refused to pay Subcontractor. Subcontractor argued that clause in subcontract was intended only to give Contractor a reasonable time to make payment, not to excuse payment altogether if Contractor didn't get paid by Owner.

The Court of Appeal of Louisiana ruled that the intended meaning of the payment clause was ambiguous. The preprinted subcontract form had obviously been drafted by Contractor. Therefore, the clause was construed against Contractor and Subcontractor's interpretation prevailed.

Cahn Electric Co., Inc. v. Robert E. McKee, Inc., 490 So.2d 647 (La.App. 1986).

Trade Usage

In any industry, and certainly in the construction industry, a number of terms take on a specialized meaning among those in the industry. Courts consider these terms to be "trade terms."

If a contract uses trade terms (and of course any set of specifications is laden with them), courts will interpret the terms according to their commonly accepted meaning within the industry. It matters not that the judge, the jury, and members of the general public don't understand the term. If the term has a widely accepted meaning in the industry, it will be interpreted accordingly.

Individuals and organizations who engage in commerce will be presumed to understand the meaning of trade terms used within their particular industry. Neither a contractor nor a project owner would benefit from arguing that it did not understand "rebar" to mean steel reinforcing bars.

Internal Contradictions

One of the primary concerns of a party putting together a set of contract documents is to avoid conflicting provisions within the documents themselves. Internal contradictions are a common source of claims and disputes. At best, they appear sloppy and unprofessional.

Internal contradictions result primarily from the widespread use of standard forms of agreement and standard sets of specifications within the construction industry. As will be described later in this chapter, the use of standard forms is generally beneficial. It is by no means a bad practice which is to be avoided.

The danger in using standard forms, however, is that they are frequently pulled off the shelf and thrown together with little forethought. They are not tailored to fit the particular project. Worse yet, they are not even carefully read in their entirety in order to ferret out ambiguities and contradictions.

For instance, an A/E working on behalf of a public owner may use the same standard form of agreement he or she has used successfully in the past. The

---

CASE STUDY 2-5

Owner awarded a contract for construction of a medical clinic. The contract included two "typical wall details" which were in conflict with each other regarding the installation of rebar.

Contractor chose to follow one drawing. Owner ordered Contractor to rip out the work and follow the other drawing which, said Owner, was consistent with local trade practice. Contractor appealed.

The U.S. Court of Appeals ruled that the drawing details were patently ambiguous. When interpreting ambiguous contract documents, it is appropriate to rely on local trade custom to determine the intended meaning. Contractor's appeal was denied.

Fortec Constructors v. United States, 760 F.2d 1288 (Fed.Cir. 1985).

A/E then learns that certain public regulations or mandatory contract provisions must be incorporated into the contract documents. If a careful effort is not made to reconcile all the documents, the A/E may end up in the embarrassing position of having prepared a contract with a number of conflicting requirements.

Similarly, the use of standardized or computerized specifications such as Masterspec can produce troublesome results if care is not taken to customize the specifications for each individual project and reconcile the specifications with the other contract documents. The blind use of "canned" specifications will frequently result in provisions which conflict with drawing notes or other documents.

The duty to avoid internal contradictions falls largely on the A/E, as the project owner typically relies on the A/E to prepare so many of the contract documents, technical and otherwise. Constant vigilance is required to avoid embarrassing or troublesome situations.

Given the length and complexity of a typical set of contract documents, however, it is inevitable that contradictions will occasionally occur. As a result, courts have developed certain rules of interpretation to be applied when one provision of the contract documents says something that contradicts a statement found elsewhere in the documents.

When a direct contradiction exists, the terms of the agreement take precedence over the terms of the general conditions. If supplementary general conditions have been incorporated into the contract documents, these supplementary conditions will prevail over the general conditions. They will not take precedence over the terms of the agreement itself, however.

When contradictions exist between the drawings and the specifications, the more specific item governs the more general item. It is frequently stated that the specifications prevail over the drawings. This is true, however, only to the extent the specifications are more detailed and specific than the information in

---

CASE STUDY 2-6

Owner awarded a contract for HUD-financed project. The contract was a standard HUD document, but it incorporated an AIA document as the general conditions of the agreement.

The HUD document and the AIA document contained conflicting definitions of when substantial completion of the work was achieved. It later became important to determine the date of substantial completion in order to compute the early completion bonus to which Contractor was entitled.

The U.S. District Court noted that the HUD document contained an "order of precedence" clause stating that the HUD document took precedence over any conflicting provisions in any other document. Therefore, the HUD definition of substantial completion was determinative.

McCarthy Brothers Construction Co. v. Pierce, 626 F.Supp. 981 (E.D.Mo. 1986).

CASE STUDY 2-7

Owner issued a written change order for Contractor to furnish and apply 130 tons of asphalt at a unit price of $180 per ton.

Owner later orally requested another 381 tons of asphalt with no discussion of price. In the subsequent dispute, Owner contended it should only have to pay the reasonable value of the additional asphalt and that value should reflect certain economies of scale.

The District Court of Appeal of Florida ruled that the oral change order was ambiguous because of the failure to establish a price. When interpreting an ambiguous provision of a contract, the past actions of the parties are the best indication of intent. Therefore, Owner must pay at the $180 per ton rate established in the original written change order.

Forest Construction, Inc. v. Farrell-Cheek Steel Co., 484 So.2d 40 (Fla.App. 1986).

---

the drawings. This is usually the case, but not always. For instance, drawing notes take precedence over the provisions in the specifications.

The general principle which is at work here is that the specific takes precedence over the general. Terms that were customized by the parties will prevail over "boilerplate" provisions of the contract documents.

As described in Chapter 1, a written contract is nothing more than a memorialization or documentation of the mutual understanding of the parties. In trying to determine what that understanding was, a court will be more persuaded by something the parties developed for this specific project as opposed to a standard document which was pulled off the shelf and incorporated into the documents with no modification whatsoever.

For instance, specifications are frequently standardized. Drawings, by definition, must be customized for each individual project. In the event of a direct contradiction between the two, it is logical to assume that the drawing more accurately reflects the intent and the understanding of the parties. It is for this reason that the old adage of specifications governing drawings is misleading.

Contract Must Be Read as a Whole

The final rule of interpretation which will be discussed here is simply common sense. When interpreting a set of contract documents, all provisions must be considered and they all must be presumed to be complementary. No provision may be considered in isolation and no provision may be presumed to be useless.

Again, the logic behind this rule is that the written contract documents are simply a reflection of the parties' mutual understanding. If the parties did not intend for a provision to have meaning, why would they include it in the contract documents?

While a provision standing alone may indicate a certain understanding, this must be modified by any other contract provisions that relate to the same matter. All provisions are presumed to reflect intent and each is considered to complement the others. This assumes, of course, that there is not a direct contradiction between two provisions, in which case the rules of interpretation described above will be applied.

This rule of interpretation is probably the one which is most frequently applied to contract documents. When a dispute arises, it is common for one of the parties to latch onto a particular aspect of the contract documents to support its argument as to what was or was not required by the contract. In interpreting the intended meaning of the contract, it is important to consider all provisions and avoid focusing solely on one isolated clause.

CONTRACTOR'S PERFORMANCE OBLIGATIONS

When discussing the interpretation of the contract documents, it is important to mention the standard of performance to which the contractor will be held. This standard is interesting because it appears to be contradictory.

On the one hand, the project owner is entitled to insist on absolute compliance with the plans and specifications. Close is not good enough. The contractor must fully perform the work in strict compliance with every specific requirement in the contract. This is what the owner bargained for and this is what the owner is entitled to get for its money.

On the other hand, courts recognize that it is unrealistic to expect a contractor to conform exactly to every single requirement on a project which may be large and complex. It would be unfair to allow a project owner to hold a contractor in breach of contract, and refuse to make payment, simply because minor aspects of the work have not been completed in strict conformance with the plans and specifications. Consequently, courts have developed the doctrine of "substantial completion." It is a legal doctrine peculiar to construction contracts.

Under this doctrine, a contractor is deemed to have fulfilled its contractual obligation once the project is "substantially complete." Substantial completion is achieved once the project is fit to be used for its intended purpose. For instance, an office building is substantially complete once the project owner can take beneficial occupancy of the building. The fact that some decorative woodwork is missing or some sinks are scratched would not prevent the owner from using the building.

What, one might ask, became of the requirement that the contractor fully perform the work in strict compliance with the plans and specifications? Courts accommodate this requirement by allowing the owner to set off sums from the final payment sufficient to cover the cost of repairing or completing any minor items. This process will be described in greater detail in Chapter 13.

In considering the contractor's performance obligations under the contract documents, then, it is important to remember that the owner can insist on strict compliance. Once the project is substantially complete, however, the owner cannot rely on lack of compliance as an excuse for failing to pay the contractor or terminating the contract. Once substantial completion is achieved, the owner's only remedy is to withhold, or set off, sufficient funds to cover the cost of repair or completion of any outstanding items.

Finally, it should be noted that determining when substantial completion is achieved is usually a judgment call. The owner and contractor may have different interpretations of when the project is fit for its intended purpose. Common sense must prevail. While lack of decorative woodwork does not prevent the beneficial use of an office building, the lack of a functioning elevator or air-conditioning system certainly does.

STANDARD AGREEMENTS

Importance of Standard Agreements

It should now be quite apparent that a typical set of contract documents for even a modest-sized construction project is a rather thick volume. If the parties to the project had to draft each contract from scratch, it would be a monumental undertaking. If the parties hired attorneys to do the drafting, it would be a very expensive undertaking.

In response to this problem, certain standardized form contracts have been developed. The use of standard form agreements is probably more widespread in the construction industry than in any other industry.

It should be noted that when one refers to "standard agreements" in the construction industry, the reference is not to the standardized specifications that were mentioned earlier in this chapter. Standard agreements spell out the legal and financial terms and conditions of the construction project. They typically consist of an agreement and a set of general conditions.

The widespread use of standardized forms in the construction industry is attributable to two compelling advantages they offer. As mentioned above, they save time. It is far more efficient to make additions, deletions, and other changes to a preprinted form than it is to draft a 20-page contract on blank paper.

In addition to saving time, standard contracts offer more certainty than individually drafted agreements. Many of the standard forms have been in use for years. Their terms and conditions have been repeatedly interpreted by the courts. When areas of ambiguity or misunderstanding have come to light, changes have been made in the forms. Considering the fact that most construction contracts are assembled by nonattorneys, the predictability that results from using standardized, widely accepted terminology is very desirable.

For these reasons, standard forms have become prevalent on both private and public construction projects. Many public project owners such as state agencies or municipalities have developed their own standard contract documents. Regardless of the particular form that is used, the use of a standardized form offers the advantages of greater predictability and less time.

Having extolled the virtues of standard agreements, it is time to again stress the dangers. As described earlier in this chapter, the careless, unthinking use of standardized contract forms can produce a disaster. At best, there will be many contract provisions which are simply irrelevant to the project at hand. At worst, there will be internal contradictions in the contract documents. Provisions in the standard form may conflict with other supplementary provisions required by law or with statements made in the specifications.

There is no substitute for a careful, thoughtful review of all the contract documents as a whole. Irrelevant provisions should be eliminated. Any particular items peculiar to the individual project must be addressed, and the documents should be consistent and clear.

The proper role of legal counsel in assembling the contract documents should also be considered. It is customary in the industry for the A/E to assemble the documents on behalf of the project owner. This is an acceptable practice. It is only prudent, however, for the A/E to ask the project owner to have its legal counsel review the completed package. This should not require a great deal of time, as the attorney is not being asked to draft the documents.

The attorney's review can be very useful, as he or she brings a different perspective and different professional skills to the contract documents. From a practical standpoint, the attorney's review will protect the A/E from a great deal of embarrassment and possibly even liability if contradictions or other problems are later discovered in the contract documents.

If a project owner declines to have its legal counsel review the standardized contract documents, that is the owner's decision. The A/E will be in a much better position nonetheless for having made the request.

Development of Standard Agreements

With the exception of contract documents developed by government entities, the standardized forms of agreement have been developed by professional and trade associations. These documents were developed as a service for members in order to offer the advantages described above.

Since the agreements were developed as a service for a particular trade or professional group, one might wonder how fair and balanced they would be. Initially, one of the primary purposes of these agreements was to protect the interests of the group's members. The forms were full of provisions designed to limit liability, maximize authority, assure payment, etc.

To the extent these forms were skewed in favor of a particular group, they met resistance from other members of the construction community. It was in the best interest of each trade or professional association to see that its forms became as widely used and accepted as possible. Consequently, compromises were made and the standardized forms became more balanced as they evolved.

In recent years, this process has been formalized. In order to foster the widespread use of its forms, an association will solicit the opinions of other industry groups and even seek the formal endorsement of the form by the other groups. For instance, standard forms published by both the National Society of Professional Engineers and the American Institute of Architects have been approved and endorsed by the Associated General Contractors of America (AGC).

It can be stated that today the commonly used standard forms are fair, balanced agreements. They are generally free of the one-sided provisions that private project owners sometimes try to impose on contractors. As a general rule, they can be considered far more balanced than a customized contract prepared by an attorney who is representing the interests of only one party to the agreement. After all, the standard forms already reflect a certain amount of compromise that was necessary to gain the acceptance of diverse industry groups.

This is not to say, of course, that the standard agreements are all the same. Each reflects a certain point of view or agenda. There are significant differences among the standard forms. Each provides a reasonable, balanced starting point for establishing an agreement, however.

The Widely Used Standard Agreements

There are four sets of standard contract documents that are widely used in the construction industry today. These standardized documents are briefly summarized below.

The American Institute of Architects (AIA) contract documents are the oldest and most widely used standard forms. Some of the documents were in use as early as 1915. AIA has developed forms governing the relationships between not only owner and contractor, but owner and architect, architect and engineer, contractor and subcontractor, and bonding company and owner. The various documents are coordinated to avoid conflicting provisions. They may be purchased from AIA's Washington office. A number of AIA documents are reprinted as appendixes to this book.

The AGC also publishes a set of contract documents. These documents are limited to relationships between owner and contractor and contractor and subcontractor. AGC has many different forms of owner-contractor agreements reflecting different business arrangements that may be made on particular projects. The AGC forms are probably the second most widely used standardized contract documents.

The Engineer's Joint Contract Documents Committee is a consortium of the National Society of Professional Engineers, the Consulting Engineering Council, the American Society of Civil Engineers, and the Construction Specifications Institute, Inc. The engineer's contract documents were published largely in response to the growing influence of the AIA documents. As yet, these documents have not become as widely used as either the AIA or AGC documents.

Finally, this book will occasionally refer to the United States government's Standard Form 23-A. Originally developed by the Army Corps of Engineers, variations of this contract form have been adopted throughout the federal government for both military and civilian construction. Standard Form 23-A has become very influential in the industry, affecting the contract documents adopted by many state and local governments.

KEY TERMS AND CONCEPTS

incorporation by reference   A reference in an agreement to other documents which are not physically part of that agreement stating that the other documents are hereby incorporated into and made a part of the agreement. Documents that are incorporated by reference into an agreement become binding terms of that agreement.

order of precedence   A statement in an agreement that in the event of internal contradictions in the agreement, certain documents or certain portions of the agreement shall take precedence over other portions of the agreement.

contra proferentem   A Latin phrase meaning "against the party who proffers a thing." Any ambiguities in an agreement will be construed or interpreted against the party who drafted the agreement.

implied warranty of the plans and specifications   The project owner impliedly warrants to the contractor that the plans and specifications are complete, accurate, and suitable for the intended purpose of the project.

substantial completion   The point at which the project is sufficiently complete to be occupied by the owner and used for its intended purpose. Once a project is substantially complete, the contractor cannot be defaulted or held in breach of contract.

CHAPTER 3

COMPETITIVE BIDDING

CONCEPT OF COMPETITIVE BIDDING

Purpose

In this country, competitive bidding is required by law on virtually all construction contracts that involve public funds. The competitive bidding requirement serves two primary purposes: conserving tax dollars and promoting fairness.

If a project is to be built with public funds, the public authorities have an obligation to accomplish the work in an economical fashion. The assumption is that the lowest possible price will be received if the contract is awarded on the basis of open competition.

The desire to minimize cost by maximizing competition is sufficiently strong to cause public authorities to reject all bids if not enough are received. For instance, if only two bids are received and they both exceed the public owner's estimate for the cost of the work, it is common for the public owner to reject the bids.

As strong as the need to conserve tax dollars is, the promotion of fairness is an even more imperative purpose of the competitive bidding system. There is a broad consensus in our society that public contracts should be awarded on the basis of the contractor's ability and willingness to offer the low price. Graft and local favoritism must not play a role in the selection of contractors.

The rigid, formalistic structure of competitive bidding which will be described in this chapter is designed to avoid not only impropriety but even the appearance of possible impropriety. In order to maintain public confidence in the system, appearances are very important. Courts frequently refer to this as "maintaining the integrity of the competitive bidding system."

The inflexible structure of the system is designed to preclude any opportunity for impropriety. As important as it is to conserve public funds, public project owners will reject a low bid due to a "technical" violation of the bidding procedures and award the contract to the second low bidder.

This is not because anything improper has actually taken place but because a failure to strictly follow the rules and compete on an identical basis violates the integrity of the competitive bidding system. Even if more public funds must be expended to accomplish the work, the integrity of the process is a priority.

When Is Competitive Bidding Required?

As stated above, competitive bidding is required on virtually every construction project which involves public funds. There are frequently statutory exceptions for very small items of work and emergency situations. Other than that, it should be assumed that competitive bidding will be required when public funds are expended.

The laws requiring competitive bidding exist at every level of our government. The federal statutes and regulations are quite elaborate and lengthy. This is the most sophisticated public procurement system in the country. A great deal of the case law that is made involving competitive bidding is made at the federal level.

States have their own laws and regulations covering competitive bidding of projects being constructed with state funds. In many of the larger states, the system rivals the federal system in its sophistication. In many smaller states the bidding statutes are surprisingly general or even simplistic.

Counties and municipalities have ordinances and regulations governing competitive bidding. Other public authorities such as school districts and sewer au-

CASE STUDY 3-1

Public Owner negotiated a contract with a firm to provide "construction management" services. These services included coordination of the bidding and coordination of several construction contractors.

Contractor argued that the sole-source, negotiated award of the construction management contract violated the competitive bidding statute. The contract should have been put out to bid.

The Court of Appeals of Indiana rejected this argument. The contract was primarily for professional services, not construction work. The firm receiving the contract did not perform construction work or guarantee a price. The competitive bidding statute does not apply to contracts for professional services because these services can only be evaluated by subjective criteria, unlike bids for construction contracts, which can be objectively evaluated.

Attlin Construction, Inc. v. Muncie Community Schools,
413 N.E.2d 281 (Ind.App. 1980).

---

thorities also promulgate competitive bidding regulations. These schemes tend to be much less elaborate than the structure that exists at the state or federal level.

Local governments frequently give themselves a great deal of discretion to waive "minor informalities" in a bid. This discretion results in a less rigid and less predictable system. To the extent local favoritism or graft exists in public procurement, it is more likely to occur at this level.

In our system of government, it is common for the federal government to make grants of funds to state and local governments. To a lesser extent, states make grants to local governments. It is common for construction projects to be built with a mixture of funds from various public sources. The question then arises, which competitive bidding statute governs the procurement?

As a general rule, the laws of the grantee, the authority that actually awards the contract and owns the project, will govern the procurement. For instance, when the federal government gives a grant to a local municipality, the federal government requires that the contract be publicly bid and that the "basic principles" of the federal procurement system be observed. The federal government does not require, however, that all the procedures and requirements of the federal system be observed. The procurement is conducted in accordance with the competitive bidding laws of the local grantee.

Public versus Private Bidding

It is common for private developers to refer to "putting a contract out to bid." Private developers are of course not subject to the requirements of public competitive bidding laws. Therefore, the process followed by private project owners bears little resemblance to that followed by public owners.

When a private owner solicits bids, it is motivated only by financial savings.

It wants the work performed at the lowest possible price. The appearance of fairness is not a consideration. Private funds are involved, and the owner is free to award the contract to any company it chooses and free to follow any procedure it chooses.

As a result, "bidding" on private contracts really consists of competitive negotiation. Usually the owner selects two or three companies it is familiar with based on experience on prior projects or based on reputation. Each company is invited to price the work. Frequently the owner makes changes in the definition of the work in order to reduce prices. Sometimes one company is played off against another in an effort to reduce the price. Contractors are sometimes required to invest in the project if they want to receive the construction contract.

All these procedures are perfectly legitimate business practices. The important thing to remember is that the private "bidding" of contracts bears no resemblance to the rigid, formal system of competitive bidding on public contracts. The remainder of the discussion in this chapter is limited to the bidding procedures followed by public project owners.

The Bid Documents

One of the primary principles of public competitive bidding is that all bidders compete on an equal footing. In preparing bid prices, each bidder must be given the same information and must be required to follow the same procedures. When the public owner evaluates bids, it must be comparing apples and apples, not apples and oranges.

In order to accomplish this, a package of bid documents must be prepared. This includes the plans and specifications defining the scope of the work and the contract, complete with general conditions, that the successful bidder will be required to sign. It also includes the bid solicitation itself.

CASE STUDY 3-2

Public Owner did not award contract to low bidder, but rather to the second low bidder.

When challenged in court, Owner said that it favored second low bidder because that company was located within the municipality, paid taxes to the municipality, and employed local residents.

City of Dayton, ex rel. Scandrick v. McGee, 423 N.E.2d 1095 (Ohio 1981).

The Supreme Court of Ohio ruled that this was not a valid reason to fail to award the contract to the low bidder. Local bidders cannot be favored unless such favoritism is authorized by law and the advantage given to local bidders is clearly stated in the bid solicitation. Owners may not apply evaluation criteria that are not stated in the bid solicitation.

Bid solicitations are frequently referred to as an "invitation to bid" or a "request for bids." This is exactly what a solicitation is. A notice or announcement is published in newspapers informing contractors that a particular contract is being put out to bid and informing them where they may obtain a bid package. The time and place of publication is frequently specified by law.

The notice is also frequently published in services such as the Dodge Reports and made available to local chapters of trade organizations such as Associated General Contractors of America. The purpose of the notice is to make as many prospective bidders as possible aware of the upcoming contract and to put bid packages in their hands.

When contractors respond to the notice, they receive a copy of the bid package including the solicitation itself. The solicitation establishes the procedures to be followed. This includes the bid form itself, the time and place the bid must be submitted, any rules or formulas that will be applied in evaluating bids, and the method for amending or clarifying the bid documents.

This last item is very important. In examining bid documents, bidders will frequently have questions regarding the definition of the work. Sometimes a bidder will discover an ambiguity or discrepancy in the plans and specifications. It is advantageous for the project owner to resolve any problems prior to bid submittal, but questions must be answered in a manner that does not give any one bidder a competitive advantage.

In order to assure that all bidders receive the same information, most bid solicitations state that all questions must be submitted in writing and answered in writing. Copies of the question and answer are provided to every prospective bidder who has requested a bid package. If any change is required in the plans and specifications or other contract documents, it will be accomplished by a formal written amendment to the bid solicitation which must be acknowledged in writing by each bidder.

It is also common for public project owners to hold a prebid conference. All prospective bidders are invited to attend. Questions may be asked regarding the bid documents, and all prospective bidders are free to be there to hear the answers. If a bidder elects not to attend the prebid conference, it does so at its peril.

Once bids are opened and the low bidder determined, a "notice of award" is issued to that bidder. The bid package usually states that a notice of award will be issued within a stated number of days of bid opening. Once the formal notice has been issued, the contractor will have a stated number of days to provide the necessary bonds and insurance certificates and execute the actual construction contract.

After contract execution, the contractor usually must wait for a formal "notice to proceed" before starting work. It is usually stipulated that the notice to proceed must be issued within a certain number of days of contract execution. With this, the bidding process and the bid documentation is complete and construction can begin.

For an example of some bid documents, see Appendix A, *AIA Document A701,* "Instructions to Bidders."

BID EVALUATION

Responsiveness

In order to be eligible for contract award, a bid must be "responsive." A bid is responsive if it is an unqualified offer to perform the work in exact accordance with the terms of the bid solicitation. If the bid deviates or takes any exceptions to the terms of the solicitation, it is considered "nonresponsive."

Examples of such deviations would be: "We will require 120 days to perform the work rather than the 110 days specified." Or: "We propose to use vinyl gutters rather than aluminum."

The reason a bid must conform exactly to the solicitation goes back to the discussion of offer and acceptance in Chapter 1. In order for a contract to be formed, there must be a mutual understanding, a meeting of the minds, regarding its terms. A bid is an offer. The project owner can either accept it or reject it. If the owner accepts a bid that deviates from the terms of the solicitation, the owner won't be getting what it asked for.

For instance, it is common for owners to amend the terms of the bid solicitation prior to bid opening. Bidders are asked to acknowledge receipt of the amendment in writing and include the acknowledgment with their bid. If a bidder fails to acknowledge an amendment and the owner accepts the bid anyway, the owner could not force the contractor to perform the work added or changed by the amendment. The contractor never offered to perform that work at the contract price. The owner would have to issue a change order and pay the contractor an additional sum. Therefore, it is a basic rule that failure to acknowledge all amendments renders a bid nonresponsive.

A bid must be responsive at the time of bid opening. Once bids are opened, problems cannot be corrected. For instance, if a bid is low but nonresponsive, it is common for the bidder then to offer to acknowledge the amendment or

---

CASE STUDY 3-3

Low bidder failed to sign bid but did sign the accompanying bid bond which incorporated the bid itself by reference.

Public Owner rejected the low bid as nonresponsive. Low bidder appealed.

The Supreme Court of Washington ruled that the signature on the bid bond incorporating the bid itself was sufficient to unequivocally bind the bidder to the terms of the bid solicitation. The low bidder did not take exception to any of the terms in the bid solicitation; so the bid was responsive.

Farmer Construction, Ltd. v. State of Washington,
656 P.2d 1086 (Wash. 1983).

---

waive the exception it took to the specifications. It is improper for an owner to allow a bidder to do this, however. A bidder gets one chance to submit a responsive bid. Once bids are opened, no bid can be altered.

While this rule seems harsh, it can be traced to one of the primary goals of the competitive bidding system: fair and open competition. If a bidder was allowed to correct a nonresponsive bid after bid opening, it would gain a competitive advantage over the other bidders. It would give that bidder the option, after seeing all the other bid prices, of either correcting its bid and receiving the contract or electing to walk away from the bid with impunity. This obviously works to the disadvantage of the other bidders who submitted responsive bids.

A final, but important, aspect of responsiveness involves the timeliness of bid submittal. Bid solicitations typically specify a precise time and place for bid opening. In order for a bid to be responsive, it must be submitted on time.

On federal procurements, this rule is sternly enforced. There are cases where bids that arrived 30 seconds late at the designated room were ruled nonresponsive. Cases involving state and local procurements have been a little more forgiving in this regard. One rule is ironclad at any level of public procurement, however: Once the first bid has been opened, no bids may be received, altered, or supplemented.

The reason for this rule is the same as stated above. A bidder could submit a nonresponsive bid, see how the first few bid prices were coming in, and then elect to cure the bid by supplementing it with the required acknowledgment, bid bond, etc., or leave the bid nonresponsive and simply walk away. This would be unfair to other bidders and a corruption of the system.

A common mistake made by project owners and their A/E's at bid openings is to receive and open untimely bids. If a bid or a supplement to a bid arrives after the first bid has been opened, the correct procedure is to refuse to physically accept or open that envelope. To open an untimely bid and "take it under advisement" creates confusion and the appearance of possible impropriety. It is also unfair to the bidder to reveal its bid price to its competitors knowing full well that the bid is not eligible for award. An untimely bid simply should not be opened.

Bidder Responsibility

In addition to submitting a responsive bid, a bidder must be deemed "responsible" in order to be eligible for contract award. The purpose is to protect the public treasury by avoiding the award of public contracts to companies or individuals that will be unable or unwilling to properly perform the work.

In determining responsibility, it is appropriate to examine a company's financial condition, its managerial competence, its production capability (does it have access to sufficient equipment and labor?), and its history of performance on similar projects.

Unlike bid responsiveness, which is a very objective determination, bidder responsibility is necessarily a somewhat subjective determination involving the exercise of discretion. Unless a public project owner is arbitrary, capricious, or unreasonable in making this determination, courts will defer to the discretion of the owner.

Certain basic steps can be taken to assure the reasonableness of responsibility determinations. If the owner has any specific responsibility criteria in mind, they should be clearly stated in the bid solicitation. If the owner wants a contractor who has successfully completed at least three similar projects in the past 2 years, that should be stated. The owner shouldn't spring this on bidders after they have already gone to the time and expense of bid preparation.

All responsibility criteria should bear a reasonable relationship to the owner's actual needs. For instance, what difference does it make to the owner if the contractor leases, rather than owns, certain necessary equipment?

In requesting information pertaining to responsibility, identical information should be requested from all bidders. Detailed documentation of the information received should be kept. This information should relate directly to the responsibility criteria being applied. If these steps are followed, it is unlikely that a court will later second-guess an owner's determination of bidder responsibility or nonresponsibility.

There are always unpleasant little surprises that can arise, for instance, discovering that the president of a company has been indicted, but not convicted, for fraud. If the project owner and its A/E can demonstrate a pattern of thorough, businesslike consideration of responsibility matters, however, they may exercise their discretion with confidence.

Bidder responsibility is determined at the time of bidding. The fact that a company had severe problems in the past may not be relevant to present responsibility.

A project owner cannot rely on past history alone in making a finding of nonresponsibility. There must be a showing that those problems exist or are

---

CASE STUDY 3-4

Public Owner refused to award contract to low bidder, saying that low bidder was not responsible.

Owner's determination of nonresponsibility was based on the fact that low bidder was "unknown" to Owner and Owner had heard that low bidder had been late completing a contract in another locale.

The Supreme Court of Georgia ruled that these were insufficient grounds for finding a contractor to be nonresponsible. Owners have broad discretion in making responsibility determinations, but they must conduct an independent, objective investigation into the contractor's financial, managerial, and technical abilities, as well as its past performance. Rumors or a lack of personal familiarity are insufficient.

Hilton Construction Co., Inc. v. Rockdale County Board of Education, 266 S.E.2d 157 (Ga. 1980).

likely to exist today. A contractor may be able to show, through current financial statements or recent performance records, that it has improved itself and is now a responsible bidder. A history of defaults is certainly relevant to the responsibility determination, but if that contractor has successfully completed its last six contracts, the owner would act at its peril in relying on prior defaults to find that contractor nonresponsible.

Unlike bid responsiveness, bidders may provide additional information or correct or clarify information after bid opening if that information pertains to bidder responsibility. Whereas modifying a bid may lend itself to manipulation of the system, there is no competitive advantage to be gained by clarifying one's financial statement after bid opening. Therefore, the general rule is that information pertaining to bidder responsibility may be furnished right up to contract award.

It is sometimes difficult to distinguish whether information pertains to responsiveness or responsibility. For instance, the solicitation may require bidders to include an equipment list with their bids. If a bidder omits the list, does that render the bid nonresponsive? Probably not. The equipment relates to the bidder's ability to perform. Failure to include the list would not enable the bidder to avoid performing the contract in the exact manner specified. Therefore, the bidder should be allowed to furnish the list after bid opening.

A final matter involving bidder responsibility is the prequalification of bidders. Sometimes public owners will conduct a responsibility inquiry before distributing bid packages. The financial, managerial, and performance records of interested, prospective bidders are examined to arrive at a so-called short list of qualified bidders. Only companies on the prequalified list receive bid packages and are eligible to bid.

The prequalification of bidders is perfectly acceptable as long as public owners adhere to necessary notice and publication requirements in order to see that no interested companies are excluded from the responsibility inquiry. And, of course, the responsibility determinations must be made in a fair, reasonable fashion as described above.

It is expensive and time-consuming to prequalify bidders. The records of a large number of companies must be examined, as opposed to a detailed examination of only the lowest two or three bidders. This procedure is primarily used on projects that are unique or extremely sophisticated because bidder responsibility is of paramount concern and there are a limited number of prospective bidders to begin with.

Unbalanced Bids

An unbalanced bid is a bid where one portion of the work does not carry its reasonable share of direct cost, overhead, and profit. This cost and profit is presumably carried in other items of work under the contract, as contractors seldom intentionally price a bid for a loss.

Unbalanced bidding occurs most commonly on unit price bids where estimated quantities of various work items are stated. It also occurs on fixed-price contracts where the work is divided into subitems which are added to arrive at the total bid price.

Unbalanced bids create tension between contractors and owners and raise questions of bid responsiveness. Contractors submit unbalanced bids for one of two reasons. The first is to "front load" the contract. That is, the bidder carries a disproportionate part of the contract price in work items that will be performed early in the job. This enables the contractor to get more money sooner and reduces the contractor's risk and financing charges.

The other reason for unbalancing a bid is to speculate on quantity overruns on a unit price contract. If a contractor thinks that the estimated quantity of item A is understated and the estimated quantity of item B is overstated, it may bid an unrealistically low price for item A and an unreasonably high price for item B. Its bid price will still be competitive because it will be computed using the owner's estimated quantities. If the contractor is awarded the contract and its hunch proves true, it will reap a windfall by performing large volumes of item B work at an inflated price.

It should be clear by now that unbalanced bids are not in an owner's best interest. If an owner pays out too much money at the front end of a project, it increases the risk the contractor will default and it increases its own construction financing charges. And of course, no owner wants to pay out a windfall on a quantity overrun.

In an attempt to avoid this problem, owners commonly state in the bid solicitation that unbalanced bids will be considered nonresponsive. This is quite easy for a private owner who is free to reject any bid for any reason it wants. Public project owners are greatly restrained in their ability to reject unbalanced bids, however.

The general rule in this country is that submission of an unbalanced bid is

---

CASE STUDY 3-5

Public Owner solicited bids for construction of sewer lines. Low bidder bid 1 cent per square foot for temporary sheeting. Owner rejected low bid, saying that it was unbalanced because the cost of the work was not appropriately allocated.

Relying on an affidavit from the bidder stating that it had temporary sheeting left over from another job, the Appeals Court of Massachusetts ruled that the low bid had not misallocated costs.

More important, said the court, the low bid was not materially unbalanced because it did not create a risk that Owner would not get the lowest price or would make progress payments in excess of the value of the completed work. The bid was not "front-loaded" to enable the bidder to derive payments in excess of the value of the work in place.

Department of Labor and Industries v. Boston Water and Sewer Commission, 469 N.E.2d 64 (Mass.App. 1984).

permissible. If a public owner is going to reject an unbalanced bid, it must show that the bid is not only "mathematically unbalanced" but also "materially unbalanced."

A mathematically unbalanced bid simply misallocates cost and profit as described above. In order to be materially unbalanced, the owner must be able to demonstrate that acceptance of that bid would result in a higher total cost to the owner than acceptance of the second low bid. This is usually impossible for the owner to prove.

There are things that owners can do to discourage the submission of unbalanced bids. These include quantity variation clauses, a formal schedule of values, and reserving the right to award a contract for only a portion of the work. These devices will be discussed in subsequent sections of this book. Suffice it to say that it is very difficult to reject a bid as nonresponsive strictly because it is unbalanced.

Computing the Bid Amount

In order to determine the low bidder, it is obviously necessary to compare the various bid amounts. This sounds straightforward, and it usually is. On a fixed-price contract, the owner or its A/E simply compares the total bid amounts. Other types of contracts require more computation, however.

On unit-price contracts, it is necessary to multiply each unit price times the estimated quantity of units stated in the bid solicitation. These subtotals are then added to arrive at the total bid price.

Frequently, the bid solicitation will list certain alternate packages of work that the owner wants the contractor to provide prices for. For instance, alternate A may require bidders to add certain work items to the total scope of work. Alternate B may retain the original scope of work but ask the bidder to price the work on the basis of using a different type of equipment.

A bidder who is low based on one alternate may not be low based on other alternates. The project owner has discretion to base contract award on any alternate or combination of alternates it chooses, as long as it is consistent with any evaluation method or formula established in the bid solicitation. This decision will not be disturbed by the courts if it is based on the owner's good faith determination of its actual needs and is not being done to manipulate the bidding system to exclude a particular contractor.

BID SECURITY

Bid Bonds

Once an owner determines the low responsive bid submitted by a responsible bidder, that owner wants assurance that the bidder will honor the bid and execute the contract. The failure of a low bidder to honor its bid would wreak havoc with the competitive bidding system and force the owner to spend more money by accepting a more expensive bid.

It is therefore customary for public project owners to require each bidder to submit a bid bond with its bid. The bond is typically in the amount of 10 percent of the total bid amount, but it may be more.

If a bidder receives a notice of award and refuses to execute the contract, the bond will be forfeited. The owner will award the contract to the second low bidder. The owner will retain, from the bond proceeds, the difference between the low bid and the second low bid. If that amount exceeds the total face amount of the bond, the entire bond is forfeited. The purpose of the bond is to compensate the owner for the additional costs incurred because of the low bidder's failure to honor its bid.

In order to understand how bid bonds work, it is important to consider the legal relationship among the owner, the contractor, and the bonding company. Within the context of this relationship, the owner is known as the "obligee," the contractor is known as the "principal," and the bonding company is known as the "surety."

The principal and the surety enter into a contract whereby the surety agrees to provide bonding, or security, for the principal's contractual endeavors. The principal agrees to honor all its contractual commitments so that the surety will not have to pay out on the bonds. The principal also agrees to reimburse the surety for any amounts paid out on bonds. Typically, the principal must pledge all its assets to the surety in order to get bonded.

The owner, or obligee, is not a party to the agreement between the surety and its principal. Each time the principal bids on a contract and submits a bid bond, the project owner is the named obligee on the bond. If the principal defaults, or fails to live up to its contractual obligations, the owner can then bring a direct legal action against the surety on the bond even though the owner and surety never entered into a contractual relationship.

In order for a bid to be responsive, it must be accompanied by a bid bond in the required amount. Usually the bid solicitation will require that the bond be furnished by a corporate surety licensed to do business in the state where the project is located.

The bond is usually signed by the surety's local bonding agent, so it must be accompanied by a valid power of attorney indicating that the corporation has given the agent authority to obligate it on the bond. If the bond does not meet all these requirements, the bidder has failed to provide adequate bid security and the bid is nonresponsive.

Owners frequently will allow forms of bid security other than bid bonds. The security may be equivalent to cash, such as a certified check in the required amount. It may also be in the form of an irrevocable letter of credit. It may never be in the form of an instrument which could be revoked or dishonored by any party. Personal checks are never adequate.

The use of a cash equivalent as bid security is generally a last resort for bidders. It ties up far less money to simply pay a bond premium to a corporate surety.

For an example of a bid bond, see Appendix B, *AIA Document A310,* "Bid Bond." Note that it recites the bidder's obligation to the owner. The surety's obligation comes into play only in the event of a default.

Owner's Right to Reject Bids

Many bid solicitations state that the owner reserves the right, at its discretion, to reject "any and all bids." The question arises as to whether or not the public project owner really has legal authority to do this.

Public owners do not have authority to reject "any" bid at their discretion. This would be contrary to the entire concept of competitive bidding. If the owner is going to award a contract, it must make that award based on the lowest responsive bid submitted by a responsible bidder.

Public owners do, however, have the right to reject all bids and decline to award a contract. Courts will allow public owners broad discretion to do this for a variety of reasons. The most common and acceptable reason is a problem with adequate appropriations. Rejection of all bids would probably be allowed, however, even if the owner simply changed its mind. Courts are reluctant to meddle in this function.

The only judicially imposed restraint on the public owner's right to reject all bids is that the owner must exercise its judgment in good faith. When public owners solicit bids, there is an implied obligation to consider all bids fairly and in good faith. The cancellation of a procurement after bid opening has a negative impact on all the bidders. The time and money expended on bid preparation have been wasted. Their bid prices have been exposed to all their competitors.

If an owner doesn't like the low bidder, rejects all bids, and then resolicits bids for an identical scope of work, this would be considered a bad faith exercise of the right to reject bids. The original low bidder could probably recover its bid preparation costs from the project owner. In the absence of such an extreme course of behavior, however, the public owner is generally entitled to reject all bids and return the bid bonds to the bidders.

It should be noted at this point that if there are problems with project financing or necessary regulatory approvals, it is more common, and preferable, for the owner to ask the bidders to extend their bid acceptance periods. For instance, if the solicitation stated that bids must be firm for a period of 60 days, the owner may ask bidders to extend that acceptance period for an additional 60 days. This will give the owner more time to resolve the problem and avoid turning the solicitation into a wasted effort for all involved.

A bidder faced with such a request may extend its acceptance period, holding its bid price firm and keeping its bid bond on line to secure that bid. Alternatively, the bidder may decline to extend its acceptance period. Once the original acceptance period has passed, the bidder may walk away from its bid with no negative consequences. The bid bond would not be in jeopardy be-

---

CASE STUDY 3-6

Public Owner solicited bids for a construction project. The bid solicitation stated that Owner reserved the right to reject all bids.

Owner did in fact reject all bids. One bidder inquired as to reason for rejection of the bids, but Owner said it had no obligation to give an explanation or show cause.

The Court of Appeals of Louisiana ruled that Owner must give reasons for rejecting all bids. Owner must act in good faith when soliciting bids and may not act arbitrarily in rejecting all bids. If Owner is not required to give an explanation for rejection of bids, it would be impossible to determine if Owner was acting in good faith.

Milton J. Womack, Inc. v. Legislative Budgetary Control Council, 470 So.2d 460 (La.App. 1985).

---

cause that bond secured a bid which was firm only for the original period of time stated in the solicitation.

MISTAKES IN BIDS

It is not unusual for a bidder to allege, after bid opening, that it has made a mistake in preparing its bid. The public project owner is then faced with the decision of allowing the bidder to correct its bid, allowing the bidder to withdraw its bid, or attempting to hold the bidder to its bid. The financial consequences of this decision can be very significant for both parties.

This issue arises with great regularity. Consequently, the courts have developed a fairly clear set of guidelines for parties to follow when dealing with bid mistakes.

What Is a "Mistake"?

In order to qualify as a "mistake" in the competitive bidding context, the mistake must be of a factual or arithmetic nature. Classic examples would be the failure to correctly total a column of subitems or the failure to properly apply unit prices to estimated quantities.

A "mistake" cannot involve an error of judgment such as the failure to properly estimate the cost of performing the work or the misreading of a section of the specifications. The failure to include the cost of a specified piece of equipment or material is usually considered factual, not judgmental, however.

Bidder's Right to Withdraw Bid

As a general rule, a bidder is entitled to withdraw its mistaken bid if (1) the mistake is both factual and "material"; (2) there is no gross negligence on the part of the bidder; (3) it would be unconscionable for the owner to enforce the

CASE STUDY 3-7

Contractor priced bid on the assumption it would not be responsible for the transportation of union workers. Contractor's bid was low.

After bid opening, Contractor learned of a union "precedent" which required it to provide transportation. Contractor asked to be allowed to withdraw its mistaken bid. Public Owner refused.

The Supreme Court of Missouri ruled that a bidder cannot obtain relief from a mistaken bid if the mistake was judgmental, rather than clerical or mathematical, in nature. This was an error of judgment; so Contractor could not withdraw the bid. Owner could recover against Contractor's bid bond because of Contractor's refusal to sign contract.

State of Missouri v. Hensel Phelps Construction Co., 634 S.W.2d 168 (Mo. 1982).

bid; (4) the bidder promptly notifies the owner of the mistake; and (5) the owner can be returned to its prior position.

The distinction between a factual and judgmental mistake has been described above. In order for the mistake to be "material," it must involve one of the fundamental aspects of the transaction. Price is always material unless one is talking about a fraction of a percent of the total contract amount. Virtually every bid mistake affects price. Therefore, it is hard to imagine a mistake in a competitive bidding context which is not material.

The requirement that the bidder not be guilty of "gross negligence" is an amorphous one. The courts have never drawn a clear line indicating when negligence becomes gross negligence. As a practical matter, this requirement is invoked by the courts only in those rare instances when the bidder's mistake resulted from such extreme carelessness or sloppiness that the bidder is not deserving of relief.

Courts also require that it be "unconscionable" to hold the bidder to its mistaken bid if the bidder is to be allowed to withdraw the bid. In some ways, this is a redundant requirement. If the mistake has a sufficiently serious impact on price to be considered "material," courts will consider it unconscionable for the owner to enforce the bid.

The final two requirements are interrelated. As soon as the bidder discovers its mistake, it must promptly inform the owner of the mistake and its desire to withdraw the bid. This usually occurs right after bids are opened and there is a large discrepancy between the mistaken bid and the other bids.

The reason for the prompt notification requirement is to inform the owner before the owner takes any steps to its detriment. If the owner has not yet made financial or other commitments based on the mistaken bid, it can simply award the contract to the lowest nonmistaken bid. It will be in the same position it would have been in if the mistaken bid had never been submitted. Therefore, there is no reason not to allow withdrawal of the mistaken bid.

CASE STUDY 3-8

Contractor submitted low bid on construction contract. After bid opening, Contractor discovered that it had made an error in transposing a subcontractor's price from a worksheet onto the bid sheet itself.

Contractor asked permission to withdraw the bid. Public Owner refused.

When Contractor declined to sign the contract, Owner sued.

The Appellate Court of Illinois said a mistaken bid may be withdrawn only if the mistake occurs despite the bidder's exercise of reasonable care. In this case, Contractor's bid checking procedures were so lax that Contractor failed to exercise reasonable care. Contractor was not entitled to withdraw mistaken bid and was liable to Owner for failure to honor bid.

Community Consolidated School District No. 169 v. Meneley Construction Co., 409 N.E.2d 66 (Ill.App. 1980).

There will be no harm to the project owner, and an inequity against the bidder will be avoided.

Bidder's Right to Correct the Bid

Sometimes a bidder will not want to withdraw its mistaken bid. It will want to correct the bid and be awarded the contract at the corrected price. In this situation, the courts are less sympathetic toward the mistaken bidder.

The general rule is that a bidder may correct its mistake and receive the award only if the nature of the mistake and the intended bid amount are clearly evidenced on the face of the bid itself.

Usually, the only mistakes that can meet this test are mathematical errors involving the addition of columns or the extension of unit prices. A mistake involving the omission of a necessary piece of equipment would not qualify, as the intended bid amount could not be clearly determined from the bid sheet itself.

It is impermissible to allow the bidder to offer any documents or other evidence other than the bid form itself if the bidder wants to receive the contract at the corrected price. If the intended amount isn't clear from the face of the bid, the best the bidder can hope for is withdrawal of its bid.

Low bidders sometimes allege mistake and seek contract award at an increased price which still leaves them as low bidder. Occasionally, a second or third low bidder will seek a downward correction of its bid to a price which makes it the low bidder. The question then arises, may a mistaken bid be corrected in a manner which displaces other bidders?

On federal contracts, the displacement of an apparent low bidder will be allowed if the intended amount of the mistaken bid is clearly and convincingly established on the face of the bid itself. Most state courts do not follow this rule, however. On state and local procurements, the general rule is that the displacement of a low bidder will not be allowed regardless of clear evidence of the intended bid amount.

Duties of Owner and Contractor

When considering bid mistakes, several well-established legal duties should be kept in mind. The first is the project owner's duty to seek the bidder's verification of its bid amount.

If the owner has any reason to believe that the bidder may have made a mistake in computing its bid, the owner must so notify the bidder and ask the bidder to check its bid and verify its accuracy.

The occurrence that causes the owner to seek verification is usually the fact that the bid is considerably lower than all other bids received and/or considerably lower than the owner's estimate for the cost of the work. There is no definitive rule as to how much lower the bid has to be in order to trigger the owner's duty to seek verification. Five percent lower probably would not cause the owner to suspect a mistake. Thirty percent lower almost certainly should. For the reasons described below, owners and their A/Es should always err in the direction of seeking verification. From the owner's standpoint, there is nothing to be lost and much to be gained.

If the owner fails to seek verification, the successful bidder may later allege mistake. If it appears that the owner should have suspected a mistake and failed to seek verification, the contractor will be able to avoid its contractual obligations or have the contract reformed to state the higher intended amount. The owner will not be allowed to exploit a known bid mistake in order to get a lower contract price.

If the owner requests verification and the bidder verifies its bid, however, it will be virtually impossible for the bidder to later argue that it made a mistake. Once the bid amount has been verified, the owner has a great deal of assurance that it can hold the bidder to that price.

The bidder has legal duties that affect its ability to allege mistake as well. The first is the bidder's duty to inspect the site prior to submitting its bid. This will be discussed in greater detail in Chapter 8, but it should be noted at this point that the bidder will be held responsible for information that could have been gleaned from a reasonable inspection of the site.

The bidder is also responsible for any information that would have been gained by attending the prebid conference with the owner's representatives. If the bidder fails to inspect the site or attend the prebid conference, it does so at its peril. It should be noted, however, that the type of ''mistake'' that results from one of these omissions is not usually grounds for correction or withdrawal of a bid anyway. This is because it would usually be considered a judgmental, not factual, error.

Finally, the bidder has a duty to notify the owner or its A/E of any "patent," or obvious, errors in the plans and specifications. If the bidder knew or should have known of an error, it cannot price its bid on the basis of the flawed contract documents and then later allege mistake or request a change order.

Just as the owner will not be allowed to exploit a known bid mistake, the bidder will not be allowed to exploit a known error in the plans and specifications. This does not mean, however, that the bidder must check calculations or independently verify other information furnished by the owner. The mistake must be obvious.

SUBCONTRACTOR PROBLEMS

When preparing a bid on a project, a prime, or general, contractor typically obtains bids or quotations from a number of subcontractors. This gives rise to several interesting issues when considering the competitive bidding process.

Holding Subcontractors to Their Quotations

Since the prime contractor is submitting a binding bid in reliance on prices quoted by subcontractors, it is essential to hold those subs to their quotations. The failure of a key subcontractor to honor its price can be the difference between a profitable and unprofitable project.

Unlike the competitive bidding system itself, the procedure for obtaining subcontractor quotations is very informal, even chaotic. Quotations are typically provided at the very last minute. This is because subcontractors don't want the general contractor to "shop around" their quotation. That is, go to subcontractor B and say "Subcontractor A offered to do the work for X dollars. Can you give me a better price?"

Not only are the quotations provided at the very last minute, they are usually provided over the telephone. There is nothing in writing. (It should now be increasingly apparent why there are so many bid mistakes.)

Given this informality, how can the general contractor accomplish the crucial task of holding its subcontractors to their quoted prices? It must rely on the doctrine of equitable estoppel.

This doctrine holds that if the bidder reasonably relies on a subcontractor's quotation in submitting a bid, the subcontractor will be "estopped," or precluded, from reneging on that quotation. The key for the general contractor who is submitting the bid is to document both the quoted price and the reliance on that price. This is usually accomplished by sending a confirming letter right after the oral quotation is received. This letter should confirm the quoted price and should state that it was the lowest received and that it has been relied upon in computing the bid amount. It need not, and from the prime contractor's standpoint should not, represent that the subcontractor will receive the subcontract if the prime contractor receives the prime contract.

CASE STUDY 3-9

Contractor obtained price quotation over the telephone from Subcontractor. Contractor relied on that price when preparing its bid on a contract.

Contractor submitted low bid and was awarded the contract. Subcontractor then refused to honor its quoted price, saying it had inadvertently omitted certain work when preparing its quotation.

The Supreme Court of Alaska ruled that the doctrine of equitable estoppel prevented Subcontractor from refusing to honor its quotation. Contractor reasonably relied on the quotation in submitting an irrevocable, fixed-price bid. Even though no formal subcontract was ever created, Subcontractor would be liable to Contractor for refusal to honor the quoted price.

Alaska Bussell Electric Co. v. Vern Hickel Construction Co., 688 P.2d 576 (Alaska 1984).

The end result of this machination is that the prime contractor can hold the subcontractor to its quoted price but is under no obligation to award the subcontract to that subcontractor. No contract has been formed with the subcontractor. Unless the sub has justifiably changed its financial position (such as ordering materials) in reliance on a representation made by the prime, the prime will be under no obligation.

This is why it is important for prime contractors to avoid making any promises or representations to subcontractors prior to bid submittal. On the other hand, the prudent subcontractor may require exactly that kind of representation prior to going to the expense of preparing a quotation.

Filed Subbids

A number of states have passed legislation pertaining to public procurement which provides structure to this free-for-all. This is a system of "filed subbids."

Under this system, the work is broken down by trade, and trade contractors, who traditionally function as subcontractors to general contractors, are invited to submit bids. These subbids are kept on file. The general contractors who bid on the prime contract are obligated to use the low subbid in each trade category unless they intend to perform that work with their own forces and are qualified to do so. The successful bidder is then obligated to award subcontracts to the low subbidders.

The filed subbid system provides greater structure and predictability to subcontracted work on public projects. This is largely a fortuitous by-product of political lobbying, however. The filed subbid systems result from the political influence of trade associations that wanted their members to have more direct access to public construction dollars and wanted to avoid the evils of bid shopping. Regardless of the motivation, however, the subbid systems have been successful in providing some structure to a chaotic aspect of competitive bidding.

Mistakes by Subcontractors

A mistaken quotation by a subcontractor may be grounds for withdrawal of the prime contractor's bid if it meets the criteria stated earlier for withdrawal of bids.

A mistake by a subcontractor will never be grounds for correction of a bid, however. This is because it is impossible to determine the intended amount of the subcontractor's quotation from the face of the prime contractor's bid.

Finally, because of the doctrine of promissory estoppel, a subcontractor will not be able to get relief from a prime contractor for the sub's mistake once the prime has submitted a binding bid in reliance on the sub's quotation. This assumes, of course, that the sub's error was not so obvious that the prime should have requested verification. As with the owner-contractor relationship, contractors will not be allowed to exploit known mistakes by their subcontractors.

BID PROTESTS

It is quite common in the construction industry for a disappointed bidder to lodge a formal protest claiming that it, not another bidder, should be awarded the contract.

Sometimes the basis of the protest is that the protester's apparent low bid was wrongfully rejected as nonresponsive. Sometimes the protester argues that another bidder's low bid should have been rejected as nonresponsive. Protests also sometimes involve the public agency's alleged failure to follow procurement regulations or alleged irregularities in the plans and specifications.

Forum and Procedure

The threshold question is where are bid protests filed? The initial protest is usually filed with the procuring agency itself. Most public agencies have an established administrative procedure for hearing bid protests. This procedure must be followed before seeking relief in court.

If the protester is unsuccessful at the administrative level, it may appeal to a court of competent jurisdiction to enjoin, or halt, the contract award or contract performance and consider the alleged improprieties in the procurement.

The bid protest procedure on federal contracts follows this basic pattern. Initially, the disappointed bidder must lodge a written protest with the procuring agency itself. If this is denied, the protester has 10 working days to file a protest with the Comptroller General's Office of the General Accounting Office. Alternatively, the protester may appeal directly to the comptroller general or may seek an injunction in U.S. District Court. The federal courts traditionally show great deference toward the comptroller general in procurement matters, however.

The 10-day filing period is worth noting. Bid protests at every level of public procurement are subject to very short filing deadlines. This is in order to avoid disruption to the procurement process and to avoid delay in government agencies obtaining the goods and services they need. Failure to file a timely protest is absolutely fatal to the protest. It won't even be considered. Any disappointed bidder considering a protest should immediately determine the filing deadline and should operate on the assumption that the protest must be filed very promptly.

Remedies

Considering the large number of bid protests that are lodged each year, it is ironic that so few meaningful legal remedies are available to the protesters. One could go so far as to say that it is the least fruitful form of litigation.

Even if the protester obtains an injunction or suspension of the procurement, it by no means guarantees that the protester will succeed on the merits of its protest. If the protester succeeds in its protest, it will not automatically be awarded the contract. The contract will be put out to bid again, and the protester will simply get another chance to bid.

If the contract has already been awarded, the court will probably just admonish the agency to adhere to procurement regulations in the future. On rare occasions, however, the comptroller general will order a federal contract terminated and put out to rebid.

Sometimes, however, when the contract has already been awarded, a successful protester will recover its bid preparation costs and protest expenses. This is because the public agency has breached the implied obligation to treat all bidders fairly, as described earlier in this chapter.

The bidder will receive only its out-of-pocket expenses, however. It will not be entitled to the anticipated profit on the contract or any other damages.

In conclusion, the best a bid protester can generally hope to receive is another chance to bid on the contract or the recovery of its bid preparation and protest costs.

KEY TERMS AND CONCEPTS

bid solicitation   An owner's invitation for contractors to submit bids for a construction project. The bid solicitation should contain a complete definition of the work to be performed, as well as a complete statement of the legal terms and conditions which will govern performance of the work.

bid responsiveness   In order to be responsive, a bid must match the terms of the bid solicitation. It may not deviate from the terms of the solicitation, take any exceptions to the terms, or place any limitations on the terms. A responsive bid also must be submitted in a timely manner and comply with any other requirements for bid submittal that are stated in the bid solicitation. If a bid is not responsive at the time of bid opening, it must be rejected. A nonresponsive bid may not be corrected, cured, or clarified.

bidder responsibility A bidder is responsible if it possesses the technical and managerial capability, financial resources, and experience necessary to perform the particular work for which a bid is being submitted. A responsibility determination must be based on a bidder's present condition. Responsibility can be determined after bid opening. If a public project owner reasonably determines that a low bidder is not responsible, the owner need not award the contract to that bidder.

unbalanced bid A bid is unbalanced if unit prices or components of a lump-sum price do not carry an appropriate share of the total direct cost, overhead, and profit. A bid is materially unbalanced if acceptance of that bid creates a risk that the project owner will not obtain the lowest possible price. Public project owners are not obligated to accept a low bid if that bid is materially unbalanced.

bid bond A bond furnished by a third-party surety guarantying that the bidder will honor its bid, if accepted by the owner, and sign the contract at the bid price. If a bidder fails to honor its bid, the owner may recover from the surety the difference between the bid price and the next lowest bid price. Bid solicitations usually require that bid bonds be furnished in the amount of a stated percentage of the bid price. A bid which is not accompanied by an adequate bid bond is not responsive.

mistaken bid A bid which contains an error of a clerical or mathematical, as opposed to judgmental, nature. If the bidder can demonstrate the existence of the mistake and show that the mistake occurred despite its own reasonable precautions, the bidder will be allowed to withdraw the bid and the bid bond will not be in jeopardy.

equitable estoppel If a contractor reasonably relies on a quotation submitted by a subcontractor and incorporates the quoted price into a firm bid, the doctrine of "equitable estoppel" will prevent the subcontractor from reneging on its quotation if the contractor's bid is accepted by the project owner and the contractor is called upon to perform the work at its bid price.

filed subbids A system used on some public projects whereby trade contractors submit bids to the project owner for specified portions of the project. The general contractor must use the low subbidders when preparing its bid and performing the work unless the general contractor intends to perform that portion of the work with its own forces.

bid protest A bidder's administrative appeal to a public authority complaining that the procurement has been conducted in a manner that violates the laws or regulations governing competitive bidding.

CHAPTER 4

ARCHITECTS, ENGINEERS, AND THE CONSTRUCTION PROCESS

THREE PHASES OF THE A/E'S WORK

As design professionals, architects and engineers (A/Es) play a unique role in the construction process. On a typical project, the A/E is the only party other than the project owner who is actively involved from beginning to end.

The A/E's responsibilities typically span the three project phases described below. It is important to note, however, that it is not unusual for A/Es to be retained for only one or two of the project phases.

Planning Phase

The planning phase of the project usually involves an examination of the general feasibility of the owner's desires as well as an examination of where and how the project will be constructed. Central to all these considerations is the issue of project budget.

The A/E's design expertise enables him or her to advise the owner of whether certain sites under consideration can physically accommodate the intended structure. Additionally, there is the question of land use regulations and other necessary permits and licenses.

In conjunction with evaluation of potential sites, there is an evaluation of the various ways of designing and constructing the facility. Developers usually have rather specific ideas about what they want the facility to be capable of, but they look to the A/E for advice on how to accomplish this. The three competing considerations are function, appearance, and cost. The A/E is best equipped to assist the project owner in arriving at a design and a site that will satisfy the owner in all three considerations.

Sometimes the owner is committed to a single site and the design must accommodate the site. Other times the owner has a number of site options and can be more rigid in its design scheme, seeking out a site that will accommodate the design.

One of the A/E's most important planning phase responsibilities is to estimate the total cost of certain designs under consideration. This is difficult, as these designs are extremely cursory and conceptual at this point. The owner cannot start to make intelligent decisions, however, until it has an idea of how much a particular project might cost. Furthermore, construction financing will not be available unless the owner is armed with reliable estimates of construction cost.

An estimate of the necessary construction schedule goes hand in hand with the cost estimate, as time truly is money in the construction industry.

When a project has been thoroughly planned, the owner should have a designated site and be familiar with the physical characteristics of the site, including subsurface conditions. The owner should know that the intended project complies with all land use regulations and other permit requirements. The owner should also have cost and schedule estimates for construction of the facility as conceptualized. The owner is then in a position to go to a lender and seek construction financing.

The owner will typically look to its A/E to pull this entire package together. Frequently, the assistance of other professionals such as attorneys, scheduling experts, estimators, and geotechnical specialists is required. The A/E is usually the party responsible for coordinating their efforts, however, in order to come up with a project plan.

Design Phase

The design phase of the project usually progresses from preliminary design to detailed working drawings sufficient to put out to bid. As this process unfolds, the twin considerations of cost and schedule are always present.

Very few project owners start out with an ironclad view of what they want. Most owners are subject to budgetary and/or scheduling restrictions. As the plans progress from the conceptual or preliminary stage to the final stage of working drawings, these considerations come into play.

A detailed description of the design process is outside the scope of this book. Two issues, however, must be stressed at this time. One is the A/E's responsibility for the work of consultants and the other is the definition of the scope of the A/E's design responsibilities.

It is customary for the prime design professional, be it an architect or an engineer, to utilize the skills and knowledge of a number of experts from specialized disciplines. Sometimes these disciplines are available within the prime designer's own firm. Other times they are hired as "consultants" or subcontractors.

Just as the prime construction contractor is fully responsible for the work of its subcontractors, the prime design contractor is fully responsible for the adequacy and competency of the work of its consultants. If a consultant makes a mistake, the prime design contractor will be just as liable to the project owner as it would be had it made the mistake itself.

This points to the need to be very cautious in selecting consultants to use in the design process. It also points out the need to see that consultants carry adequate levels of professional malpractice insurance and agree to indemnify the prime designer in the event of a claim involving the adequacy of the consultant's work. The improper selection, monitoring, and coordination of consultants is a major source of problems during the design phase.

The other important issue to keep in mind regarding the design phase is the definition of the A/E's scope of work. The agreement between the project owner and the A/E should precisely spell out the A/E's responsibilities. If the A/E is being asked to rely on certain information such as a survey, the agreement should so state. In fact, any time an A/E is asked to utilize data which the A/E is not being hired to verify independently, the agreement should indicate that the A/E is relying on the accuracy and adequacy of this owner-furnished information.

This concern should always be paramount in preparation of an A/E agreement. If the scope of work is not detailed and precise, how can anyone determine if a particular item is extra work? More important, if a problem develops, how will it be determined whether the A/E was responsible for dealing with this particular matter?

A well-conceived, detailed scope of work can save the A/E a world of trouble as the design phase progresses.

Construction Phase

The A/E's responsibilities during the construction phase of the project vary greatly. It is therefore important again to have a detailed scope of work, as this will be relied on to determine responsibility and liability if a problem arises.

The A/E's construction phase responsibilities usually begin with preparation of bid packages. These consist of the final plans and specifications, the construction contract, the general conditions, bid forms, and instructions to bidders. Bids are solicited by advertisement or otherwise, and bid packages are given to prospective bidders.

Prior to bid opening, the A/E may be responsible for issuing amendments to the bid package and conducting prebid site inspections and prebid construction meetings where bidders' questions are answered. When bids are opened, the A/E frequently serves as the owner's representative, determining the low bidder and announcing the contract award.

Once work begins, the A/E usually monitors the contractor's performance. This is the riskiest and most controversial aspect of the A/E's construction phase services. It will be addressed in detail later in this chapter.

When work is complete, the A/E conducts a final inspection, prepares a punch list of remaining items, authorizes release of final payment, and otherwise assists the owner with the tasks of closing out the project.

If all goes reasonably well, the A/E has the satisfaction of guiding and participating in the project from its earliest conceptualization through detailed design, construction, and completion. The A/E has been instrumental in turning vague ideas into a functioning physical facility.

A/E'S OBLIGATIONS TO THE OWNER

An A/E on a typical project is wearing several hats. First and foremost the A/E is functioning as an independent professional providing professional services for a fee. The A/E also functions from time to time as an agent of the owner and as an arbitrator of disputes between the owner and the contractor.

The A/E's role as agent and arbitrator will be discussed in the claims process section at the end of this chapter. This section of the chapter will focus on the A/E's professional obligations to his or her client, the project owner.

Standard of Care

The A/E's obligation is to exercise the degree of care, skill, and knowledge that is generally expected within the profession. This is true during all three phases of the project. It is the same standard applied to doctors, lawyers, and other providers of professional services.

An A/E's service or advice need not reflect superlative brilliance in the field, but it must meet a certain minimum level of expertise that is vaguely defined as "acceptable" or "average." When performing design calculations, for instance, the A/E must follow certain procedures that are generally accepted in the profession. The failure to do so will probably be considered negligence or professional malpractice.

It is important to note that an A/E who holds himself or herself out as possessing particular expertise in a field will be held to a standard of care applied to such experts. For instance, if a civil engineer takes it upon himself or herself

---

CASE STUDY 4-1

Owner awarded Contractor a contract for construction of a sewer project. The contract stated that neither Owner nor Engineer assumed responsibility for Contractor's ability to meet the specified infiltration limits and if Contractor felt the design was inadequate to meet the limits, Contractor must notify Engineer in writing.

Contractor was unable to meet the infiltration limits. Contractor sued Owner for breach of implied warranty of the specifications and sued Engineer for negligent preparation of the specifications. Defendants relied on the disclaimer in the construction contract.

The Appellate Court of Illinois ruled that all owners extend an implied warranty to contractors that the plans and specifications are accurate, complete, and suitable for the completion of the project. The A/E in turn assumes a duty to prepare design documents that meet this standard. These fundamental obligations cannot be disclaimed or shifted to the contractor. The language in the contract was unenforceable.

W. H. Lyman Construction Co. v. Village of Gurnee, 403 N.E.2d 1325 (Ill.App. 1980).

---

to evaluate subsurface data or perform structural calculations, the civil engineer will be expected to possess and exercise the same degree of care, skill, and knowledge expected of a geotechnical engineer or a structural engineer. Once an A/E undertakes a particular endeavor, it is no excuse to later argue that this was really outside the A/E's field of expertise. This explains the widespread use of technical consultants and subcontractors.

Over the years, a few court decisions have held that an A/E extends an implied warranty that its design documents are complete and accurate and suitable for their intended purpose. Although doctors and lawyers have never been asked to warrant the successful outcome of their services, some courts have reasoned that the design professions are more empirical and more subject to perfection.

These court decisions have been greeted with alarm in the design professions. It must be stressed, however, that these decisions are anomalies. They do not represent the mainstream of judicial thinking regarding the A/E's standard of care. In the absence of contractually assumed liability, which is discussed below, the A/E is held only to a standard of due care, and that standard is measured by the skills and knowledge of the average practitioner. This is the rule that is applied in virtually every jurisdiction in the United States. Cases imputing an implied warranty have been overruled, discredited, or limited in their effect.

A/E's Contractual Obligations

In addition to the A/E's general obligation to exercise due care, the A/E has a number of specific contractual obligations established in its agreement with the project owner.

CASE STUDY 4-2

Owner retained Engineer to design wastewater treatment plant. Engineer based design on use of cement-bentonite slurry wall. Engineer relied on Supplier's representations regarding the compressive strength of the product and conducted no independent investigation into the properties of the product.

The wall failed and caused extensive damage to the treatment plant. Owner sued Engineer for professional malpractice.

The U.S. District Court ruled that Engineer failed to exercise the skill and judgment expected of a design professional. An A/E does not guarantee the sufficiency of its design. Nor is an A/E expected to conduct an extensive independent testing program on every product it specifies. It was negligent, however, for this engineer to blindly rely on Supplier's representations without seeking some independent verification.

City of Columbus v. Clark-Dietz & Associates—Engineers, Inc.,
550 F.Supp. 610 (N.D.Miss. 1982).

An architectural or engineering services agreement bears little resemblance to a construction contract. To begin with, it is always negotiated, not competitively bid. Additionally, there are not the large number of contingencies that need to be addressed in a construction contract.

A typical A/E agreement addresses the basic issues of fee, schedule, insurance, and use of consultants. The agreement then devotes most of its space to defining the scope of the A/E's work.

As mentioned earlier, the definition of the scope of work is crucial in defining the A/E's contractual obligations. Without a detailed, complete, and understandable scope of work, it is impossible to determine where the A/E's responsibilities began and where they ended. It is also impossible to identify and recover payment for extra work items not included in the original scope.

Most A/Es use a standard, preprinted form of agreement for their contracts with project owners. This may be a form prepared by their attorney for their use, or it may be one of the forms published by the professional organizations. Both the American Institute of Architects and the Engineers' Joint Contract Documents Committee publish such forms. These forms have been officially approved by their respective organizations, and they avoid the serious pitfalls of A/E agreements that are described below. See Appendix C for *AIA Document B141*, "Standard Form of Agreement between Owner and Architect."

There are two serious pitfalls that should be avoided by A/Es when entering into agreements with project owners. They are two forms of contractually assumed liability: warranties and indemnification clauses.

As described earlier, courts have refused to read an implied warranty into an A/E agreement. The A/E has a duty to exercise due care in carrying out his or her professional responsibilities, but the A/E does not impliedly warrant to the owner that the work product is flawless or will accomplish everything the owner wanted the A/E to.

Even though courts have refused to find an implied warranty, it is still possible for the A/E to extend an express, or written, warranty to the owner. This is seldom labeled as a warranty in the A/E services agreement, but it occurs nonetheless. For instance, the designer of an industrial facility may be asked to guarantee that the facility as designed will be capable of meeting certain performance standards. This would be considered an express warranty.

The problem with warranties is twofold. First of all, an A/E may exercise due care and even professional excellence at all times, and still have a project fall short of expectations because of variables beyond the A/E's control. With a warranty, the A/E is liable nonetheless, and this greatly expands the A/E's liability exposure.

The second problem with warranties is insurance coverage. There simply isn't any. The insurance companies who write "errors and omissions" or professional malpractice policies for A/Es are alarmed at any contractually assumed liability. They are only willing to cover the risk that the A/E will fail to meet the required professional standards. The policies invariably exclude coverage for liability resulting from warranties. It is therefore in the best interest of both owner and A/E that warranties be kept out of the agreement.

The second form of contractually assumed liability is the indemnification clause. Again, the problems are the expansion of liability exposure and the lack of insurance coverage.

An agreement to indemnify another party is an agreement to protect them, pay them, and otherwise make them whole in the event a claim is asserted against them. To the extent the indemnification clause is limited to claims against the owner arising solely out of the A/E's negligence, this is not a problem, as the A/E would be liable for its negligence anyway.

The problem is that indemnification clauses are frequently written in such a way that the A/E's liability is contractually expanded to include claims not arising out of its own negligence. The most common example is the indemnification clause which refers to claims arising "in whole or in part" from the A/E's services. In other words, the A/E may be 10 percent responsible for the problem, but it has agreed to fully compensate the project owner.

As with express warranties, insurance companies are not willing to cover expanded liability resulting from indemnification clauses. There are almost always exclusions in the insurance contracts, although these exclusions can sometimes be removed or reduced through the purchase of indemnification riders.

While on the subject of contractually assumed liability, there is one other topic which should be addressed. This is the A/E's effort to contractually limit its liability for its own negligence.

These "limitation of liability clauses" typically state that the A/E's liability to the owner shall not, under any circumstances, exceed a certain stated amount. The use of these clauses, which are legally enforceable, has been pushed by some A/E insurance carriers and professional associations.

Just as A/Es and their insurers have been reluctant to agree to a contractual expansion of A/E liability, project owners have been reluctant to agree to the contractual limitation of the A/E's traditional liability. It is fair to say that the use of limitation of liability clauses is not gaining widespread acceptance in the industry.

Sufficiency of the Plans and Specifications

Probably the single most important obligation the A/E has toward the project owner is the obligation to prepare a complete, accurate, and unambiguous set of plans and specifications.

It was stated earlier that implied warranties are not read into A/E service agreements. It is so well established, however, that an A/E has a professional obligation to produce sufficient plans and specifications that it almost rises to the level of an implied warranty.

The plans and specifications should not omit anything that is necessary or include anything that is redundant. They should be free of conflicts and ambiguities. They should be accurate regarding existing site conditions. And it should be possible to construct the project as designed using commercially acceptable construction methods in order to end up with a functioning facility.

As will be seen later, the sufficiency of the plans and specifications is crucial regarding the A/E's liability to the owner, the owner's liability to construction contractors, and the A/E's liability to construction contractors.

Liability for Cost Estimates

It is common, at the planning stage of a project, for the owner to tell the A/E that there is a certain maximum budget for the project. This is obviously a crucial consideration throughout the design phase of the project. The A/E must estimate the construction cost of the facility he or she is designing. This is difficult, because it involves assessing such intangibles as the local competitive bidding climate.

The question arises, what happens when all the bids or quotations come in and the project, as designed, is over its budget? What are the A/E's responsibilities in this situation?

To begin with, the A/E is expected to use ordinary professional skill in estimating construction costs but is not expected to predict costs with dead accuracy. It is unusual for a construction cost overrun to be successfully asserted as a malpractice claim against an A/E.

Most A/E service agreements address this issue. Typically, they state that the A/E's sole responsibility if bids come in over budget is to provide redesign work at no additional charge in order to bring the project within budget. The A/E cannot be held liable for monetary damages. Sometimes the agreement will state that the A/E's obligation to provide free redesign services will accrue only if the low responsive, responsible bid exceeds the budget by a certain stated percent. In any event, the A/E's obligations in this situation should be expressly established in the A/E service agreement. For an example, see Subparagraph 3.2.4 in Appendix C.

A/E'S LIABILITY TO THIRD PARTIES

Traditionally, the A/E's only responsibilities were owed to the project owner, the client with whom the A/E did business. Evolving legal trends have changed all that. Along with every other participant in our economy, the A/E now finds itself exposed to liability to third parties with whom the A/E never did business.

The Demise of "Privity"

"Privity of contract" means that a direct contractual relationship exists between two parties. They have entered into an agreement.

Traditionally, the law held that an A/E could not be sued by a construction contractor or any other third party not in privity with the A/E. The A/E's professional obligations were owed strictly to its client, the project owner. It was the owner that the A/E contracted with and the owner who paid the A/E. Therefore, the A/E need consider only the interests of the project owner.

The past 40 years have seen the near total demise of privity as a requirement for maintaining a lawsuit for commercial damages. The trend began in the context of product liability litigation and spread to every area of law including A/E liability.

Today, it is safe to say that the lack of privity of contract will rarely protect an A/E in a suit alleging the negligence or professional malpractice of the A/E. As a result, A/Es are being sued by contractors, subcontractors, bonding companies, construction lenders, and other parties on the construction project with whom the A/E has no contractual relationship.

Foreseeable Harm

With the demise of privity, the new operative phrase is "foreseeable harm." Today's rule can be summarized as follows: In carrying out its professional

---

CASE STUDY 4-3

Mechanical Engineer prepared drawings pursuant to agreement with Owner. Contractor later complained that the drawings were inaccurate and sued Engineer for the increased cost of performing the construction work.

Engineer responded that its only obligation was to its client, the Owner. Engineer said it had no contract, and therefore no legal obligations, with regard to Contractor.

The Superior Court of New Jersey ruled that Contractor could sue Engineer for its increased costs. Privity of contract is no longer required in order to maintain a suit of this nature. A/Es may be held liable to any party for the economic consequences of their professional negligence if it was reasonably foreseeable that the injured party would be affected by the A/E's performance of its professional duties.

Conforti & Eisele, Inc. v. John C. Morris Associates, 418 A.2d 1290 (N.J.Super. 1980).

responsibilities, the A/E has a duty to exercise ordinary skill and due care. That duty is owed to all parties who could foreseeably suffer economic harm as a result of the A/E's failure to exercise due care. If one of those parties is harmed as a result of the A/E's lack of due care, that party may maintain an action against the A/E for negligence.

Common Claims against A/Es

The most common source of third-party claims against A/Es is the A/E's inspection and certification role in the construction process. This is discussed in detail below. The other two common sources of third-party claims are design deficiencies and delayed response to requests or submittals.

Design deficiencies would include inaccuracies or conflicts in the plans and specifications, as well as any insufficiencies in the design documents. The plans and specifications must be complete and sufficient so that if they are adhered to by a construction contractor, a complete, operational project will result.

Contractors are entitled to rely on the plans and specifications when bidding and planning a job. To the extent design deficiencies increase the cost of the contractor's performance, the A/E may well be held liable to the contractor.

An A/E's delayed response to requests or submittals is another source of claims by contractors. When a contractor seeks clarification or direction from the A/E when faced with an unanticipated problem, the A/E has an implied obligation to respond within a reasonable period of time. If the A/E does not, and the lack of a response delays the contractor or extends its total performance time, the A/E may be held liable to the contractor for its delay damages.

Submittals typically involve product catalogs, shop drawings, and other things

---

CASE STUDY 4-4

Engineer prepared plans and specifications for wastewater treatment plant pursuant to agreement with Owner. The specifications required certain internal components in the sludge pumps.

Contractor prepared its bid in reliance on a quotation from Supplier. Engineer refused to accept the particular model pump being offered. Supplier had to furnish Contractor with a more expensive pump in order to obtain Engineer's approval. Supplier then sued Engineer for the increased cost, arguing that Engineer had negligently drafted and incorrectly interpreted the specification. Engineer responded that it owed no duty to an equipment supplier.

The Court of Appeals of Minnesota ruled that Engineer did owe Supplier a duty to exercise due care in the drafting and interpretation of specifications. An A/E's obligation to exercise appropriate professional skill and judgment extends to all parties who may foreseeably rely on the A/E's services.

Waldor Pump & Equipment Co. v. Orr-Schelen-Mayeron & Associates, Inc., 386 N.W.2d 375 (Minn.App. 1986).

---

that must be approved by the A/E before the contractor incorporates them into the project. Sometimes the construction contract stipulates that these documents will be turned around in a certain minimum time. Even if the contract contains no such provision, there is an implied obligation for the A/E to make a decision within a reasonable period of time. Prompt decisions on these matters are frequently crucial to the contractor's ability to maintain its schedule.

A/Es are also called upon to make decisions regarding contractors' change order proposals. This will be discussed at the conclusion of this chapter.

THE A/E'S INSPECTION RESPONSIBILITIES

During the construction phase of a project, it is common for the A/E to inspect the contractor's work on behalf of the project owner. This gives rise to questions regarding the scope of the A/E's inspection responsibilities and the A/E's liability for shortcomings in carrying out those responsibilities.

Scope of Responsibility

The scope of the A/E's inspection responsibilities is primarily established in the written agreement between the A/E and the project owner. A very precise and well-considered scope of work is therefore necessary in order to avoid misunderstanding on the owner's part and unintended liability exposure on the A/E's part.

Very few owners are willing to pay an A/E to station personnel at the job site 50 or 60 hours a week to observe every move of the contractor. Nor are owners willing to pay to have every piece of material used by the contractor laboratory-tested.

Most owners are seeking periodic inspection of the work. The owner-A/E agreement should reflect this. The scope of work should be explicit as to how

---

CASE STUDY 4-5

Contractor awarded purchase order to Fabricator for exterior metal stairway. Fabricator submitted shop drawings to Contractor, who in turn submitted the drawings to Architect for approval.

Architect was slow reviewing the shop drawings. The delay increased Fabricator's costs. Fabricator sued Architect for unreasonably withholding approval of the shop drawings. Architect argued that its only duty in reviewing shop drawings was to protect the interests of its client, the Owner.

The Court of Appeal of Louisiana disagreed. It was foreseeable that subcontractors such as Fabricator would be economically affected by Architect's performance of its functions. Architect therefore owed a duty to those parties to exercise due care in carrying out its responsibilities.

Gurtler, Hebert & Co., Inc. v. Weyland Machine Shop, Inc., 405 So.2d 660 (La.App. 1981).

many times a week or a month the A/E is expected to visit the site. If particular materials or installations are to be tested, this should be clearly spelled out. The agreement should then make it clear that the A/E's inspection and testing responsibilities do not extend beyond those specifically listed and the A/E does not guarantee the sufficiency of the contractor's work. For an example, see Paragraph 1.5 of Appendix C.

In recent years, a somewhat semantical debate has arisen regarding the use of the term "monitoring" rather than "inspection." The rationale is that if an A/E "inspects" the work, the A/E will be liable for failing to detect problems, whereas if the A/E only "monitors" the work, it will be held to a lower standard of observation.

This distinction has its genesis in several arcane court decisions, but it is generally lacking in validity. It is unlikely that a modern court would allow the question of an A/E's liability to turn on the use of the verb "inspect" rather than "monitor."

There is certainly no harm in the cautionary use of the term "monitor." Many A/Es, influenced by their liability insurers, have become more comfortable with this parlance. This is fine, but A/Es should not be lulled into believing that the use of the term "monitor" will excuse the failure to meet professionally accepted standards or otherwise lessen their obligations.

Even if the owner-A/E agreement calls for the A/E to monitor the contractor's work, the A/E will still be required to authorize release of payments and acceptance of the work. This authorization requires an affirmative determination on the part of the A/E. The A/E will not be able to hide behind the somewhat passive connotations in the term "monitor."

CASE STUDY 4-6

Owner awarded architectural agreement to Architect using the AIA Standard Form of Agreement between Owner and Architect. Architect prepared specifications requiring liquid mortar to be poured in a particular fashion.

Contractor had trouble with the pours and poured mortar in a manner that deviated from the specifications. Architect observed these pours but did not object. When the walls developed problems, Owner sued Architect for failing to inspect Contractor's work in the manner required by the AIA architectural agreement.

The Supreme Court of Arkansas noted that the AIA agreement does not require the architect to make continuous or exhaustive inspections and does not make the architect the guarantor of the contractor's compliance with the plans and specifications. However, the agreement does require the architect to "guard the owner against defects and deficiencies in the work." If Architect observed nonconforming work being performed and failed to object, Architect breached its inspection duties under the agreement.

Dan Cowling & Associates, Inc. v. Board of Education of Clinton District School, 618 S.W.2d 158 (Arkansas 1981).

A/Es who are concerned about the liability exposure arising from construction phase activities should focus their attention on the preparation of a detailed, explicit scope of work in the owner-A/E agreement. This is the best precaution to take against expansive liability exposure.

Conformance with Plans and Specifications

One of the A/E's primary inspection responsibilities is to determine whether the contractor is conforming to the plans and specifications for the project. The owner is entitled to strict conformance with the plans. This is what the owner is paying the contractor for. If the contractor is deviating from the plans and specs, it is important for the owner to know so that the owner may take protective measures such as withholding payment.

When inspecting the contractor's work for conformance to the plans and specifications, the A/E is expected to use the skill and care generally accepted within the profession. The A/E is not expected to perform material tests or take other elaborate measures unless this is called for in the agreement with the owner.

There are two common pitfalls for A/Es when inspecting the work. The first is a lack of familiarity with the contract requirements. This is particularly inexcusable, as the A/Es usually have prepared the plans and specifications themselves. If the A/E is not thoroughly familiar with the detailed requirements of the construction contract, it will be impossible for the A/E to determine whether the contractor is conforming to those requirements.

The second pitfall is the failure to inspect work before it is covered up. Most construction contracts prohibit the contractor from covering up work before the owner or its representative have inspected it. A/Es must be alert to strictly enforce this provision. It is impossible for an A/E to reach a responsible professional opinion regarding the sufficiency of the work if the work is now under 4 feet of backfill or concealed by a new wall.

Frequently, the plans and specifications require a certain amount of interpretation. Plans that require a great deal of interpretation are probably sloppy or incomplete. Nonetheless, it is inevitable that questions will arise regarding the intended meaning of the plans and specs or their application to particular field conditions. In rendering these interpretations, the A/E is expected to be objective and to avoid an expansive reading of the contract requirements.

Because plans and specifications require a certain amount of interpretation, it is customary for the owner to hire the same A/E who designed the project to perform construction phase activities. The rationale is that the designer is in the best position to interpret the design and judge the contractor's conformance to that design.

There is a countervailing school of thought, however. Some large institutional project owners, including several agencies of the federal government, prefer to hire a separate A/E for construction phase activities. The concern is that the A/E who designed the project will have a vested interest in defending the adequacy and integrity of the design. If there are problems with the design, the A/E will not be objective in arriving at an appropriate solution. Still, the prevailing practice is for the project owner to hire the designer to inspect the contractor's work.

Occasionally, matters of artistic interpretation arise during construction. For instance, this could involve the approval of a particular shade of paint. Construction contracts typically give the architect broad discretion to make these determinations.

A/Es should not confuse the unfettered discretion they have in making artistic determinations with their role in interpreting the plans and specifications. Properly prepared design documents should speak for themselves and require a minimum of elaboration. The A/E's inspection responsibility is to render an opinion regarding the contractor's conformance with those objective requirements. The A/E is not allowed to embellish the design as the work progresses.

A final issue involving conformance with the design has to do with the A/E's approval of shop drawings and other submittals. Shop drawings are drawings submitted by construction contractors to project owners depicting the way certain aspects of the work are to be performed. Shop drawings typically address such matters as the fabrication or assembly of a particular item or the form and fit of a particular aspect of the work.

Shop drawings are necessary, particularly on large or complex construction projects. It is impossible for even the most complete set of plans and specifications to depict every detail of every installation throughout the project. Furthermore, there are certain aspects of the work where the owner and A/E look to the contractor to provide expertise in fabrication or installation of an item or even selection of a particular proprietary product.

In reviewing and approving shop drawing submittals or submittals proposing the use of a particular product, the A/E should be guided by a desire for conformance with the expressed intentions of the plans and specifications. This is what the A/E's approval of a shop drawing submittal indicates. The work as depicted in that drawing will conform to the plans and specifications.

Much has been made of the choice of language used in approving shop drawings. A/Es are concerned that when approving shop drawings, they will inadvertently waive or alter contract requirements, thereby exposing themselves to a liability claim by the project owner. They therefore use very equivocal, noncommital language in "approving" shop drawing submittals.

One typical statement, found on a stamp affixed to a shop drawing submittal, reads as follows: "Review is only to check for compliance with the design concept of the project. Approval does not indicate the waiver of any contract requirement. Changes in the work may be authorized only by written change order."

The use of this language does little to protect the A/E but a great deal to create confusion. Under the terms of the typical contract documents, the contractor cannot proceed with the work until it receives approval of submittals. Either the submittal was approved or it wasn't approved. Once it was approved, contractors are entitled to act in reliance on that approval. Courts are not sympathetic to an A/E's after-the-fact, self-serving explanation of what he or she really meant to say when he or she approved a shop drawing submittal.

A/Es who are concerned about inadvertently waiving contract requirements can take solace from one basic legal principle. If a contractor submits a shop drawing which entails any deviation from the plans and specifications, this deviation must be prominently noted on the drawing itself. If the drawing involves a change which the contractor fails to flag, the A/E's approval of the drawing will not constitute a waiver of the contract requirements.

Contractor's Percentage of Completion

Another of the important inspection functions of the A/E during the construction phase of the project is to determine the amount of progress the contractor has made. This is crucial, as it relates to the owner's release of payment to the contractor.

Most construction contracts call for periodic progress payments from the owner to the contractor. Typically, payment is to be made based on the contractor's percentage of completion, as measured by the value of the work. For instance, if the total contract price is $1 million and the contractor has completed work at the site with a value of $150,000, the contractor is entitled to be paid the $150,000 less the stipulated "retainage" (usually 10 percent). The job would be said to be 15 percent complete.

It should be apparent that the determination of percentage of completion involves a fair amount of subjective judgment on the part of the A/E. Additionally, the A/E is subject to conflicting pressures from the owner, who wants to make sure the contractor is not receiving advance payment for work not yet performed, and the contractor, who is hungry for maximum cash flow. It is far easier for the A/E on a unit-price contract, where an objective measurement of quantity or number of items can be applied.

When determining percentage of completion, A/Es should rely on any schedule of values which was established in the contract between the owner and the contractor. In fact, the progress payment issue is a very good reason to insist that a schedule of values be agreed upon in advance. Without such a schedule, the A/E must apply its subjective judgment to a matter that is fraught with potential litigation.

The legal ramifications of an A/E's authorization of release of a progress payment are significant. If the A/E fails to exercise due care in determining the contractor's percentage of completion and the contractor is paid in excess of the value of the work in place, the A/E could be held liable.

If the overpaid contractor becomes insolvent or disappears, the A/E could be held liable to the owner, the owner's construction lender, and the contractor's bonding company. It was foreseeable that all these parties would rely on the A/E's determination to avoid overpayment. And all these parties would foreseeably be harmed if the contractor was overpaid and then defaulted. Funds

---

CASE STUDY 4-7

Owner awarded Contractor a lump-sum construction contract. Contract called for Owner to make monthly progress payments to Contractor based on Architect's certification of Contractor's percentage of completion.

Architect certified a particular percentage of completion, but Owner refused to make a progress payment for that amount unless certain changes were made in the terms of the contract. Contractor sued Owner for breach of contract.

The Missouri Court of Appeals ruled that Owner did breach the contract. When a contract establishes Architect as the party responsible for determining Contractor's percentage of completion, that determination is binding on both Owner and Architect. Owner was not entitled to ignore Architect's certification or to impose additional preconditions before making the progress payment.

Hart and Son Hauling, Inc. v. MacHaffie, 706 S.W.2d 586 (Mo.App. 1986).

---

exceeding the value of the work in place would have been irretrievably disbursed. The A/E could be held liable for the difference between the value of the work in place and the total payments to the contractor authorized by the A/E.

Certification of Completion

The conclusion of a construction project is marked by two significant milestones: substantial completion and final acceptance. Each carries certain legal ramifications.

When the contractor has achieved substantial completion of the project, the project is suitable for its intended purpose. The project owner can take occupancy of the project and make use of the project. The risk of loss due to casualty is shifted from the contractor to the owner. Typically, the contractor is entitled to receive payment of the contract balance except for enough retainage to cover the cost of any "punch list," or last-minute completion items.

Once the punch list is completed by the contractor, the owner is ready to finally accept the project. The contractor is paid the remaining contract balance. Upon final acceptance and final payment, the owner waives the right to bring any claims against the owner for defective work unless the defective work was "latent," or hidden, or was covered by a warranty. Conversely, the contractor loses the right to assert any claim for additional compensation if it was not asserted prior to final acceptance and payment.

Not surprisingly, it is the A/E who is called upon to certify that the contractor has achieved substantial completion or final completion of the project. This certification typically is issued to the project owner. It is also common, however, for the A/E to certify to public authorities such as a building inspector that a project is substantially complete in accordance with the plans and specifications and the applicable building codes.

If construction defects are discovered after the A/E's certification of completion, litigation may result. For instance, in recent years there have been a rash of lawsuits by condominium associations against A/Es who certified to public authorities that the project had been completed in accordance with the plans and specifications.

There is not a great deal A/Es can do to avoid this problem. Public authorities, construction lenders, and others customarily require an architect's certificate before issuing an occupancy permit or authorizing the release of a final construction loan disbursement.

The only thing the A/E can do is to try to convince project owners to use certification language which accurately reflects the A/E's limited role during the construction phase of the project. Rather than blankly certifying that the contractor's work complies with all plans, specifications, and ordinances, A/Es could more appropriately be asked to certify that to the best of their knowledge and belief this is the case. A/Es might also want to state that they are not and cannot be guarantors of the sufficiency of the contractor's work.

A/E'S ROLE IN THE CLAIMS PROCESS

Considering the A/E's intimate involvement with a typical project from beginning to end, it is not surprising that A/Es become very involved in the claims process. The claims process refers to the process whereby the construction contractor requests additional compensation or other benefits under the contract from the project owner.

The A/E's responsibilities during the construction phase make it almost inevitable that the A/E will get involved in claims situations. Many construction contracts recognize this reality and specifically delineate a certain role for the A/E. This section examines the role of the A/E in the claims process.

A/E as Agent of the Owner

If the A/E is given responsibilities during the construction phase of the project, the A/E carries out those responsibilities as the agent of the owner. This is a crucial factor, as the agency relationship has a number of legal ramifications.

A construction contractor has the right to rely on the words and actions of the A/E if the A/E is acting within its actual or apparent authority on the project. An owner cannot designate an A/E as an on-site representative and then disown the remarks or directives of that representative.

The law recognizes this by holding that the project owner, as "principal," will be bound by the acts of its agent, the A/E.

A/Es must constantly keep this in mind during the construction phase. Every directive and every interpretation must be consistent with the terms of

CASE STUDY 4-8

Owner solicited bids for construction contract. The contract drawings contained a conflict regarding responsibility for relocation of a gas line. One bidder telephoned Owner's Engineer and asked for a clarification. Engineer said the utility would take care of it.

Bidder was awarded the contract. Owner then required Contractor to relocate the gas line. Contractor sued Owner for additional compensation, saying it had been entitled to rely on the prebid oral statement by Engineer.

The Court of Special Appeals of Maryland acknowledged that under similar circumstances, it had held project owners accountable for the prebid statements of A/Es functioning as agents of the owners. In this case, however, the bid documents expressly stated that all clarifications must be in writing and oral explanations would not be binding. Therefore, Engineer was acting outside the scope of his agency authority in giving an oral explanation and Contractor was not entitled to rely on that explanation.

Mass Transit Administration v. Granite Construction Co., 471 A.2d 1121 (Md.App. 1984).

the contract the construction contractor agreed to. If the A/E's directives are inconsistent with the terms of the contract, the contractor may very well be entitled to additional compensation or some other remedy under the contract. The owner will pay for this remedy, as the owner is bound by its agent's actions.

Conversely, any information that comes to the attention of the A/E during the construction process will be imputed to the project owner. If a contractor points out a differing physical condition at the site to the A/E or informs the A/E of a problem that is delaying progress, the A/E has a duty to promptly inform its principal, the owner. Even if the A/E fails to transmit this information to the owner, the knowledge will still be imputed to the owner because of the agency relationship. The contractor has the right to assume that anything said or given to the owner's designated representative will be transmitted to the owner.

The legal impact of this agency doctrine is significant. An A/E, as agent of the owner, has the ability to inadvertently waive contract rights possessed by the owner or grant certain contractual remedies to the contractor. It is crucial that any change in the legal relationship between owner and contractor result from a thoughtful, deliberate decision which the project owner has expressly authorized. An owner which discovers that its A/E has inadvertently waived certain contractual rights will not be pleased.

In order to protect itself and its client the owner, an A/E must be thoroughly familiar with the construction contract. This includes not only the technical aspects of the contract but the general provisions and other "legal" aspects as well. If the A/E is not familiar with the rights and responsibilities of each party, how can it appreciate the ramifications of its actions or directives?

CASE STUDY 4-9

Construction contract specified a particular product "or equal." Contract also stated that Engineer was responsible for determining Contractor's compliance with the plans and specifications.

Contractor proposed an alternate product and Engineer approved the substitution. Owner later refused to allow Contractor to install the approved alternate product. Contractor installed the more expensive product named in the specifications and sued Owner for the increased cost.

The Appeals Court of Massachusetts ruled that Engineer was the authorized agent of Owner in matters of compliance with the specifications. Once Engineer had approved the product in accordance with the procedure established in the contract, Owner was bound by that determination and could not rescind the approval.

E. A. Berman Company v. City of Marlborough, 419 N.E.2d 319 (Mass.App. 1981).

While discussing agency, it is necessary to note the importance of the scope of the A/E's authority. Frequently, the A/E is not designated as the owner's on-site representative. The A/E's construction phase responsibilities may be limited to monthly inspections and a final certificate of completion.

The A/E's agreement with the owner should make this clear. So should the construction contract. There is nothing worse for an A/E or an owner than working with a construction contract which implies the A/E has broad job site authority when in fact the owner has given the A/E very little authority. All the contract documents should accurately reflect the A/E's scope of authority. All parties will know where they stand, and there will be no problem with the contractor relying on apparent authority which the A/E actually does not possess.

A/E as Arbitrator

It is common for construction contracts to state that any claim for a price increase or extension of time must first be presented to the A/E for a decision. When presented with such a request, the A/E is expected to make an independent judgment as a professional, not a parochial decision based on the A/E's loyalty to the project owner.

This is a difficult task, as the A/E is being asked to function simultaneously as agent of the owner and as a neutral arbitrator. Furthermore, the A/E may be faced with a direct conflict of interest if the claim relates to the sufficiency or accuracy of the A/E's work product.

For instance, a contractor may claim that the drawings inaccurately portrayed site conditions or failed to address the fit of particular components. The sufficiency of the A/E's professional work product is called into question. It is difficult for the A/E to be entirely objective, knowing that a favorable recommendation on the contractor's claim will raise questions from its client, the project owner. Nonetheless, the A/E has an obligation to make an objective determination and give the contractor that which it is entitled to under the contract.

The effects of this conflict are mitigated by the fact that when the A/E functions as an arbitrator during construction, it is usually just dispensing a preliminary administrative remedy. The contractor must, under the terms of the contract, seek the A/E's decision first, but it is not ultimately bound by that decision.

Typically, the decision can be appealed to an administrative board or a court. Frequently, an arbitration clause calls for formal, binding arbitration of the dispute. This is separate from the A/E's "arbitration" role during the construction phase, and the A/E would never serve on a panel of arbitrators if the A/E had been involved in the project.

In the past, some public contract documents purported to give the A/E final authority to resolve all claims. These so-called engineer decision clauses stated that there could be no appeal from the A/E's decision on a claim.

Courts were hostile toward these clauses, recognizing the inequity of allowing the owner's agent or employee to make unappealable decisions. Although the clauses were considered enforceable, courts were resourceful at finding ways to limit their effect. Today, engineer decision clauses are rare in public construction contracts. Most jurisdictions have established administrative boards to decide contractor's claims.

While the A/E's opinions and the A/E's initial response to the claim will certainly be considered, the board will have authority to make independent findings of fact, rulings of law, and a decision on the claim.

CASE STUDY 4-10

Construction contract stated that Engineer "will decide all questions which may arise...as to the acceptable fulfillment of the contract on the part of the contractor."

Owner and Contractor got into a dispute over late completion of the project. Engineer made a determination regarding the amount of liquidated damages that Owner could withhold from Contractor's final payment. Contractor sued to recover the money withheld. Owner argued that the terms of the contract made Engineer's decision final and binding on all the parties.

The Court of Appeals of Arizona ruled that an engineer's resolution of a dispute will be final and unappealable only if the construction contract expressly states that the engineer will be the final arbitrator. In this case, the contract contained no such statement. Engineer's authority was limited to interpreting the contract documents and making decisions during the performance of the work. Engineer was not the final arbitrator of disputes.

New Pueblo Constructors, Inc. v. State of Arizona, 696 P.2d 203 (Ariz.App. 1985).

The Claims Process

In concluding this chapter on A/Es and claims, it is useful to summarize the process by which claims are usually asserted.

Typically, a contractor will orally convey a problem to the owner's representative, precipitating a certain amount of give and take. If the owner agrees that a change order is appropriate, the contractor will be asked to submit a change order proposal putting prices on the changed or additional work.

There is frequently extensive negotiation regarding the price of changed work. Once this has been resolved, the change order is executed by both the owner (or its representative) and the contractor. A contractor who proceeds with changed or extra work without a signed change order proceeds at its own risk.

If the owner does not agree that a particular work item or a particular directive is a change in the original scope of work, the owner may direct the contractor to proceed with the work. The contractor is obligated to proceed but will proceed under protest and later submit a claim for the increased cost. A court, board, or panel of arbitrators will ultimately decide whether this was a change and whether the contractor is entitled to additional compensation. This process will be described in detail in Chapter 6.

A similar process occurs regarding requests for an extension of time. The owner's representative will be called on to determine whether a particular delay is excusable, nonexcusable, or compensable under the terms of the contract. Typically, excusable delay is beyond the control of both owner and contractor, entitling the contractor to an extension of time. Compensable delay is the fault of the owner or its agents, entitling the contractor to an extension in the schedule and an increase in the contract price to cover the increased costs of performance resulting from the delay.

If an agreement is reached regarding any extension or price increase the contractor is entitled to, a change order is issued and executed. If the parties can't agree, the contractor will be forced to submit a formal claim. These matters will be discussed in detail in Chapter 6.

KEY TERMS AND CONCEPTS

standard of care   In carrying out its responsibilities, the A/E is required to possess and exercise the level of skill and judgment that is accepted among similarly situated design professionals.

warranty of plans and specifications   The owner extends an implied warranty to the contractor that the plans and specifications are accurate, complete, and suitable for the successful construction of the project. The A/E therefore has an obligation to furnish the owner with design documents that meet this standard.

privity of contract   A direct contractual relationship. There used to be a legal requirement, now virtually obsolete, that a party be in privity of contract with another party before the party could be held liable to that other party.

foreseeable harm   The contemporary legal doctrine that has replaced privity of contract. If a party is negligent in the performance of its duties, it may be held liable to any party who suffered harm that was foreseeable at the time the duties were undertaken. Therefore, an A/E may be held liable to contractors or subcontractors despite the lack of privity of contract.

limitation of liability   A contractual provision whereby the two parties to a contract agree to establish an upper limit of liability for certain specified shortcomings or breaches of contract. The clause cannot limit liability toward parties who did not sign the contract.

construction monitoring   A general term referring to the services provided by the A/E to the project owner during the construction phase of the project. The specific scope of the A/E's responsibilities must be established in the owner-A/E agreement. The scope of responsibilities will determine the degree of liability exposure.

agency   A legal relationship whereby one party gives another party authority to represent and act on behalf of the former party. An A/E is frequently the agent of the owner on a construction project. The owner is therefore bound by the actions of the A/E and the knowledge of the A/E is imputed to the owner.

certification   A written statement that something has occurred. A/Es are frequently called upon to certify to the owner (and any other party that may foreseeably rely on the certification) that the contractor has achieved certain milestones in its performance of the construction work.

OWNER'S ASSURANCE OF PERFORMANCE

The primary concern of the owner of any project, large or small, is to see that the project is completed properly. Owners are all too familiar with tales of shoddy workmanship, unexpected costs, and contractors that walk off the job. The construction process is complex and capital-intensive. The successful completion of a project is never a foregone conclusion.

In order to improve the odds that the contractor will perform as agreed, construction contracts typically contain a number of provisions designed to give the owner some leverage. This chapter will focus on the most important of these provisions: performance bonds, termination clauses, payment provisions, and warranties and guarantees. Each of these provisions is designed to give the project owner some assurance that it will be protected from an unscrupulous or incompetent contractor.

PERFORMANCE BONDS

A performance bond is a legal instrument whereby a third party, usually a corporate surety, guarantees the contractor's performance to the project owner. Performance bonds provide a significant benefit in terms of assurance of performance, although the project owner must directly or indirectly pay the premium on the bond.

Nature of the Relationship

A performance bond involves a three-way arrangement whereby a bonding company (the "surety") agrees to issue bonds on behalf of a contractor (the "principal") on various construction contracts in exchange for a premium computed as a percentage of the face amount of the bond. The contractor in turn agrees to indemnify, or reimburse, the surety if the surety is forced to pay out on any bond due to the contractor's default. This indemnification agreement usually includes a pledge of assets by the contractor.

Performance bonds are issued on a project by project basis. Each bond names the specific project owner, who is the "obligee," or beneficiary of the bond. The bond states that if the contractor/principal fails to fully complete the project in compliance with the terms of the contract and the plans and specifications, then the bonding company/surety will complete the project for the owner/obligee at its expense.

The surety's obligation is limited to the "face amount" stated on the bond. Regardless of how the surety elects to complete the project, it cannot be required to spend more than the face amount of the bond. This is the limit of the risk it has agreed to assume in exchange for the premium.

On public construction projects, the bond is usually required to be in the amount of the full contract price. In some ways this is overkill because once a project gets underway, the cost of completion starts to decline. The project owner is indirectly paying for more protection than it needs in the event of a contractor default. For this reason, privately financed projects sometimes require a performance bond only for 60 or 80 percent of the contract price.

There is resistance to this arrangement among corporate sureties, however, who feel that as a practical matter they have the same amount of risk but less premium. Some sureties will not write bonds for less than the full contract amount.

Sometimes a performance bond will name two or more obligees. These

---

CASE STUDY 5-1

Contractor furnished a performance bond naming Owner of public project as obligee. After completion of the work and acceptance of the project, Owner discovered latent deficiencies in the work.

Owner sued Surety on the performance bond, arguing that bond served as a guarantee of faithful performance and the defects in the work were the result of Contractor's failure to fully and faithfully perform.

The District Court of Appeal of Florida agreed with Owner and allowed recovery against Surety. In so doing, the Court disagreed with an earlier Florida case which had held that a performance bond guarantees only the physical completion of the project and the bond obligation ended upon the owner's acceptance of the project.

School Board of Pinellas County v. St. Paul Fire & Marine Insurance Co., 440 So.2d 872 (Fla.App. 1984).

bonds are known as "dual obligee" bonds. Typically, the obligees are the project owner and the construction lender whose loan to the owner is secured by the project itself. The lender in this situation wants the same assurance of contractor performance as the owner. See Appendix D, *AIA Document A311,* "Performance Bond."

Advantages for the Owner

The primary advantage of a performance bond has already been stated. If the construction contractor walks off the job, goes bankrupt, or otherwise fails to faithfully complete the project, the owner has a corporate institution, presumably solvent, it can look to to complete the work. There is a second, more subtle, advantage as well.

Corporate sureties will not agree to bond just any contractor who walks through the door. In order to keep their level of risk reasonable, sureties try very hard to write bonds only for contractors that will complete their projects.

As a result, contractors must undergo a thorough evaluation by sureties before sureties agree to issue performance bonds. This evaluation focuses on the past history of the contractor and its principals. Do they have a history of successfully completing projects of this nature? Do they have the technical and administrative expertise that will be required for successful completion? And finally, does the company have access to sufficient capital to complete the project?

This extensive evaluation of a contractor's history, abilities, and financial situation can only benefit a project owner. By requiring a contractor to furnish a performance bond, the owner is getting a surety to prequalify the contractor. The owner knows that at least one reputable corporate surety has sufficient faith in the contractor to take that contractor on as a risk.

Sureties frequently possess the resources and knowledge to investigate a contractor's financial and technical situation in a way that most project owners could not. They are familiar with the contractor's overall situation. For instance, each contractor has a specific bonding limit based on the contractor's financial resources. The bonding company will not allow the total amount of outstanding performance bonds to exceed that limit. It would be difficult for the average project owner to accomplish this type of financial evaluation independently.

If a project owner elects to award a contract to an unbonded contractor, the burden of evaluating the contractor falls squarely on the owner. Most owners are unable or unwilling to carry out this function. And the ramifications of an error in judgment will be severe if the owner ends up with an unbonded contractor who defaults on the contract.

What Triggers the Surety's Obligation?

The surety's obligation on the bond arises only if the contractor/principal fails to fulfill its obligations under the construction contract. This failure is commonly referred to as a "default."

In order for the contractor to be considered in default, its shortcomings under the contract must be sufficiently serious to be considered a breach of contract. In other words, the project owner cannot expect the surety to get involved every time the contractor's workmanship leaves something to be desired.

Usually, an owner who is experiencing persistent problems with a contractor will first threaten to notify the surety and then, if necessary, actually put the surety on notice that the contractor is not performing as required by the contract. When a surety receives such a notice, it contacts the contractor and prods the contractor to improve its performance. Contractors are very responsive to this type of pressure, as their business depends on maintaining a good working relationship with a corporate bonding company. If a contractor cannot get bonded, it is precluded from bidding on a great deal of work.

As a practical matter, a surety will work with a contractor to the maximum extent possible to see that the contractor lives up to the contractual obligations guaranteed by the bond. This is in everyone's best interest. It usually requires a catastrophic occurrence, such as a contractor's abandonment of the work, before the surety will formally declare the contractor to be in default and get actively involved in the completion of the project.

In the event of a contractor default, the surety has three options. The first is to provide the contractor with a line of credit in order to give it the capital necessary to complete the contract. This is the surety's preferred course of action, but it is feasible only if the contractor's problems are strictly financial. Frequently, by the time a contractor has defaulted on a contract, the surety has lost confidence in the administrative and/or technical abilities of the contractor and is unwilling to commit substantial sums to that contractor.

The surety's second option is to contract with another construction company to complete the contract. There are disadvantages to this option, however. If the original contractor is in default, the project is usually in total disarray and the project owner is upset and suspicious. Recognizing this, contractors are reluctant to step into someone else's mess. Additionally, equipment and crews must be mobilized and there will be a learning curve as supervisors and crews master an unfamiliar project. For all these reasons, a replacement contractor will charge a premium to come in and take over a job that has gone bad. These increased costs will have to be picked up by the surety, not the project owner.

The third option exists more in theory than in practice. The surety of a defaulted contractor can bring its own forces, its own employees, in to finish a contract. Sureties, however, are in the financial service business, not the construction business. Few corporate sureties have the ability or the interest to complete contracts with their own forces, and this option is seldom exercised.

In considering the three options of the surety of a defaulted contractor, it is important to remember the concept of the face amount, or penal amount, of the performance bond. This face amount establishes the surety's maximum liability exposure on the bond, regardless of how it elects to complete the contract. If it appears to the surety that the penal amount of the bond will be insufficient to complete the contract, the surety will simply tender that amount to the project owner. The project owner will have no choice but to accept it, as the surety's obligation cannot possibly exceed that amount.

What Discharges the Surety of Its Obligations?

Once a contractor has completed a contract, the surety is relieved of any obligations on the bond that applies to that contract. There are a few instances where courts have allowed owners to recover from performance sureties for workmanship problems discovered well after completion. The general rule, however, is that the surety's obligation ends when the construction contract is completed and the project accepted by the owner.

There are also certain occurrences during the construction of the project that can relieve the surety of its obligations under a performance bond. All these occurrences involve action or inaction by others that prejudices the surety's ability to protect its legitimate interests.

If a contractor is in default, the project owner/obligee has a duty to give the contractor's surety prompt notice of the default. This enables the surety to evaluate its options and select the most expedient way to complete the contract. If the owner fails to give prompt notice, and the surety suffers some sort of financial harm or prejudice as a result, the lack of timely notice may discharge the surety of its obligations under the performance bond.

During the course of construction the owner and contractor frequently agree to a number of changes. It is expected that change orders will be issued and the performance bond will apply to the construction contract as modified. Sometimes, however, the changes will be so major that they completely alter the nature of the project and greatly expand the nature of the risk.

An example would be a change order which doubles the price of the construction contract or adds extensive work by trades not covered in the original contract. This is not a risk that the surety contracted to assume, even given the limitation of the penal amount of the bond, because it increases the likelihood of a contractor default. If a change is so major that it is considered a "cardinal change" in the contract, the surety will be discharged from its obligation on the bond.

Finally, a surety will be partially discharged if the owner negligently releases payment to the contractor and it turns out that the contractor had not performed the work for which it was being paid. This is because the performance surety has an equitable interest in undisbursed construction funds until the contract is completed. If that money had not been released to the defaulted contractor, it would be available to help pay for completion of the contract. To the extent the owner negligently overpays a contractor who later defaults, the surety's obligation on the bond is reduced accordingly.

OWNER'S RIGHT TO TERMINATE THE CONTRACT

One of the most important tools reserved by project owners to assure the contractor's compliance with the terms of the construction contract is the right to terminate that contract. Construction contracts typically allow for "termination for default" and "termination for convenience."

Termination for Default

It is customary for construction contracts to state that if the contractor fails to perform fully and faithfully in accordance with the terms of the contract, the owner may terminate the contract for default and the contractor will be entitled to no additional compensation.

Termination for default clauses usually contain a long list of offenses, shortcomings, and omissions which will constitute default. For an example, see Paragraph 14.2 of *AIA Document A201,* "General Conditions of the Contract for Construction," shown in Appendix E. This document is incorporated by reference into *AIA Document A101,* "Standard Form of Agreement between Owner and Contractor" (see Appendix F).

It is important to keep in mind that despite this threatening language, not every shortcoming will support a default termination. The ramifications of a default termination for the contractor are severe, as will be seen below. Therefore, courts usually require that the contractor's shortcomings amount to a material breach of contract.

For instance, most default termination clauses contain a provision requiring the contractor to adhere to the agreed construction schedule. It is unlikely, however, that a court would uphold a default termination if the contractor was 1 week behind schedule halfway into an 18-month project. The problem is not sufficiently serious to warrant it.

Certain problems are sufficiently serious to warrant a default termination, however. The most common is the failure to pay subcontractors or suppliers. If unpaid parties begin asserting mechanic's liens against the owner's property, the owner may very well exercise its right to terminate the contract for default.

Similarly, a persistent failure to adhere to the plans and specifications may warrant a default termination. Minor problems are inevitable on any project, and a certain amount of corrective work is to be expected. If the contractor intentionally deviates from the contract requirements, however, or persists in providing shoddy workmanship, the owner may consider it a breach of contract and terminate for default.

The third common ground for default is the failure to follow the schedule. As mentioned earlier, a modest delay by the contractor will not be considered an act of default. The test is whether, at that particular time, the contractor has a reasonable chance of completing the work by the contractually stipulated date. The completion date should be adjusted, if necessary, to allow for any ex-

CASE STUDY 5-2

Owner terminated Contractor under the termination for default provision of a contract, citing Contractor's tardy performance of the work. Contractor challenged the termination, arguing that it should have been given an administrative hearing prior to being terminated.

The New York Supreme Court, Appellate Division, rejected Contractor's argu-ment. A default termination is a contractual right which the owner may exercise when justified by the facts.

The Court said that although a contractor may be entitled to an opportunity to tell its side of the story and an opportunity to cure the defects in its performance, this does not mean the contractor is entitled to an adversarial, administrative hearing before the contract may be terminated for default.

Albert Saggese, Inc. v. Town of Hempstead, 474 N.Y.S.2d 542 (N.Y.A.D. 1984).

---

cusable delay the contractor may have encountered. If the contractor has no chance of finishing the work by the required completion date, the contractor may be considered to be in breach and the contract may be terminated for default.

It should be noted at this point that most default termination clauses require both notice and the opportunity to cure the default. Typically, the owner is required to give the contractor written notice that it is considered to be in default. The contractor is then given a stated number of days, established in the contract, to "cure" the default. This may involve performing corrective work or working overtime to bring the job back on schedule. If the contractor fails to cure the default within the stated period, the owner sends a second notice which actually terminates the contract for default.

The requirements for a notice and opportunity to cure are consistent with the concept that a contract should be terminated for default only if the contractor has materially breached the agreement. If the problems can be promptly cured when they are brought to the contractor's attention, they were not serious enough to warrant a default.

The owner's right to terminate for default should be exercised only when there are serious problems, because the financial ramifications for the contractor are severe. If a contract is terminated for default, the contractor may be held liable for what are commonly referred to as "excess reprocurement costs." That is, to the extent the owner's cost of having the work completed according to the original plans and specifications exceeds the original contract price, the defaulted contractor, or its surety, will be liable for the difference.

Given the problems with bringing in a substitute contractor, these excess costs can be significant. The delay and difficulty can be harmful to the owner, as well. Therefore, it is not only fair to the contractor but also in the owner's best interest, to give a contractor notice and an opportunity to cure its default prior to terminating a contract for default.

Termination for Convenience

Most construction contracts also contain a clause giving the owner the right to terminate the contract for its own convenience. This provides crucial protection to the owner because it is the only way the owner can maintain any flexibility.

The termination for convenience clause allows the owner to terminate the contract for any reason or for no reason at all. It essentially allows for termination "without cause." All the owner has to do is give the contractor notice of termination. As discussed below, the owner will also have to pay the contractor. An example of a termination for convenience clause appears below.

The owner may, at its sole discretion, terminate all or part of the work covered by this contract at any time the owner concludes such termination is in its own best interest. Termination shall be accomplished by delivery of a written notice of termination to the contractor. Upon receipt of such notice, the contractor shall immediately stop work and shall expeditiously cease incurring obligations relating to the performance of the terminated work. The contractor shall be entitled to payment for work performed prior to receipt of the notice of termination. Such payment shall be based on the percentage of the total work completed multiplied times the total contract price. This sum shall be presumed to include the pro rata share of overhead and profit on the completed work. The owner shall be credited with all payments made prior to the effective date of termination.

The termination for convenience clause allows the owner to terminate the contract without breaching the contract. The owner needs this flexibility because a variety of things can imperil a project after the construction contract has been signed. Financing may fall through. There may be problems with public regulatory authorities. The owner's need for the additional space may change.

In the absence of a termination for convenience clause, the owner would breach the contract by "canceling" its commitment to the contractor. This would subject the owner to liability to the contractor for lost profit and other damages. The termination for convenience clause is the only vehicle which will give the owner the flexibility it needs. The owner will be able to terminate the contract at any time for any reason.

Termination for convenience clauses usually allow the contractor to recover the contract costs it has incurred prior to the effective date of termination. The direct cost of labor and material is almost always paid. Indirect costs such as home office overhead and profit on the completed work may or may not be recoverable. All these items must be addressed in the termination clause. Sometimes even the cost of administering the termination may be recovered.

Lost profit on the terminated work is never recoverable. Termination clauses usually make this emphatically clear. After all, the purpose of a termination for convenience clause is to give the owner the flexibility to terminate the contract without having to pay this type of damage settlement. In return for this flexibility, however, the owner is expected to reimburse the contractor

CASE STUDY 5-3

Owner awarded Contractor a lump-sum contract for rehabilitation of a bridge. Serious structural deterioration was discovered after work started. Owner elected to terminate the contract for convenience while it evaluated the bridge's condition.

Contractor submitted its actual costs incurred prior to termination. Owner insisted that Contractor should be compensated based on the percentage of contract completion rather than actual costs incurred.

The Court of Appeals of Ohio ruled in favor of Contractor. The language of the contract determines the form of compensation in the event of a convenience termination. This contract referred to the contractor's "reasonable costs." It was therefore improper for Owner to base Contractor's recovery on the percentage of completion.

Conn Construction Co. v. Ohio Department of Transportation, 470 N.E.2d 176 (Ohio App. 1984).

for its costs in order to keep the contractor from being harmed by the owner's unilateral decision.

OWNER'S RELEASE OF PAYMENT

The flow of cash on a construction project typically runs from the construction lender to the project owner to the prime contractor and then to the subcontractors and suppliers. As the disburser of funds to the contractor, the owner is in an excellent position to structure payments in a manner that will assure proper performance by the contractor.

Progress Payments

Construction contractors are not expected to wait until final completion of a project to receive payment. The capital requirements of a project are usually so large that few companies could afford to work on this basis. The financing charges on borrowed capital would have to be passed through to the owner at considerable cost.

To avoid this problem, the construction industry has traditionally used a system of progress payments from the owner to the contractor. The basic concept is that each month the contractor will be paid for the value of the work it has completed during that period. The owner is paying only for work that is in place on the construction site; it is paying only for value received. This is crucial from an owner's standpoint. If it pays for more than the value of the work in place, it loses a certain amount of leverage with the contractor and increases its exposure in the event of a default.

The value of some work items is easily determined. On a unit price contract, for instance, it is simply a question of measuring the units and applying the unit prices. Frequently, progress payments cover the value of material delivered and stored at the job site. This value can be determined from supplier invoices.

On a fixed-price, lump-sum construction contract, however, the task becomes more difficult. A single dollar figure has been established for a large and complex project. How can the owner reasonably determine the value of one month's work?

The method that is commonly used is the percentage of completion method. If the project architect certifies to the owner that 15 percent of a $1 million contract is complete, the contractor is entitled to receive $150,000, less any amounts received in previous progress payments.

Although simple in theory, this method becomes difficult in application. There are inherent conflicts in determining the percentage of completion at any given time. The owner wants to pay as little as possible, preserving its capital and its leverage with the contractor. Construction lenders are notoriously conservative in authorizing loan disbursements which are also based on the work in place. Contractors, on the other hand, are eager to be paid as much as possible. They are seldom happy with the owner's estimate of the percentage of completion. All in all, the determination of the proper amount of a progress payment is a contentious affair.

To mitigate this problem, many construction contracts call for the establishment of a "schedule of values." This schedule assigns dollar values to the various segments of the work, either by phase or by trade. In essence, it allocates the lump-sum price among a large number of identifiable work items. This makes the task of determining progress payments much simpler and less divisive.

Usually, a schedule of values is determined after the contract has been ex-

---

CASE STUDY 5-4

Owner awarded Contractor a contract for sewer construction. Contract called for periodic progress payments based on the value of completed work.

Because of inaccurate determinations by its own engineer, Owner made progress payments to Contractor for pipe that had not been installed. Contractor then defaulted on its contract. Owner brought action against Contractor's Surety on the performance bond.

The U.S. Court of Appeals, Ninth Circuit, ruled that Surety's obligation on the performance bond was partially discharged to the extent Owner had overpaid Contractor. Overpayment deprives Surety of contract funds which would otherwise be available for completion of the project. To the extent that premature progress payments are financially harmful to Surety, Surety will have its obligation on the performance bond reduced.

Transamerica Insurance Co. v. City of Kennewick, 785 F.2d 660 (9th Cir. 1986).

ecuted. The contract simply states that a schedule will be negotiated between the parties. Some project owners attempt to allocate the price among the various segments of the work within the contract itself. Although this avoids the uncertainty of negotiating a schedule of values after the contract has been signed, it is not a recommended procedure.

A contractual schedule of values can be a potent weapon for a contractor seeking additional compensation for alleged changes in the work. It also violates the principle that the contractor is responsible for determining what is required and how much it will cost to perform the work. A schedule of values is a useful tool for determining the amount of progress payments, but it should not be included in the contract.

The last two important topics regarding progress payments are retainage and setoffs. Retainage is a percentage of each progress payment which is retained by the project owner until completion of the project and release of final payment. The purpose of retainage is to protect the owner against latent defects or other problems which were undetected at the time the progress payment was made.

Typically, 10 percent of each progress payment is retained until final payment. On large, long-term projects, it is common to reduce retainage after the contractor achieves 50 percent completion, as the owner's risk declines as the value of work in place increases. It is unusual, and from the owner's standpoint imprudent, to retain less than 5 percent of the progress payments under any circumstances. The amount of retainage must be established in the construction contract itself.

A setoff serves the same purpose as retainage: protection for the owner against shortcomings in the contractor's performance. Like retainage, the owner's right to assert a setoff should be established in the contract. Unlike retainage, setoffs are not applied automatically. They are applied only when there is a specific problem the owner is aware of and seeks to protect itself against.

For instance, if the prime contractor fails to pay a subcontractor who in turn puts a mechanic's lien on the owner's property, the owner may withhold, or setoff, the amount of the lien from the contractor's next progress payment. This setoff would be in addition to the normal retainage called for in the contract. If the prime contractor fails to correct a particular problem prior to conclusion of the project, the owner could setoff an appropriate amount from final payment.

Lien Waivers

Chapter 10 of this book discusses the statutory right of unpaid contractors, subcontractors, and material suppliers to place a lien on the property of the project owner. Liens resulting from the prime contractor's failure to pay its subcontractors or suppliers are of particular concern to project owners.

As a result, it is customary for owners who are making progress payments

CASE STUDY 5-5

Contract allowed Owner to retain 10 percent of each progress payment until "all work" was completed. Contractor finished all work except some minor "punch list" items. Owner continued to hold 10 percent retainage and was challenged by Contractor.

The Court of Appeal of Louisiana ruled that the retainage provision should not be interpreted literally. The purpose of retainage is to protect the owner against incomplete work. Therefore, an owner should not be allowed to hold 10 percent of the total contract price to secure the completion of a few minor items.

The Court said that once a contractor achieves substantial completion of the work, the retainage should be reduced to reflect the cost of the remaining punch list items.

State v. Laconco,
430 So.2d 1376 (La.App. 1983).

---

to contractors to ask for lien waivers. These waivers basically acknowledge that the party has been paid in full for labor furnished or materials supplied during the applicable period. The document goes on to state that the party waives its statutory right to assert a lien against the property of the project owner.

Every time a progress payment is made, lien waivers should be obtained from the prime contractor and every subcontractor or supplier who furnished labor or materials during the applicable time period. The prime contractor should be required to certify that no other parties furnished labor or materials during that period and that all parties have been paid in full. The prime contractor should also be required to agree to indemnify, or reimburse, the owner

---

CASE STUDY 5-6

Contract required Contractor to furnish Owner with lien waivers from all subcontractors and suppliers prior to receiving payment.

Owner refused to make payment to Contractor unless Contractor provided lien waiver from plumbing subcontractor. Subcontractor signed the waiver even though it had not actually been paid yet by Contractor. When Contractor failed to pay Subcontractor, Subcontractor placed a lien on Owner's project. Owner argued that the lien was barred by Subcontractor's prior execution of lien waiver.

The California Court of Appeal ruled that Subcontractor's lien waiver could not be enforced against Subcontractor because it had been coerced in order to secure payment from Owner to Contractor. Subcontractor was allowed to maintain its lien on Owner's project.

Bentz Plumbing & Heating v. Favaloro,
180 Cal.Rptr. 223 (Cal.App. 1982).

if any liens are asserted due to the prime contractor's failure to make full payment.

If a party has completed its work on the project, it should be required to sign a full waiver and release of lien rights. If it still has more work to do, it should sign a partial release covering all labor and materials furnished through a stated date. By the time the owner makes final payment to the prime contractor, it should have full waiver and release forms from the contractor and from every subcontractor or supplier who furnished labor or materials to the project.

In order to avoid misunderstandings or disagreements as to the form or nature of the lien waivers that will be required, this should be established in the construction contract itself. An example of a lien waiver is printed below.

Release of Lien

WHEREAS, _____ (Contractor) has been paid in full by _____ (Owner) for labor, materials, and/or equipment furnished under a contract dated _____ .

AND WHEREAS, said labor, materials, and/or equipment was applied to real property located at _____ (Project) which is owned by Owner.

THEREFORE, in consideration of the reliance of Owner upon this agreement and final payment by Owner, the Contractor does hereby:

1. Certify to Owner that all subcontractors and suppliers to the project have been paid in full.

2. Release, waive, and forever quitclaim unto the owner any and all manner of liens Contractor now has or may acquire in the real property associated with Project.

3. Agree to indemnify and hold harmless Owner, its successors or assigns, against any loss claim or lien asserted by a subcontractor or supplier against Owner or against the real property associated with Project.

IN WITNESS WHEREOF, Contractor has caused this release to be signed by its duly authorized owner, partner, or corporate officer on the _____ day of _____ , 19_____ .

WARRANTIES AND GUARANTEES

Warranties and guarantees are contractual commitments extended by the contractor to the contract owner. As a practical matter, the two terms are synonymous in the context of construction contracting.

Warranties may be "express," that is, stated in writing in the construction contract itself. Some warranties are "implied." Although they are not stated in writing, they are implied as a matter of law.

The Uniform Commercial Code (UCC), which has been adopted in almost every state, contains an elaborate system of warranties. The UCC applies only to the sale of goods, however; so these warranties do not apply to construction contracts. Material suppliers are subject to the UCC when they sell goods to contractors or project owners. The UCC warranties will be briefly reviewed in Chapter 10.

Warranties

The most basic warranty extended by contractors is the warranty of workmanlike construction. Most construction contracts include a statement that the contractor extends such a warranty. The wording varies, of course, but typically the contractor warrants that it will use construction methods and techniques that are recognized as acceptable within the trade or industry. The contractor also warrants that the materials it will use will be new and will be suitable for the successful accomplishment of the work.

If a construction contract does not contain an express warranty of workmanship, courts will be quick to read an implied warranty into the contract. The rationale is that acceptable workmanship is essential to the contract, and it is implicitly understood by both parties that the project owner would not contract for anything less that acceptable workmanship.

When reading an implied warranty into a contract, courts are somewhat restrained in determining the scope of the warranty. An express warranty of workmanship will probably be broader than the implied warranty a court would find. Therefore, express warranties are more useful for owners and may enable the owner to hold the contractor to a higher standard.

As a practical matter, the implied warranty of workmanship comes into play only on small projects, typically residential. Commercial construction contracts usually contain express warranties and detailed plans and specifications. These explicit contractual statements provide the owner with a far more viable remedy than a general, implied warranty. In situations where the contract doc-

---

CASE STUDY 5-7

Contract contained an express warranty of the Contractor's materials and workmanship. Owner informed Contractor that it was dissatisfied with the quality of Contractor's work and would be forced to withhold future progress payments.

Contractor treated this as a breach of contract and walked off the job. Owner argued that Contractor breached the contract first by breaching the express warranty of the workmanship.

The Court of Appeals of Indiana ruled that Owner breached the contract. Before a workmanship warranty problem becomes a material breach of contract, the contractor must be given a reasonable opportunity to correct the problem. Owner never gave Contractor that opportunity. Therefore, Owner was not justified in unilaterally changing the payment terms of the contract. Owner, rather than Contractor, breached the contract.

Burras v. Canal Construction and Design Co.,
470 N.E.2d 1362 (Ind.App. 1984).

---

uments are sparse or even nonexistent, the implied warranty of workmanship does give the courts an opportunity to provide the owner with a remedy for egregiously poor workmanship.

Express warranties of labor and material generally run for a stated period of time, usually 1 year. This means that if during the 1-year period the owner notifies the contractor of a defect in the materials or the work, the contractor must return to the job site and correct the problem at no charge to the owner. If there is a dispute as to whether the item falls under the warranty, the owner has the burden of establishing that the problem does in fact result from defective workmanship.

A common question that arises regarding warranties is the expiration date. As the express warranty typically runs for 1 year, the determinative factor is the date the warranty starts to run.

Some contracts state that the warranty runs for 1 year from the date of substantial completion. This is the date when the project becomes suitable for its intended purpose and the owner is able to take occupancy and make use of the structure.

Other contracts state that the warranty runs for 1 year from final completion and acceptance of the project. In other words, all the punch list items have been completed and the owner has made final payment to the contractor. Contractors are understandably reluctant to have a warranty start to run upon final acceptance. The process of completing the punch list and closing out the contract can be a lengthy one. In effect, the warranty period is extended for far more than 1 year from the owner's beneficial use and occupancy of the project. Contractors have a limited ability to speed up project close-out, as so much depends on the owner's efficiency and reasonableness. Contractors therefore prefer to have the warranty commence upon substantial completion.

If the contract fails to establish the date when the warranty starts to run, the courts are left with the difficult task of establishing the date. There is no clear-cut rule. Some courts have reasoned that the warranty should start to run upon substantial completion. The owner has use and occupancy of the building and will have the opportunity to discover any defects in the workmanship. Other courts have adopted the stricter rule that the warranty period cannot begin to run until final payment and final acceptance. In order to avoid uncertainty, construction contracts should always clearly state the date upon which the 1-year warranty of labor and materials will start to run.

There is one final item of importance regarding the warranty period. It is well established that the warranty period is not extended by the contractor's performance of corrective work under the warranty. In other words, if the contractor repairs something 6 months into the warranty, that item is still under warranty for only another 6 months. The warranty does not extend for 1 year from the date the corrective work was performed.

In addition to the express warranty of workmanship, construction contracts sometimes contain other express warranties. It is common for a contractor to warrant, or guarantee, the roofing system, sometimes for periods of 10 years or more. Expensive equipment such as mechanical systems or elevators are also commonly warranted for periods in excess of 1 year.

As mentioned earlier, in the context of construction contracting the terms warranty and guarantee are functionally synonymous. There are two situations where the term "guarantee" is widely used.

When a contractor warrants a roof or other system for a long period of time, it is common for the owner to require the contractor to furnish a "guarantee bond." This is a contractual promise by a third-party corporate surety to pay for the correction of defective labor or materials during the stated warranty period. The owner requires it because there is no certainty the contractor will still be in business 6 or 8 years after completion of the work. The guarantee bond makes the long-term warranty a more meaningful form of protection for the project owner.

The term "guarantee" is also used in design/build contracts, which will be discussed in Chapter 11. When a single entity is going to both design and construct a project, it is common for the owner to require that entity to guarantee that the completed project will be capable of meeting certain performance standards. This is most common on industrial projects, and the performance guarantee is usually stated in terms of production capability.

KEY TERMS AND CONCEPTS

performance bond A contract entered into between a contractor (referred to as the "principal") and a bonding company (referred to as the "surety") whereby the bonding company guarantees to the project owner (referred to as the "obligee") the contractor's faithful performance of its contractual duties and completion of the project.

The project owner is not a party to the suretyship agreement (or "bond") but is named as an obligee in the bond. The surety's obligation under the bond arises only if the contractor defaults on the contract by failing to complete the work in accordance with the contractual requirements. In the event of a contractor default, the

---

CASE STUDY 5-8

Roofing contractor extended a special guaranty to Owner whereby Contractor agreed to maintain the watertight integrity of the roof for a period of 5 years regardless of the cause of any leak.

Owing to a design flaw in the roof, leaking occurred. Contractor argued that it should not be held responsible because it did not cause the problem.

The Court of Appeals of North Carolina acknowledged that normally a contractor is not responsible for problems caused by inadequate design. In this case, however, Contractor failed to limit its guaranty to workmanship problems. Under the terms of the special guaranty, Contractor was obligated to correct the problem regardless of its cause.

Burke County Public Schools v. Juno Construction Corp., 273 S.E.2d 504 (N.C.App. 1981).

surety must complete the work or reimburse the owner for the cost of completing the work.

termination for default   A project owner's right, established in the terms of the contract, to remove the contractor from the project because of the contractor's material breach of contract.

In the event of a termination for default, the owner has no further contractual obligations to the contractor. The contractor, however, is obligated to reimburse the owner for costs incurred in completing the work to the extent such costs exceed the original contract price.

termination for convenience   A project owner's right, established in the terms of the contract, to remove the contractor from the project despite the absence of any contractor wrongdoing. Termination for convenience clauses are intended to give the owner the flexibility to abort a project for reasons of its own convenience.

In the event of a termination for convenience, the owner must pay the contractor for all work completed prior to the effective date of termination, as well as other contractually stipulated termination costs. The contractor has no right to sue for breach of contract or to recover lost profit on work it was unable to perform.

progress payment   Interim payments made to the contractor reflecting the value of work completed to date. The value is usually determined by the "percentage of completion" method but may be measured according to contractually stipulated unit prices or a schedule of values.

retainage   A contractually stipulated amount, usually 5 or 10 percent, which is withheld, or retained, by the project owner from each progress payment. The purpose of retainage is to provide the owner with security in the event of defective or incomplete work by the contractor. Retainage is released to the contractor upon final acceptance of the completed project.

lien waiver   A document whereby the contractor acknowledges it has been paid for completed work and waives its statutory right to assert a mechanic's lien against the owner's project. Generally, a contractor is required to furnish partial lien waivers upon receipt of progress payments and a final lien waiver upon final payment. Contractors are also usually required to furnish the owner with lien waivers from all the subcontractors and suppliers with whom the contractor has done business.

warranty   A contractual commitment to replace or repair any defective work. All construction contracts contain an implied (or unstated) warranty that the workmanship will meet the accepted standards of the construction industry. Most construction contracts contain an express (or stated) warranty that the contractor will correct any defective work discovered within 1 year of completion of the project.

guarantee   A contractual obligation to replace or repair defective items for a stated period of time. Guarantees usually apply to specific pieces of equipment or specific portions of the work, such as the roof. Guarantees are frequently backed up by bonds. Guarantees are commonly furnished by equipment or material suppliers to the prime contractor, who in turn assigns the guarantee to the project owner upon completion of the work.

CHANGES IN THE WORK

One of the factors that makes the construction process a challenging and fascinating field of endeavor is that it defies standardization. Every construction project is truly unique. Even if the design has been used dozens of times before, site variations assure uniqueness.

Factors such as financing and regulatory matters also inject a certain degree of uncertainty into the project. Given the number of variables, it is no surprise that changes occur during the course of the project.

Changes in the definition of the contractor's work fall into two basic categories: directed and constructive. Directed changes are changes that are expressly ordered by the project owner or its A/E. Constructive changes are changes caused by factors other than a change order. Usually the contractor seeks additional compensation for constructive changes.

This chapter examines directed and constructive changes and then discusses the pricing of changed work.

WHY CHANGES OCCUR

As stated above, changes in the definition of the work are almost inevitable because the construction process is complex and subject to a large number of variables. Unfortunately, many in the industry refuse to treat changes as a matter-of-fact business occurrence. Changes become a major source of contention and even a debilitating distraction on some projects.

Complexity of the Process

Even a relatively small construction project involves a tremendous number of components. A thorough set of drawings and specifications tends to be a rather thick volume. Yet even the most carefully prepared set of contract documents cannot possibly address every piece of material or every method of installation or application.

It is inevitable that from time to time the contract documents will require some interpretation from the owner or its A/E. If the documents are silent or ambiguous on a particular item, the A/E's interpretation of the requirements may differ from the contractor's reasonable interpretation. This may be a constructive change in the work.

Differing site conditions, which are discussed in detail in Chapter 8, almost always require a change in the definition of the contractor's work. The drawings and specifications are prepared based on certain assumptions regarding the site. Despite exhaustive site investigation, these assumptions may not prove true. Changes will be required.

Additionally, the complexity of the process results in a risk that errors will be made in the design of the project. Frequently, these errors are first discovered by contractors in the field trying to accomplish the work as specified. If this occurs, it will be necessary to make changes in the definition of the contractor's work.

Changes in Development Plans

A number of factors having nothing to do with design or construction can also cause the project owner to make changes in the work. The owner may encounter unexpected problems with project financing, causing it to scale back the project. Similarly, a changing real estate market may cause an owner to scale back or alter a project in midstream.

Regulatory problems can also force a project owner to make changes in the work. Ideally, all regulatory hurdles should be cleared before a construction contract is awarded. It is not unusual, however, for owners to encounter regulatory problems during the course of construction itself. This may result from the owner's oversight, but it also may result from citizen opposition or lawsuits.

Finally, the owner may simply change its mind regarding a certain aspect of the project. As discussed below, a changes clause is an important tool for a project owner who wants to maintain maximum flexibility in order to cope with new factors. These factors may be imposed on the owner, but they may be purely subjective, as well.

Traditional Attitudes toward Changes

Despite the fact that a changes clause provides the owner with important flexibility, owners and A/Es have traditionally viewed the change process with suspicion.

No one questions the owner's right to direct changes in the scope of the contractor's work. They resist and resent the contractor's request for change orders, however. The reason, of course, is money.

If a contractor claims that a certain set of circumstances or a certain directive in the field amounts to a constructive change in the work, the contractor will usually ask for a price adjustment to compensate it for that work. Too many successful claims for price adjustments will threaten the integrity of the project budget. Owners are understandably concerned about this matter.

The inherent conflict between owners and contractors regarding constructive changes has caused owners to view claims for additional compensation as an unethical practice by contractors. Although owners want the flexibility to direct changes in the work, they want the contractor to honor its original contract price if changes result from something other than an owner's directive. And owners also frequently feel that their directives do not increase the contractor's performance costs and should not cause a price increase.

In fairness to owners, part of the tainted view toward claims for additional compensation has resulted from the practices of contractors on competitively bid jobs. When competition is stiff, bidders must pare their bids to the bone. By not carrying any contingency funds in their bid prices, contractors place themselves in a position where they are not prepared to cope with any unexpected occurrence. An item that otherwise might have been absorbed by the contractor in order to maintain good relations with the owner and keep the job running smoothly may become the source of a claim. And it is true that some unscrupulous contractors have bid jobs with the intent of making a profit from claims for extras.

The A/Es have a unique perspective on claims for extras. Frequently a claim arises out of an alleged inaccuracy or omission in the drawings or specifications. The integrity of the A/E's professional work product is being challenged. Under these circumstances, it is understandable that the A/E will be defensive and suspicious of the contractor when addressing the merits of a claim for additional compensation.

All the attitudes described above are counterproductive to the successful completion of a project. Every party on a construction project should recognize that changes, both directed and constructive, are an inevitable part of the process. An objective, businesslike approach to the process will be in everyone's best interest.

As described below, the contract should establish a procedure to be followed. That procedure should include safeguards to protect owners against "claims-hungry" contractors. But it should also recognize the contractor's right to a price adjustment if the contractor can prove it was required to do something that deviated from the original scope of work and can itemize and document its increased costs.

DIRECTED CHANGES

As its name indicates, a "directed change" is a change in the definition of the contractor's work that is ordered, or directed, by the project owner or its representative. The change may add new work to the scope of work or deduct certain tasks from the original scope of work. A directed change is typically accomplished by the issuance of a written change order.

Owner's Need to Make Changes

If a construction contract lacked a changes clause, the project owner would be in a very difficult situation indeed. It is axiomatic that the owner may strictly enforce the contractual work requirements, but the owner may not require anything not called for in the contract. Considering the owner's need for flexibility, discussed above, a contract without a changes clause would be a very impractical form of agreement on a construction project.

Without a changes clause, an owner who wanted to expand the scope of the work would have to negotiate with the contractor to amend the contract. The contractor would have tremendous leverage in negotiating with the owner. The project would be delayed until the parties could reach an agreement. If they couldn't reach an agreement, the owner would be forced to bring in a second contractor to perform the extra work. This in turn would create severe scheduling and coordination problems. In short, the owner's need to expand the scope of work would disrupt the entire project.

Conversely, if a project owner needed or wanted to delete some of the work in the contract, it would be unable to do so in the absence of a changes clause. The owner's failure to allow the contractor to complete all the work in the contract and pay for that work would be a breach of the construction contract. For these reasons, it is imperative that the owner include a changes clause in the contract.

Before examination of the specific elements of a changes clause, it should be noted that there is one important limitation on the owner's right to direct changes, even when there is a changes clause in the contract. If the owner awards the contractor a $100,000 contract to build a warehouse and then issues a $1.4 million change order to build an attached office building, the contractor will be in a difficult position. It may lack the resources or ability to perform the vastly expanded scope of work. This may force it into a breach of the contract.

To avoid this inequity, courts will not allow owners to issue change orders that are considered "cardinal changes." If the nature of the project is completely transformed by a change order, it will be considered an impermissible cardinal change. If the change order is consistent with the original nature of the project, however, the contractor will be required to honor the directive.

Elements of an Effective Changes Clause

The starting point of an effective changes clause is the establishment of the owner's right to order changes in the definition or the scope of the work.

These changes can be ordered at any time prior to final completion and acceptance of the work.

Usually the clause specifies the manner in which the directives are issued, e.g., in writing. The clause should also establish which individuals have authority to issue written changes. This is imperative if confusion and misunderstanding are to be avoided. Contractors should act only on proper change orders signed by an authorized individual. Owners should be expected to pay only for extra work performed pursuant to such change orders.

The changes clause should also make it clear that the contractor has an obligation to proceed promptly with any change order work. Even if the parties have not agreed on the appropriate price increase or time extension, the contractor must obey the change order. It may not withhold performance until all its terms are met. This would defeat the purpose of having a changes clause from the owner's standpoint.

The clause should go on to state that if the parties are unable to agree on the terms of the change order, the contractor may submit a formal claim that will be resolved in accordance with the "disputes" provision of the contract. In other words, the contractor must perform the work now and arbitrate or litigate its claim for additional compensation later.

If possible, the changes clause should establish a formula or method for pricing the changed work. On some contracts, such as unit-price contracts, this is relatively easy. Other contracts are more difficult to quantify in advance. The pricing of changed work is covered at the end of this chapter.

The changes clause should also provide for an appropriate extension of time for the performance of changed work. The basic principle here is that if the change order will extend the contractor's performance period by a certain number of days, the contractual completion date should be extended by a corresponding amount.

The appropriate extension is not necessarily limited to the amount of time required to perform the changed work alone. Sometimes the change order will have a ripple effect on other, unchanged aspects of the work, forcing the contractor to perform work out of sequence or pushing the contractor into a period of inclement weather. The time extension should take the total impact of the change order into consideration.

Usually the owner looks to the contractor to make the initial proposal regarding the pricing and time extension for changed work. After all, the contractor is in the best position to have this information. The changes clause frequently specifies the format and content of the contractor's change order proposal or submittal. Once the submittal is received by the owner, there is often intense negotiation regarding price and schedule. It is the contractor's duty, however, to assemble the original proposal and to document or itemize its anticipated costs in order to support its proposed price.

Finally, a changes clause should place upon the contractor the duty to give the owner prompt notice of any directive, interpretation, or situation which the contractor considers to be a change in the work. These are the "constructive changes'' that are described below. The owner has the right to receive prompt notification of these matters in order to make a decision. For instance, if the A/E interprets the specifications in a manner the contractor considers to be a change, the owner will want the opportunity to evaluate the situation. If the owner agrees that this would be a change in the definition of the work, the owner may want to override the A/E's directive in order to avoid paying for a change. A typical changes clause can be found in Article 12 of Appendix E, *AIA Document A201,* "General Conditions of the Contract for Construction."

CONSTRUCTIVE CHANGES

A "constructive change" is a change in the scope or definition of the contractor's work that is directed by the owner or the owner's authorized representative. A constructive change can be distinguished from a directed change by the fact that the owner or its representative does not acknowledge, at least at the outset, that the directive calls for a change in the work.

When an owner issues a change order, it is implicitly acknowledging that the scope or definition of the work is being altered. Only price and time extensions need to be resolved.

If an owner issues a "directive" in a form other than a change order, however, the owner is not acknowledging that this entails a change in the work. The owner may very well contend that the directive was within the original scope of work; the work required by the directive was already called for in the contract.

Constructive changes must be distinguished from differing site conditions, which are covered in Chapter 8. With differing site conditions, it is a physical condition in the field, either natural or manmade, which forces the contractor to perform additional or altered work. Constructive changes result from an order or a directive issued by the owner or its representative. If the directive is issued in response to unanticipated conditions in the field, the contractor's claim could be more accurately characterized as a differing site condition claim. If the directive reflects the owner's interpretation of the work requirements, the contractor's claim is based on a constructive change in the work.

What Is a Directive?

A directive is an unequivocal order to the contractor from the owner or its authorized representative calling for the contractor to perform a particular item of work or directing the contractor to perform work in a particular manner.

Sometimes the directive is in writing. This might be in the form of a field order directing the contractor to do something but not acknowledging that extra or altered work is involved. More often, however, these directives are oral and are issued on an informal basis in the field.

In order for there to be a constructive change, there must be an unequivocal order. If the owner or its representative is simply requesting something or expressing a nonbinding opinion, it is not a directive. A contractor will be allowed to recover additional compensation only if it can show it was required to perform the additional or altered work. If the contractor simply volunteered to do the work or acquiesced in order to maintain good business relations, it will not be a compensable constructive change.

Most constructive change claims result from differing interpretations of the contract. Sometimes provisions of the drawings or specifications are subject to two or more interpretations. If there is an obvious ambiguity or a direct conflict among the provisions, the contractor has a duty to inform the owner prior to submitting a bid or signing a contract. If the ambiguity is subtle, or "latent," however, the contractor has no such duty.

The rule regarding latent ambiguities is that if the contractor's interpretation of the contract requirements was reasonable, any directive which alters the contractor's intended method of performance is a constructive change. This is the most common source of constructive change claims. The owner or A/E assumed or believed that the contract called for certain work to be performed in a certain way. The contractor assumed otherwise. If the drawings or specifications are latently ambiguous and the contractor's interpretation was reasonable, directives requiring the contractor to alter its performance will constitute constructive changes.

It is important to keep in mind that the owner, A/E, or other owner's representative has no right to tell the contractor *how* to perform the work. The "means and methods" of construction are left to the discretion of the contractor, who is presumably expert in these matters. The contract simply defines, in an objective, verifiable manner, the end result the contractor must produce. As long as the contractor complies with these requirements, the method used is generally none of the owner's business.

CASE STUDY 6-1

Owner awarded Contractor a contract for construction of bridges over a canal. Contract included construction of concrete barrier rail at a unit price of $42 per linear foot.

Rather than using fixed forms, as Owner expected, Contractor used slip forms to build the barrier rail. Owner claimed it was entitled to a price reduction, because the use of slip forms saved Contractor a great deal of money.

The Court of Appeals of North Carolina ruled that Owner had no right to take a credit. The contract simply referred to the use of "forms." When a contract does not specify a particular method of performance, the contractor is free to choose any method so long as it achieves compliance with the specifications. If the contractor complies with the specifications, the owner cannot treat the contractor's method of performance as a deductive change in the work.

Hardaway Constructors, Inc. v. North Carolina Department of Transportation, 342 S.E.2d 52 (N.C.App. 1986).

This, too, is a source of constructive change claims. Sometimes A/Es or other job site representatives disapprove of or disagree with the contractor's method of construction. While the owner certainly has the right to insist on strict compliance with the specifications for the completed work, the owner and its representatives must be careful not to confuse the means with the end result. If the owner's representative directs the contractor to employ certain methods of performing the work and the contractor can later show that it would and could have employed a less expensive method of achieving compliance with the specifications, the contractor will be entitled to recover its increased costs under the theory of a constructive change.

The Changes Clause

Most changes clauses contain two provisions important to constructive change claims. They are the notice requirement and the written change order requirement.

The notice provision simply states that anytime the contractor receives a directive which it considers to be a constructive change, it must give the owner or its representative prompt, written notice. If the contractor proceeds to perform the allegedly changed work without giving the owner notice, the contractor will not be entitled to any additional compensation for the work. For instance, see Subparagraph 12.3.1 of Appendix E.

The purpose of the notice requirement is to give the owner the opportunity to make a judgment as to whether the directive entails a change in the work. If the owner concludes that it does, the owner may want to override or rescind the directive rather than paying the contractor extra for the work. Or the owner may consider it worth the extra money and try to negotiate a price with the contractor and then issue a formal, written change order for the work.

Finally, the owner may not agree that the directive entails changed work. The owner may stand behind the directive, require the contractor to perform it, and let the contractor pursue a constructive change claim under the dispute resolution provisions of the contract.

The written change order provision simply states that any changed or extra work must be authorized in advance by the owner. In other words, a written change order is required.

Despite the seemingly harsh language of these requirements, there are severe limitations on their enforceability. To begin with, a party to a written contract may, by its conduct, waive a contract requirement. This means that an owner may waive the written change order requirement by authorizing changes orally or by recognizing oral changes authorized by its representatives. An owner cannot avail itself of the speed and informality of oral changes and then rely on the written change order requirement to defend a claim for a constructive change. This is true even though the contract states it can be modified only by written instrument signed by both parties.

CASE STUDY 6-2

Contract for construction of condominium project included clause requiring prior written authorization from the project owner before the contractor performed any extra work.

Owing to errors in Owner's plans, it was necessary for Contractor to make changes in the roof and trusses. Owner's superintendent orally directed Contractor to proceed and assured Contractor that the extra work would be paid for. No written change order was issued, however.

When Contractor sought to recover payment for the extra work, Owner argued that it was not obligated to pay in the absence of a written change order. The Supreme Court of Nevada disagreed. By issuing an oral directive and standing by while Contractor followed that directive, Owner waived the contract requirement that all changes be authorized in writing in advance.

Udevco, Inc. v. Wagner,
678 P.2d 679 (Nev. 1984).

Even if the owner does not waive the written change order requirement by its actions, it still may be unable to rely on the absence of a change order to defend a constructive change claim. In order to rely on this defense, the owner must be able to show that it suffered some prejudice, or economic harm, as a result of the contractor's failure to follow the contractually required procedures.

For instance, if a contractor did not give the owner or its representative notice that it considered a directive to be a constructive change and then went ahead and performed the work, the contractor may not be able to prevail on a constructive change claim. The owner could argue that had it been notified of the alleged change, it would have investigated the situation and possibly done something different. The owner has suffered prejudice as a result of the lack of notice; so the lack of notice will be a viable defense to the constructive change claim.

A more common constructive change scenario is that the contractor is directed to do something and protests to the owner that it involves a change. The owner or its representative deny that it involves any change in the work and order the contractor to proceed as directed. The contractor proceeds. There is no written change order, of course, as the owner denies that change has taken place. If the contractor requests a change order, the owner refuses to issue one.

In this situation, the owner may not rely on the lack of a written change order as a defense. The owner was notified that the contractor considered the directive to be a change. The owner had an opportunity to consider the contractor's contention and respond to it. The owner was in no way prejudiced by the lack of a written change order. To enforce that requirement under these circumstances would enable the owner to reap a windfall at the contractor's expense. The contractor will be allowed to pursue its claim for a constructive change under the dispute provision of the contract.

Quantity Variations

This is a unique type of change that bears little resemblance to either a constructive change or a directed change. It arises on unit price contracts where the contractor has bid or agreed to stated unit prices for estimated quantities of items, for instance, a bid of $4 per cubic yard for the excavation of a particular classification of soil.

Problems arise because the owner's quantity estimate may be inaccurate. After all, it is only an estimate. On a unit-price contract, the contractor is paid only for the units of work actually performed. And the contractor's unit price was based on the estimated quantity. If the quantity proves to be much less than estimated, the contractor could suffer a loss on that item because it would not even recoup its mobilization or start-up costs. If there is a significant quantity overrun on the item, the contractor might receive a windfall. After all its initial costs were recouped on the estimated quantity, the overrun would be gravy.

To mitigate this problem, many contracts state that the unit price will be "equitably adjusted" if actual quantities vary from estimated quantities by more than a stated percent, frequently 20 percent. Overruns would presumably call for a downward adjustment of the price. Underruns would call for an upward adjustment. The concept of "equitable adjustment" is discussed in the next section of this chapter.

If the contract does not include a quantity variation clause, the contractor will be paid the original unit price regardless of the actual quantity of work performed. If there is a substantial shortfall, it will be virtually impossible to get a unit-price increase. Contracts typically disclaim the accuracy of quantity estimates and state they are "for bidding purposes only." And a quantity underrun hardly qualifies as a constructive change. There has been no directive from the owner requiring anything that wasn't required in the original contract.

PRICING CHANGED WORK

The most difficult and contentious aspect of changed work is establishing the price to be paid to the contractor. Even assuming the owner agrees that a change has occurred, the owner may not agree with the price proposed by the contractor. Owners tend to feel that changes have a minimal effect on the contractor's costs, while contractors tend to see every change as having a widespread ripple effect. The problem is compounded by the fact that usually the work must be performed right away. There is no time for lengthy negotiations prior to performance of the work.

When to Price Changed Work

Under a normal changes clause, the contractor has a duty to proceed immediately in response to any change order or other directive issued by the owner.

It may be possible to quickly agree on a price before the contractor starts the changed work. This is referred to as "forward pricing" a change order.

Forward pricing is usually accomplished by having the contractor assemble estimates or quotations for the various items of work included. If the amounts seem reasonable and authentic, the owner may agree to them, and a total price for the change order will be established in advance.

The advantage of forward pricing is the certainty it produces and the avoidance of disputes. For the owner, in particular, it is desirable to know exactly what the change order is going to cost. The contractor can also benefit, however, from having a certain price before performing the work and knowing that the change order will not result in a price dispute.

There are serious disadvantages for the contractor, though. During performance of the changed work, the contractor may incur costs it did not anticipate. These may be direct labor and material costs that were either underestimated or inadvertently omitted. More commonly, they are so-called impact or ripple costs. These are the indirect costs that result from the change order. They include extended job site supervision and delay and disruption to the unchanged portions of the work.

Impact costs are difficult to estimate in advance and sometimes difficult to quantify even after the fact. On some projects, the impact costs of a change order can be very significant. For this reason, many contractors prefer not to forward price change orders. They prefer to keep detailed cost and schedule records as they perform the changed work and then submit a proposed price based on actual costs after completion of the changed work.

Even when the work is not forward priced, however, the measurement or determination of change order costs is far from clear-cut. The parties and, if

---

CASE STUDY 6-3

During the course of construction of a public building, Owner issued 81 change orders. Each change order stated that the price increase covered "all charges direct or indirect arising out of this additional work." Contractor signed each change order.

Contractor later sought to recover its increased costs caused by the cumulative impact of the numerous changes. When confronted with the change order language, Contractor said it would have been impossible to determine the cumulative impact during the course of the work and it is customary in the construction industry to bring these claims at the conclusion of the project.

The California Court of Appeal rejected Contractor's argument. If Contractor wanted to reserve the right to seek its cumulative impact costs, it should have stated so in writing when acknowledging each change order. In the absence of such a written reservation of right, Contractor is deemed to have waived the right to any additional compensation arising out of the changes.

Vanlar Construction, Inc. v. County of Los Angeles, 217 Cal.Rptr. 53 (Cal.App. 1985).

CASE STUDY 6-4

While attempting to lay a sewer line across a river, Contractor discovered that the specified method of weighting the pipe was inadequate. Contractor notified Owner's Engineer of the problem and requested guidance. Engineer was slow responding.

Contractor, eager to accomplish the work while water levels were favorable, proceeded with the work. Contractor made necessary modifications in the ballast scheme without receiving a written change order.

Contractor later attempted to recover its increased cost of performance resulting from the ballast modifications. The Court of Appeals of Tennessee ruled that even though the modifications may have been necessary and even though the problem resulted from Owner's defective specifications, Contractor could not recover because it failed to obtain a written change order as required by the contract.

J. M. Humphries Construction Co. v. City of Memphis, 623 S.W.2d 276 (Tenn.App. 1981).

necessary, courts or arbitrators, must look to the pricing formula established in the changes clause of the contract.

Equitable Price Adjustment

Many changes clauses, including the ones used on federal construction contracts, simply state that a change will entitle the contractor to an "equitable price adjustment." This is basically a price adjustment that will leave the contractor in the same economic position it would have been in had the change order not been issued. It is intended to "make the contractor whole."

An equitable price adjustment should certainly include the direct cost of labor and materials required to perform the work. These items tend to be rela-

CASE STUDY 6-5

Owner awarded Contractor a contract for construction of the foundation for an electrical generating plant. The plans called for piles to be driven through 24 feet of granular fill which Owner was having placed at the site.

Owner was unable to obtain the type of fill it wanted and substituted clay. Contractor's pile-driving operations were made considerably more difficult by the change in fill.

The Supreme Court of Nebraska held that the new fill was a constructive change in the scope of Contractor's work. Owner had represented that the piles would be driven through gravel. Driving piles through clay was outside the original scope of work, so Contractor was entitled to additional compensation.

Omaha Public Power District v. Darin and Armstrong, Inc., 288 N.W.2d 467 (Neb. 1980).

tively easy to document and measure. It should also include the impact of the change order on the cost of performing other unchanged work. As mentioned above, this is difficult to document and measure and is a common source of disputes.

There have been many disputes regarding a contractor's entitlement to overhead and profit markups on changed work. The large majority of courts and administrative boards that have addressed the issue have concluded that these markups should be allowed.

Although home office overhead is a fixed amount which is not affected by a change order, certain overhead expenses can be directly attributed to the change and should be recovered by the contractor. These expenses include increased or extended job site supervision and also the administrative effort of pricing and preparing a change order proposal for the owner. The administrative costs are not always recognized, although the federal boards of contract appeals recognize them as recoverable costs.

It is well established that a contractor is entitled to mark up the direct and indirect costs to allow for a profit. After all, the original contract price presumably allowed for a profit on the work. It would hardly be equitable to allow an owner to order the contractor to perform extra work at cost. This would diminish the overall profitability of the contract and amount to asking the contractor to work "for free."

Ideally, once all the various factors are considered, the owner and contractor can agree on an "equitable price adjustment" as compensation for the change order. Although a great number of itemized costs are taken into consideration in arriving at that figure, the change order itself usually expresses it as a single lump sum.

The process is difficult, however, as the concept of equitable price adjustment is inherently loose and subject to differing interpretations. For this reason it is desirable to establish a formula for pricing changed work in the contract itself.

CASE STUDY 6-6

Contractor was awarded contract for sandblasting and painting bridge spans. Contract stated that if Contractor considered any order or directive to entail extra work, Contractor must so notify Engineer before beginning the work.

Owner's supervisor required Contractor to sandblast to a finish higher than that required in the specifications. Contractor complained to the supervisor but failed to give written notice to Engineer.

When Contractor sought payment of additional compensation for the sandblasting, the Court of Appeals of Indiana ruled that the failure to give written notice barred any such recovery. This was true despite the fact the supervisor's directives clearly exceeded the contractual scope of work.

State of Indiana v. Omega Painting, Inc., 463 N.E.2d 287 (Ind.App. 1984).

CASE STUDY 6-7

Owner's bid documents estimated that contract would require the use of 195 ounces of "expansive admixture." Believing that this estimate was grossly understated, Contractor bid $10 per ounce even though its direct cost for the material was only 3 cents per ounce. Contractor submitted low bid and was awarded the contract.

When Owner discovered that the project would actually require 35,324 ounces of admixture, it had to terminate the contract for the owner's convenience. The contract contained no clause permitting an adjustment in the unit price to compensate for estimating errors; so Owner had no alternative if it was to avoid paying a windfall to Contractor.

Commonwealth, Department of Transportation v. Anjo Construction Co., Inc., 487 A.2d 455 (Pa.Cmwlth. 1985).

Pricing Formulas in the Contract

Many construction projects defy the use of preestablished formulas for pricing changed work. Some contracts lend themselves to this approach, however.

Unit-price contracts are ideal, as the work is being paid for according to measurable quantities. If additional quantities are ordered, the unit prices can continue to apply, or a quantity variation clause may be used as described earlier in this chapter.

Even on lump-sum contracts, it is possible to eliminate some areas of disagreement by establishing a formula in the contract. For instance, it is common for a changes clause to state that change orders will be priced according to direct costs plus a stated percentage markup for overhead and a stated markup for profit. This may or may not adequately compensate contractors for impact costs, but it is an approach that is widely used and is appealing in its simplicity.

Another effective technique is the use of cash "allowances" in the contract. When bidding or quoting a price, the contractor is instructed to state that its price includes an allowance of so many dollars for certain items of work or items of equipment. If the owner later decides to delete one of these items from the scope of work, the contract price is simply reduced by the amount of the allowance. This is a very effective device to use if the owner is seriously considering such a deletion at the outset.

Finally, the contract may call for changed work to be performed on a "time and materials" basis, that is, the direct cost of materials plus a stated hourly rate for labor. Sometimes a stated percentage markup is allowed on the material costs. This is an effective method on small projects, but not desirable on major projects. Owners are uncomfortable with the approach because it resembles writing the contractor a blank check. The argument can be made, however, that there is no less uncertainty in paying for changed work on a time and materials basis than in ordering a contractor to proceed with the promise of an "equitable price adjustment" upon completion.

KEY TERMS AND CONCEPTS

change in the work A change in the scope of work established in the contract documents at the time of contract execution. A change may involve the deletion of work, the addition of new work, or an alteration in the materials or equipment to be used.

directed change A change ordered by the project owner and acknowledged by the owner to be a change in the scope of work.

constructive change A change in the work which the contractor alleges to have been caused by an act or directive of the owner or owner's representative. The owner denies that a change in the scope of work has occurred and contests the contractor's entitlement to additional compensation.

deductive change A directed change whereby the owner deletes work from the original scope of work established in the contract documents.

change order A document issued by the project owner and signed by both owner and contractor acknowledging that the contract has been modified to reflect a change in the scope of work. A change order generally reflects the change in the contract price that has been agreed upon as a result of the changed work. Change orders frequently contain language whereby contractors waive and release the right to any further added compensation as a result of the change.

quantity variations A variation, usually on a unit-price contract, between the estimated quantities of work stated in the contract and the actual quantities encountered in the field. A significant underrun can pose a financial hardship for the contractor, whereas an overrun can produce a financial windfall. Consequently, many unit-price contracts call for a price adjustment if the actual quantity varies from the estimated quantity by more than a stated percentage amount.

equitable price adjustment A general term, frequently used in construction contract changes clauses, referring to the price increase (or decrease, in the event of a deductive change) that will leave the contractor in the same financial position it would have been in but for the change in the scope of work.

forward pricing The assignment of a contract price adjustment to a change order before the actual costs of the change are known. Forward pricing is based on estimates. The owner and contractor agree on the price adjustment before the changed work is actually performed.

SCHEDULING AND DELAY

In the construction industry, there is a great deal of truth to the old cliché that "Time is money." The vast amount of capital, labor, material, and equipment required for a construction project makes it inevitable that any lengthening of the process will result in higher costs for owner and contractor alike.

For the owner, there is the cost of financing the construction. Construction loans are typically written at a much higher interest rate than permanent, long-term financing. But the permanent mortgage is not available until the project is complete. Additionally, a project cannot be put to productive use and cannot start generating revenue until it is complete.

The contractor has a similar interest in prompt completion. The longer the project lasts, the greater the contractor's supervisory and overhead costs are. Labor rates and material costs may escalate. The contractor's bonding capacity is impaired, and the opportunity to bid on new jobs is lost.

Given the keen financial interest of all involved, it is not surprising that scheduling and delay problems are a major source of disputes on construction projects. This chapter examines the way schedules are established, modified, and enforced. It also discusses the remedies available to owners and contractors when schedules are not honored.

ESTABLISHING THE CONSTRUCTION SCHEDULE

As with almost every other aspect of the relationship between owner and contractor, scheduling must be established in the contract. If a construction contract contains no schedule or no completion date, courts will infer that a "reasonable time" is allowed for the contractor to complete the project. Needless to say, few project owners are willing to trust the fate of their project to such an amorphous standard of performance.

The Contractual Schedule

Most construction contracts contain the statement that "Time is of the essence." To understand the purpose of this statement, it is necessary to recall the distinction between material and immaterial breach of contract discussed in Chapter 1.

By stating that time is essential, the owner is putting the contractor on notice that a failure to meet the completion requirements will be a material breach of contract which would justify a default termination of the contract. As a practical matter, an owner would be on shaky ground if it kicked a contractor off a job simply because the contractor was a few days behind the established progress schedule. However, if the owner could show that the contractor has no reasonable chance of completing the project on time, a default termination would be upheld.

Establishing a completion schedule is quite simple. Sometimes the owner simply states the date by which the work must be completed. The preferred method, however, is to state the number of calendar days the contractor will be allowed for performance of the work. This method is superior because it allows for greater flexibility and specificity when it becomes necessary to make adjustments in the completion date. These matters will be discussed later in this chapter.

If a contractor is allowed a certain period of time to perform the work, for instance, 420 calendar days, it is obviously necessary to establish when the period starts to run. Some construction contracts state that the performance period starts to run on the date of the contract itself.

Frequently, however, the contractor is not authorized to begin work immediately upon contract signing. Problems with site access or project financing may force the contractor to wait weeks before actually beginning work. It is common for contracts to state that the contractor will receive a "notice to proceed" within 30 or 60 days of contract execution, and the contractor must commence work within 5 days of receipt of that notice. When a contract is structured in this manner, it usually states that the contractor's performance period starts to run upon the owner's issuance of the notice to proceed.

Construction contracts should also establish how the date of completion will be established. Considering the financial consequences of late completion, this should not be determined on an ad hoc basis.

The most prevalent and appropriate benchmark for a contractor's completion of the work is "substantial completion." Substantial completion is achieved when the project is sufficiently complete so that the owner can take occupancy and put the structure to use for its intended purpose. There may be a large number of remaining "punch list" items which the contractor is contractually obligated to complete, but if the contractor achieves substantial completion within the stated number of calendar days, it has met its completion obligation. The fact that certain finish work needs to be touched up or certain hardware is missing should not enable the project owner to levy harsh financial penalties against the contractor. The owner received that which it bargained for. It is occupying and making productive use of the project within the stipulated period of time.

Sometimes construction contracts will state that the contractor must achieve "final completion" of the project within the stipulated number of calendar days. This means that all the punch list must be complete and the owner must formally accept the project and release final payment.

This arrangement is quite unfair to contractors. As will be seen in the final chapter on project closeout, a great deal must be done between substantial completion and final completion and acceptance of the project. Many of these matters are beyond the control of the contractor. Why should the contractor be held financially responsible, for instance, by way of liquidated damages, for this period of time, particularly when the owner has the beneficial use of the project? For this reason, courts prefer to interpret "completion" of the project to mean substantial completion. If a contract explicitly requires final completion and acceptance within the stated number of calendar days, however, this requirement will be enforced.

The Contractor's Construction Schedule

Considering the complexity and extent of a typical construction project, it is apparent that a great deal of planning and scheduling is required. A detailed examination of scheduling techniques is beyond the scope of this book, but a basic understanding is useful.

Until recent years, most construction scheduling was performed using simple, manually prepared bar charts. Each bar represented a particular activity and indicated when it must commence and when it must be completed. These milestones are usually expressed as the number of elapsed calendar days of work on the project. The timely commencement of follow-on activities would of course be contingent upon the timely completion of the earlier ones.

Some bar charts are quite crude, breaking the activities down only according to trade. Some are quite elaborate, however, with separate bars for virtually every identifiable activity.

In recent years, the use of bar charts has been largely replaced by the use of computerized "critical path method" (CPM) schedules. These schedules are based on the same concept as a bar chart, but the activities are tracked on a computer-generated network drawing. CPM schedules tend to break the activities down with far greater specificity than even the most elaborate bar chart, thereby giving contractors greater ability to monitor their progress and properly coordinate the various activities.

The term "critical path" refers to that sequence, or path, of activities which is critical to the timely completion of the project. For some activities, the scheduling constraints are not severe, as little or no follow-on work is dependent upon their timely completion. Other activities, such as the pouring of the foundation, are sure to be on the critical path.

The fact that CPM schedules are computerized adds greatly to their usefulness. It is common for contractors to generate an "as-planned" CPM schedule prior to starting work. As work progresses, an "as-built" schedule is maintained. This enables the contractor to carefully monitor its own progress. As will be seen later in this chapter, it also provides a powerful tool for documenting the extent of various delays, their effect on the critical path, and their effect on the actual completion of the project.

Traditionally, progress schedules were prepared by contractors strictly for their own use. The attitude of contractor and owner alike was that the contractor was responsible for the proper scheduling and coordination of its work. As long as it met the completion date, this scheduling was no one else's business.

In recent years, however, project owners have insisted on getting into the act. It is now common for contracts to require that the contractor submit a proposed progress schedule to the owner within so many days of contract execution. This schedule is to be reviewed and formally approved by the owner. Adherence to this schedule is a requirement of the contract.

Project owners feel that by reviewing and approving a contractor's schedule, they will gain more control over the contractor and be in a better position to hold the contractor accountable for its progress or lack thereof. From a managerial standpoint, this is probably true. From a legal standpoint, however, this is a dubious proposition.

As mentioned earlier in this chapter, an owner will not be able to terminate a contract for default simply because a contractor has fallen behind its approved schedule. The owner must be able to prove that the contractor was so far behind schedule that it had no reasonable chance to complete the project on time. In the absence of that showing, the owner must give the contractor an opportunity to pick up its pace and complete the work on schedule.

The owner's formal approval of a contractor's progress schedule is also a double-edged sword which can come back to harm the owner. On any construction project, the owner has certain obligations which must be met in a timely manner. The site must be accessible. Decisions and approvals must be made. The work of separate contractors must be properly coordinated. If the owner fails to carry out its responsibilities in a timely fashion, it may very well be held liable to the contractor for delay damages.

By formally approving the contractor's progress schedule submittal and making it a part of the contract, the owner has gained a slightly higher degree of leverage with the contractor. It has also made a contractual representation that it will carry out its responsibilities in a manner which will enable the contractor to meet the approved schedule. If the owner fails to do so and the contractor's performance is delayed as a result, the approved progress schedule will be Exhibit 1 in the contractor's delay claim against the owner.

Categorizing Delay

Before examining the relationship between owner and contractor regarding delay, it is useful to discuss the three basic categories of delay. All construction delay can be characterized as excusable, nonexcusable, or compensable.

Excusable delay is delay which occurs due to factors beyond the control and without the fault of either party. Bad weather is the most common example. Generally speaking, excusable delay will entitle the contractor to an extension of the performance period, but no additional compensation.

Nonexcusable delay occurs as the result of the contractor's failure to meet its contractual obligations. For instance, material was not procured on time or insufficient labor was furnished. If nonexcusable delay results in the contrac-

---

CASE STUDY 7-1

Contract allowed Contractor 290 days to complete construction of fire station. Some of the drawings furnished by Owner proved to be defective. This delayed Contractor's performance of the work.

Owner became dissatisfied with the pace of Contractor's progress and terminated the contract for default. Contractor contested the termination.

Chaney Building Co. v. City of Tucson, 716 P.2d 28 (Ariz. 1986).

The Arizona Supreme Court ruled that Contractor's delays were beyond its control and therefore excusable. Owner was obligated to extend the performance period to compensate for the delay. If the proper extensions had been granted, Contractor's progress would have been satisfactory. Therefore, the default termination was reversed.

tor's failure to complete the contract within the stipulated number of days, the contractor will be held financially responsible to the project owner for the delay.

Compensable delay is delay caused by the owner's failure to meet its obligations. For instance, the owner failed to provide timely access to the site or failed to review shop drawings within the contractually allowed period. Generally speaking, compensable delay entitles the contractor to an extension of the performance period and an increase in the contract price to compensate it for the increased costs caused by the owner's delay.

Sometimes, two separate causes of delay occur concurrently. If an excusable or compensable delay occurs concurrently with a nonexcusable delay, the contractor will not be entitled to a time extension or increased compensation for the period of nonexcusable delay. The rationale is that the contractor would have been delayed anyway because of its own shortcomings. Similarly, if an excusable delay occurs concurrently with a compensable delay, the contractor will be entitled to a time extension, but no compensation, for the period of excusable delay. After all, the contractor would have been unable to work notwithstanding the owner's shortcomings.

To understand the concept of concurrent delay, consider these illustrations:

1 The owner denies timely site access to the contractor. Ten days later, unusually severe rain begins to fall. Ten days after commencement of the rain, the rain stops and the owner provides site access. The first 10 days of delay would be compensable. The next 10 days of concurrent delay would entitle the contractor to an extension of time for the excusable delay but would not be compensable.

2 The contractor is unable to obtain a piece of equipment necessary to perform the excavation. The owner, however, has not provided access to the site. The occurrence of the nonexcusable delay cancels the effect of the owner's

---

CASE STUDY 7-2

Contract called for construction of an air traffic control tower. Inadequate Government specifications for fasteners resulted in problems with installing masonry panels. Work was halted.

As soon as work stopped, serious deficiencies in the workmanship of Contractor's masonry subcontractor were discovered. These problems were corrected while Government resolved the problems with its specifications. Contractor later brought a claim alleging that the entire period of delay was compensable.

The U.S. Claims Court ruled that the delay was initially compensable because it was the fault of Government. As soon as the deficient workmanship was discovered, however, the compensable delay became concurrent with a nonexcusable, contractor-caused delay. Contractor was not entitled to any additional compensation for the period of concurrent delay.

Toombs & Co., Inc. v. United States, 4 Cl.Ct. 535 (1984).

compensable delay. The contractor would not be entitled to a time extension or additional money.

3 The contractor fails to obtain the necessary piece of equipment, and no work takes place for 10 days. Unusually severe rain then begins to fall and continues for 10 days. By the time the rain stops, the contractor has obtained the equipment and is ready to start work. The first 10 days of delay are non-excusable, and to the extent this delay causes late completion, the contractor will be liable to the owner. The contractor will not be responsible for the next 10-day period of concurrent delay, however. The excusable delay negates the effect of the contractor's shortcomings, as the contractor would not have been able to work anyway. The contractor will not be entitled to an extension of time for any period when it did not have the equipment available, however, as it would have been delayed notwithstanding the rain.

CONTRACTOR'S ENTITLEMENT TO EXTENSION OF TIME

It is important to emphasize that a contractor's entitlement to an extension of time is dependent on the terms of the contract. If the contract does not expressly authorize time extensions, the owner will be in a position to argue that the contractor is obligated to complete the project on schedule regardless of any occurrences. The owner will not necessarily prevail in this argument, as courts sometimes recognize that an act of God will excuse nonperformance of a contract. But the door will be open for the owner to make the argument.

The contractor's entitlement to an extension of time is usually dependent on the definition of excusable delay; so the examination of this issue must begin there.

Excusable Delay

As stated earlier in this chapter, excusable delay results from occurrences which are beyond the control and without the fault of either owner or contractor. Most construction contracts spell out the occurrences which will entitle the contractor to an extension of time. This is seldom labeled "excusable delay," but the fact the contractor is allowed additional performance time indicates that the delay was recognized as being beyond the contractor's control.

In the absence of a contract clause authorizing extensions of time, there will be great confusion as to what, if any, events will justify an extension of time. Courts would probably excuse the delay only in the face of catastrophic natural disasters. A time extension clause is therefore crucial from a contractor's point of view.

These clauses vary as to the events which will entitle the contractor to an extension of time. An example is Paragraph 8.3 in Appendix E. Many contracts are less expansive in their definition of excusable delay, however.

Weather, of course, is the most common cause of excusable delay. It is also the most misunderstood.

In order for adverse weather to be an excusable delay, it must be so severe or unusual that it could not have been reasonably anticipated. When bidding and scheduling their jobs, contractors are expected to anticipate bad weather. It would be foolish, and certainly not beyond the control of the contractor, to price and schedule work on the assumption that every day will be warm and dry. Normal seasonal and geographic factors must be considered. A week of rain in April might be "adverse," but in most locations, spring rain should be anticipated.

To prove entitlement to a time extension, contractors must rely on the weather records for the locale of the project. The weather occurrences for the period in question must be compared with the historical weather data for that time of year. Ultimately, it comes down to the inherently subjective judgment call as to whether or not the weather conditions were so severe or unusual for that location at that time of year that the contractor could not have reasonably anticipated their occurrence.

Another misunderstood cause of excusable delay is acts of governmental authorities. Again, the key is foreseeability. If a contractor knows it is required to get certain permits from public authorities, it must anticipate that a certain lead time will be required. Delay in obtaining these permits will usually not be excusable. The delay will be excusable only if the contractor was without fault and the nature or extent of the delay could not have been anticipated. A classic example would be when an environmental organization files suit and obtains an injunction shutting down the project.

Notice Requirements

Most contract clauses authorizing extensions of time for excusable delay require that the contractor give the owner prompt notice of the delay. For instance, AIA Document A201 requires the contractor to make a claim in writing within 20 days of the commencement of the delay or the right to a time extension will be waived. Many contracts require written notice within a much shorter period of time.

The question arises, does the contractor's failure to give the owner timely written notice actually result in a waiver of the right to a time extension? The answer is, it depends on whether or not the owner was prejudiced by the lack of written notice.

If the owner was aware of the delay, it is hard to see how the lack of a written notice would affect the owner's options or decisions. This is frequently the case, as an owner's representative usually visits the site regularly and would be aware of a work stoppage. Even if the owner was unaware of the delay, the lack of written notice may not prejudice the owner's interests, particularly if the delay is caused by bad weather. Even if the owner had been given notice, what could it have done?

In order for the failure to give written notice to operate as a waiver of the right to an extension of time, the owner must be able to show that had it been given notice, it would have taken certain actions to mitigate the problem. Then, the lack of notice did adversely and irrevocably affect the owner's interests. In this situation, courts will enforce the written notice requirement against contractors.

Effect of a Time Extension

The effect of a time extension is quite simple. The contractor is allowed to complete the project at a later date without incurring financial liability to the owner. As will be discussed later in this chapter, most contracts call for liquidated damages to be assessed against the contractor for every day the project remains incomplete after the stipulated completion date. A time extension enables the contractor to avoid liquidated damages for that period of delay attributable to excusable causes.

OWNER'S DAMAGES FOR CONTRACTOR'S DELAY

As stated earlier, in the construction industry time truly is money. This is just as true for project owners and developers as it is for construction contractors. A contractor's late completion costs an owner considerable amounts of money in increased financing charges and lost revenue. Most construction contracts therefore hold contractors accountable for such delay.

Definition of Nonexcusable Delay

Nonexcusable delay is a delay in the completion of the project which is attributable to the fault of the contractor. Contractors are responsible for the scheduling of the work, the means and methods of construction, and the proper performance of subcontractors and suppliers. Shortcomings in any of these categories are generally considered nonexcusable delay.

By the process of elimination, nonexcusable delay may be defined as any delay which is not compensable (i.e., the fault of the owner) or excusable (i.e., not the fault of either party). As mentioned earlier, not all contracts recognize the existence of a contractor's right to an extension of time for excusable delay. Under these contracts, contractors would have to show that the delay was the fault of the owner in order to avoid contractor responsibility for the delay.

Liquidated Damages

If a contractor is late in its completion of a construction project, it is difficult for the owner or a court to accurately compute the amount the owner has lost owing to the late completion. Extended finance costs and lost rent may be determined with some accuracy. Other factors, such as lost production, failure to open during peak season, and loss of visibility, defy computation.

Because of the amorphous nature of owner's damages for late completion, it is customary to stipulate "liquidated damages" in the construction contract. These damages, stated as a per diem amount, establish the owner's damages for late completion. The owner can recover no more and no less.

The owner need not prove the actual damages it incurred as a result of the contractor's late completion, so the damages are said to be liquidated, or reduced to an established amount in advance. All the owner needs to prove is the number of days of late completion attributable to the contractor. This number is then multiplied by the per diem rate to arrive at the liquidated damages to which the owner is entitled.

It is common in the construction industry to refer to liquidated damages as a "penalty." This is ironic because liquidated damages are not automatically enforceable and one thing that will render them unenforceable is the fact that they are intended as a "penalty" for late completion.

In order for liquidated damages to be enforceable, two basic requirements must be met: (1) The actual damages must be inherently difficult to measure. This is always the case with delay damages on a construction project. (2) The stipulated amount must reflect a good faith effort, at the time of contract execution, to estimate what those damages might be. The amount cannot be intended as a penalty or a sword to be held over the contractor's head. If these requirements are met, the owner will be entitled to recover liquidated damages for the contractor's late completion and will not have to worry about proving its actual damages.

Actual Damages

A widely held misconception in the construction industry is that if a contract does not call for liquidated damages, the contractor cannot be held liable for its late completion of the project. Nothing could be farther from the truth.

In the absence of the stipulation of liquidated damages, a project owner is allowed to sue a tardy contractor for its actual delay damages. As discussed

---

CASE STUDY 7-3

Contract for construction of water works improvements called for liquidated damages of $50 per day for late completion. Contract was completed 1138 days behind schedule. Owner and Contractor each blamed the other.

It was determined that some of the delay was the fault of Contractor and some the fault of Owner. Contractor argued that because Owner contributed to the delay, Owner could not assess liquidated damages against Contractor.

The U.S. District Court ruled that it was necessary to apportion the delay between the parties. If the project would not have been completed on time even in the absence of Owner-caused delay, then Contractor is liable for liquidated damages for the portion of the delay attributable to Contractor.

Aetna Casualty and Surety Co. v. Butte-Meade Sanitary Water District, 500 F.Supp. 193 (1980).

---

earlier, it is often difficult to prove with reasonable certainty what those damages are. On some projects, it may be impossible to prove delay damages, but the owner is always free to attempt to do so. Sometimes the owner may have provable, actual delay damages which are astronomical.

The basic rule regarding recovery of actual delay damages is that any loss which is foreseeable at the time of contract execution is recoverable. Contractors usually have a very accurate idea of the intended use for a completed project. They may not have access to financial projections for the project, but they certainly know whether the building will be used as a shopping mall or a paper mill. Knowing the intended use of the facility, they will be liable for any lost revenue resulting from the owner's inability to make timely and appropriate use of that facility.

When one considers the foreseeable actual damages that can flow from late completion of many construction projects, it is apparent that a liquidated damages clause can benefit contractors just as much as owners. It is therefore surprising that contractors commonly refer to liquidated damages as a "penalty" and consider it a sword in the hands of the owner. In fact, a liquidated damages clause can be just as much a shield in the hands of the contractor.

For instance, consider a contract for the construction of an industrial facility with the capacity to produce $20,000 worth of product per day. Would liquidated damages of $500 per day be beneficial to the contractor? Recalling that liquidated damages set an absolute ceiling on the owner's recovery for late completion, and that in the absence of such a clause the owner could recover all foreseeable actual damages, one would have to conclude that this would be very beneficial for the contractor.

With this in mind, liquidated damages should not be thought of as a penalty or an owner's weapon. Liquidated damages should be a reasonable attempt by both parties to establish in advance those damages which should be paid by a contractor if the contractor is responsible for the late completion of the project. The purpose is not to give the contractor an incentive to complete the work on time. The purpose is to avoid the difficult and treacherous process of proving the actual damages that may result from late completion.

One final point needs to be made regarding liquidated damages. They are a stipulation of delay damages only. They do not liquidate, or limit, the owner's recovery of damages for contractor breaches other than late completion. If a contractor finished a project late and failed to comply with the plans and specifications, the owner could withhold liquidated damages for the late completion and sue to recover the cost of bringing the work into compliance with the contract documents. Liquidated damages are strictly a stipulation of the owner's delay damages. They do not preclude or limit any remedies the owner might have for other types of breach of contract by the contractor.

CONTRACTOR'S DAMAGES FOR OWNER'S DELAY

One of the most common claims by contractors for a price increase is the delay claim. Contractors price their bid or quotation on the assumption they will be able to complete the work during a certain period of time. If that time period is extended, and labor, equipment, capital, and office support are tied up for a longer period of time, it is very expensive. To the extent the delay is attributable to the acts or omissions of the project owner, the contractor may be able to recover compensation.

Compensable Delay

Unlike excusable delay, compensable delay is rarely defined in the construction contract itself. In fact, it can almost be said that it is unheard of for a contract to expressly address the issue of compensable delay. All contracts do, however, contain a number of express and implied obligations which the owner owes the contractor. These include providing timely access to the work site, providing complete and accurate plans, and properly coordinating the work of any separate prime contractors. To the extent the owner breaches any of these duties, the resulting delay may be considered compensable.

This is not to say that any breach of duty by the owner results in an automatic price increase for the contractor. As this section will show, there are many hurdles the contractor must clear before it recovers delay damages. Additionally, owners frequently include disclaimers of liability for delay in the construction contracts. All this makes contractor delay claims one of the most complex and hotly contested issues in construction contracting.

Causes of Compensable Delay

The possible causes of compensable delay defy an exhaustive listing, as any breach of an owner's duty may result in a delay for the contractor. Certain causes are so common, however, that they deserve mention.

A project owner always has an implied duty to provide the contractor with timely access to the job site. This is fundamental, as a contractor cannot perform its function if it is not physically present on the site.

Sometimes owners fail to provide timely site access because earlier, separate prime contractors have not completed their work. For instance, it may be necessary for an earth-moving contractor to complete roads or bridges before other contractors can get their equipment onto the site. The owner's failure to obtain necessary regulatory approval for the project can also result in denial of timely site access. If the project involves improvements to an existing facility, the owner's continued use and occupation of the facility can result in denial of site access.

The owner also has an implied duty to provide the contractor with a set of plans and specifications which are complete and accurate. Errors or omissions in the design documents are a common source of compensable delay claims. When errors are discovered in the field, it is frequently necessary to halt construction work pending resolution of the problem. It is logical that the cost of this delay should be borne by the project owner.

The owner's inadequate coordination of separate prime contractors is also a cause of compensable delay. This was alluded to in the discussion of site access. If an owner elects to award more than one prime contract, the owner has an implied duty to properly schedule and coordinate the work of these contractors. If a contractor can't start work when scheduled because other contractors have not completed necessary preparatory work, the resulting delay will generally be considered compensable.

Sometimes contracts state that the owner will be furnishing the contractor with certain equipment or material. This is not an implied obligation, as contracts usually state that the contractor will furnish all labor and material necessary for completion of the work. When the owner elects, usually for financial reasons, to furnish certain equipment or materials, it has a duty to make them available on the site at the proper time. Failure to do so may result in a compensable delay.

Finally, the owner's slow review of and response to contractor submittals is a common cause of compensable delay. These submittals may be shop drawings, material samples, or anything else where owner approval is required under the contract. Sometimes contracts state the number of days that will be allowed for the owner to review and respond to a submittal. More frequently, the contract is silent on this matter. In that case, courts rule that the owner is allowed a "reasonable" amount of time for submittal review. If the owner is tardy in reviewing necessary submittals, and delay results, this will be the owner's responsibility. This does not mean, of course, that the owner is under any compulsion to approve submittals which are not consistent with the intent and requirements of the contract.

Notice Requirements

It is common for construction contracts to state that the contractor must give the owner prompt written notice of the commencement of any delay which the contractor considers to be compensable. Failure to give timely written notice results in a waiver of the contractor's right to a price increase.

The enforceability of these notice requirements is much the same as discussed regarding excusable delay. Generally, the contractor will lose its right to compensation only if the owner can show prejudice. That is, the owner had no actual knowledge of the delay and the contractor's failure to give timely notice prevented the owner from taking steps to avoid or mitigate the financial harm caused by the delay. If the owner can't show that it was prejudiced by lack of notice, most courts will not allow the notice requirement to be used by owners to avoid responsibility for owner-caused delay.

A qualifying word is necessary, however. In some states there is a judicial history of hostility toward contractor claims for additional compensation. In these jurisdictions, courts may latch onto something like the failure to give timely written notice as appropriate grounds for denial of a contractor's delay claim, regardless of the absence of any actual prejudice to the owner.

CASE STUDY 7-4

Contract for construction of condominium project called for Owner to furnish Contractor with certain patented molds. Contract required Contractor to give Owner written notice of any delay claim within a "reasonable" time after the delay was experienced.

Owner furnished an inadequate number of molds, delaying Contractor's work. Contractor wrote a letter to Owner stating that it was being delayed and would "submit our billing to you at a later date." When Con-

tractor later pursued a delay claim, Owner argued that Contractor failed to comply with the written notice requirement in the contract because Contractor had not stated the extra costs it alleged to be incurring.

The Supreme Court of Nevada ruled that the notice was adequate. The purpose of the notice was to alert the owner to the problem. It was not necessary, or feasible, for the contractor to itemize its increased costs at the time of giving notice. The Court affirmed a lower court award of $544,386 against the owner.

Eagle's Nest Limited Partnership v. S. M. Brunzell, 669 P.2d 714 (Nev. 1983).

Documenting Compensable Delay

In order for a contractor to recover additional compensation for an owner-caused delay, it is not enough to show that there was delay and the contractor's cost of completing the work was higher than expected. Contractors seeking delay damages have the burden of proving their claim. This requires detailed documentation, usually in the form of written records maintained during the course of the project.

One of the best ways to document the cause and extent of delay is to maintain "as-built" progress schedules. These can later be compared with the "as-planned" schedule prepared by the contractor when planning the work. As mentioned earlier in this chapter, the advent of computerized scheduling techniques has greatly facilitated the use of this technique.

It is not enough, however, to simply show the extent of an owner-caused delay. The contractor must be able to document the increased costs that were caused by this delay. The fact that costs increased proves nothing. The contractor must be able to show that the increase was caused by the owner's delay. Detailed labor and equipment records are usually necessary, not only to show the amount of the cost increase but also to show that the increase was caused by the delay. Some of the specific items which need to be documented will be discussed below in the section on delay damages.

One basic legal principle deserves mention at this point. Unless otherwise stated in the construction contract, a contractor has the right to complete the project ahead of schedule. Early completion will of course save the contractor money, just as late completion will cost the contractor money. This means that a contractor may suffer compensable delay even though it finishes the project on or before the contractual completion date. If the contractor can show that it would have finished even earlier but for owner-caused delay, it will be entitled to any lost savings that it can document and prove.

Delay Damages

A contractor's delay damages usually fall within certain well-defined categories. Keeping in mind that delay, in itself, does not alter or expand the scope of work to be accomplished, many of these damages are in the form of escalated costs.

Escalated labor costs may result if a contractor is delayed in its performance of the work. The work may be pushed back into a period of increased wage rates under a collective bargaining agreement. Similarly, the cost of fringe benefits such as medical insurance or pension fund contributions may increase.

Material and equipment costs may also escalate as a result of a delay. It is common for suppliers of equipment and material to quote prices that will be firm only for a stated period of time. Delay may mean that prices the contractor relied on when pricing its bid are no longer available.

Other costs are not escalated but are simply extended because of the period of delay. The most common are extended job site costs, which include supervisory costs and items such as the trailer and utilities. It is readily apparent that the costs of maintaining a field office and paying a supervisor will be greater if a project extends months beyond its scheduled completion date.

Other costs may be extended, as well. If the contractor is working with borrowed money, its financing costs are extended. The same is true of premiums paid for insurance policies required under the terms of the contract.

One cost deserves special mention because it is so controversial and so widely misunderstood. This is the item of unabsorbed or underabsorbed home office overhead. Generally speaking, a contractor's home office expenses are fixed and quite consistent regardless of the contracts the contractor is currently working on. That being the case, one might wonder how the delay in completion of one contract could cost the contractor any money at the home office.

When a contractor is awarded a contract, the contractor justifiably assumes that for the scheduled period of construction, those contract billings will absorb a certain percentage of the home office expenses. That percentage could be stated as the ratio between that contract amount and total contract billings during the scheduled period of construction.

If performance of the contract is delayed, the contractor will receive its contract payments more slowly over an extended period of time. Therefore, the contract will not absorb as large a percentage of the home office expenses as planned. This is why this item is referred to as unabsorbed or underabsorbed home office overhead.

Project owners have vociferously resisted paying this item of delay damages for years. They argue that home office expenses have not gone up because of the extended performance period, so why should the contractor receive any additional money? Despite this argument, courts have gradually come to recognize unabsorbed home office overhead as recoverable. The formula used to compute the amount is called the "Eichleay formula," originally stated by the federal Armed Services Board of Contract Appeals in the Appeal of Eichleay Corporation, 60-2 BCA Paragraph. 2688. The formula can be stated as follows:

$$\frac{\text{Contract billings}}{\text{Total billings for contract period}} \times \text{total overhead for contract period}$$

$$= \text{overhead allocable to the contract}$$

$$\frac{\text{Allocable overhead}}{\text{Days of performance}} = \text{daily contract overhead}$$

$$\text{Daily contract overhead} \times \text{number of days of delay} = \text{total unabsorbed home office overhead}$$

Project owners and many courts have criticized the Eichleay formula as arbitrary and unrealistic. Nevertheless, its use has been endorsed by the federal courts and boards of contract appeals. Many state courts are influenced by the federal arena when it comes to construction litigation, so the use of Eichleay continues to spread.

A final item of delay damages that needs to be mentioned is lost efficiency. If a contractor is forced to perform work in a stop-and-start fashion, it is simply not as efficient. These costs are very difficult to document and prove; how

---

CASE STUDY 7-5

Contractor on federal project brought a delay claim. Contractor attempted to use the Eichleay formula of computing unabsorbed home office overhead during the period of government-caused delay. This formula computes the percentage of the contractor's fixed daily administrative expenses which would have been absorbed by contract billings if contractor had not been delayed in the performance of that contract.

An administrative board ruled that the use of the Eichleay formula was imper-missible because a delay in performance of one contract does not increase the contractor's home office expenses.

The U.S. Court of Appeals reversed. When a contractor bids a job, it computes its overhead costs on the basis of the time that will be required to complete that job. If government-caused delay extends the performance period, less fixed overhead is absorbed by those contract billings than originally planned. Contractors are entitled to recover this unabsorbed overhead and are entitled to use the Eichleay formula to compute it.

Capital Electric Co. v. United States, 729 F.2d 743 (Fed.Cir. 1984).

---

ever, the costs of idle equipment or the costs of remobilizing crews and equipment may be itemized. Costs such as lost labor efficiency are far more difficult to document. If provable, however, lost efficiency is a well-recognized item of delay damages.

Owing to the difficulty in itemizing and proving delay damages, many contractors would simply like to show the cost of the work as originally bid or estimated and compare it with the actual cost of performing the work affected by the delay. The increase is arguably attributable to the delay and constitutes the contractor's delay damages.

Courts are understandably hostile to this so-called total cost method of computing delay damages. There is no showing that the delay actually caused the cost increase and there is no breakdown of the elements of the cost increase. Many courts will allow the use of the total cost method under limited circumstances, however.

First, the factual circumstances of the case must reasonably preclude any itemization of delay damages. Second, all delay must be attributable to the owner's shortcomings. There cannot be any contractor-caused delay or other factors which could account for the cost increase. And third, the contractor must be able to show that its original bid price was a reasonable and accurate projection of the cost of performing the work as originally scheduled.

NO-DAMAGE-FOR-DELAY CLAUSES

The discussion of contractors' damages for owner-caused delay should make it amply clear that delay can be very expensive. It is not surprising, then, that project owners frequently attempt to contractually disclaim liability for delay.

These "no-damage-for-delay" clauses usually state that the contractor will

---

CASE STUDY 7-6

Subcontractor filed suit against Owner and Contractor for delay it experienced in performance of a concrete subcontract. Subcontractor attempted to prove its delay damages using the "total cost" method. That is, Subcontractor attributed the entire difference between its estimated costs at time of bid preparation and its actual costs to the delay.

The Supreme Court of Utah said that damages must be computed and documented with some specificity. The "total cost" method of computing delay damages can be used only if (1) the nature of the damages make it highly impractical to accurately measure them; (2) the contractor's bid estimate was reasonable; (3) the contractor's actual costs were reasonable; and (4) the contractor was not responsible for any of the increased costs.

Contractor in this case could not meet this standard, so it was denied recovery of delay damages.

Highland Construction Co. v. Union Pacific Railroad Co., 683 P.2d 1042 (Utah 1984).

be entitled to an extension of time for delay beyond the control of the contractor, but this shall be the contractor's sole remedy for delay. The contractor shall not be entitled to additional compensation for delay, regardless of the source or cause of that delay. An example is printed below.

> In the event the contractor is delayed by factors that are beyond the control of and without the fault of the contractor, the contractor may be entitled to an extension of the contractual performance period. This extension of time shall be the contractor's sole remedy in the event of a delay. The contractor shall not be entitled to an increase in the contract price as a result of any delay of any nature whatsoever, including delay caused by the acts or omissions of the owner.

The obvious question is: Can these clauses be enforced against contractors? The answer is yes, but with certain limitations.

Risk Allocation

In the first chapter of this book, it was stated that a written contract is simply an expression of the intent of the parties. Our legal system places great emphasis on the freedom to contract. Two business entities bargaining on an arm's-length basis are free to strike just about any deal they choose. One of the primary purposes of a contract is to allocate risk between the parties, and this is just as subject to bargaining as the price.

On a construction contract, one of the primary risks is the risk of delay. Courts recognize that the parties are free to allocate this risk as they choose. If it is agreed that the contractor shall bear the sole financial risk of delay, courts will enforce this provision.

Courts read no-damage-for-delay clauses with a sharp and cautious eye, however. No-damage clauses are considered "exculpatory clauses" because they exculpate or excuse a party (in this case the project owner) from liability

---

CASE STUDY 7-7

Sewer construction contract stated that Contractor "agrees to make no claim for damages for delay in the performance of this contract occasioned by any act or omission to act of the City or any of its representatives."

City declared a moratorium on street openings, thereby delaying Contractor's performance of its work. When Contractor brought a delay claim, City relied on the "no-damage-for-delay" clause as a defense.

The New York Court of Appeals ruled that disclaimers of owner liability for delay are an acceptable business practice and are legally enforceable. Contractor's delay claim was denied.

Corrino Civetta Construction Corp. v. City of New York, 493 N.E.2d 905 (N.Y. 1986).

---

which it would otherwise have. As mentioned in Chapter 1, a basic legal principle is that exculpatory clauses will be strictly construed. That is, courts will interpret them narrowly in order to limit their effect.

The reason for this is that courts recognize that parties seldom bargain on truly equal ground. On construction contracts, the project owner usually has more leverage than the contractor. This is particularly true on competitively bid projects where the contract terms are presented on a take-it-or-leave-it basis. Since owners impose no-damage-for-delay clauses to protect their own interests, courts will interpret the clauses narrowly in order to limit their effect.

For instance, if a no-damage clause refers to "ordinary delays," a court would be likely to rule that the clause was not intended to apply to delays caused by the owner, as these are not ordinary. Therefore, owners prefer clauses that are more expansive and refer to "any and all delays of any cause whatsoever, including the acts or omissions of the owner or its agents."

Because of the doctrine of strict construction, the analysis of the enforceability of a no-damage-for-delay clause must begin with a careful reading of the language of the clause itself. Additionally, several well-recognized exceptions to the enforceability of these clauses have evolved over a period of time.

Exceptions to Enforceability

The exceptions to the enforceability of no-damage-for-delay clauses tend to overlap, as they all result from judicial efforts to restrict the impact of the exculpatory clauses. In many instances they are simply different ways of saying the same thing. Certain basic categories of exceptions have become widely recognized, however.

The legal rationale (some would say legal fiction) behind these exceptions is that there must be a limit to the intended effect of these exculpatory clauses. The reason courts have developed the exceptions is the same as the reason behind the doctrine of strict construction. Courts want to avoid the harsh impact on a contractor of an exculpatory clause which was imposed by the project owner.

Interference by the Owner　An owner's active interference with the contractor's ability to perform its work is recognized as an exception to the enforceability of no-damage clauses. Courts reason that a contractor would not intend to agree to a contract whereby the owner would be allowed to impede its ability to carry out its performance of the work. Denial of site access is the most common example of active interference. An owner's failure to coordinate multiple prime contractors or failure to provide adequate plans is also sometimes characterized as active interference.

Delays Not Contemplated by the Parties　This is really yet another corollary of the doctrine of strict construction. If a no-damage-for-delay clause does not refer to a particular cause of delay, a court may say that the delay was not contemplated by the parties when agreeing to the contract and is therefore not covered by the clause.

Delays of Unreasonable Duration Even when a particular type of delay is specifically referenced in the no-damage-for-delay clause, a court may say that the clause was only intended to apply to delays of reasonable duration. Parties should not be presumed to have intended to agree to something unreasonable. Therefore, if the delay extends for an "unreasonable" period of time, courts may refuse to apply the no-damage clause to the delay.

Fraud by the Owner This exception is based more on considerations of public policy than on the strict construction of an exculpatory clause. If a delay is caused by the fraudulent or bad faith acts of the owner, courts are loath to allow the owner to hide behind an exculpatory clause. As stated earlier, these exceptions are not mutually exclusive. Nor are they universally recognized. In states with a judicial legacy of hostility toward contractor claims for extra compensation, the only exception that might be recognized is fraud by the owner. In other jurisdictions, courts are quick to rule that a particular delay was not contemplated by the parties and is therefore not covered by the clause.

In all jurisdictions, courts are influenced on a case-by-case basis by the relative reasonableness of each party's conduct and the relative harm that would result from enforcing or refusing to enforce the no-damage-for-delay clause.

ACCELERATION, DISRUPTION, AND SUSPENSION

Acceleration, disruption, and suspension are all related to the topic of delay because each involves the same precious commodity: time. This section of the chapter examines each of these issues.

Acceleration

As its name implies, acceleration is a hastening of the pace of work by the owner. A construction contract assigns a precise quantity of work to the contractor and gives the contractor a stated period of time to perform that work. The contractor is allowed to use that entire period to perform the work. If the owner gives the contractor less than the agreed amount of time or requires additional work to be performed within the original period of time, the owner is said to have accelerated the contractor's work. This entitles the contractor to recover its provable increased costs.

In order for there to be a compensable acceleration of the schedule, there must be a directive from the owner. If the contractor simply picks up the pace, for instance, adding a second crew, because it is running behind schedule, this is not a compensable acceleration. Usually, the directive from the owner is not an explicit order to accelerate the work, but the owner must take some affirmative action which reduces the contractor's performance period.

The contractor also must be able to show that this affirmative act by the owner actually forced it to perform within a shorter period of time and that as a result it incurred higher costs. If these three elements, an owner directive, an acceleration of the work, and increased cost of performance, can be shown, the contractor may recover its damages. The damages for acceleration almost always consist of increased labor costs, as a contractor will be forced to add additional crews or pay existing crews overtime in order to accelerate the work.

The issue of "constructive acceleration" arises when a contractor is forced to perform an increased amount of work, by change order or otherwise, but the owner refuses to grant additional performance time. The contractor is required to perform an increased quantity of work within a period of time which was agreed to in the context of the original scope of work. If this forces the contractor to accelerate its work by adding crews or working overtime, this is compensable.

Disruption

Once a performance period is established in the contract, it is the contractor's responsibility to plan and organize its work so that it will be able to meet that schedule. Assuming the absence of a contractual provision to the contrary (and such a provision would be very unusual), the contractor has unfettered discretion to schedule its work in a sequence of events which it considers most efficient and economical.

If the project owner, through its affirmative acts or the breach of its con-

---

CASE STUDY 7-9

Contract for construction of a new high school allowed 1000 days for completion of the work. In an effort to achieve an earlier occupancy date, Owner issued a change order moving the completion date ahead by 5 months.

Contractor brought claim for its acceleration costs, using the "total cost" method of computing its increased expenses. A trial court awarded Contractor the difference between its estimated costs and its actual costs. Owner appealed.

The Superior Court of Pennsylvania reversed the trial court. Although contractors who have their work schedule accelerated are entitled to recover their increased costs, the "total cost" method is an inappropriate way to measure those costs unless the contractor can prove that both its estimated and actual costs were reasonable. Contractor in this case failed to do so.

John F. Harkins Co., Inc. v. School District of Philadelphia, 460 A.2d 260 (Pa.Super. 1983).

---

tractual duties, forces the contractor to perform work out of sequence, the owner is said to have disrupted the contractor's work. The impact of the disruption usually affects the proper coordination and sequencing of the various trades. Sometimes, however, disruption occurs when a particular task is interrupted and must be performed in a "stop-and-start" manner.

Disruption can be distinguished from owner-caused delay in that a contractor may have the sequence of its work disrupted and still be able to finish the project as originally scheduled. This does not mean the contractor has not been harmed, however, as a disruption in the planned sequence of work may result in lost efficiency and may force the contractor or its subcontractors to increase crews or work overtime.

In order for a contractor to recover from an owner for disruption of the work, the contractor must first establish the sequence of work it originally planned. This is usually accomplished with the as-planned schedule. The actual impact, or disruption, caused by the owner's breach is usually demonstrated with as-built schedules and daily job logs.

The damages themselves usually prove to be the toughest hurdle for a contractor who has been disrupted. The damages are in the form of lost efficiency and increased labor costs. As mentioned earlier in the section on delay damages, lost efficiency tends to be difficult to quantify and document.

Suspension of Work

Many construction contracts give the project owner the right to order the contractor to suspend all or a portion of its operations. This is a valuable tool for the owner, as it gives the owner flexibility in dealing with various problems or contingencies which might arise during the course of the work. Without a "suspension of work" clause, the owner would be in breach of contract if it issued a "stop work" order and forced the contractor to temporarily shut down its operations.

CASE STUDY 7-10

Contract called for installation of meters in apartments housing military personnel. Government approved Contractor's submittals for construction sequence and schedule.

Government failed to provide access to the apartments in an orderly fashion. This disrupted the sequence of Contractor's work and made it impossible to properly coordinate the work of various trade subcontractors. Contractor had to backtrack to complete the project.

The U.S. Court of Appeals ruled that the failure to provide access to the apartments in a logical, sequential fashion was a disruption of Contractor's work. Contractor was entitled to recover the increased costs caused by this disruption.

Blinderman Construction Co., Inc. v. United States, 695 F.2d 552 (Fed.Cir. 1982).

Many suspension of work clauses, including the ones used on federal government contracts, give the owner the right to suspend work for a "reasonable" period of time without compensating the contractor. It is only when the suspension becomes "unreasonable" that the owner must compensate the contractor.

A common interpretation of this "reasonableness" standard is that the suspension is reasonable if it does not extend the contractor's total performance period. If the performance period is extended, the contractor must be compensated. A suspension order of several hours' duration in order to address some unexpected occurrence in the field would probably be considered reasonable. A suspension order of a week's duration would probably require compensation.

The federal suspension of work clause, and most other suspension clauses, state that the contractor may recover its documented increased costs but may not apply any markup for profit on those costs. The contractor is entitled to be reimbursed or made whole for the cost of the owner's stop work order but not to profit from the order. Unlike a change order, which generally authorizes a profit markup, a stop work order does not require the contractor to perform any extra work. The federal clause is printed below.

Suspension of Work

(a) The contracting officer may order the contractor in writing to suspend, delay, or interrupt all or any part of the work for such period of time as he may determine to be appropriate for the convenience of the government.

(b) If the performance of all or any part of the work is, for an unreasonable period of time, suspended, delayed, or interrupted by an act of the contracting officer in the administration of this contract, or by his failure to act within the time specified in this contract (or if no time is specified, within a reasonable time), an adjustment shall be made for any increase in the cost of performance of this contract (excluding profit) necessarily caused by such unreasonable delay, suspension, delay, or interruption and the contract modified accordingly. However, no adjustment shall be made under this clause for any suspension, or interruption to the extent (1) that performance would have been so suspended, delayed, or interrupted by any other cause, including the fault or negligence of the contractor or (2) for which an equitable adjustment is provided for or excluded under any other provision of this contract.

KEY TERMS AND CONCEPTS

compensable delay   A delay in the contractor's performance of the work which results from the owner's failure to fully and faithfully perform an obligation under the contract. In the absence of a contract provision to the contrary, the contractor is entitled to recover its increased performance costs resulting from the owner-caused delay.

excusable delay   A delay in the contractor's performance of the work which results from a factor which is beyond the control and without the fault of either owner or contractor. Unforeseeably severe weather is the classic example of excusable delay. If an excusable delay occurs, the contractor is entitled to an extension of the performance period for a commensurate amount of time but is not entitled to any additional compensation.

nonexcusable delay   Delay which results from the contractor's failure to properly carry out its obligations under the contract. The contractor receives no additional compensation and no extension of the performance period.

concurrent delay   Delay resulting from two separate causes at the same time. If excusable or compensable delay occurs concurrently with nonexcusable delay, the delay will be treated as nonexcusable. If compensable delay occurs concurrently with excusable delay, the delay will be treated as excusable.

liquidated damages   A per diem amount, stipulated in the contract, which the owner will recover from the contractor if the contractor substantially completes the project later than the date required by the contract and the delay is not excusable. Liquidated damages are enforceable if they represent a reasonable effort to forecast, at the time of contract formation, the actual damages the owner might incur as a result of the delayed use of the project. Liquidated damages serve as the owner's exclusive damages for late completion.

escalation   The increase in the contractor's cost of labor and materials that occurs during a period of delay. If the delay is compensable, this price escalation will be a major component of the contractor's recoverable delay damages.

unabsorbed home office overhead   The portion of the contractor's daily fixed office overhead costs that would have been absorbed by billings to a particular contract but for an owner-caused delay in the contractor's performance of that contract. Unabsorbed home office overhead is a major component of a contractor's delay damages in a compensable delay situation.

no-damage-for-delay clause   A contractual clause whereby the owner disclaims any liability for the contractor's damages or increased performance costs resulting from delay of any nature, including delay caused by the owner's breach of contract. With certain exceptions, no-damage-for-delay clauses are enforced against contractors.

acceleration   A directive from the project owner which forces the contractor to accelerate its work schedule by completing the project earlier than originally required. Generally, the increased costs caused by acceleration can be recovered by the contractor.

disruption   An act, failure to act, or directive from the owner which forces the contractor to perform work in a sequence that varies from the conventional or logical sequence in which the contractor had planned to perform the work. Generally, the contractor is entitled to recover the increased costs resulting from the disruption.

suspension   An owner's directive to the contractor to suspend operations. The owner's right to suspend work is usually established in the construction contract itself. Frequently, the owner is not required to pay additional compensation if the suspension is only for a "reasonable" period of time. The reasonableness of the duration of a suspension is a case-by-case factual determination.

DIFFERING SITE CONDITIONS

Differing site conditions are physical conditions at the job site which differ materially from the conditions represented in the construction contract or the conditions that normally could be expected in a job of that type.

This chapter examines the various ways construction contracts treat differing site conditions. The chapter also discusses the ways in which the conduct of the owner or contractor can affect the parties' respective rights.

THE DIFFERING SITE CONDITIONS CLAUSE

Not all contracts contain a differing site conditions clause. Those that do generally authorize an equitable price increase to cover the contractor's cost of coping with unanticipated site conditions.

The definition of a differing or unanticipated site condition varies. Although it is difficult to quantify, some contracts require a higher degree of variation than others. Some clauses are limited to conditions which differ from those depicted in the contract documents and do not apply to conditions which are simply very unusual and unexpected. A typical clause can be found in Paragraph 12.2 of Appendix E.

No Implied Right

The crucial aspect of a differing site conditions clause is that it is necessary in order for the contractor to be entitled to any additional payment under the contract. There is no implied right to additional compensation for differing site conditions. The contractor has agreed to construct a certain facility and the owner has agreed to pay a stipulated price. If the contractor runs into unexpected physical conditions, that is the contractor's problem. The contractor still must complete the work and will be entitled to only the original contract price.

Fifty years ago, differing site conditions clauses were rare. When contractors sought additional payment for physical problems on the job site, courts applied the draconian rule stated above. Courts did not apply this rule in all situations, however, as will be seen below.

Breach by the Owner

Occasionally, courts were confronted with situations which assaulted their sense of fairness or justice. Project owners had either intentionally or negligently misrepresented the physical conditions at the job site to such a degree that the project bore little resemblance to the project the contractor had agreed to build. Yet the contract did not authorize additional compensation and the project owner was insisting the contractor honor its price.

In these situations, courts began to rule that project owners had materially breached the contract. The ramifications of such a ruling on an owner are severe. Whereas a differing site conditions clause may authorize recovery of the increased costs of performance, a breach by the owner will entitle the contractor to cease performance and recover damages far exceeding anything that would be authorized under a site conditions clause. Rulings such as these provided part of the impetus for owners to include differing site conditions clauses in their contracts.

Purpose of the Clause

The most fundamental purpose of a differing site conditions clause is to allocate risk between the parties. The allocation of risk is one of the most important functions of any contract of any nature. Other than establishing the product to be delivered and the price to be paid, there is nothing more important than determining which party will bear which risks.

Most aspects of a construction project can be objectively defined and quantified. The competent contractor can estimate with reasonable accuracy what it will cost to perform the work. Some aspects of the project cannot be defined or quantified, however. Hidden site conditions are one of these aspects. Who bears the cost of this risk?

As mentioned earlier, the traditional approach was for owners to attempt to place all the risk on the contractor. Except in extreme circumstances, this approach usually worked. It produced some undesirable results from the owner's standpoint, however.

Faced with the burden of all the risk of differing site conditions, contractors began carrying large "contingencies" in their bid prices. This was the only way they could protect themselves against a catastrophic loss in the event of a serious site condition problem. If no site condition problems were encountered, the contingency funds carried in the contract price became a windfall for the contractor.

This phenomenon was particularly noticeable on public, competitively bid projects. In an effort to avoid paying excessive prices, public project owners began to include differing site conditions clauses in their contracts. The federal government in particular has been an influential pioneer in this area. The nature and influence of the federal clause is discussed later in this chapter.

Although the use of site condition clauses first became widespread in the public sector, it eventually gained acceptance in the private sector. Private project owners came to realize that it was more economical in the long run to share the risk of differing site conditions and avoid paying hidden contingency prices on every single construction contract.

By agreeing to share the risk, owners received another important benefit mentioned earlier. If the contract authorizes increased payment for differing site conditions, the contractor cannot very well argue that those conditions constitute a material breach of contract by the owner. The project owner, whether public or private, minimizes the risk of being held in breach of contract for failing to adequately describe the physical conditions at the job site.

Today, it can be stated that the majority of construction contracts contain some form of a differing site conditions clause. As will be seen later in this chapter, however, this is by no means a universal practice. Some project owners not only fail to include such a clause, they go to great lengths to disclaim any responsibility for the conditions at the site or the accuracy of their depiction of those conditions.

DETERMINING SITE CONDITIONS

If one is to consider "differing" site conditions, it is first necessary to objectively describe the physical conditions that were reasonably anticipated on the project. The contractor makes this determination based on a combination of information provided by the owner and information garnered by the contractor.

What Are Site Conditions?

Site conditions are any physical conditions at the job site which may affect the cost or manner of performance. They may be somewhat arbitrarily categorized as subsurface conditions, existing utilities, and existing structural components.

Subsurface soil conditions are probably the most common source of differing site condition disputes. Sometimes the owner or its A/E has performed extensive subsurface investigation prior to putting a contract out to bid. The contract documents may include the results of numerous test borings and test pits. On other projects, no subsurface investigation has been performed and the contract documents make no representations regarding subsurface conditions. The contractor must rely on its experience and visual observations of the surface to deduce what might be reasonably expected in that locale.

In consideration of subsurface soil conditions, the primary areas of concern are the composition and consistency of the various soils (frequently called "soil classifications"), the depth to bedrock, the presence of buried boulders or debris, and the presence of troublesome materials such as clay or peat.

Subsurface water conditions are also a common source of disputes. As with soil conditions, the degree of information in the contract varies considerably from project to project. If subsurface investigation has been performed, the contract may reveal factors such as depth to groundwater and the presence of saturated soil. If no subsurface investigation has been performed, the contractor will have to base its expectation on experience and the appearance of surface conditions.

Existing utilities are another common site condition problem. This is particularly true of buried utilities such as sewer, water, and gas lines. The utilities may have been installed decades earlier. Accurate "as-built" plans showing the location of these lines may not be available. Sometimes there are public records of utility locations. Other times the contractor is totally reliant on the project owner for any information regarding the location of subsurface utilities.

Existing structural components are a serious problem when an existing building is being renovated. As walls are removed, unexpected structural impediments may be encountered. An accurate "as-built" drawing will warn the contractor in advance of these problems. Even if such drawings are not available, the owner's A/E may have performed extensive investigation as a necessary part of the design process. If none of this information is available, the contractor will have to rely, once again, on experience, common sense, and visual observation to determine what physical conditions might be expected.

One other physical condition should be mentioned at this point, the problem of quantity variations which was discussed in Chapter 6. A quantity variation occurs when a contractor encounters an actual quantity of subsurface material which differs substantially from the quantity estimated in the contract. Although this appears to be a differing site condition, it can more accurately be thought of as a constructive change in the scope of the work. The qualitative nature of the physical conditions do not differ from those represented in the contract, simply the quantity of certain known materials.

The distinction can be more than simply semantic. Under a differing site conditions clause, contractors are typically entitled to an "equitable adjustment" in the contract price. In the context of site conditions, this is generally interpreted to mean that they will recover their costs and be made whole, but they will not be allowed to profit from the problem. (On federal contracts, however, profit may be added to the increased costs in determining an equitable adjustment.) Under a changes clause, contractors are usually entitled to receive a profit markup on extra work. Therefore, if a contract is priced on a lump-sum basis, a contractor on a nonfederal project could probably recover more for a quantity variation under a changes clause than under a differing site conditions clause.

To reiterate briefly a point made in Chapter 6, as a practical matter, the distinction is seldom called into play. Most contracts involving extensive excavation price work on a unit-price basis. The contractor is paid for the number of cubic yards removed, regardless of the actual quantity.

If actual quantities vary significantly from estimates, however, this can be a problem even on a unit-price contract. A substantial shortfall may cause a loss for the contractor, as it will be unable to receive payment on enough units to recover the cost of renting or mobilizing its equipment. An overrun can be a windfall to the contractor. Having bid the work on the assumption of a modest quantity, the contractor will recoup its costs early and the rest of the work will be gravy.

In order to remove this gamble from the contract and protect the contractor against a loss and the owner against paying a windfall, most unit-price contracts contain a quantity variation clause. This clause simply says that if the actual quantity varies from the estimate, either up or down, by more than a certain percent (usually 20 or 25 percent), then the unit price will be equitably adjusted. If the adjustment is in the contractor's favor, the contractor would recover its direct and indirect costs but would not be able to increase the profit on the contract.

Owner's Description of Site Conditions

The primary source of site condition information is the data portrayed in the contract documents by the owner. Of the two parties to the construction contract, the owner is in the better position to know what the site conditions are. The owner owns the site and has had an extended period of time to investigate conditions. The owner has probably hired expert assistance in the planning and design of the project. This necessitates a certain amount of subsurface investigation.

Usually, there is not one single section of the contract documents which comprehensively portrays the site conditions. Rather, representations of physical site conditions are scattered throughout the drawings and specifications.

Many drawings contain dimensions and elevations representing the location of features on the face of the earth. Drawings also frequently portray the location of existing subsurface utility lines. On a renovation project, they reflect the location of various items in the existing building.

Soil boring logs may be found in the contract. These present the results of subsurface test borings. Boring logs portray the subsurface conditions by indicating the nature and depths of the various materials. Additionally, the specifications frequently classify the soil conditions according to standard geological categories.

CASE STUDY 8-1

Contractor was preparing to bid on road construction contract. The contract documents contained no soil boring logs and gave no indication of subsurface soil conditions. They did indicate a compaction factor, however.

Relying on the compaction factor, Contractor inferred that certain soil conditions would be found and priced its bid accordingly. When Contractor started work, it discovered far more rock than it anticipated. Contractor brought claim for differing site conditions, arguing that actual conditions differed materially from the conditions indicated by the compaction factor stated in the contract.

The U.S. Claims Court ruled that Contractor was not entitled to rely on the compaction factor as a representation of subsurface conditions. The compaction factor was averaged and covered a large area. As the compaction factor was not an affirmative representation of site conditions, actual conditions did not vary from those represented in the contract, and the claim was denied.

A. D. and G. D. Fox v. United States, 7 Cl.Ct. 60 (1984).

In short, the contractor must gather site condition information from throughout the contract documents and will be responsible for being familiar with that information regardless of where it may be found.

The owner has responsibilities regarding the site condition information as well. It has long been recognized by the courts that a project owner extends an implied warranty of the accuracy of any affirmative site condition representations. If the representations are not accurate, a differing site condition has occurred. If there is no differing site conditions clause in the contract, the contractor may argue that there has been a material breach of contract by the owner. Although owners frequently try to disclaim responsibility for site condition representations, as will be discussed later in this chapter, the implied warranty is something that is taken very seriously by the courts.

It is important to note that the implied warranty extends only to affirmative representations in the contract. To the extent the contract documents make any statement, by word or number, regarding physical conditions, the owner extends an implied warranty that those statements are accurate. This does not mean that the owner warrants that the site condition information is a complete, comprehensive, or accurate statement of what actually exists in the field. The warranty applies only to things which are said, not things which are left unsaid. The owner does have an implied obligation to disclose relevant site data in its possession, however.

Prebid Site Inspection

Although the owner is in a better position to know what the site conditions are, the owner does not bear sole responsibility for making this determination. The contractor also must get involved.

CASE STUDY 8-2

Owner solicited bids for repair of a damaged bridge pier and fender. Owner had previously had an adjacent bridge pier repaired and had in its possession detailed information on problems the previous contractor had encountered with tides and currents.

Owner failed to disclose the information from the earlier project. Contractor encountered problems with tides and currents. Contractor sued Owner for breach of contract.

The California Court of Appeals ruled that failure to disclose the information was a breach of contract, even if the nondisclosure was unintentional. Owner has an implied duty to furnish Contractor with all site condition data within Owner's control or possession.

Welch v. State,
188 Cal.Rptr. 726 (Cal.App. 1983).

Before submitting a bid or committing itself to a price, the contractor must conduct an inspection of the job site. Usually the contract expressly requires the contractor to make such an inspection and states that the contractor will be responsible for any conditions observed in the field. Even if the contract does not contain such a clause, there is an implied duty for the contractor to visually inspect the site prior to committing itself to a price.

A common source of disputes is the appropriate scope of the contractor's inspection. When an unexpected condition is discovered, the owner argues that the contractor should have detected this condition during its prebid site inspection. The contractor responds that there was no way it could have detected the problem.

The general rule is that while the contractor is required to make a "reasonable" site inspection, the inspection need not be an exhaustive one. Courts recognize that prior to bidding, the contractor has neither the time nor the resources to conduct the kind of investigation the owner could or should have made. The contractor will be responsible for observing patent, or obvious, conditions, but not latent, or subtle, conditions.

The contractor will be expected to possess the judgment of an experienced contractor when observing and interpreting the physical site conditions but will not be required to conduct an independent technical investigation. Nor will the contractor be required to hire expert assistance in interpreting the situation.

For instance, if outcroppings of ledge can be observed at the site, the contractor will be on notice that ledge can be expected. The contractor is not required, however, to make its own test borings or to hire a geotechnical engineer to interpret boring logs provided by the owner. Similarly, the presence of cattails on the site will alert the contractor to a shallow water table. In the absence of such indications, though, the contractor would not be responsible for a latent condition such as the level of the water table.

With regard to drawing dimensions, the general rule is that the contractor

---

CASE STUDY 8-3

Bid documents required Contractor to conduct prebid inspection of the job site and stated that Contractor would be responsible for any observable conditions.

Contractor performed inspection but failed to notice clogged culverts. As Contractor performed the work, it encountered problems with inadequate drainage and soggy soil. Contractor brought a differing site conditions claim.

The Court of Appeals of Arkansas denied the claim, saying that a reasonable site inspection would have alerted Contractor to the particular condition in question.

Crookham & Vessels, Inc. v. Larry Moyer Trucking, Inc., 699 S.W.2d 414 (Ark.App. 1985).

---

can rely on these dimensions without confirming them in the field. Sometimes the contract documents expressly require the contractor to confirm all dimensions in the field. This requirement will be enforced against the contractor unless the dimensions are so numerous that it would have been impracticable to confirm them all in the short period of time allowed before bid submittal.

The ramification of a contractor's failure to conduct an appropriate prebid site inspection is simple. If, in the scope of a reasonable inspection, the contractor failed to observe a condition or appreciate the significance of a condition, the contractor will not be entitled to any increase in the contract price due to the cost of coping with that condition. This failure to detect a condition in the field will shift the economic risk caused by that condition from the owner to the contractor. From a contractor's standpoint, it is therefore crucial that a careful, thoughtful inspection of the site be conducted prior to submitting a bid or quotation. Courts have no sympathy for contractors who submit blind bids.

Prebid Meeting

A final source of site condition information is the prebid meeting. Contract documents frequently call for a meeting among all prospective bidders, the owner's representative, and the owner's design professionals prior to bid submittal. The purpose of the meeting is to answer any questions that have arisen or to provide clarifications where necessary.

It is crucial that this be done in an organized manner with all prospective bidders present. Otherwise, some bidders will gain a competitive advantage by being privy to information that other bidders don't possess. It is extremely bad form, and legally damaging, for owners or their A/Es to respond to telephone inquiries from prospective bidders. Any inquiry, whether by telephone or letter, should be responded to in the open forum of the prebid meeting with all prospective bidders present.

Attendance at the prebid meeting is mandatory for all bidders, as they will be held responsible for any information conveyed at that meeting, regardless of whether or not they were actually in attendance. Failure to attend the prebid meeting has the same effect as failure to conduct a reasonable site inspection. The contractor will not be entitled to any increase in the contract price due to conditions which were revealed at the prebid meeting.

FEDERAL GOVERNMENT CONTRACTS

As mentioned earlier, the federal government was a pioneer in the use of differing site conditions clauses. As a result, the federal clause has become a model for many other site condition clauses on both public and private contracts. It is useful to examine the clause and discuss the two different categories of site conditions it recognizes.

Differing Site Conditions

(a) The contractor shall promptly, and before such conditions are disturbed, notify the contracting officer in writing of: (1) subsurface or latent physical conditions at the site differing materially from those indicated in this contract, or (2) unknown physical conditions at the site, of an unusual nature, differing materially from those ordinarily encountered and generally recognized as inhering in work of the character provided for in this contract. The contracting officer shall promptly investigate the conditions, and if he finds that such conditions do materially so differ and cause an increase or decrease in the contractor's cost of, or the time required for, performance of any part of the work under this contract, whether or not changed as a result of such conditions, an equitable adjustment shall be made and the contract modified in writing accordingly.

(b) No claim of the contractor under this clause shall be allowed unless the contractor has given the notice required in (a) above; provided, however, the time prescribed therefor may be extended by the government.

(c) No claim by the contractor for an equitable adjustment hereunder shall be allowed if asserted after final payment under this contract.

Type 1 Conditions versus Type 2 Conditions

The first type of differing site condition recognized by the federal clause is the type that has been discussed so far in this chapter. This is the physical condition which differs materially from the condition indicated in the contract. This is the same type of condition which would arguably be considered a breach of contract in the absence of a differing site conditions clause.

The type 2 condition recognized under the federal clause is more controversial. It authorizes additional compensation for unknown conditions which differ materially from those conditions which would ordinarily be encountered on a project of that nature. There is no precedent for compensation for conditions of this nature. In the absence of such contract language, these conditions would be at the sole risk of the contractor. Therefore, many project owners, both public and private, do not recognize type 2 differing site conditions in their contracts.

As with the prebid site inspection, the contractor is expected to possess the judgment of an experienced, prudent contractor. A contractor cannot rely on its own ignorance or inexperience to recover for a type 2 site condition. The condition must be so truly unusual that it simply could not have been anticipated.

While many differing site conditions clauses do not go as far as the federal clause, a good argument can be made for recognition of type 2 differing site conditions. If the purpose of the clause is to share the risk and avoid the need for contractors to carry large contingencies in their bid prices, then there is no practical distinction between a physical condition which simply could not have been anticipated and a condition which differed from a representation in the contract documents.

DISCLAIMERS OF SITE INFORMATION

Considering the owner's implied warranty of the accuracy of all affirmative representations regarding the physical condition of the site, it is not surprising that project owners sometimes attempt to disclaim responsibility for that information. This section examines those disclaimers and their enforceability.

The Disclaimer

If a project owner wants to place all the risk of differing site conditions with the contractor, the owner will omit a differing site conditions clause from the contract and disclaim responsibility for the accuracy of any site information in the contract.

This disclaimer typically states that subsurface data and other site information is provided to bidders as general guidance and not as a representation of fact. The clause goes on to disclaim the owner's responsibility for any conditions encountered in the field and states that the contractor shall not be entitled to any additional compensation as a result of such conditions. An example of a typical disclaimer is shown below.

> The soil boring logs and other site condition data are provided solely for the informational use of bidders. The owner does not warrant the accuracy or sufficiency of this information. Bidders are responsible for thoroughly familiarizing themselves with the physical conditions at the site. The eventual contractor shall not be entitled to an increase in the contract price as a result of any physical condition encountered at the site.

Enforceability of the Disclaimer

The obvious question is whether courts will enforce this type of disclaimer. The answer is affirmative. As "exculpatory language," the clause will be strictly construed against the owner, but given the comprehensive nature of the language quoted above, this will be of little benefit to the contractor. If the disclaimer is not as broadly worded, however, a court may rule that a particular piece of contested information was outside the scope of the disclaimer.

Although the disclaimers are generally enforceable, certain exceptions to their enforceability have evolved. The most widely recognized exception is the owner's intentional withholding of relevant site information. If the owner is aware of the existence of site data, for instance, old soils surveys or blueprints showing the location of subsurface utilities, and fails to disclose that information to prospective contractors, the disclaimer will not enable the owner to avoid liability for those particular differing site conditions.

Another, less recognized exception is the owner's negligent misrepresentation of the site conditions. In other words, the owner didn't intentionally withhold information but was negligent in seeking out available information. Perhaps the owner's engineer was negligent in performing its subsurface investigation.

Many courts have ruled that the disclaimer will not apply to this kind of negligent misrepresentation. There is less consensus, however, than with the case of intentional withholding of information. Sometimes the disclaimer expressly states that the owner has not conducted a complete or exhaustive survey of site conditions, thereby reducing the likelihood that a court will rule that the disclaimer does not apply to negligently omitted information.

There is one other exception to the enforceability of these disclaimers. Occasionally, courts will rule that there was insufficient time between release of the bid documents and bid submittal for bidders to independently verify or determine site conditions.

This exception is not as widely recognized as the two mentioned above. It is usually applied when the contractor must rely on a large quantity of detailed, owner-furnished data, yet the owner has disclaimed responsibility for the accuracy of those data. An example might be a piping job in an existing building

---

CASE STUDY 8-4

Owner solicited bids for construction of a sewer line. Bid documents stated that subsurface data "are incomplete, are not a part of the contract documents, and are not warranted to show the actual subsurface conditions."

Contractor encountered unanticipated rock formations which caused its tunnel-boring equipment to fail. Contractor sought to recover its increased costs, arguing that the disclaimer of the accuracy of subsurface data was illegal and unenforceable.

The Supreme Court of Ohio ruled that an unambiguous disclaimer such as this is enforceable so long as Owner did not withhold any pertinent information. There was no evidence of withheld information; so the disclaimer was enforced against Contractor.

S & M Constructors, Inc. v. City of Columbus, 434 N.E.2d 1349 (Ohio 1982).

CASE STUDY 8-5

Owner solicited bids for repairs to concrete piers. Bid documents contained a great deal of detailed subsurface data but stated that data were provided for informational purposes only, that they did not purport to represent actual physical conditions, and that bidders had responsibility for verifying all site conditions.

Contractor encountered subsurface conditions that differed substantially from the conditions indicated in the bid documents. Contractor argued that it was enti-

tled to rely on Owner's subsurface data despite the contractual disclaimer.

The Court of Special Appeals of Maryland said that while these disclaimers are generally enforceable, there are exceptions. One exception arises when an owner's affirmative representations of fact cannot reasonably be verified by the bidders. That was the case here. Owner had assembled subsurface data over a 4-year period. Contractor could not have confirmed those data within the short period of time allowed for bid preparation. Contractor was therefore allowed to rely on data despite the disclaimer.

Raymond International, Inc. v. Baltimore County, 412 A.2d 1296 (Md.App. 1980).

---

where the owner furnishes thousands of dimensions and the contractor has 7 days to prepare its bid. In a situation such as this, courts may be reluctant to enforce the disclaimer against the contractor.

CONTRACTOR'S WAIVER

It is not only possible for the project owner to disclaim liability for differing site condition claims, it is also possible for the contractor to inadvertently waive its right to such a claim. This primarily occurs when the contractor fails to give timely notice of the site condition, but it can also occur in other ways.

Notice

Almost all differing site conditions clauses require the contractor to give the owner or its representative prompt notice when the contractor discovers any condition in the field which it considers to be a differing site condition. This notice requirement is found in the federal clause printed above.

The purpose of the notice requirement is to give the owner an opportunity to respond to the condition in an expeditious and economical manner. The owner may elect to redesign a portion of the project and issue a change order to the contractor. Or the owner may ask the contractor to submit price proposals for several alternative methods for dealing with the problem. The owner may even elect to delete major portions of the project because of the unanticipated site condition.

Whatever the owner chooses to do, it must have the opportunity to examine the physical condition before it is disturbed and then make a choice before the contractor has incurred additional expenses as a result of the condition. If the owner is not given that opportunity, it suffers economic harm, or prejudice.

In Chapter 7, the concept of prejudice was discussed with regard to a contractor's notice that it has encountered delay. It was stated that these notice requirements are frequently not enforced against contractors because the owner is already well aware of the delay and suffers no prejudice due to the lack of notice.

In the matter of differing site conditions, the opposite is true. The owner can almost always show that it suffered prejudice due to the lack of prompt notice; so the notice requirement is almost always enforced against the contractor. The contractor is in a unique position in the field to detect differing physical conditions. Prompt notice is crucial to avoiding economic harm to the owner by keeping the owner's options open. If a contractor fails to comply with the notice requirement in a differing site conditions clause, most courts will rule that the contractor has waived its right to any additional compensation under the clause.

Waiver in General

There are two other ways in which a contractor may inadvertently waive its right to compensation under a differing site conditions clause. The first is acceptance of final payment under the contract. Most clauses state that no site condition claim may be asserted after acceptance of final payment. Even in the absence of such language, a contractor would be held to have waived the right to the claim if it failed to assert the claim prior to final payment and failed to expressly reserve the claim upon acceptance of final payment.

A more subtle waiver occurs when a contractor acknowledges a change or-

---

CASE STUDY 8-6

Contractor was performing excavation and encountered soil conditions differing from the conditions indicated in the contract documents.

The actual conditions forced Contractor to alter its method of construction, increasing the cost of performance. Contractor later attempted to recover the increased costs from Owner pursuant to the differing site conditions clause.

The U.S. Court of Claims denied Contractor any recovery because Contractor failed to give timely notice of the conditions to Owner. When a contractor encounters differing site conditions in the field, it may not simply improvise and then recover its increased costs from the project owner. The project owner must be given prompt notice before the conditions are disturbed and then be given the opportunity to make design changes or otherwise respond to the conditions in the field.

Schnip Building Co. v. United States, 645 F.2d 950 (Ct.Cl. 1981).

---

der arising out of a differing site condition. A change order typically states that the authorized price increase shall be the total compensation for the changed work and the contractor shall assert no further claim arising out of the matter in question. Once the contractor signs off on the change order, it is bound by those terms.

If the change order was necessitated by a differing site condition, this poses problems for the contractor. Although the change order pays the contractor for the increased cost of performing that aspect of the work, the site condition may have an impact on the cost of performing other aspects of the work later in the project. For instance, a soil condition may not only necessitate redesign of the foundation, it may affect construction of the septic waste system.

If a contractor anticipates this kind of subsequent impact, it must be sure to expressly reserve the right to assert claims relating to the site condition's effect on other aspects of the work. If the contractor fails to reserve this right when acknowledging a change order caused by a site condition, the acknowledgment in the change order may operate as a waiver of the right to assert any other claim arising out of that particular physical condition.

KEY TERMS AND CONCEPTS

site condition   A physical condition, existing at the site where the work is to be performed, which may affect the performance of the work. Site conditions include subsurface soil and water conditions, existing utilities, and conditions in existing structures.

differing site conditions clause   A clause in a construction contract authorizing the contractor to receive an equitable price adjustment if the contractor encounters differing site conditions. In the absence of such a clause, the contractor must complete the work in accordance with the contract documents at the contract price, regardless of the physical conditions encountered in the field. A material misrepresentation of physical conditions may be a breach of contract by the owner, however.

type 1 differing site conditions   Actual site conditions which differ materially from conditions affirmatively represented in the contract documents. The name is derived from the differing site conditions clause found in federal government construction contracts.

type 2 differing site conditions   Actual physical conditions which differ materially from the conditions which a prudent, experienced contractor would reasonably expect to encounter on a project of that nature. The name is derived from the differing site conditions clause found in federal government construction contracts.

quantity variations   Actual quantities of material which differ substantially from the estimated quantities stated in the contract documents. Strictly speaking, quantity variations are not differing site conditions. Any price adjustment to compensate for quantity variations is usually authorized by a quantity variations clause or the changes clause.

prebid site inspection   The contractor's obligation, established in the bid documents or other contract documents, to thoroughly inspect the job site prior to submitting a bid. Contractors are held responsible for any site information which could have been determined during a reasonable site inspection, regardless of whether the contractor actually conducted such an inspection. Contractors are not expected to determine the nature of hidden, or latent, conditions and are not expected to conduct independent tests.

disclaimers of site information   A contract clause inserted by the owner stating that the owner does not warrant the accuracy of the site condition information and the contractor is responsible for making all site condition determinations and responsible for completing the work at the contract price regardless of the actual conditions encountered in the field.

exceptions to site condition disclaimers   There are four widely recognized exceptions to the enforceability of site condition disclaimers: (1) negligent misrepresentation by the owner, (2) withholding of information by the owner, (3) physical conditions outside the scope of the disclaimer, and (4) lack of time for contractor to conduct a prebid site inspection.

waiver   The contractor's waiver of the right to receive additional compensation under the differing site conditions clause. The most common form of waiver is the contractor's failure to give the owner prompt notice of a differing site condition prior to disturbing that condition.

PAYMENT AND SECURITY

Construction is a capital-intensive activity. Large sums of money must be expended over an extended period of time in order to produce a completed project. Furthermore, it is usually necessary for contractors to place binding orders for materials and equipment well ahead of the time the materials or equipment will be incorporated into the project.

These conditions create a great deal of financial risk for a contractor undertaking a construction project. It is crucial for the contractor to know that it will receive timely payments in accordance with the terms of the construction contract. This chapter examines contractors' entitlement to payment and the legal devices that are available to secure that payment.

PAYMENT SCHEDULE

In Chapter 5, the release of payment was discussed from the perspective of the project owner seeking to assure proper performance by the contractor. This section examines the payment schedule from the standpoint of the contractor seeking to maintain adequate cash flow to prosecute the work.

Progress Payments

It has long been customary on construction projects for the owner to make periodic payments to the contractor. The reason is simple. Considering the large capital expenditure and the extended period of construction, it would be difficult for even the most fiscally strong contractor to finance the entire project until completion. Additionally, construction work in place, even on a partially completed project, represents a tangible asset which the owner has received. The use of periodic progress payments recognizes these realities.

All the details of progress payments must be established in the construction contract. In the absence of a provision calling for periodic progress payments, the contractor could not get paid until substantial completion of the project.

Typically, progress payments are made on a monthly basis. This varies, of course, and it is not unusual for a contract to call for payments on a weekly or biweekly basis. Generally, however, monthly payments make the most sense. Payments of greater frequency create a blizzard of paperwork. A financially sound contractor should be in a position to finance its work on a month-to-month basis; so a request for more frequent payments may seem unreasonable in the absence of special circumstances.

The most difficult aspect of progress payments is determining the amount to which the contractor is entitled. Construction contracts usually refer to the value of the completed work in place. If work is being paid for on a unit-price basis, this is not difficult to determine. The owner's representative simply measures or counts the completed units of work.

More frequently, however, work is being paid for on a lump-sum basis. The contractor's progress payment should be based on the percentage of completion applied to the total contract price. This is difficult to measure with precision, particularly on a large project. It is therefore common for the owner and contractor to agree on a "schedule of values" to be used for the purpose of computing progress payments.

The schedule of values breaks down a lump-sum contract price and assigns prices to various identifiable segments of the work or milestones in completion of the work. The use of such a schedule will greatly reduce the likelihood of disagreements regarding the size of progress payments.

Sometimes a simple schedule of values is incorporated right into the progress payment provision of the construction contract. For instance, it is common on smaller jobs for the contract to state that the contractor will receive stated amounts upon the accomplishment of certain milestones (i.e., completion of the foundation, framing of the structure, etc.).

On larger projects, it is difficult to do this, so a more elaborate schedule of values is necessary. Although the schedule may be made a part of the contract itself, this is not advisable. The incorporation of a schedule of values into the contract can have unintended consequences for both owner and contractor. A schedule which was intended only to facilitate periodic progress payment determinations can suddenly have an impact on matters such as pricing change orders, determining termination costs, or computing damages for breach of contract.

It is preferable for the contract to simply state that upon execution of the contract, the owner and contractor will negotiate a mutually agreeable schedule of values. The contract should also state that the schedule will be used for the sole purpose of computing progress payments and will not become a part of the contract or be used for any other purpose under the contract.

Once a detailed schedule of values has been established, the determination of progress payments becomes relatively straightforward. The contractor submits periodic requisitions for the work completed during the payment period in question. The A/E or other owner's representative inspects the completed work in the field and certifies the accuracy of the requisition. Payment is issued according to the schedule of values as applied to the completed work.

Contractors do not usually receive 100 percent of the value of the completed work when they receive a progress payment, however. It is customary for construction contracts to allow the owner to withhold a percentage of each progress payment as "retainage." This percentage varies but is usually 5 or 10 percent.

The purpose of retainage, as discussed in Chapter 5, is to give the owner some assurance that any improper or incomplete work will be corrected by the contractor. Retainage gives the owner some margin of error in avoiding a situation where the cost of completing the project exceeds the amount of undisbursed construction loan proceeds. Retainage is held until release of final payment when the owner is satisfied that all work has been accomplished in accordance with the contract documents.

CASE STUDY 9-1

Contract called for project owner to retain 10 percent of each progress payment until "all work" was completed. Contractor achieved substantial completion but failed to complete the punch list items. Owner refused to release any of the retainage.

The Court of Appeal of Louisiana said that despite the literal language of the contract, Owner was not entitled to retain 10 percent of the contract amount once

Contractor achieved substantial completion. Owner was only entitled to retain sufficient funds to cover the cost of the outstanding punch list items.

The Court said: "If corrective work is required, the owner is entitled to deduct the cost of this work from the retainage and withhold it until the work is satisfactory. However, the owner is not entitled to withhold the entire retainage until every minor deficiency is taken care of. He can only retain as much as reflects the cost of uncompleted work."

State v. Laconco, Inc.,
430 So.2d 1376 (La.App. 1983).

While retainage serves a legitimate and important function in terms of protecting the owner's interest, contractors have a countervailing interest in maximizing cash flow during construction. It is common for contractors to request that the progress payment provision allow for a reduction of retainage when a certain percentage of completion has been achieved.

The rationale is that as the project gets closer to completion, the risk to the owner decreases. Yet the total amount of retainage continues to grow with each periodic progress payment.

It is therefore common on larger projects for the contract to call for 10 percent retainage on all progress payments up to 50 percent completion, with 5 percent retainage on all subsequent progress payments. This would leave the owner holding at least 7½ percent of the contract price upon final acceptance. This is generally sufficient to protect the owner's interests, and it assists the contractor by giving it better cash flow than would be achieved with a straight 10 percent retainage.

Final Payment

A contractor's entitlement to final payment is, of course, dependent upon the successful completion of the project. Because of the complexity of a typical construction project, however, it is not easy to definitively identify when that completion has been achieved. Consequently, the release of payment during the final stages of the project is determined by the language of the contract and the legal principle of "substantial completion."

Substantial completion is one of the most critical milestones in the course of a construction project. Substantial completion is achieved when the project is suitable for the owner's occupancy and use of the project for its intended purpose. This does not mean the project has been completed in full accordance with the plans and specifications. There may be a large number of items to be corrected or completed, but if these items don't prevent the beneficial use and occupancy of the structure, then the project is considered substantially complete.

Once substantial completion has been achieved, the project owner is not legally entitled to withhold payment from the contractor for failure to complete the work. The owner may withhold enough contract funds to cover the cost of completing the remaining "punch list" of minor items, but the owner may not refuse to make any payment under the contract. The contractor has substantially performed and has earned its payment under the contract, less the cost of completing the punch list.

Despite the principle of substantial completion, many construction contracts state that the contractor will not receive its final progress payment until final completion of the work, that is, completion of the punch list and formal acceptance of the project by the owner. The result of such payment provisions is that the owner holds, after substantial completion, sums of money that far exceed the cost of completing the punch list items. Although these contract provisions are generally enforceable, the owner will not be able to hold the

---

CASE STUDY 9-2

Under the terms of a construction contract, Owner withheld $25,000 in retainage from Contractor's progress payments.

The completed facility never functioned properly. Owner spent $70,000 correcting the problem and then sued contractor to recover that amount. Contractor argued that it should be credited with the retainage, reducing its liability to $45,000.

The Supreme Court of North Dakota rejected Contractor's argument. The contractor "earns" the retainage only when it has substantially completed the project. Here, the facility was never suitable for its intended purpose, so Contractor never became entitled to the retainage. Owner was allowed to keep the retainage and recover the cost of correcting the problems.

Merrill Iron & Steel, Inc. v. Minn-Dak Seeds, Ltd., 334 N.W.2d 652 (N.D. 1983).

---

funds indefinitely, even if the contractor never completes the punch list. If the contractor has achieved substantial completion, it is entitled to the contract sum less the cost of completing punch list items.

A better way to structure the release of final payment is for the contract to state that upon substantial completion, the contract balance (the final progress payment plus accrued retainage) will be released to the contractor *except* for an amount sufficient to cover the cost of completing the punch list.

Frequently, contracts will authorize the owner to retain 1½ or 2 times the estimated cost of completing the punch list. This is an appropriate practice, as it gives the owner some needed security and ensures that the contractor won't lose interest in the project after substantial completion.

Once the punch list has been completed and the project has been inspected and formally accepted by the owner, the contractor then receives a final payment of the retainage that was held to cover the punch list items. This release of final payment significantly alters the legal relationship between the owner and the contractor. These issues will be examined in Chapter 13.

PRECONDITIONS TO PAYMENT

As stated above, the most basic legal precondition to the contractor's entitlement to contract payment is the achievement of substantial completion. Other "conditions precedent" may exist, however, some resulting from contract provisions and some resulting from state licensing statutes.

Contractual Conditions Precedent

The most common contractual precondition to final payment is the contractor's presentation of lien waivers. Contracts frequently state that the contractor must present its own waiver of lien, an affidavit swearing that it paid all subcontractors and suppliers it dealt with, lien waivers from all those subcontractors and suppliers, affidavits from the subcontractors and suppliers swearing that they paid their lower tier subcontractors and suppliers, and lien waivers from the lower tier subcontractors and suppliers.

Clauses such as this are enforced by the courts. It is crucial for the project owner to know that all parties have been paid and the project is in no jeopardy of being subjected to liens. If the contractor is unable or unwilling to present the lien waivers and affidavits, it is not entitled to receive final payment.

The same applies to progress payments. The furnishing of affidavits and partial lien waivers pertaining to the work covered by the progress payment can be an enforceable condition precedent to the contractor's entitlement to receive a progress payment.

Another condition precedent is occasionally written into construction contracts. This precondition states that if the project owner is unable to obtain construction financing in accordance with certain specified terms, the contractor will not be obligated to perform and the owner will not be obligated to pay. This precondition would come into play after a contract has been signed by the parties but before the owner has issued a notice to proceed with the construction work. It is analogous to a termination for the convenience of the owner, but it would be a "no cost" termination, as no work would have been performed by the contractor.

State Licensing Requirements

Most states in the United States have enacted statutes requiring contractors to obtain state licenses before engaging in the business of construction. Usually a particular license is required for general contractors and other licenses are required for the various trades. Sometimes a license will authorize a contractor to perform contracts up to a certain maximum amount, with more stringent licensing requirements applied to contractors performing larger jobs. Home improvement contractors are also frequently subject to specialized licensing requirements.

In order to put some teeth in these licensing requirements, many state statutes say that possession of an appropriate license is a condition precedent to the contractor's entitlement to receive payment. In other words, a contractor may fully and faithfully perform the construction contract, but if that contractor does not have the right state license, the project owner has no legal obligation to make payment.

Many states have adopted a rule of strict compliance with the licensing statutes. Contractors who believe they have the correct license and later discover that they do not may be denied payment. Sometimes change orders push the total contract amount over the contractor's licensed maximum. Even though the contractor has fully performed the work, the owner may simply refuse to pay. This seems to be a rather harsh and inequitable rule, but many state legislatures believe it to be necessary in order to achieve compliance with the licensing statutes.

Some states, however, have sought to soften the effect of the licensing stat-

CASE STUDY 9-3

Contractor did not possess license required by the North Carolina statutes. Contractor entered into agreement and fully performed the work.

Owner refused to pay Contractor on grounds Contractor lacked the proper state license. Contractor argued that it would be unjust to allow Owner to benefit from Contractor's labor yet refuse to pay for it.

The Court of Appeals of North Carolina ruled that Contractor could not recover payment under the contract because a contract signed by an unlicensed contractor is illegal. Nor could Contractor recover under another theory such as "unjust enrichment," as it would weaken the effectiveness of the licensing statute to allow such recovery.

Revis Sand & Stone, Inc. v. King,
270 S.E.2d 580 (N.C.App. 1980).

---

utes. These states require only substantial compliance with the licensing statute. If a contractor makes a good faith effort to comply but fails to comply because of a misunderstanding or bureaucratic delay, the contractor will still be entitled to payment for work performed. Some states will allow a contractor to comply by obtaining a license during the course of the project rather than prior to contract execution. States that allow substantial compliance will deny payment only to those contractors who make no effort to comply with the licensing statute.

LIENS

A contractor's entitlement to receive payment is meaningless if there are no funds or assets available to satisfy the owner's obligation to make that payment. Sometimes developers become insolvent without having paid the prime contractor. Sometimes prime contractors become insolvent without having

---

CASE STUDY 9-4

Contractor, as a corporate entity, did not have a California contractor's license. The corporation's president and principal shareholder did have a California contractor's license, however.

Contractor, in its corporate capacity, signed a construction contract and fully performed the work. Owner later refused to pay, saying that Contractor lacked the necessary license.

The California Court of Appeal ruled that although a technical violation of the contractor licensing statute had occurred, Contractor had substantially complied with the statute because the person responsible for managing the work had a license. Contractor was allowed to recover payment under the contract.

Knapp Development & Design v. Pal-Mal Properties,
219 Cal.Rptr. 44 (Cal.App. 1985).

paid their subcontractors and suppliers. Mechanic's lien and materialman's lien statutes were enacted to address these problems.

The lien statutes create a mechanism whereby parties who furnish labor or materials to a project may, by carefully following certain prescribed steps, obtain a security interest in the owner's property. The rationale is that the labor and materials have increased the value of the owner's property, so the unpaid contractor or supplier should be able to look to that property as security for eventual payment.

A fully perfected lien is very much like a mortgage on the property. It must be satisfied, or paid, before free and clear ownership of the property is transferred. This gives the party possessing the lien, the "lienor," a great deal of leverage with the project owner. Liens are frequently the best hope for an unpaid contractor or supplier.

Statute Strictly Construed

In the eyes of the law, liens are considered an "extraordinary remedy." The right to place a lien on a project does not exist by virtue of common, or judge-made, law. Liens are the creatures of statute. They subject project owners to liability to parties with whom the owners have never contracted. They were enacted to solve a perceived social ill, that is, honest tradesmen being denied payment for their labors. But they are contrary to the basic concept that one should not be liable to pay an obligation which one never directly incurred.

As a result, liens may be perfected only if the lienor strictly complies with all the requirements of the lien statute. The failure to comply with a single requirement will defeat the lien, regardless of the good faith efforts of the would-be lienor. All in all, any would-be lienor must be able to show that it dotted every "i" and crossed every "t" in order to bring itself into compliance with the lien statute.

This reliance on the precise language of the particular statute makes it difficult to discuss liens in a general sense. Each state has its own lien statute. While there are a number of similarities and consistencies, it is also fair to say that each state lien statute is unique. The validity of any lien must be determined by carefully examining the requirements of the lien statute in the state where the project is located. This should be kept in mind while reading the general discussion of liens in this chapter.

What Is Lienable?

As a general rule, labor and materials used to improve the project give rise to a lienable interest. This general rule is not always easy to apply, however.

To begin with, there is the matter of the language of the lien statute. Each statute has different wording which gives rise to different interpretations as to what is lienable. For instance, is equipment which is affixed to, but not actually incorporated into, the project lienable? How about the cost of fuel and electricity expended during performance of the construction work? Can the leasing of equipment during the performance of the work be considered labor or materials incorporated into the project? These questions can be answered only by examining the applicable lien statute and the court opinions interpreting that statute.

It should be noted that few lien cases get involved with the question of the "value" of the labor and materials the lienor has furnished to the project. It is generally recognized that the contract price is presumed to reflect that value, even though the contract price includes a markup on direct costs for overhead and profit. The project owner can attempt to rebut that presumption and show that the actual value is less than the contract price. If the lienor has performed its work in accordance with the contract requirements, however, it will be difficult for the owner to prevail in this argument.

Another crucial question which arises is the scope of subcontractor lien rights. This is a sensitive issue for project owners because of the risk of double payment. If an owner pays the prime or general contractor and the prime contractor fails to pay its subcontractors and suppliers, any liens perfected by those subs and suppliers may force the owner to pay twice for the construction services.

The lien statutes in some states are structured so that the lien rights of the subcontractors and suppliers are "derivative" of the rights of the prime contractor. That is, the subcontractor has lien rights only to the extent the prime contractor has lien rights for that same item of work. If the prime contractor has been paid for the work, the subcontractor can have no lien rights for the work, regardless of whether or not the sub has been paid by the prime contractor.

Most states, however, give subcontractors and suppliers "primary" lien rights. The rights are not derivative of the prime contractor's lien rights, and the subcontractors and suppliers may assert a lien regardless of whether the prime has already been paid for the work. These states frequently provide special protection for homeowners, shielding them from the risk of double payment. For commercial property owners, however, any protection against double payment has to come from the prudent use of lien waivers and affidavits.

Material suppliers face special problems with regard to liens. These liens,

---

CASE STUDY 9-5

Owner failed to pay Contractor for work performed on project. Contractor placed a mechanic's lien on Owner's project for the amount it claimed it was owed.

Owner argued that Contractor's lien included amounts for overhead and profit, whereas the lien statute only authorized liens for money owed for "labor performed or furnished or for materials furnished."

The Supreme Court of South Carolina ruled that the cost of supervising the work and profit on the work may be included in the lien amount. So long as the lien amount did not include damages claimed for breach of contract, it was valid.

Sentry Engineering and Construction, Inc. v. Mariner's Cay Development Corp., 338 S.E.2d 631 (S.C. 1985).

CASE STUDY 9-6

When Owner failed to pay Contractor the full contract balance, Contractor placed a lien on Owner's project.

Owner argued that Contractor's lien included an amount for interest on late payments which was not authorized in the contract. Owner also said that the lien amount included damages for delay and other damages for breach of contract.

The District Court of Appeals of Florida agreed with Owner. Amounts which are not authorized by the contract may not be included in a lien, nor may damages claimed for breach of contract. Contractor willfully exaggerated its lien, so the lien was dismissed as being unenforceable.

Hobbs Construction & Development, Inc. v. Presbyterian Homes, 440 So.2d 673 (Fla.App. 1983).

---

sometimes labeled "materialman's liens," are identical to mechanic's liens with regard to the manner in which they are perfected. The problem arises because of the requirement that a lien secure a debt owed for labor or materials incorporated into the project. How can a material supplier, who sells large quantities of materials to numerous customers for use in a variety of projects, prove that the materials in question were actually incorporated into a particular project?

There is no simple answer to this question. Material suppliers must keep accurate records and track the use of the materials to the best of their ability. Recovery against payment bonds usually only requires the good faith belief that the materials were destined for a particular project, but assertion of a materialman's lien generally requires proof of actual incorporation of the materials into the structure. Detailed record keeping is the supplier's only recourse.

One final issue regarding lienable interests deserves mention. Can architects and engineers assert a lien on a project if they are not paid for their design services or other professional services? The answer, once again, depends largely on the language of the lien statute in the state where the project is located.

Some state lien statutes specifically authorize liens for professional A/E services. In states where the statute doesn't address the issue, courts are divided in their interpretation of the intended meaning of the statute. Some courts have held that professional design services provide no direct, tangible benefit to the value of the real estate in question, so A/E services are not lienable in the absence of explicit statutory authorization. Other courts have held that despite the absence of "nuts and bolts" enhancement to the value of the property, A/E services do increase the value of the project and are therefore lienable.

Perfecting a Lien

As described earlier in this section, the method of properly perfecting a lien is entirely dependent on the language of the lien statute in question. There are, however, certain steps which are commonly required.

The first step is usually the issuance of a notice of lien to all interested parties. Generally, the lien statute requires that the notice be filed within a certain number of days after the last date upon which labor or materials were provided to the project.

As a lien is the assertion of a right to real estate, the notice usually must be filed in the appropriate registry of deeds. This notice puts all potential purchasers and lenders on notice of the fact that a contractor or supplier claims a lien interest in the property in question. Many statutes also require notice by certified mail to parties who may be affected by the lien. This is particularly common when the party asserting the lien has no direct contractual relationship with the property owner.

After the issuance of a lien notice, the next step, under many lien statutes, is the filing of a formal lien complaint in the appropriate court. Again, the complaint usually must be filed within a specified number of days of the last date the lienor provided labor or materials to the project. This provides the project owner and its lenders with assurance that after a certain point in time, no liens may be asserted against the project.

The lien complaint usually alleges nonpayment for labor or materials furnished to the project and demands that the real estate be sold at auction with the resulting equity applied to satisfy the lien.

As a practical matter, lien foreclosure sales are very rare. The project owner usually obtains other sources of financing to satisfy any valid liens. Owners may also bond off a lien. Many lien statutes authorize owners to post a bond in lieu of lien. This bond serves as substitute security for the contractor or supplier's claim for payment. As long as the bond is in effect, the property is free and clear of any lien.

CONTRACTOR'S RELIANCE ON THIRD PARTIES

If a project owner becomes insolvent and unable to pay a contractor for work performed, the question arises as to where else the contractor might look for satisfaction. The general answer is that there is nowhere else to look for payment. The contractor may assert a lien against the owner's property, as described above, but the only party who has promised to pay the contractor is the project owner.

Occasionally, however, exceptions to this general rule can be found. This section of the chapter examines some of the circumstances which may arise and which may enable the contractor to recover from a third party.

Recovering from the Construction Lender

When a project owner obtains construction financing from a bank or other lender, the lender makes a commitment to loan a stipulated amount of money. These funds are not turned over to the owner all at once, however. The funds are disbursed as needed for the owner to pay for completed work. Usually, the disbursement of construction loan proceeds coincides with the owner's progress payments to the contractor.

Just as the owner does not want to release contract funds that exceed the value of the work the contractor has completed, the lender does not want to disburse loan proceeds that exceed the value of the completed work. The reason is similar. The construction loan is secured by a mortgage on the real estate under development. The lender does not want to disburse loan proceeds that exceed the value of the security.

If a project owner becomes insolvent, the construction lender is frequently holding an undisbursed portion of the construction loan proceeds. This pool of funds is a tempting target for a contractor who has not been paid by the project owner. It is a difficult target to reach, however.

The construction loan agreement between the lender and the project owner usually states that the construction contractor is not a party to the loan agreement and is not a third-party beneficiary of the loan agreement. The contractor is asked to sign the loan agreement, but this is for the limited purpose of acknowledging that it will complete the work for the lender and honor the original contract price if the project owner defaults on the loan agreement. It does not make the contractor a beneficiary of the loan agreement.

As a result, contractors are usually not successful in their argument that the lender is obligated to pay them for completed work. As a practical matter, however, the lender often will step in for a defaulted project owner and pay the contractor to continue the work. The reason is simple. An incomplete building does not offer the same value as security on the defaulted loan as a completed building offers. Therefore, even though a construction lender has no obligation to pay a contractor for completed work or pay a contractor to continue the work, it may be in the lender's best interest to do exactly that.

CASE STUDY 9-7

Contractor performed considerable work on project. Owner then became insolvent, leaving Contractor unpaid.

Contractor tried to recover payment from the undisbursed construction loan proceeds being held by Owner's bank. Contractor argued that it was a beneficiary of the loan agreement between bank and Owner. Bank refused to make payment.

A Pennsylvania court ruled that Contractor's agreement was with Owner only and Contractor had relied on the creditworthiness of Owner alone. Nothing in the construction loan agreement indicated an intent to guarantee payment to Contractor or otherwise benefit Contractor. Contractor could not recover payment from the undisbursed loan proceeds.

R. M. Shoemaker Co. v. Southeastern Pennsylvania Economic Development Corporation, 419 A.2d 60 (Pa.Super. 1980).

Third-Party Guarantors

If, at the time of contract formation, the contractor has reservations about the project owner's ability to pay for the work, the contractor may ask a third party to guarantee the owner's payment obligation.

This guarantor may be a larger corporation or a wealthy individual. If the owner fails to pay for properly completed construction work, the contractor may then call on the third-party guarantor to honor its guarantee. The guarantor's obligation only arises, however, once the owner has defaulted on its obligation to pay the contractor and is in material breach of contract.

It should be noted that the guarantor's obligation only extends to making payments which have already been earned under the construction contract. The guarantor generally has no obligation to pay the contractor to complete the project or compensate the contractor for the lost profit and other damages incurred as a result of being unable to complete the project.

Escrow Accounts

Sometimes, when a construction lender discovers that contractors are not being paid properly by the project owner, the lender will hold undisbursed loan proceeds in escrow. These funds will not be paid to the owner, who is in breach of the construction loan agreement, but the funds will be available to pay contractors for completed work. The rationale, again, is that the lender wants to enhance the value of the real estate that serves as security for the defaulted loan agreement.

Some states have enacted statutes pertaining to publicly funded projects which say that in the event of a default by the prime contractor, the public project owner will hold any undisbursed funds in escrow to be used for paying subcontractors and suppliers who have not been paid by the prime contractor. Unlike the situation described in the preceding paragraph, the rationale here is that unpaid subs and suppliers should be protected on a public works project. This type of escrow fund does nothing to enhance the value of the project itself.

PAYMENT BONDS

For unpaid subcontractors and suppliers, payment bonds offer the most effective method of recovery. Payment bonds offer no solace to an unpaid prime contractor, however, as it is the prime who must furnish the payment bond.

A payment bond is furnished by the prime contractor pursuant to the requirements of its contract with the project owner or, on public projects, pursuant to the requirements of a statute. The prime contractor's bonding company, or surety, promises to pay the designated obligees (in this case, subcontractors and suppliers) in the event the prime contractor fails to do so. As with performance bonds, the surety's obligation only arises once the prime contractor has defaulted on its contractual obligations.

On private projects, the purpose of a payment bond is to protect the project owner's interests. If the prime contractor fails to pay its subs and suppliers, the owner doesn't want those parties asserting liens against the project. The owner therefore requires the prime to furnish a payment bond.

Although the presence of a bond does not preclude the assertion of liens, the owner can call upon the bonding company to satisfy the prime contractor's obligations and have the liens removed. Also, as a practical matter, it is generally easier for unpaid subcontractors and suppliers to collect from a payment bond than to recover payment by way of a lien.

On public projects, payment bonds serve a different purpose. Publicly owned buildings are not subject to liens. They are legally immune. This means that if a prime contractor goes bankrupt without paying its subcontractors and suppliers, those subs and suppliers have nowhere to turn for payment. Legislatures have concluded, as a matter of public policy, that it is unfair for the public to benefit from the labor and materials furnished by these parties without providing some means for assuring payment. Therefore, statutes have been enacted requiring prime contractors on public projects to furnish payment bonds to protect subcontractors and suppliers.

As will be seen below, the different purposes of payment bonds on private and public projects affect the determination of which parties may recover against the bond.

Who May Recover?

Since a bond is simply a contract (a "suretyship agreement," to be precise) between the prime contractor ("principal") and the bonding company ("surety"), the scope of a bond's coverage is determined by the language of the specific bond in question. In order to determine who may recover, one must look at the named "obligees" under the terms of the bond. Those are the parties who are protected by the bond and may recover against the bond in the event of a default by the prime contractor.

On private projects, the bond is designed to keep the project free of liens. It is therefore common for these payment bonds to state that only those parties that are legally entitled to perfect a lien may recover against the payment bond. If a party had no lien rights or failed to perfect its lien rights, it will not be able to recover against the bond. Not all payment bonds on private projects are worded this way, however. Some use broader language allowing recovery by any unpaid subcontractor or supplier who furnished labor or materials to the project.

On public projects, the scope of the payment bond is mandated by state or federal statute. Generally, these statutes are designed to protect any party who has enhanced the value of the public project by furnishing labor or materials. Lien rights, in the public project context, are irrelevant.

It is common for payment bonds on public projects to simply cite the applicable statute and state that all parties protected under that statute are obligees under the payment bond. This ensures that the bond will provide the coverage mandated by the statute, without inadvertently providing coverage to the parties who are not protected by the statute.

What May Be Recovered?

An unpaid subcontractor or supplier may recover the contract balance it is owed for work it has performed. The bonding company is free, of course, to argue that the payment bond claimant failed to fully or adequately perform in accordance with its contract. To the extent this can be proved, the cost of completion or correction can be set off against the contract balance.

As with mechanic's lien claims, payment bond claims generally do not get into the question of the "true value" of the labor and materials furnished to the project. The contract price creates a strong presumption regarding the value, even though the contract price includes a profit component. If the bond claimant fully performed in accordance with the contract requirements, it will be entitled to recover the contract balance.

If change orders have been issued during the course of a subcontractor's performance, the sub will be entitled to recover the increased amounts authorized by the change orders. If there are alleged constructive changes or disputed extra work, the subcontractor can recover the fair value of that work from the payment bond, assuming the introduction of adequate evidence to support the claim.

Material suppliers have a somewhat easier task recovering against payment bonds than they do when asserting materialman's liens. With bond claims, suppliers usually only need to show that they sold the material in the good faith belief it was destined for the bonded project in question. They need not prove actual incorporation of the materials into the project.

Finally, it should be noted that very few payment bonds and only a few public works payment bond statutes authorize the recovery of attorney's fees by successful bond claimants. As with almost every other aspect of the American judicial system, each party pays for its own counsel, win or lose.

Notice and Limitation Requirements

The most common reason for denial of recovery by payment bond claimants is the failure to comply with the notice or limitation provisions of the bond. Again, the specific requirements vary with the language of each bond or the language of the applicable public works payment bond statute, but virtually every payment bond contains such provisions.

The notice requirement states that bond claimants must give the prime contractor written notice of the claim within a stated period of time, frequently 90 days, of the last date the claimant furnished labor or materials to the project. Sometimes

CASE STUDY 9-8

Unpaid material supplier sought to recover from public works payment bond. The applicable statute stated that the payment bonds applied to "every claimant who has furnished labor or materials in the prosecution of the work provided for in such contract."

The bonding company argued that under the language of the statute, Supplier had to prove that the materials it sold were actually incorporated into the bonded project.

City Electric v. Industrial Indemnity Co., 683 P.2d 1053 (Utah 1984).

The Supreme Court of Utah disagreed. The federal Miller Act contains identical language and all that is required under the Miller Act is the supplier's good faith belief the materials are destined for the bonded project. Unfortunately for Supplier in this case, however, it could not even make that showing. Supplier had been selling on an open account, and the records were insufficient to show what Supplier's reasonable belief might have been with regard to the destination of particular materials.

---

notice is required only from parties who had no direct contractual relationship with the prime contractor. Other times, notice is required of all claimants.

The limitation requirement states that any court action for recovery against the payment bond must be initiated within a certain period of time, frequently 1 year, of the last date the claimant furnished labor or materials to the project. Sometimes the limitation period starts to run upon substantial or final completion of the entire project.

As stated earlier, the interpretation and application of payment bonds is a matter of contract. If a bond claimant fails to comply with either the notice requirement or the limitation period in a payment bond, it will be denied recovery even though it is an unpaid obligee under the terms of the bond.

The Miller Act

The most influential public works payment bond statute in the country is the federal "Miller Act," 40 U.S.C. sec. 270a–270f. This statute governs payment bond requirements on federal construction projects all over the country. Enacted in 1935, the Miller Act has also served as the model for most state payment bond statutes, many of which are nicknamed "Little Miller Acts." Because it is the archetypal public works payment bond statute, a detailed description of the Miller Act is warranted.

When Is It Required?   Miller Act bonds are required on any prime contract exceeding $25,000 "for the construction, alteration or repair of any public building or public work of the United States."

For contracts in excess of $5 million, the payment bond must be in the amount of $2.5 million. For contracts of $1 million to $5 million, the payment

CASE STUDY 9-9

Payment bond stated that unpaid subcontractors could not file claim against bond until at least 90 days after the date they last furnished labor or materials and no later than 1 year after that date.

Unpaid Subcontractor filed payment bond claim 1 year and 13 days after last furnishing labor and materials. Subcontractor argued that the 1-year period shouldn't start to run until the 90-day period expired, as subcontractors were not allowed to file suit during the 90-day period.

The Supreme Court of Michigan ruled that the bond should be limited to the time period expressly stated. The 90-day provision is designed to keep the bonding company from getting involved in every single late payment dispute. The 1-year limitation period sets an outside limit on the bonding company's potential liability on the payment bond. The two provisions serve different purposes. Therefore, the 1-year period starts to run when labor or materials are last furnished, not when the subcontractor can first file suit on the bond.

W. R. Armand v. Territorial Construction, Inc., 322 N.W.2d 924 (Mich. 1982).

---

bond must be in the amount of 40 percent of the contract price. The payment bond must be in the amount of 50 percent of the contract price if the contract is for $1 million or less.

Who Is Protected?   The statute simply says that bond claims will be allowed by "every person who has furnished labor or material in the prosecution of the work provided for in such contract." This is deceptive, however, as this broad language has been narrowed over the years by judicial interpretation.

The basic rule is that any "first tier" subcontractor or material supplier who has a contract directly with the prime contractor may recover. Second tier subcontractors who have a contract with a subcontractor may also recover. Second tier suppliers may not recover. They and all other parties are considered to be "too remote."

What Is Covered?   Miller Act payment bond claimants can recover money owed for labor or materials used in performing the work. Fuel and other consumables are also covered. The cost of leased equipment is covered if it can be shown that it was used on the bonded project. Equipment repair costs, but not equipment replacement costs, are also covered.

Material suppliers need not prove that the materials were actually incorporated into the bonded project. They need only show that the materials were sold in the good faith belief the materials were intended for the project.

Notice and Limitation Requirements   Bond claimants who had a direct contractual relationship with the prime contractor need not give formal notice of their claims. Second tier claimants must send a notice by registered mail to the prime contractor within 90 days of last furnishing labor or materials to the project. The notice must state the amount owed and identify the party with whom the second tier claimant contracted.

For both first and second tier claimants, suit must be filed in federal court no sooner than 90 days after the last date labor or materials were furnished and no later than 1 year after that date. Both the notice and limitation periods are strictly enforced.

KEY TERMS AND CONCEPTS

progress payments Payments made periodically, usually monthly, by the project owner to the contractor. The payments reflect the value of the construction work completed to date and in place. This value is usually determined by applying a percentage of completion to the total contract price. Sometimes progress payments are determined by an agreed schedule of values or by unit prices.

retainage A percentage of each progress payment, usually 10 percent, which is retained by the project owner until final contract payment. The purpose of retainage is to provide the owner with protection in the event the contractor fails to fully complete the work or otherwise fails to fully honor its contractual obligations.

substantial completion That time when the project is sufficiently complete to enable the owner to occupy the project and make beneficial use of the project for its intended purpose. Once substantial completion has been achieved, the contractor cannot be considered to be in material breach of contract. The contractor has earned the contract price, less the cost of completing or correcting any remaining items of work.

punch list The list of items that remain to be completed or corrected after the contractor has achieved substantial completion. These are usually minor items which do not prevent the beneficial use and occupancy of the project but which must be completed in order for the contractor to fully perform the work.

final payment The project owner's last payment to the contractor upon the contractor's completion of the punch list work. The final payment usually consists of the accrued retainage. It may also include the last progress payment.

licensing requirements The licensing required by each individual state for individuals or organizations performing construction work within that state. Many states require separate licenses for the various trades or for general contractors undertaking very large projects.

The possession of a valid state license is usually a legal precondition to a contractor's recovery of payment under the contract. Some states strictly enforce this requirement. Others accept a contractor's good faith effort at substantial compliance.

lien A right created by state statute which allows parties furnishing labor or materials to a project to obtain a security interest in the real estate in order to protect their entitlement to payment. Liens are generally available to prime contractors, subcontractors, and material suppliers. Unpaid parties may perfect liens only by fully and carefully complying with the requirements of the applicable state statute.

lien waivers Documents whereby parties waive and release any lien rights they may have gained by virtue of furnishing labor or materials to a project. Lien waivers are frequently accompanied by affidavits where the party swears it has fully paid all other parties with whom it did business.

Many construction contracts make the furnishing of lien waivers and affidavits from the prime contractor and all subcontractors and suppliers a legal precondition to the owner's obligation to make final payment to the prime contractor. Partial lien waivers may be required before progress payments are made.

payment bonds   A bond furnished to the owner by the prime contractor whereby a corporate surety promises to pay any unpaid subcontractors or suppliers in the event the prime contractor defaults and fails to meet its payment obligations.

On private projects, payment bonds are designed primarily to protect the owner by keeping its project free of liens. On public projects, which are generally not subject to liens, payment bonds are required by statute and are designed to protect unpaid subcontractors and suppliers who would otherwise have no recourse.

Miller Act   A federal statute requiring prime contractors on federal construction projects in excess of $25,000 to furnish payment bonds protecting subcontractors and suppliers. The Miller Act served as the prototype for most state public works payment bond statutes.

SUBCONTRACTORS AND SUPPLIERS

The construction process requires a wide array of skills. Very few companies possess all the specialized abilities required for construction of an office building or a sewage treatment plant. Even smaller projects require labor from a variety of trades and disciplines. And, of course, it is always necessary to purchase the materials and equipment for a construction project.

For these reasons, it has long been customary for the prime contractor or general contractor on a project to award a number of subcontracts and purchase orders. The widespread use of subcontractors and suppliers offers certain efficiencies. Many contractors who customarily function as subcontractors have specialized expertise and experience in a particular trade or even on a particular type of project. It is far more efficient for general contractors to make use of this established expertise rather than attempt to perform this work with their own forces.

The use of subcontractors creates problems, as well. It greatly increases the number of independent entities involved in the project. Scheduling and coordinating the work becomes a challenge. A proper chain of command and channel for communication must be maintained at all times. The funds being used to finance the project must pass through more hands.

This chapter examines the important issues that arise out of the use of subcontractors and suppliers.

NATURE OF THE RELATIONSHIP

A prime or general contractor (the terms are used synonymously in this chapter) has a contract with the project owner. The subcontractors and suppliers have no contractual relationship with the owner, only with the prime contractor. Out of this basic arrangement arise a number of questions as to who is responsible for what.

Prime Contractor's Sole Responsibility

When a project owner awards a contract to a prime contractor, it is the prime contractor and the prime contractor alone who promises to complete the project in accordance with the contract documents. The prime contractor may elect to perform all the work with its own forces. The prime may also elect to subcontract out certain aspects of the work or even virtually the entire project.

The decision to subcontract is largely within the discretion of the prime contractor. Sometimes the contract with the owner will place certain restrictions on subcontracting, however. The prime contract may require the prime to perform at least a certain percentage of the contract with its own forces. The contract may also require the owner's prior approval of the individual subcontractors. By and large, though, the decision to subcontract is left up to the prime contractor and is dictated by economic and technical factors.

When a prime contractor elects to award subcontracts, it by no means absolves itself of the legal obligation to perform that work. The prime retains total responsibility to the owner for adequate completion of the project. The prime is responsible to the owner for any deficiencies or shortcomings in the work of its subcontractors and suppliers.

If a subcontractor or supplier fails to comply with the project specifications, the prime contractor cannot simply tell the owner that it wasn't the prime's fault. The prime has sole responsibility, vis-à-vis the owner, to see that the work is properly performed. If a particular subcontractor can't get it done, it is the problem of the prime contractor, not the owner. The prime will have to replace the subcontractor and see that the work is completed. If this increases the prime's costs, that is not the owner's problem. It is strictly a matter between the prime and the defaulting subcontractor.

The prime has agreed to construct a certain specified project at a certain stipulated price. The prime has probably also agreed to warrant its workmanship. The project owner has the right to look solely to the prime contractor to honor these obligations. If subcontractors or suppliers cause problems, the prime may have some recourse against them, but its obligations to the owner remain unchanged.

Just as the prime contractor retains sole responsibility for the proper completion of the work, the prime is also solely responsible for maintaining the project schedule. Typically, the prime is allowed a certain number of days to complete a job. If the slow performance of a subcontractor delays the prime's performance, this is not the owner's fault. Likewise, slow delivery of crucial equipment by a supplier is not the owner's fault. It is the responsibility of the prime contractor. Delay by a subcontractor or supplier is considered nonexcusable delay as far as a project owner is concerned. The prime contractor will not be allowed an extension of the performance time. The prime contractor will be assessed liquidated damages for the late completion, even though the delay was caused exclusively by a subcontractor or supplier. As with the sufficiency of the work, the prime has sole responsibility, vis-à-vis the project owner, for timely completion of the project.

Chain of Authority

One of the most difficult aspects of subcontracting is the need to establish and maintain a proper chain of authority. Since the prime contractor has sole responsibility to the project owner, it follows that the prime must also have sole authority over the subcontractors and suppliers.

Although it happens with surprising frequency, it is an absolute disaster on a project for the owner's representative to communicate directly with subcontractors or for subcontractors to communicate directly with the owner. If the owner starts issuing directives to a subcontractor, it creates tremendous confusion. Is the work within the scope of the prime contract? If not, is the owner asking the sub to perform the work pursuant to a direct side agreement with the owner? If the work is within the scope of the prime contract, how does the owner know it is the responsibility of this particular subcontractor?

Similarly, subcontractors should never seek clarification or direction directly from the owner's representative. It creates the risk of confusion regarding changes in the scope of the prime contract or changes in the scope of a particular subcontract. It also raises questions regarding who is responsible for paying for particular items of work.

The only proper way to handle these matters is to make sure that all parties honor the proper chain of command. If the owner wishes to issue a directive or change the scope or definition of the work, it should tell the prime contractor. The prime contractor will in turn tell the appropriate subcontractor, if necessary.

All change orders or directives should be issued from the owner to the prime contractor. The prime can then, at its discretion, issue directives or change orders to the appropriate subcontractors.

CASE STUDY 10-1

Owner awarded Contractor a contract for construction of a dike. Contractor subcontracted a portion of the work to Subcontractor.

Difficult soil conditions were encountered during the course of construction. In response, Owner's engineer issued a number of directives to Subcontractor. Subcontractor performed as directed and later requested additional compensation from Contractor for work outside the scope of the subcontract agreement.

The Court of Appeals of Indiana ruled that Contractor was not liable to Subcontractor for the extra work, as Contractor did not issue the directives. A prime contractor cannot be held responsible when the owner's representative bypasses the contractor and issues orders directly to subcontractors.

Thatcher Engineering Corp. v. Bihlman, 473 N.E.2d 1022 (Ind.App. 1985).

The same applies to inquiries from subcontractors. Any request for clarification or any material sample or shop drawing submittal should be sent from the subcontractor or supplier to the prime contractor. The prime contractor will then send the request or submittal to the owner's representative. The owner's response will be directed to the prime, who will pass it on to the subcontractor or supplier. This is in keeping with the basic legal premise that it is the prime contractor alone who has total responsibility to the owner for the completion of the project.

Subcontractors Distinguished from Suppliers

Subcontractors perform construction work. Although they necessarily also furnish materials and equipment as part of their work, their primary role is to provide labor. Usually, subcontractors provide specialized types of labor in accordance with traditionally recognized trades, such as electrical, mechanical, or masonry. It is also common, of course, to award subcontracts that do not fall within a traditional trade category or a particular section of the specifications.

Suppliers sell materials or equipment to prime contractors. They do not perform construction work. If they do perform any labor at the job site, it is minor and incidental to the installation of equipment they have sold to the prime contractor.

As will be seen in the next section of this chapter, this distinction is not simply semantical. It affects the way in which the agreement with the prime contractor is formed and the legal rules which govern the interpretation of that agreement.

CONTRACT FORMATION

The formation of a contract between a prime contractor and subcontractors or suppliers lacks the formality of the competitive bidding process, or even the structure of private, negotiated construction contracts. This informality gives rise to a completely different set of legal issues.

Subcontractors

The formation of subcontracts is chaotic. Prime contractors obtain quotations of prices from subcontractors for certain designated sections of the work. These quotations are usually provided orally over the telephone at the very last minute before submittal of a bid on the prime contract.

There are two reasons for this practice. The first is that the time constraints of preparing a bid on a complex project force prime contractors to pull together a great deal of information within a limited period of time. The second reason is subcontractors' fears of "bid shopping."

Bid shopping is a practice where prime contractors obtain a quotation from a trade contractor or subcontractor and "shop it around" to competitors to see if they can get a lower price. In an effort to avoid being played off against one another, trade contractors have made a practice of submitting quotations only at the last minute before bid submittal.

As a result of this practice, formal, written subcontract agreements are usually signed only after the prime contractor has been awarded the prime contract. This creates problems, because the prime contractor has priced its binding bid on the basis of certain subcontractor prices which have not yet been agreed to in writing. What happens if a key subcontractor attempts to renege on its price?

Prime contractors in this situation must rely on the equitable doctrine of "promissory estoppel." This doctrine holds that if one party reasonably relies to its detriment on the promise of another, the other party must be held to its promise in order to avoid harm to the first party.

Applied to the prime contractor–subcontractor relationship, if the prime contractor reasonably relies on the promised price of a subcontractor in submitting a binding bid, the subcontractor will be forced to honor that price or pay the resulting extra cost. This is not based on a breach of contract, as no contract has yet been formed. It is based on the reasonable reliance on a promise.

The problem for prime contractors is that they must be able to prove reasonable reliance. Sometimes subcontractor quotations are less than unequivocal. The subcontractor may have conditioned its quotation on certain contingencies.

Prime contractors attempting to lock in the prices of their subcontractors frequently send a confirming telegram or mailgram to subs. The message states that the prime contractor appreciates the quotation from the sub and the quoted price has been incorporated into the bid on the prime contract.

In order to establish promissory estoppel, the message need not state that the subcontract will be awarded to that particular company in the event of a prime contract award. From a prime contractor's standpoint, it is obviously preferable to avoid making this commitment. The prime contractor has the best of both worlds in this situation. The subcontractor is committed on the

---

CASE STUDY 10-2

Contractor, preparing to bid on project, solicited a quotation from Subcontractor. Subcontractor gave an oral quotation and then, at Contractor's request, followed it up with a written breakdown of the quotation.

Contractor was awarded the prime contract, but Subcontractor refused to enter into a subcontract agreement, citing changes in its workload. Contractor sued Subcontractor for the increased cost it incurred in subcontracting out that portion of the work.

The U.S. Court of Appeals ruled that Subcontractor was liable to Contractor even though no subcontract agreement had been formed. Under the doctrine of "promissory estoppel," a subcontractor will be bound to honor its quotation if the prime contractor reasonably relied on the quotation in preparing its bid on the prime contract.

Preload Technology, Inc. v. A. B. & J. Construction Co., Inc., 696 F.2d 1080 (5th Cir. 1983).

---

price, but the prime is not committed to doing business with the subcontractor. It is not until after award of the prime contract that the prime contractor enters into formal written subcontract agreements with its trade contractors.

On public contracts, a new system has been established for the award of subcontracts or trade contracts. It involves the use of "filed subbids." This arrangement is mandated by the public works statutes in some states and has been enacted in response to the political influence of subcontractor trade associations who want more direct access to public works dollars.

The filed subbid system works as follows. Trade contractors submit subbids to the public project owner for certain designated sections of the work. These subbids are kept in a file available to any general contractor interested in bidding on the prime contract. In pricing their bids, prime contractors must rely on the prices established in the subbid file because the successful bidder will be required to award subcontracts to the low subbidder in each designated category. The only exceptions are when the prime contractor plans to perform that portion of the work with its own qualified personnel or the prime contractor can show cause that it cannot work harmoniously with a particular subcontractor.

It is interesting to note that most filed subbid statutes do not address the general terms and conditions that will be used when the successful bidder on the prime contract awards subcontracts to the low subbidders. Therefore, the prime contractor may comply with the statute by offering subcontracts to the low subbidders but may try to impose harsh conditions on the subs.

A final observation must be made regarding subcontract award. Although the process is unstructured and chaotic, there are a number of standard, preprinted subcontract agreement forms which are widely used in the industry. As mentioned earlier, these written agreements are not usually executed until after the prime contractor has been awarded the prime contract.

To reduce the uncertainty this presents to subcontractors, subs can at least

CASE STUDY 10-3

Contractor was preparing to bid on a public school project. State law required bidders to use the lowest filed subbids for certain designated trades.

Contractor did not list the low subbidder for the metal window portion of the work, listing itself instead. Contractor was awarded the prime contract, but Subbidder sued Contractor for failing to award it the metal window subcontract.

The Appeals Court of Massachusetts ruled in favor of Subbidder. The prime contractor can only refuse to award a subcontract to the low filed subbidder if the prime contractor customarily performs work in that trade with its own qualified personnel. That was not the case here, so Subbidder was entitled to recover its anticipated profit on the subcontract from Contractor.

Roblin Hope Industries, Inc. v. J. A. Sullivan Corp., 413 N.E.2d 1134 (Mass.App. 1980).

try to establish the form of agreement which will be used in the event of a subcontract award. If the sub knows that a particular form will be used (for instance, *AIA Document A401*, "Standard Form of Agreement between Contractor and Subcontractor," in Appendix G), the subcontractor will have a better idea of the terms and conditions it will be expected to honor during the project.

Suppliers

The formation of agreements between prime contractors and material suppliers differs a great deal from the formation of subcontracts. Most sellers of standardized, "off-the-shelf" products simply have a price list. Contractors place orders against that list, usually receiving a discount of 10 percent or so for being trade customers. The seller of the product may or may not have some boilerplate terms and conditions preprinted on the back of its sales receipt or invoice. That is the extent of the written documentation.

For larger purchases, such as equipment or customized products, the contractor usually negotiates a price over the telephone and then issues a "purchase order" for the equipment. The purchase order generally contains detailed terms and conditions which the contractor seeks to impose on the transaction.

The problem is that when the supplier furnishes the equipment or materials, the supplier's invoice contains different terms which the seller seeks to impose on the transaction. Each party usually asks the other to acknowledge its form. Neither form is usually acknowledged. Each form states that it takes precedence over any conflicting provisions or terms offered by the other party.

This process creates great confusion as to exactly the legal provisions that were intended to govern the purchase and sale. As will be seen in the next section of this chapter, it causes great problems for the prime contractor, who wants to see that the supplier's commitment to the prime is no narrower or no less than the commitment the prime has assumed toward the owner with regard to the piece of equipment being furnished.

The other important distinction between subcontract formation and the purchase of materials or equipment is the Uniform Commercial Code (UCC). The UCC is a statute which has been adopted in virtually every state to govern the sale of goods. It does not apply to construction contracts or subcontracts, as these are primarily for the sale of service, with the furnishing of goods incidental to the construction services being furnished.

The UCC establishes basic rules governing offers, counteroffers, and contract formation. It also recognizes certain implied warranties extended by sellers of goods and establishes rules for the effective disclaimers of these implied warranties.

A detailed description of the UCC is outside the scope of this book. The important thing to remember is that the sale of goods by a supplier to a contractor is governed by a statutorily imposed set of rules which differs greatly from the legal principles governing construction contracts. Unfortunately, however, the UCC is not altogether successful in resolving the conflicting terms that were described earlier.

RIGHTS OF THE PRIME CONTRACTOR

When a prime contractor submits a binding bid or signs a construction contract, it takes on a wide assortment of obligations to the project owner. As far as the owner is concerned, the prime contractor has sole responsibility for meeting those obligations. Yet the contractor relies on a large number of subcontractors and suppliers to accomplish the work.

The challenge for the prime contractor is to see to it that the subs and suppliers assume toward the prime the same obligations the prime has assumed toward the owner with regard to the portion of the work being performed by any particular subcontractor or supplier.

CASE STUDY 10-4

Contractor requested price quotation from Supplier. Supplier sent a quotation with preprinted terms and conditions. The terms and conditions disclaimed any implied warranty of Supplier's product.

Contractor issued its standard purchase order to Supplier. The purchase order made no reference to any limitation of implied warranties. A dispute later developed as to whether or not the implied warranties had been effectively disclaimed by Supplier.

The Court of Appeals of South Carolina ruled that the warranties had been disclaimed. Contractor's purchase order did not sufficiently alert Supplier to the fact that Contractor did not accept the disclaimer as a term of the sale.

Mace Industries, Inc. v. Paddock Pool Equipment Co., Inc., 339 S.E.2d 527 (S.C. 1986).

Prime contractors use three basic devices to accomplish this: "flow-down" clauses, warranties, and performance bonds.

Flow-down Clauses

A flow-down clause in a subcontract generally states that the subcontractor agrees to accept toward the prime contractor all the obligations the prime has accepted toward the owner. An example of such a clause is shown below.

> Subcontractor agrees to adhere to and be bound to contractor by all of the provisions of the general contract dated _____ and executed by contractor and owner. Subcontractor assumes toward contractor all of the duties, obligations, and liabilities that contractor assumes toward owner. With regard to any requirements of the general contract for submission of written notices within specified time periods, it is agreed that subcontractor will submit such notices to contractor promptly enough to enable contractor to submit them to owner or architect within such specified time periods.

It is readily apparent that if a clause such as this is enforced according to its literal language, the subcontractor has agreed to construct the entire project. Yet the subcontract as a whole makes it clear that the sub is only agreeing to perform a certain part of the work. How, then, are these clauses to be interpreted and enforced?

Courts recognize that a flow-down clause does not expand the subcontractor's scope of work. The clause applies only to the work obligations encompassed by the section or sections of the specifications for which the sub is responsible. The clause is also interpreted, however, to impose the prime contract's administrative procedures on the subcontractor.

If the prime contract contains notice requirements pertaining to differing site conditions, for instance, a flow-down clause forces a sub to give a prime contractor the same notice the prime must give the owner. The same can be said of written change order requirements, shop drawing submittals, requests for extensions of time, and numerous other contract administration requirements.

If a subcontract contains a flow-down clause, it is of paramount importance to the subcontractor that it carefully review the terms of the prime contract documents. These documents, even more than the subcontract itself, may establish the rules pertaining to the administration of the contract and the procedure to be followed in the event a claim arises. The subcontractor must play by the same rules that have been imposed on the prime contractor, and this is precisely what the prime intended to accomplish by inclusion of a flow-down clause.

On federal construction projects, the rule is different. The courts have long held that general flow-down clauses on federal projects impose only the requirements pertaining to the definition of the work. They do not apply to the legal terms and conditions of the prime contract or the administrative procedures that exist between the prime contractor and the federal government. These matters must be independently established in the subcontract itself.

CASE STUDY 10-5

A subcontract contained a general flow-down clause stating that the terms and conditions of the prime contract were incorporated into the subcontract by reference.

Subcontractor was delayed by the lack of certain drawings. Subcontractor brought a claim for delay damages, but the claim was denied because Subcontractor failed to give written notice of the delay within 15 days, as required by the terms of the prime contract. Subcontractor appealed, arguing that the flow-down clause incorporated only the work requirements, not the procedural requirements, of the prime contract into the subcontract.

The Court of Appeals of Washington ruled that the flow-down clause imposed the procedural requirements of the prime contract on Subcontractor. Failure to give notice within 15 days was therefore fatal to Subcontractor's claim.

Sime Construction Co., Inc. v. Washington Public Power Supply System, 621 P.2d 1299 (Wash.App. 1980).

The federal rule has not been followed by many state courts. On nonfederal jobs, subcontractors should assume that a general flow-down clause incorporates the terms and conditions of the prime contract into the subcontract.

Warranties

In order to protect itself vis-à-vis the project owner, a prime contractor wants to make sure that its subcontractors extend warranties of their work that are comparable with the warranties the prime must extend to the owner. This does not mean that in the event of a problem the owner will look to the subcontractor for a solution. The prime contractor is solely responsible as far as the owner is concerned. If the prime is forced to honor its warranty to the owner, however, it wants to be in a position to require the responsible subcontractor to come back in and perform warranty work or reimburse the prime for any additional costs it incurred.

Subcontracts typically include a standard 1-year warranty of labor and materials. This is the same workmanship warranty the prime contractor extends to the owner. From the prime contractor's standpoint, it is important that subcontractor warranties do not start to run until final completion and acceptance of the entire project. This is when the prime's warranty period usually commences. If the subcontractor warranties start to run upon completion of each sub's portion of the work, the prime may find itself in a position where it is still obligated on a warranty to the owner, but the warranty of the subcontractor who performed the work in question has expired.

Prime contractors must also be careful to see that any special warranties or guarantees, for instance, on the roof, are covered in the subcontract. Any warranty obligation the owner imposes on the prime contractor should be carefully imposed by the prime on the appropriate subcontractor.

Supplier warranties pose special problems. The project owner's A/E sometimes specifies a particular proprietary product. The specification may result from promotional literature or other representations the sellers of the product have made. The prime contractor is obligated to furnish this product, and the prime extends a warranty on all material and workmanship.

When the prime contractor issues a purchase order to the supplier, however, the supplier responds with its "standard" sales terms. These terms frequently not only omit any performance representations but also disclaim or limit supplier liability in the event the product fails. This puts the contractor in a difficult situation. It is committed to purchasing a product from one particular supplier and committed to extending a warranty on the product's performance. Yet the supplier with whom the contractor must do business will not warrant the product to the contractor.

Under the terms of the Uniform Commercial Code, these supplier disclaimers are generally enforceable. The only thing a contractor in this situation can do is attempt to create confusion as to which set of "standard" terms and conditions govern the transaction. By refusing to acknowledge the supplier's terms and sending out its own purchase order, the contractor will be able to later argue that the supplier's disclaimers did not apply. It is not a very desirable solution, but it is the best that can be accomplished under the circumstances.

Subcontractor Performance Bonds

Just as it is possible for prime contractors to obtain guarantees of performance from corporate sureties, qualified subcontractors can obtain performance bonds as well.

A subcontract performance bond operates just as a prime contract performance bond. The prime contractor is the named obligee in the bond. If the subcontractor/principal fails to perform its contractual obligations, the surety can be called upon to complete the work.

It is always a judgment call for prime contractors as to which subcontracts should be bonded. Subcontract performance bond premiums are an expense which cannot be passed directly through to the project owner. While it might be ideal to require a performance bond from every subcontractor, this would make the prime contractor less cost-competitive.

Usually, prime contractors elect to require performance bonds only from key subcontractors. If a sub's performance is crucial to the successful accomplishment of the work or if the sub's work constitutes a major portion of the work, the prime contractor may be inclined to require a performance bond. Other subcontractors are usually allowed to work unbonded. Suppliers are rarely bonded.

PRIME CONTRACTORS' COORDINATION RESPONSIBILITIES

As stated earlier in this chapter, the prime or general contractor has sole responsibility for the timely completion of a project in accordance with the contract requirements. The prime's decision to subcontract out certain portions of the work does not alter this obligation.

When the prime contractor elects to award subcontracts, it automatically assumes legal responsibility for the proper coordination of subcontractors. This is necessary in order for the prime to fulfill its obligations to the project owner. These coordination responsibilities fall into the two general categories of division of the work and coordination of schedules.

Division of the Work among Subcontractors

When a prime contractor awards subcontracts, it is the prime's responsibility to divide the work in such a way that there are no omissions and no overlap. The project owner and the subcontractors themselves have no obligations in this regard.

The division of work is a deceptively difficult task. Although the sections of the specifications are divided more or less along traditional trade lines, as described in Chapter 2, this cannot be relied on. When preparing the plans and specifications, neither the project owner nor the architect/engineer has any obligation to arrange them in a manner which will facilitate the award of subcontracts. The owner and A/E can organize the contract documents any way they please. It is the prime contractor's job to divide the work among subcontractors and establish the scope and definition of each sub's responsibilities.

If a prime contractor blindly relies on the division of the specifications, problems can result. It is common for certain types of electrical work, for instance, to be found in the mechanical section of the specifications. If the prime simply referred to each section of the specs when awarding subcontracts to the electrical and mechanical subcontractors, the electrical sub wouldn't be obligated to wire the equipment. The mechanical sub may or may not be obligated, depending on how its subcontract was worded.

All in all, this is not a desirable situation. At a minimum, it causes disruption and confusion when the subcontractors are not certain of their exact scope of work. At its worst, the situation results in the prime contractor's being subjected to a number of costly claims by subs who allege that they were forced to perform work outside the scope of their subcontracts or were unable to properly perform their work because other trade matters were not taken care of.

From a prime contractor's standpoint, there is no substitute for carefully going through the plans and specifications and thoughtfully crafting each subcontractor's scope of work. The careless, broadside incorporation of specifications by reference is almost certain to produce the problems described above.

It is also important to note that the prime contractor is responsible for interpreting the plans and specifications for the subcontractors. If any question arises regarding the intent of the documents, the subs are entitled to look to the prime, who in turn should seek a directive from the owner's authorized

---

CASE STUDY 10-6

Contractor on a wastewater treatment project awarded a subcontract for mechanical work and a subcontract for the force main work. Each subcontract referenced a particular division of the project owner's specifications.

Each division of the specifications referred to particular gate valves. The two subcontractors argued with Contractor over which sub was responsible for the valves.

The mechanical subcontractor eventually performed that work under protest and sued Contractor for additional compensation.

The Supreme Court of Minnesota ruled that Contractor must pay the mechanical subcontractor for the gate valve work. "One aspect of a prime contractor's duties is to coordinate the work of its subcontractors and eliminate gaps and overlaps in their work."

Lamb Plumbing & Heating Co. v. Kraus-Anderson of Minneapolis, Inc., 296 N.W.3d 859 (Minn. 1980).

---

representative, usually the A/E. Subcontractors are entitled to rely on the guidance they receive from the prime. If the prime contractor's interpretation or directive turns out to be inaccurate, it is the prime, not the sub, who must bear the cost of correcting the problem.

Coordination of Schedules

The prime contractor is responsible not only for dividing the work among the subcontractors but also for determining and coordinating the schedule for each subcontractor. This is a crucial task, because the work must be performed in the proper sequence. The site preparation sub must be finished before the foundation sub can work. The foundation sub must be finished before the framing sub can work. The framing sub must be finished before the mechanical or electrical work can be roughed in. And so on. Additionally, equipment and materials must be ordered, leaving sufficient lead time so that they arrive in time to be installed without creating delay.

As with the division of the work, the prime contractor has sole responsibility for determining the schedule for each subcontractor. The failure to properly coordinate the schedule may not only delay a particular sub, it may delay completion of the entire project.

Ideally, each subcontractor should be given an explicit schedule showing the date it will be able to start its work and the date it is expected to be finished. Each subcontractor should also be shown the entire project schedule so that it knows how its efforts fit into the overall scheme of things. With this explicit schedule established, the sub will know what is expected and the prime will have something it can enforce in its dealings with the sub.

Unfortunately, this type of precise subcontractor scheduling is frequently omitted. This is not an oversight by prime contractors. They do not want to commit themselves to having the project ready for subs at certain dates, fearing claims for delay and disruption if the dates are not met.

Instead, prime contractors frequently state in subcontracts that the sub will work at the direction of the prime contractor, performing its work whenever the prime tells it to. These contract clauses also state that a certain amount of delay and disruption can be expected and the prime contractor disclaims any liability for such delay or disruption.

Subcontract clauses such as these are generally enforceable, subject to the same exceptions to no-damage-for-delay clauses discussed in Chapter 7. Subcontractors are reluctant to agree to these terms, as they should be, because it gives the prime contractor authority to force the sub to work in a very inefficient fashion. Frequently, however, the superior bargaining position of the prime contractor enables it to force these scheduling provisions on subcontractors.

If the subcontracts do not contain specific dates for commencing and completing the work, how can the prime contractor hold the subs responsible for delay? The most common solution for prime contractors is to include a subcontract clause stating that to the extent the subcontractor's slow performance delays the completion of the project and subjects the prime contractor to liquidated damages, the sub shall be liable to the prime for those liquidated damages.

These clauses are enforceable, although it becomes a challenge for the prime contractor to prove that the sub caused the late completion when the subcontract did not contain any precise schedule. If such delay can be proved,

---

CASE STUDY 10-7

Contractor on hospital project awarded a subcontract for fireproofing work. Subcontract required Subcontractor to perform work "as directed" by Contractor. Subcontract also disclaimed any Contractor liability for delay to Subcontractor's work.

Contractor prepared a critical path method schedule for the project, but the steel erector failed to follow it. Subcontractor was forced to perform work out of sequence, with the work of other subcontractors interfering with the fireproofing

application. Subcontractor sued Contractor for its increased costs of performance. Contractor argued that the language of the subcontract shielded it from liability for the out-of-sequence work.

The District of Columbia Court of Appeals ruled that despite the language of the subcontract, Contractor did not have the right to force Subcontractor to work in an improper sequence. Although the subcontract gave Contractor a certain amount of discretion in scheduling the work of its subcontractors, it did not permit Contractor to force subs to work in an illogical sequence which was contrary to their reasonable expectations.

Blake Construction Co., Inc. v. C. J. Coakley Co., Inc., 431 A.2d 569 (D.C.App. 1981).

however, courts will uphold the pass-through of liquidated damages to tardy subcontractors.

It is really more fair and more businesslike for prime contractors to establish precise schedules in each subcontract and include liquidated damage clauses reflecting the anticipated effect of late subcontractor performance. As long as prime contractors prepare subcontract agreements, however, with one eye over the shoulder looking for delay and disruption claims from subs, it is likely that most subcontracts will continue to give the prime great discretion in directing the timing and scheduling of subcontractor performance.

PAYMENT OBLIGATIONS TO SUBCONTRACTORS AND SUPPLIERS

A prime contractor's payment of its subcontractors and suppliers involves a similar procedure and similar issues to a project owner's payment of a prime contractor. Subcontractors and suppliers are one step farther down the contractual chain, however, one step farther removed from the source of the construction funds. This poses certain unique payment problems for subs and suppliers.

Conditions Precedent

The most basic legal precondition to a subcontractor's entitlement to payment is substantial compliance with the contract requirements. The prime contractor may hold the subcontractor to the same objective standard of contract compliance that the owner holds the prime contractor to. This is reasonable, of course, as the essential purpose of a subcontract is the completion of a designated portion of the work in accordance with the owner's plans and specifications.

A more controversial type of legal precondition is a contract clause making the prime contractor's obligation to pay the subcontractor contingent on the prime's receipt of payment from the owner. An example of such a subcontract payment clause is shown below.

> Contractor shall pay subcontractor within 10 days of the date contractor receives payment from owner for the work performed by subcontractor. Final payment to subcontractor shall be made within 10 days of contractor's receipt of final payment from owner.

Prime contractors argue that these clauses are fair and reasonable because the prime contractor is dependent on the flow of contract funds from the project owner. Subcontractors, say the primes, must share in the inherent risk that the flow of project funds will be disrupted.

Subcontractors argue that these clauses are unreasonable because the subs have no contractual relationship with the project owner and no leverage with regard to the release of contract funds. Subcontractors contract with the prime contractor and rely on the prime's creditworthiness in recovering payment. If

they fully perform their work in accordance with the subcontract requirements, say the subs, they should be paid in full by the prime regardless of
whether the prime has been paid by the owner.

The courts seem to agree with the subcontractors, as these payment clauses
are strictly construed. A subcontract payment clause such as the one quoted
above is generally interpreted to mean that the prime contractor has a reasonable amount of time to try to recover payment from the owner before the prime
must pay the sub. The prime cannot delay payment indefinitely, however.
Even if the owner never pays for the work in question, the prime must pay the
sub within a reasonable period of time after the sub's payment was due.

Courts rule that the only way a prime contractor will be excused from paying a
subcontractor owing to nonpayment by the project owner is if the subcontract
payment clause expressly states that payment by the owner is a "condition
precedent" to the prime's legal obligation to pay the sub. Any subcontractor
confronted with a payment clause such as this must realize that it may not be
paid because of problems that have nothing to do with the sufficiency of its
own performance.

Progress Payments and Retainage

Progress payments are not as prevalent on subcontracts as they are on prime
contracts. The work is usually performed over a shorter period of time; so it is
not unusual for the sub to receive a single payment. On large subcontracts
where work will be performed over a period of months, however, it is common
for subcontracts to call for periodic progress payments based on the percentage of completion. The procedure for submitting requisitions and receiving
payment is basically the same as with prime contracts.

If a subcontract calls for periodic progress payments, it will invariably allow
the prime contractor to withhold retainage, usually 10 percent, from each pay-

---

CASE STUDY 10-8

Contractor awarded a subcontract which
stated: "Retained percentages will be paid
to [Subcontractor] as and when [Contrac-
tor] receives such payment from [Owner]
and in the same proportions."

Owner failed to release final payment
to Contractor, so Contractor refused to
release retainage to Subcontractor. Subcontractor sued Contractor, who relied on
the subcontract language as a defense.

The highest court of New York, the
Appellate Division of the Supreme Court,
ruled that Owner's nonpayment did not
excuse Contractor's refusal to pay Subcontractor. The subcontract language entitled Contractor to a reasonable period of
time before releasing Subcontractor's retainage, but it was not sufficiently explicit
to make payment by Owner a "condition
precedent" to Contractor's obligation to
pay Subcontractor.

Grossman Steel & Aluminum Corp. v. Samson Window Corp.,
426 N.E.2d 177 (N.Y. 1981).

ment. The purpose is the same as prime contract retainage. The prime contractor wants to make sure that the total subcontract payments to date do not exceed the value of the subcontract work in place. The prime also wants to be sure that if problems develop with the subcontractor's work prior to final payment, the prime is holding enough subcontract funds to cover the cost of correction.

Final Payment

The question of when a subcontractor receives final payment is also a controversial one. Prime contractors like to hold subcontractors' retainage until final completion of the entire project and receipt of final payment from the project owner. This offers obvious advantages from a cash-flow standpoint. Prime contractors also argue that it is reasonable protection for them because the owner's final inspection of the work may turn up problems relating to the performance of one or more subcontractors. Prime contractors want some financial insurance against this type of situation.

For subcontractors, it is frequently a hardship to wait until completion of the entire project before receiving their final payment. On large projects, subcontractors involved in the early phases may have to wait months or even years before final payment. Subs argue that once their portion of the work is complete, the prime contractor has the opportunity to carefully inspect the work. If they have fully complied with their subcontract requirements, they should be paid the subcontract balance.

Either way of structuring final subcontract payment is legally enforceable so long as the clause is clearly written. Subcontract payment terms are essentially the product of business negotiations between the prime and the sub. The extent to which the sub is willing to postpone receipt of final payment usually reflects how eager the sub is to receive the work.

Payment of Suppliers

The payment of suppliers is very different from the payment of subcontractors. This is a sale of goods. Payment in full is usually required within no more than 30 days of delivery. Retainage is highly unusual in these transactions. The prime contractor has the opportunity to inspect the equipment or materials before accepting them. Once they are accepted, the prime is usually obligated to make full payment. If a problem later surfaces, the prime can rely only on any express or implied warranties the supplier has extended with regard to its product.

Liens and Payment Bonds

If a subcontractor or supplier does not receive full payment from the prime contractor, its best remedy is to seek recovery against the prime's payment bond, if any, or to place a lien on the owner's project. These devices were discussed in detail in Chapter 9.

KEY TERMS AND CONCEPTS

promissory estoppel   An equitable doctrine which holds that if one party changes its economic position in reasonable reliance on the promise or affirmative representation of another party, the second party is precluded from reneging on its promise. In construction contracting, this doctrine is applied to enable prime contractors to hold subcontractors to their oral, prebid quotations, even though no subcontract agreement has yet been formed.

filed subbids   A statutory system used on public construction projects whereby trade contractors submit bids on designated portions of the work. These bids are then filed. General contractors bidding on the prime contract must utilize the lowest filed subbid in each trade category unless the general contractor plans to perform that work with its own qualified personnel or the general contractor has a reasonable objection to working with that particular subcontractor.

flow-down clause   A clause included in some subcontracts which states that the subcontractor assumes toward the prime contractor all the duties and obligations the prime contractor has assumed toward the project owner under the terms of the prime contract. Generally, this is interpreted to include notice requirements and other procedural aspects of the prime contract. On federal construction projects, however, it is interpreted to apply only to the definition of the construction work itself.

Uniform Commercial Code   A model statute which has been adopted in virtually every state and covers the purchase and sale of goods. It does not apply to construction contracts but does apply to agreements between contractors and their equipment or material suppliers. The Uniform Commercial Code addresses vital matters such as offer and acceptance, implied warranties, and the disclaimer of warranties.

division of work   The prime contractor's allocation of work among the various subcontractors. The prime contractor has sole responsibility for dividing the work among subcontractors in such a way that there is no duplication and there are no gaps. The project owner and its architect or engineer have no obligation to prepare plans and specifications in a way that facilitates the award of subcontracts.

sequence of work   The prime contractor's scheduling of subcontractors' work in such a way that the project is constructed in a logical, orderly fashion and no subcontractor is delayed or disrupted by the untimely performance of another subcontractor. The prime contractor has sole responsibility for scheduling and coordinating the work of its subcontractors.

condition precedent   An occurrence which must take place before a party incurs the legal obligation to do something. In the context of construction subcontracting, this issue arises when a subcontract states that the prime contractor's obligation to pay the subcontractor is contingent on the prime receiving payment from the project owner.

　　If the subcontract expressly states that this is a "condition precedent," the payment clause will be enforced according to its literal terms. If the subcontract is less explicit, the clause will be interpreted only to give the prime contractor a reasonable amount of time before the obligation to pay the subcontractor arises.

EMERGING FORMS OF CONSTRUCTION CONTRACTING

In the first chapter of this book, the traditional method of organizing a construction project was described. The project owner awards a single prime contract to a "general contractor" for a project that is fully designed and very well defined. The general contractor in turn awards a number of subcontracts to specialty or trade contractors. The general contractor has sole responsibility, vis-à-vis the project owner, for the completion of the project. This has been the prevalent method of organizing construction projects for generations.

In recent decades, new methods of organizing construction projects have emerged. These new contractual arrangements have been developed primarily in response to changing economic conditions. To a lesser extent, they reflect changes in the organization of the construction industry itself. This chapter examines the three most common forms of nontraditional construction projects: construction management projects, design/build projects, and turn-key projects.

CONSTRUCTION MANAGEMENT

The construction management method of organizing a construction project involves the award of multiple prime contracts by the project owner. Rather than award a single prime contract to a general contractor who will have sole responsibility for scheduling, coordinating, and completing the work, the owner elects to award a series of prime contracts to various trade and specialty contractors. Each contractor is given responsibility for a certain defined portion of the project. Other aspects of the project may not even have complete working drawings at this point.

In the absence of a single, general contractor, the project owner necessarily assumes responsibility for the scheduling and coordinating of the work of the various prime contractors. As a practical matter, this is handled by the owner's agent, the construction manager. The role of the construction manager is discussed in some detail later in this chapter.

The construction management technique (but not the name) was first used during wartime periods earlier in this century. Projects of military and industrial significance had to be completed in a short period of time. By awarding multiple prime contracts for various phases of the project, the government could start work on the preliminary phases while its architects and engineers were still completing the design for later phases of the project.

Construction management in the private sector gained prominence during the decade of the 1970s. Once again, the motivation was to shorten the duration of the design and construction process. Rather than military emergency, the problem in the seventies was high construction loan interest charges and rapidly escalating costs for labor and materials. Construction management offered an opportunity to mitigate those factors.

It should be apparent by now that a construction management project involves different contractual relationships and a different chain of command than a traditional construction project. This arrangement is illustrated in Figure 11-1.

Role of the Construction Manager

The term "construction management" or "construction manager" is used very loosely. It is no wonder that many people, including those in the construction industry, are unclear as to exactly what the responsibilities of a construction manager are.

In "pure" construction management, the construction manager (or CM) is an independent professional serving as the agent of the project owner. The CM is

FIGURE 11-1
Contractual relationship on a construction management project.

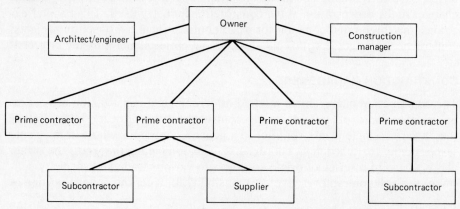

responsible for scheduling the work of the various prime contractors, coordinating the division of work and the performance of work in the field and administering the business and financial aspects of the project. In other words, the CM carries out most of the functions of the traditional general contractor.

This is necessary because the project owner, by electing to award multiple prime trade contracts, has implicitly assumed an obligation toward those contractors to properly schedule and coordinate the work. Yet most project owners lack the resources and expertise to perform this function—thus the advent of the professional construction manager.

In a pure construction management situation, the CM is retained strictly as an independent, professional consultant. The CM is paid a fee for this service. The CM plays no entrepreneurial role in the development, design, or construction of the project and has no financial interest in its outcome. All contracts are awarded by the owner directly to the trade contractors, with the CM simply advising the owner.

As construction management evolved, the pure form of this method quickly fell by the wayside. The two groups with the most to offer project owners were the architects and engineers (A/Es) and the traditional general contractors. These two groups actively marketed their services as "construction managers" and developed standard contract forms defining their role as CM. In so doing, they developed two forms of hybrid construction management which are prevalent today.

The contractors' approach to construction management is reflected in the Associated General Contractors of America Document No. 8, "Standard Form of Agreement between Owner and Construction Manager." Under this arrangement, the CM guarantees a total maximum construction cost to the owner. The CM, not the owner, enters into contracts with the trade contractors. The CM also has the option of performing extensive construction work with its own forces. In other words, the CM functions much like the traditional general contractor. The primary distinction is that construction work is commenced before final working drawings are ready for all phases of the project. The CM guarantees a maximum price based on conceptual drawings and explicit design parameters.

The A/E's approach to construction management is reflected in the Engineers' Joint Contract Documents Committee Publication No. 1910-15, "Standard Form of Agreement between Owner and Project Manager for Professional Services." Under this arrangement, the "project manager," as it is referred to, is responsible for providing all architectural and engineering services. The project manager does not guarantee the maximum cost of the project and does not enter into any contracts with the construction trades. In fact, the project manager disclaims any responsibility for construction methods or techniques. The project manager performs a function much like the traditional A/E. Again, the primary distinction is that construction contracts are awarded before final working drawings are complete for the entire project, enabling a "phased" approach to the work and a shorter total elapsed time.

Both the general contractors and the A/Es have modified the pure construction management method to make it more similar to their accustomed roles. Yet each arrangement maintains some of the key characteristics of pure construction management.

Advantages of Construction Management

The primary advantage of construction management has already been referred to. It is the opportunity to "fast-track" a project. This means that construction can commence on early phases of the project while working drawings are still being completed on later phases. This means that the design and construction overlap, thus reducing the total elapsed time for the entire process.

It is impossible to fast-track a traditional construction project because a general contractor cannot agree to a fixed price until all the details of the work requirements have been established. If an owner wants to fast-track a project, it must be willing to forgo a fixed price and deal with numerous contractors. The potential benefit is that by reducing the elapsed time of the design and construction process, the owner reduces its construction financing costs and mitigates future labor and material cost escalation.

The other advantage of the construction management system is that by awarding trade contracts directly, the project owner avoids the general contractor's markup on subcontracted work. This advantage may be somewhat illusory, as the owner will have to pay a CM to perform many of the general contractor's traditional functions. Additionally, the general contractor's markup of subcontracted work is usually not as large as many owners assume. Nonetheless, the avoidance of general contractor markup has a strong emotional appeal to many developers and project owners.

Risks of Construction Management

The construction management method of organizing a project creates certain risks. On a traditional project, the owner awards a fixed-price contract for a thoroughly described facility. If all goes well, the owner knows exactly what it will receive and exactly what it will have to pay for that product.

With construction management, the owner starts with only conceptual plans and design parameters. Although the various trade contracts are usually of a fixed-price nature, the owner has no fixed price for the entire project. The use of construction management therefore results in less control over the nature of the completed project and less control over the total price.

The absence of a general contractor creates other risks as well. There is no single point of responsibility and authority for the construction work. In theory, the construction manager has authority to coordinate the work of the trade contractors. The degree of authority will depend, however, on the nature of the agreement between the owner and the CM and the language in the construction contracts between the owner and the trades.

On a traditional project, the general contractor has ultimate responsibility for the timely and sufficient completion of the work. If there are problems with delay or shoddy work, the general contractor cannot simply point its finger at its subcontractors. Any problems with subcontracted work are the responsibility, and liability, of the general contractor. The project owner need only make contact with a single party.

A construction management project, on the other hand, lends itself to reciprocal finger pointing. With no single source of responsibility, the owner is faced with a situation where the trade contractors blame each other, or the CM, for the problems which arise. It is harder for the owner to get problems resolved when it must act as fact finder and mediator of every dispute.

Construction management also increases the legal liability exposure of the project owner. Having elected to forgo the general contractor, the owner has assumed the responsibility for the proper scheduling and coordination of the project. The fact the owner has retained a CM to perform this function does not protect the owner. It is usually the owner, not the CM, who has contracted with the trade contractors. They will look to the owner when problems arise. The owner may then seek recourse against the CM for doing a poor job, but this may not be much solace if the project is coming unraveled and the owner is facing claims from numerous trade contractors.

This liability exposure is greatest in the area of scheduling and delay. There have been a large number of lawsuits by trade contractors against project owners alleging that the owner, through its CM, failed to properly schedule or coordinate the work, thereby delaying the trade contractor. Many of these suits have been successful. In response, owners have started using no-damage-for-delay clauses in their trade contracts, as well as clauses stating that the trade contractors are responsible for coordinating the work among themselves. Some owners have even designated a single trade contractor as having primary responsibility for coordinating all the work.

These clauses have had varying degrees of effectiveness in insulating project owners against liability for delay of trade contractors. If nothing else, they

---

CASE STUDY 11-1

Owner awarded numerous prime contracts for construction of an automobile assembly plant. Owner retained construction manager (CM) to serve as its agent for the scheduling and coordination of the project.

CM allowed several contractors to discharge water through partially completed storm drains. This flooded the sole access road and prevented other contractors from getting their equipment on site. The concrete contractor sued Owner and CM for delay damages.

The U.S. District Court ruled that Owner, having elected to award multiple prime contracts, had an obligation to coordinate the contractors so that no contractor would be denied timely site access. The concrete contractor received a $750,000 judgment against Owner and CM jointly.

R. S. Noonan, Inc. v. Morrison-Knudsen Co., Inc., 522 F.Supp. 1186 (D.C.La. 1981).

CASE STUDY 11-2

Owner retained construction manager (CM) using the form of agreement published by the Associated General Contractors of America (AGC). Under this agreement, the CM guarantees a maximum price and contracts directly with the trade contractors.

After completion of the project, problems developed with the air-conditioning

system. Owner sued CM. CM responded that it was not responsible for the work of the mechanical contractor.

The District of Columbia Court of Appeals ruled that under the AGC construction management agreement, the CM is responsible for the work of the trade contractors because the relationship between CM and trade contractor is essentially the same as the relationship between general contractor and subcontractor on a traditional construction project.

Phoenix-Georgetown, Inc. v. Charles H. Tompkins, Inc., 477 A.2d 215 (D.C.App. 1984).

---

call attention to a fundamental weakness in the construction management method. Without a single source of authority and responsibility for construction, greater responsibility falls on the owner, and the likelihood of delay and coordination problems increases.

Outlook for Construction Management

It is fair to state today that construction management has not lived up to its promise of the 1970s. Many large project owners, both public and private, have found that CM projects generate a disproportionate amount of delay

---

CASE STUDY 11-3

Owner of industrial facility awarded a number of separate trade contracts. Each contract contained a "no-damage-for-delay" clause stating that if the contractor was delayed by other contractors, it would not be entitled to any additional compensation.

In an effort to speed up the project, Owner gave an equipment supplier priority access to the building. This impeded the mechanical contractor's site access and

delayed the mechanical contractor. Contractor filed suit against Owner.

The Court of Appeals of Michigan ruled that the delay damage disclaimer is generally enforceable. On a multiple prime contract project, however, the contractors are completely dependent on the owner for proper scheduling and coordination of the work. Owner's failure to fulfill these obligations amounted to intentional interference with Contractor's work. Intentional interference is an exception to the enforceability of the delay damage disclaimer, so Contractor could recover.

Phoenix Contractors, Inc. v. General Motors Corp., 355 N.W.2d 673 (Mich.App. 1984).

---

claims and other litigation. Cost overruns have been a problem as well.

As inflation and interest rates have declined, so has the appeal of construction managed projects. The need for certainty and control may now exceed the need to avoid cost escalation and finance charges.

Despite these factors, however, construction management in its various forms is here to stay. Construction will always be a very capital-intensive endeavor. Anything that can be done to reduce the total elapsed time of design and construction has an innate economic appeal. When inflation and interest rates rise once again, many project owners will again prefer to take their chances with phased construction rather than wait to design an entire project and put it out to bid.

DESIGN/BUILD

Under the "design/build" method of organizing a construction project, the owner contracts on a cost-plus basis with a single entity to provide the entire project. This includes planning, preliminary design, final design, and construction. Usually the design/build contractor is a general construction contractor, although it is sometimes a joint venture of a general contractor and an architectural/engineering firm.

Design/build has two important distinctions from the construction management method. First, the owner contracts with a single entity rather than contracting with numerous trade contractors. Second, the owner of a design/build project does not contract directly with an independent A/E. The A/E is usually a subcontractor to the prime design/build contractor. Many large engineering/construction firms have sufficient professional staff to perform virtually all the design in-house. The contractual arrangement on a design/build project is illustrated in Figure 11-2, on p. 196.

CASE STUDY 11-4

Owner awarded numerous prime contracts for construction of medical school. The general building contractor was designated as the party having responsibility for the overall coordination of the project. Each contract disclaimed Owner liability for delay.

The project ran 25 months behind schedule and the electrical and plumbing contractors brought delay claims against Owner. Contractors argued that despite the contract language, Owner was the only party that had actual authority to properly schedule and coordinate the work.

The Supreme Court of New Jersey ruled that under this contractual arrangement, Owner was not liable for delay of the various contractors. If Owner had failed to designate a party with coordination responsibility, the contractors' argument might be persuasive. Owner had effectively delegated the responsibility, however, and could not be held liable under these circumstances.

Broadway Maintenance Corp. v. Rutgers University,
447 A.2d 906 (N.J. 1982).

Defining Scope of Work and Payment

Initially, a design/build contractor usually performs a feasibility study for the project owner. This study would probably include some very preliminary cost estimates. If the project is deemed feasible, the design/build contractor, through the A/E, would begin to design the project.

The initial design documents are usually very general. They define the basic parameters of the project in terms of size, capability, and design standards. These documents are not sufficiently precise to be used in awarding trade contracts, but they are vital to the design/build process. This is because the owner and design/build contractor rely on these documents to negotiate a guaranteed maximum price. This preliminary design work is usually paid for on a lump-sum basis, as the owner may or may not contract for a completed project.

If the parties agree on a guaranteed maximum price, the actual design/build contract is executed. Allowable costs are defined in this contract. The contractor receives all allowable costs plus a stipulated fee. If costs exceed the guaranteed maximum, they are taken first from the contractor's fee and, if necessary, from the contractor's pocket. There is usually a "shared savings" provision which applies to a cost underrun. By giving the contractor a share of any savings under the guaranteed maximum price, the owner maintains the contractor's incentive to run an efficient project.

Once the design/build contract has been executed, the contractor, through the A/E, begins to prepare working drawings and complete specifications for the various trades. Bid packages are assembled and subcontracts awarded much the same as on a traditional construction project. Design/build contractors frequently have expertise in particular types of industrial or utility projects and may elect to perform substantial portions of the construction work with their own forces.

Advantages of Design/Build

Unlike a construction management project, design/build offers the project owner a single source of responsibility and authority for the successful com-

FIGURE 11-2
Contractual relationship on a design/build project.

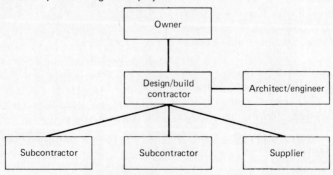

pletion of the entire project. If there is any problem with the design or the construction, the owner can look to the design/build contractor. As the sole prime contractor, the design/build contractor is liable for the work of all its subcontractors, including the A/E.

Design/build projects also offer the opportunity to fast-track the design and construction of a project. It is common for design/build contractors to be constructing early phases of the project while working drawings are still being prepared for later phases. The economic advantages of fast-tracking were discussed in the section on construction management. These advantages are even more attractive on the heavy industrial and utility projects which are very capital-intensive and are the most likely projects to be arranged on a design/build basis.

The final advantage of a design/build project is the opportunity for the owner to rely on the specialized expertise of the design/build contractor. As mentioned earlier, many design/build contractors specialize in certain types of heavy, engineered construction projects. They usually have a large number of technical experts on their staff. On a complex, capital-intensive project, it can be reassuring for the owner to deal with a specialist who has a track record of performing that particular type of project.

Disadvantages of Design/Build

The biggest disadvantage of a design/build project is the owner's inability to precisely define the project. As described earlier, the owner signs a contract based on only a preliminary design which establishes certain design parameters. No matter how many standards, parameters, and "statements of intent" the agreement has, the owner still cannot be sure of the exact details of the completed project.

This problem is not too severe on an industrial project, where the parameters can be objectively stated in terms of production capacity per hour or per day. The owner is far more concerned with production capacity than it is with interior wall finishes. On other types of projects, however, the lack of detailed working drawings can be a source of disappointment and disputes.

Considering the lack of a precise contractual definition of the work, it is not surprising that change orders are a problem on design/build projects. The contractor may consider the owner's directive to call for something more than what was required by the design parameters. The contractor would understandably want an increase in the guaranteed maximum price. The owner, on the other hand, may think its directive is consistent with what the contractor promised to deliver. The lack of precise contractual drawings and specifications makes these disagreements very hard to resolve. A large amount of cooperation and mutual confidence is required. The owner usually does not have an independent A/E and is therefore highly dependent on the expertise and integrity of the design/build contractor.

Design/build projects also do not provide the owner with as much cost control and cost certainty as a traditional fixed-price contract. A shared savings provision gives the contractor a strong incentive to control costs, however, and the guaranteed maximum price sets an outer limit on the owner's obligation. Nevertheless, there can be a wide gap between estimated price in the cost-plus contract and the guaranteed maximum price.

Finally, it must be mentioned that the design/build method of organizing a construction project poses greater liability exposure for the contractor than the traditional method of construction. Traditionally, the contractor is given detailed plans and specifications to follow. The owner has warranted the accuracy and sufficiency of those documents. If the contractor faithfully performs in accordance with those documents, it will have satisfied its legal obligations. Design problems will be a matter between the owner and its A/E.

On a design/build project the contractor has responsibility for design, either because it designed the project with its own personnel or because the A/E who designed the project was working as a subcontractor to the design/build contractor. If the project doesn't function as promised, the problem is in the contractor's lap. This liability for design problems also complicates the matters of obtaining insurance and performance bonds.

TURN-KEY DEVELOPMENTS

The third type of emerging construction project has actually been around a long time. It is the "turn-key" project where the contractor serves as developer of the project.

The contractor basically agrees to design and construct a completed project on land the contractor owns or will obtain. The contractor is responsible for financing the construction and land acquisition.

The project can be defined in great detail and a fixed price placed on the entire package. Turn-key projects are seldom fast-tracked, as the end user is motivated more by certainty and simplicity than by a desire to compress the

---

CASE STUDY 11-5

Owner awarded design/build contract to Contractor for development of a fertilizer plant. The project was completed and Owner gave Contractor final payment and a general release pertaining to all obligations "arising from or in any way related to the contract."

The air compressor train later failed and Owner filed suit against Contractor.

Contractor moved for summary judgment, arguing that the release barred any action by Owner.

The U.S. District Court ruled that the release did not apply to Contractor's alleged negligence in providing professional design services to the project. Although Owner could not sue for construction problems, it was still entitled to sue for breach of a professional obligation.

Kaiser Aluminum & Chemical Corp. v. Ingersoll-Rand Co., 519 F.Supp. 60 (S.D.Ga. 1981).

CASE STUDY 11-6

Owner awarded a contract to Contractor to design and build an industrial plant capable of meeting certain production standards. Contractor awarded subcontract to A/E for the design of the facility. The subcontract incorporated the terms of the prime design/build contract.

The completed plant was unable to meet the performance criteria. Owner sued Contractor and A/E for breach of warran-ty. Contractor and A/E responded that the production requirements were simply a way of defining the scope of work and that they never warranted the performance of the plant.

The U.S. Court of Appeals, Eighth Circuit, ruled that the design/build contract was set up in such a way that Contractor and A/E had an obligation to produce a plant capable of meeting the production criteria. Anything less was a breach of warranty.

Arkansas Rice Growers Cooperative Association v. Alchemy Industries, Inc., 797 F.2d 565 (8th Cir. 1986).

---

design and construction process. Once the project is completed in accordance with the contract requirements, the owner closes on the purchase of the land and buildings and walks in the door—thus the term "turn-key."

For the end user, the turn-key method offers the certainty of knowing exactly what it will get for a completed project. Also, the end user is spared headaches of being involved in the construction process. The end user need not obtain construction financing or monitor progress payment requests. Of course, the financing costs are hidden in the total purchase price. The contractor is assuming the entrepreneurial risk of a real estate developer and is pricing the contract in a way that will allow for a profit. The buyer of a turn-key project is unlikely to obtain as low a price as it would if it developed the project itself.

KEY TERMS AND CONCEPTS

construction management A method of organizing a construction project where the owner awards multiple prime contracts to various trade contractors. The project is usually phased, with construction starting on early phases before final working drawings have been completed for the later phases of the project.

In the absence of a single "general" contractor, the owner is responsible for the scheduling, coordination, and management of the project. The owner usually retains the services of a professional construction manager to perform these tasks. The term "construction management" is used loosely in the industry; so the role and compensation of construction managers varies greatly.

design/build A method of organizing a construction project where the owner awards a single contract to one firm which designs and builds the facility. After conceptual design documents and a preliminary cost estimate have been prepared, the parties negotiate a guaranteed maximum price for a cost-plus-fixed-fee contract. At this stage, the project is defined only in terms of design parameters and standards. As work progresses, the owner pays all allowable costs up to the guaranteed maximum price. Design/build techniques are used primarily on heavy, engineered construction projects such as industrial facilities and utility plants.

turn-key development A method whereby the contractor not only designs and builds the project but purchases the land and finances the construction. When the project is complete, the buyer purchases the land and buildings in accordance with a contract which defined the project and established a price.

DISPUTE RESOLUTION

If a construction dispute cannot be resolved through negotiation and compromise between the owner and contractor, it will become necessary for an impartial third party to resolve the disagreement. The same is true, of course, for disputes involving architect/engineers (A/Es), subcontractors, and other parties on a construction project.

The manner in which a dispute is resolved depends on the applicable state and federal statutes as well as the provisions of the contract between the parties themselves. This chapter examines the various forums which are available for the resolution of construction disputes: administrative boards, the courts, arbitrators, and mediators. It also discusses the problems which arise when the various agreements among parties on a project contain inconsistent dispute resolution provisions.

ADMINISTRATIVE REMEDIES

Many construction contracts involving public project owners call for disputes to be resolved by administrative boards. This forum is usually faster and less expensive than litigation in court. Additionally, the board members hear a great number of construction disputes and gain an expertise and understanding that is rare among the judiciary.

The widespread use of administrative tribunals reflects a recognition by public authorities that disputes on construction projects are inevitable and frequent. As will be seen, however, the use of administrative remedies sometimes raises questions regarding the objectivity of the decision makers.

Role of the A/E

In the past, it was common for public works construction contracts to contain what is known as an "engineer decision" clause. This clause typically requires the contractor to submit all claims for additional compensation under the contract to the project engineer or architect. The A/E's decision on the claim is final and binding on all parties unless it was fraudulent or made in bad faith. In other words, there is no appeal from the A/E's decision.

The problem with this type of clause is readily apparent. The project A/E is usually an employee of the public project owner. The A/E is being asked to render an objective decision on a matter that may have a significant economic impact on his or her employer. Furthermore, the dispute may involve the conduct or the work product of the A/E itself. At a minimum, the engineer decision clause creates the perception of a lack of objectivity.

These clauses are far less common than they were 30 years ago. The reason is twofold. Contractors, both individually and through their trade associations, have objected to having their contract claims decided by the public project owner's employee. The perception that the project owner is stacking the deck in its own favor creates an unfavorable bidding climate by reducing the number of bids received and increasing the bid amounts. Public authorities have responded to this sentiment by removing contract language which makes the project A/E's decision final and binding and by creating the administrative boards which are discussed below.

The second reason for the decline of engineer decision clauses is hostility from the courts. Recognizing the inherent unfairness of such a dispute resolution mechanism, courts have gone out of their way to limit the effect of the clauses. Some courts have ruled that while the project A/E's decision may be binding as to findings of fact, the decision can be appealed to the courts if the A/E has made an error of law. Other courts have gone farther, ruling that the engineer's "binding" decision does nothing more than create a rebuttable presumption as to the facts of the dispute.

Engineer decision clauses are still found in some public works construction contracts. Generally, however, the clauses have been modified to reflect the reality that the A/E's decision is not final and binding in every regard. Even in those jurisdictions where the clause purports to give the A/E such authority, the courts have pared back the enforceable effect of the contract language.

Today, the role of the A/E in resolving disputes between the contractor and the project owner resembles the role of a mediator. Many construction contracts, both public and private, call for the contractor to initially submit a claim for more time or more money to the project A/E.

For instance, Article 2 of *AIA Document A201,* "General Conditions of the

CASE STUDY 12-1

State awarded Contractor contract for highway construction. State's standard contract form said the state engineer "will decide all questions which may arise...as to the acceptable fulfillment of the contract on the part of the contractor."

Contractor submitted a claim to the state engineer, but the engineer denied the claim. Contractor then filed suit, and a jury awarded it the amount it demanded. State appealed, arguing that under the terms of the contract, the engineer's decision had been final and Contractor had no right to go to court.

The Court of Appeals of Arizona rejected State's argument. The Court said an engineer can be the final arbiter of disputes only if the contract makes this very clear. The language in question was not sufficiently explicit to make the engineer's decision final and binding. The contract language served only to define the engineer's authority during construction of the project.

New Pueblo Constructors, Inc. v. State of Arizona,
696 P.2d 203 (Ariz.App. 1985).

Contract for Construction," in Appendix E of this book, requires all claims under the contract to be submitted initially to the architect for a review and a decision. The architect's decision is not final and binding, however. Either the owner or the contractor may submit the dispute to arbitration, and the arbitrators will be free to disregard any opinions, findings, or rulings by the architect. Only architect decisions involving "artistic effect" are binding on the parties, and then only if the decision is consistent with the "intent of the contract documents."

Public contracts also usually call for the initial submission of a dispute to the project architect or engineer but allow for an appeal to an administrative board which is not bound by the A/E's findings.

CASE STUDY 12-2

State awarded contract to Contractor for highway construction. The contract incorporated regulations requiring claims for additional money under the contract to be submitted to the State Highway Administrator. The Administrator's final decision could be appealed in court.

Contractor sued State for failing to relocate a pipeline as required by the contract. Contractor never submitted the claim to the Administrator. State argued that in the absence of a final decision by the Ad-ministrator, the courts had no jurisdiction to hear the claim.

The Supreme Court of North Carolina agreed with State. A contractor must exhaust the administrative remedies established in the contract before bringing its claim into court. The case was dismissed without prejudice, and Contractor was instructed to bring the claim before the Administrator. If Contractor was then dissatisfied with the Administrator's final decision, Contractor could appeal that decision in court.

Huyck Corporation v. C. C. Mangum, Inc.,
309 S.E.2d 183 (N.C. 1983).

This arrangement is appropriate. As a party intimately familiar with the overall project, the A/E is in a good position to judge the validity of the contractor's claims. It is also appropriate that the A/E, as the owner's agent and representative at the site, be given prompt notice of any contractor complaints. In practice, many claims, particularly smaller ones, are resolved by the A/E to the mutual satisfaction of the owner and the contractor.

By allowing for the resolution of any unsettled claims by an objective tribunal, however, construction contracts avoid the appearance of unfairness. The contracts recognize that while the A/E may be in the best position to have all the facts, the A/E has an inherent conflict of interest when asked to serve as the ultimate authority on disputes. The A/E's opinion may be persuasive evidence to arbitrators, jurors, or an administrative board, but it should not be binding. It must be recognized that the A/E may have a loyalty to an employer or client and may be defensive if the A/E's own conduct or work product is called into question. The two-tiered approach of an initial submittal of a claim to the A/E for a nonbinding decision, with an appeal to an objective tribunal, balances the interests and needs of all parties on the construction project.

Administrative Boards

The federal government, as well as a number of states, have created administrative boards with authority to resolve disputes between construction contractors and the public project owner. As mentioned earlier, these boards hear a large volume of claims and become quite efficient and expert at applying the standard public contract documents and resolving the disputes. The federal system serves as a model for many state claims boards and will be described as an example of the way administrative remedies are applied.

The disputes clause found in standard federal contract documents requires the contractor to first submit a claim to the "contracting officer." This is the government's designated agent and project representative. The contracting officer makes a formal decision on the contractor's claim. If the contractor is dissatisfied with the claim, it may appeal to the appropriate board of contract appeals.

Most large procuring agencies of the government have a board of contract appeals (i.e., Armed Services Board of Contract Appeals, General Services Administration Board of Contract Appeals, Interior Board of Contract Appeals, etc.). Some smaller agencies simply designate one of the other boards to hear disputes arising out of their construction contracts.

When a contracting officer's decision is appealed to a board of contract appeals, the board is not bound by any of the contracting officer's factual findings or applications of the contract language itself. The contracting officer's testimony may be persuasive evidence, but it will not be binding on the board in any way.

Once a board has made its formal, written decision, that decision may be appealed to federal court only on questions of law. The board's factual findings are final. Only an error of law may be challenged.

As a practical matter, the federal boards of contract appeals make very few errors of law. Over the years, the boards have earned an excellent reputation among contractors and others for fairness and competency. They have a large body of precedential decisions and administrative judges who possess great expertise in the field of government contract law. State administrative boards do not have the same lengthy tradition and have not yet earned the same acceptance in the construction community, but all indications are that they will become as well accepted as the federal boards. Virtually all observers agree that the administrative boards are a far superior form of dispute resolution than the old "engineer decision" clauses.

LITIGATION

Unless a private construction contract calls for binding arbitration, which will be discussed below, any disputes will probably have to be resolved in court. The choice of court will depend on the factors discussed below.

Jurisdiction

Most construction disputes are tried in one of the 50 state judicial systems. A particular state court gains jurisdiction over a case if one of the parties is based in that state or if the project itself is located in that state. If the two parties to the dispute are based in different states, there may be two state court systems which could have jurisdiction. In that situation, whichever party initiates the litigation will be able to choose the "forum," or the court which will hear the case. Generally speaking, so long as the court where the suit is initiated has proper jurisdiction, the suit will remain with that court even though there may be one or more other state court systems which could also have jurisdiction.

Federal courts gain their jurisdiction over construction disputes primarily through a doctrine known as "diversity of citizenship." If the two parties are based in different states and the amount in dispute is $10,000 or more, either party may initiate the suit in federal district court.

A special federal court, the U.S. Claims Court, hears claims of contractors who did business with the federal government. A contractor on a federal construction project may elect to bypass the board of contract appeals and appeal the contracting officer's decision directly to the Claims Court.

Finally, it is not uncommon for private construction contracts to contain a choice of forum clause. These clauses state that the contract shall be governed by the law of the state of X and all disputes arising under the contract shall be tried in the courts of the state of X. With certain limitations, these clauses are enforceable.

Advantages of Litigation

Litigation offers the opportunity to engage in very thorough, pretrial discovery of factual matters. Depositions can be taken from potential witnesses. Written interrogatories can be submitted to the other party to be answered. Documents must be produced and can be examined. In other words, a thorough attorney can learn virtually all there is to be learned regarding the factual history of the dispute. There is no excuse for being surprised in the courtroom.

Litigation also offers the opportunity to bring in additional parties and have the entire matter heard in the same forum at the same time. This is particularly important in construction disputes where three or more parties may be involved. For instance, the contractor may sue the owner for a differing site condition. The owner may feel the A/E was negligent in preparing the drawings and file a "third party complaint" against the A/E. The A/E, in turn, may feel that its geotechnical consultant is to blame for the problem and may want to bring the consultant into the suit. When there is a common factual basis for disputes involving numerous parties, it is very advantageous and efficient to have everything heard at once in the same forum. Litigation offers this opportunity. As will be seen later in this chapter, arbitration does not.

When compared with arbitration, litigation also offers the advantage of having formal legal principles stated and applied to the dispute. If the court is incorrect in its statement or application of legal principles, the litigants have an avenue of appeal. With arbitration, on the other hand, there are no formal statements of legal principles and virtually no avenue of appeal. The arbitrators' decision is final, even if they may have misunderstood the law.

Disadvantages of Litigation

The disadvantages of litigation can be summed up in two words: time and money. Depending on the jurisdiction, a complex construction dispute may take anywhere from 2 to 6 years before it reaches trial. This can be a very long time to wait for payment.

The prolonged, detailed factual discovery process also makes litigation very expensive. Huge amounts of attorneys' time are consumed during pretrial discovery and in the resolution of pretrial motions. Although this process results in great specificity and few surprises, it makes litigation a very expensive undertaking.

ARBITRATION

Arbitration is a method of dispute resolution which is created by contract. The parties to the contract agree to submit any dispute arising under the contract to binding arbitration by a third party. The parties to the contract are free to designate any arbitrator or arbitrators they choose, as well as the rules which will govern the arbitration proceeding.

The arbitration clause found at paragraph 7.9 of *AIA Document A201,* "General Conditions of the Contract for Construction" (Appendix E of this book), is the most widely used arbitration clause in the industry. It is found in a number of standard forms, and variations of this clause are frequently used in contracts which are drafted from scratch.

Note that the clause calls for binding arbitration of "all claims, disputes and other matters in question between the contractor and the owner arising out of, or relating to, the contract documents or the breach thereof...." Parties sometimes seek to avoid arbitration by arguing that the particular matter in dispute is not arbitrable because it is not covered by the arbitration clause. Courts give the broad language of this arbitration clause proper effect, however, making it difficult for a party who has signed such an agreement to avoid arbitration.

It should also be noted that the clause in *AIA Document A201* calls for arbitration "in accordance with the Construction Industry Arbitration Rules of the American Arbitration Association...." The American Arbitration Association (AAA) is a not-for-profit organization which administers arbitration proceedings and maintains a panel of prequalified individuals to serve as arbitrators. The AAA has published a detailed set of procedural rules which govern arbitration proceedings held under its auspices. The AAA is headquartered in New York City and maintains regional offices throughout the country.

Traditionally, the biggest problem with arbitration clauses was getting the parties who signed the contract to honor the clause. Many parties viewed arbitration as something they would or would not use, depending on the needs of the moment. Courts fostered this attitude by finding all kinds of reasons the arbitration clause was not in effect. For instance, courts would rule that an arbitration clause in an "executory contract," e.g., a contract where performance has not yet begun, could not be enforced. Some courts also ruled that if a party had been in breach of contract, it lost the right to enforce the arbitration clause.

These rulings created great uncertainty regarding the enforceability of arbitration clauses. In response, statutes were enacted recognizing the validity and enforceability of arbitration clauses. These statutes state that binding arbitra-

---

CASE STUDY 12-3

Construction contract consisted of an AIA form containing a standard arbitration clause. The contract stated that change orders were anticipated, but the total contract price would in no event exceed $700,000.

A dispute developed regarding extra costs, and Contractor demanded arbitration. Owner opposed arbitration, saying that Contractor was demanding money in excess of the $700,000 ceiling. Owner said these claims were for alleged work outside the scope of the construction contract and therefore not covered by the arbitration clause.

The Court of Appeals of New York ruled that all the claims were covered by the arbitration clause. Arbitration clauses are interpreted broadly to apply to any disputes arising out of the project. The fact the demand exceeded the cost ceiling did not mean the arbitration clause did not apply.

Sisters of St. John the Baptist v. Phillips R. Geraghty Constructor, Inc., 494 N.E.2d 102 (N.Y. 1986).

tion is a favored form of dispute resolution. The courts will compel parties who have signed contracts with arbitration clauses to arbitrate, and the courts will enforce the arbitrator's decision. The old grounds for avoiding arbitration have been abolished. At the federal level, the Federal Arbitration Act accomplishes this purpose. Most states have enacted a version of the Uniform Arbitration Act which accomplishes the same thing at the state level.

Advantages of Arbitration

Arbitration is a faster remedy than litigation. Generally speaking, a hearing will be held in a matter of months, rather than the years which are consumed while waiting to get to court.

Arbitration is also cheaper than litigation. The informality of the process means that less lawyer time will be involved, particularly on smaller cases. This is less true, however, on large, complex cases where investigation and preparation will consume a great deal of time regardless of whether the case is being litigated or arbitrated.

When a dispute is arbitrated, the parties know that the arbitrators will be people with experience and expertise in the construction industry. The AAA's pool of arbitrators consists of contractors, architect/engineers, and attorneys who are very conversant with the construction process and construction disputes. They speak the language. Judges and juries generally do not. This means that disputes may be resolved faster than they might be in court. It also makes arbitration an ideal forum for disputes involving the interpretation of technical documents or the application of trade customs.

Finally, the decisions of arbitrators are not published or reported anywhere. They are confidential. To some parties in some circumstances, this is important.

Disadvantages of Arbitration

As arbitration is less formal than litigation, there is less opportunity to narrow the scope of the hearing. When a dispute is arbitrated, usually everything is admitted into evidence regardless of its relevancy. This informality produces a degree of uncertainty. Surprising results can occur.

Unlike court decisions, the arbitration results cannot be appealed. Arbitrators are not required to make findings of fact or rulings of law. They may simply announce a result, such as the contractor is awarded $56,344 and the owner's counterclaim is denied. If a party feels aggrieved by the result, there is no avenue of appeal. The arbitration statutes allow courts to overturn arbitration results only in situations involving fraud, bad faith, or a conflict of interest.

Arbitration fees can be a disadvantage as well. The filing fees required by AAA are quite steep, much higher than a typical court filing fee. If the case is settled and withdrawn, the parties will not be able to get a full refund. Additionally, after the first 2 days of the arbitrators' services, the parties themselves will be responsible for compensating the arbitrators. Unlike judicial employees, arbitrators are not paid by the taxpayers.

CASE STUDY 12-4

Subcontract called for binding arbitration, with Contractor and Subcontractor each selecting one arbitrator and those two arbitrators selecting a third member of the arbitration panel.

A dispute developed and was submitted to arbitration. The arbitrators made an award in favor of Contractor. Subcontractor then learned that the arbitrator selected by Contractor was an individual who owed Contractor money and had ongoing business dealings with Contractor. Subcontractor went to court to have the arbitration award vacated.

The New Jersey Superior Court, Appellate Division, said that arbitration awards are normally not subject to appeal. A conflict of interest or evident partiality on the part of an arbitrator is a basis for reversing an award, however. The Court therefore vacated the arbitration award.

Barcon Associates, Inc. v. Tri-County Asphalt Corp., 411 A.2d 709 (N.J.App.Div. 1980).

The biggest disadvantage of arbitration, however, is the inability to get all parties into a single forum for a single hearing. When a dispute is litigated, a party who believes there are other parties who share responsibility for the problem may implead those parties into the litigation, regardless of whether or not the party had a contract with those other parties. This means that when a dispute involves a common set of facts affecting the interest of three or more parties, all parties will be heard and the conduct of all the parties will be considered when arriving at a result.

Many arbitration clauses expressly preclude the consolidation of the arbitration proceeding with any other arbitration proceeding involving a third party. This is particularly common in agreements between A/Es and project owners. The A/E does not want to get dragged into every owner-contractor dispute and therefore agrees to arbitration only on the condition that it be required to arbitrate with no one but the owner. For instance, note the prohibition of consolidation in paragraph 9.1 of *AIA Document B141,* "Standard Form of Agreement between Owner and Architect," found in Appendix C of this book.

Even when the contract does not expressly forbid consolidation, many courts refuse to compel consolidation unless it is expressly authorized in the contract or by statute.

This inability to get all involved parties together in the same forum is a serious drawback to arbitration. The problem is discussed in greater detail in the final section of this chapter.

MEDIATION

Like arbitration, mediation is a form of dispute resolution which is created by contract. The parties agree, in advance, that any disputes arising under the contract will be submitted to mediation.

CASE STUDY 12-5

Owner entered into an architectural services agreement with Architect and a construction contract with Contractor. Each contract called for arbitration under the American Arbitration Association rules. Each contract was silent regarding the consolidation of the arbitration proceeding with any other arbitration proceeding.

Contractor brought a delay claim against Owner and demanded arbitration. Owner in turn demanded arbitration with Architect, alleging that Architect's negligence caused the delay. Owner attempted to have the two arbitration proceedings consolidat-

ed, as they involved a common set of facts. Contractor opposed arbitration.

The Court of Appeals of Maryland addressed the question of whether arbitration proceedings can be consolidated in the absence of a contractual authorization or prohibition of consolidation. The Court's majority ruled that in the absence of a contractual prohibition, the arbitration proceedings could be consolidated. Three justices filed a dissenting opinion, arguing that the Court should follow the rule applied in several Western states and only order consolidation if the contract expressly authorized consolidation.

Litton Bionetics, Inc. v. Glen Construction Co., Inc.,
437 A.2d 208 (Md.App. 1981).

Unlike arbitration, mediation is not binding and final. It is not sanctioned by statute. It is simply an attempt to avoid a formal dispute by having an objective third party facilitate an amicable resolution of the dispute. If this effort fails, the parties will have to resort to a formal, binding form of dispute resolution such as litigation or arbitration.

The parties are free to designate any mediator they choose. Ideally, the mediator should be trained in facilitating dispute resolution. A number of organizations train mediators and administer mediation proceedings much as AAA administers arbitration proceedings. The largest such organization is the National Academy of Conciliators located in Washington, D.C.

Advantages and Disadvantages of Mediation

The advantages of mediation are that it is fast, inexpensive, and confidential. The disadvantage is that it is nonbinding. If an agreement cannot be worked out, the mediation proceeding will have been a waste of time and money.

THE PROBLEM OF INCONSISTENT DISPUTE PROVISIONS

The largest problem in the area of dispute resolution is the problem of inconsistent dispute provisions in the contracts among the various parties on the construction project. This problem was referred to in the section on arbitration. If all the concerned parties cannot be brought into the same forum at the same time, it is difficult for any party to achieve a prompt, economical remedy. The problem can be illustrated with the following hypothetical situation.

A project owner retains an architect to design a building. The owner-architect agreement calls for binding arbitration under the AAA rules but prohibits consolidation of the arbitration proceeding with any proceeding involving a third party. The architect designs the project and specifies certain electrical equipment.

The owner then awards a construction contract to a contractor. The construction contract does not contain an arbitration clause; so any disputes will have to be litigated in court. The contractor awards an electrical subcontract to the subcontractor, using a preprinted form which calls for binding arbitration under the AAA rules. The subcontractor issues a purchase order to the supplier for certain electrical equipment specified by the architect. The supplier insists on using its own standard terms and conditions which call for binding arbitration under the rules of its trade association and limits the supplier's liability to the purchase price of the equipment. The subcontractor acquiesces, having no other source for the specified equipment.

The electrical equipment fails to function properly, rendering the entire mechanical system inoperative. The owner files a demand for arbitration against the architect. The architect defends the action by saying there was nothing wrong with its design, so the problem must be with the manufacture of the equipment or the installation by the contractor. The owner then files suit against the contractor.

The contractor takes the position that the problem is the responsibility of the subcontractor. The contractor tries to bring a third-party complaint against the subcontractor to bring the subcontractor into the litigation. The subcontractor insists on arbitration pursuant to the terms of the subcontract and is granted a stay of litigation pending outcome of the arbitration proceeding with the contractor. The subcontractor blames the supplier for the problem and demands that the supplier join the arbitration proceeding with the subcontractor and contractor. The supplier successfully argues, however, that its arbitration clause calls for a separate proceeding under a different set of rules.

In the meantime, the litigation between owner and contractor is heating up. The contractor initiates a third-party claim against the architect alleging negligence. The owner wishes to join in this claim but is precluded from doing so by the arbitration clause in the owner-architect agreement.

It is easy to see that in this type of situation, a prompt, economical resolution of the dispute will be impossible. Once all the various matters have been heard, it is possible that there will be inconsistent results. For instance, the owner may lose its arbitration claim against the architect on the ground that the problem resulted from poor installation and not poor design. But the owner may also lose its lawsuit against the contractor if the contractor can convince a jury that the problem was caused by poor design. Or the owner may win its suit against the contractor based on a finding that the equipment was defective and the contractor was responsible for all equipment furnished to the project. The contractor, however, may not be able to pass this liability down the line to the supplier because of the convoluted nature of the dispute resolution mechanisms.

CASE STUDY 12-6

Owner awarded construction contract to Contractor. Contract contained a standard arbitration clause. Contractor then awarded a number of subcontracts, none of which included arbitration clauses.

A dispute developed, and Owner refused to pay Contractor. Contractor in turn failed to pay subcontractors. Fifteen subcontractors liened Owner's property. Owner sued Contractor for breach of contract. Contractor moved to compel arbitration.

Owner argued that it should not be required to arbitrate with Contractor while its property was exposed to the subcon-

tractors' liens. Owner said that inconsistent results might ensue, forcing Owner to make double payment. Owner complained that it was not its fault Contractor failed to include arbitration clauses in the subcontracts.

The Appellate Court of Illinois ruled that Owner must arbitrate notwithstanding the liens on the property. If Owner wanted to avoid this problem, it should have required Contractor, under the terms of the construction contract, to use only subcontractors who agreed to binding arbitration of any dispute. Having failed to do so, Owner could not avoid arbitrating with Contractor and then litigating the lien claims with the subcontractors.

J & K Cement Construction, Inc. v. Montalbano Builders, Inc.,
456 N.E.2d 889 (Ill.App. 1983).

The only way to avoid this type of problem is to give some advance consideration to the dispute resolution provisions of all the agreements. For instance, if the owner-architect agreement calls for arbitration, the owner should include an arbitration clause in the owner-contractor agreement as well. The owner should insist that none of the arbitration clauses preclude consolidation. The owner-contractor agreement should also require that the contractor include identical arbitration clauses in all its subcontracts and require its subcontractors to do the same when entering into agreements with suppliers and lower tier subcontractors.

As a practical matter, it is frequently impossible to get all the parties to agree on the same dispute resolution provision. Regardless of which method of resolution is selected, however, it is always desirable to strive for consistency.

KEY TERMS AND CONCEPTS

administrative remedies Resolution of a dispute by a designated administrative tribunal or designated individual. Administrative remedies are used only on public works construction contracts. There is generally a judicial appeal from the administrative decision which is available to dissatisfied contractors.

litigation The resolution of disputes through the use of the judicial system. State and federal statutes define the jurisdiction of the various courts, determining where lawsuits may be initiated.

arbitration A method of dispute resolution whereby the parties to a contract agree, in the contract, to submit any disputes arising out of the contract to binding arbitration.

The agreement may prescribe the method of selecting the arbitrators and the rules which will be followed during any arbitration proceeding. Arbitration awards are enforceable in court and may be appealed only on narrow grounds involving fraud or conflict of interest.

mediation   An attempt by an objective third party to negotiate or facilitate a resolution of a dispute. The recommendation of the mediator is not binding on the parties.

inconsistent dispute provisions   A problem which arises when the various contracts on a construction project call for different methods of resolving disputes. This makes it impossible to get all parties into the same forum at the same time, even though all the disputes are based on the same factual occurrences. It also increases the likelihood of inconsistent or unjust results.

PROJECT CLOSEOUT

The conclusion of a construction project is a welcome occasion for all parties involved. It involves a lot more than handshakes and ribbon cutting, however. The process of closing out a project involves matters which affect the basic rights of owner and contractor alike.

This chapter examines the crucial milestones of "substantial completion" and "final acceptance" and describes the legal effects of each. It also discusses the topic of waivers and releases, and describes the contractor's continuing warranty obligations which survive the owner's acceptance of the project.

SUBSTANTIAL COMPLETION

The concept of substantial completion is peculiar to construction contracts. With other types of contracts, each party must fully and faithfully perform every detail of the agreement. If a party "substantially" meets all its obligations but fails to complete some of the minor details of the work, it will not have complied with the contract and may be considered to be in breach of the contract. In the field of contract compliance, close is not good enough.

This doctrine created problems in the area of construction contracts. Most construction projects are so large and contain such elaborately detailed work requirements that it may be a physical impossibility to strictly comply with every requirement. In recognition of this problem, the courts developed the concept of "substantial completion" of a construction contract.

214

Definition of Substantial Completion

A construction project is substantially complete when the project owner is able to occupy the facility and use it for its intended purpose. The project must be functionally complete but need not have all the required details of work in place.

In determining whether substantial completion has been achieved, it is necessary to look at the intended purpose of the project. For instance, if the carpet and other interior finishes are not complete in an industrial facility, this may not impede the occupancy and use of that facility. The lack of carpets in a hotel or office complex would generally be considered to prevent the use of the facility for its intended purpose, however.

The legal effect of achieving substantial completion is significant. Once the contractor has reached substantial completion, it may not be considered to be in breach of the contract. This does not mean that the contractor is entitled to receive the full contract price, as will be seen below in the section on punch lists. It does mean that the contractor may not be terminated for default. The owner may withhold the money necessary to complete any unfinished items of work, but it may not terminate the contract for default and assess damages against the contractor for failure to honor its contractual commitment.

There is one other important legal ramification of achieving substantial completion. Once the project is substantially complete, the owner may no longer assess liquidated damages against the contractor for late completion. Liquidated damages are intended to compensate an owner for the lost use of the facility caused by the contractor's slow performance. If the project is substantially complete, e.g., suitable for occupancy and use for its intended purpose, the owner is no longer being harmed by loss of use. An attempt to assess liquidated damages even after the project is substantially complete makes the liquidated damages assessment look like a penalty. As discussed in Chapter 7, this calls the enforceability of the liquidated damages clause into question.

Establishing a "Punch List"

When a contractor feels it has achieved substantial completion, it usually requests the architect/engineer or other authorized owner's representative to inspect the work and certify the accomplishment of this milestone. In inspecting the work, the owner's representative makes a list of incomplete or incorrect items. This list is traditionally referred to as the "punch list," because it was common for the owner's representative to punch a hole through the item on the list with a paper punch once it was completed. Today it is more common for the parties to initial the items on the list.

As mentioned earlier, it is invariably a judgment call as to whether the contractor has achieved substantial completion. If the list of unfinished items includes things that directly affect the use and function of the project, the project may not be substantially complete. Items on a typical punch list, prepared on a substantially complete project, tend to be aesthetic in nature. Although all systems are operational, there may be items which need to be touched up or repaired. The contractor may not have turned over certain operating manuals or installed certain hardware or fixtures. These are the types of items which usually are found on a punch list.

Once it is agreed the project is substantially complete and the punch list has been established, the contractor will normally be entitled to a significant reduction in retainage. This matter is usually addressed in the contract itself. Once the project is substantially complete, the contractor is entitled to receive the contract sum less retainage sufficient to protect the owner against any outstanding obligations. Many contracts call for the owner to retain 1½ or 2 times the estimated cost of completing the punch list items. This retainage is released upon final acceptance of the project.

FINAL ACCEPTANCE OF THE PROJECT

Once the punch list is complete, the contractor requests a final inspection by the owner's representative. The scope of the inspection by the owner's representative is significant because of the legal ramifications of final acceptance.

When an owner finally accepts a project, the owner loses the right to hold the contractor responsible for defects in the work which could have been detected during a reasonable final inspection. The owner may come back to the contractor for only those "latent" defects which could not have been detected. The owner, or its representative, is only required to perform a reasonable inspection, however. It is not required to expose or uncover work which is not readily apparent to the naked eye. Nor is the owner expected to perform tests or laboratory analyses in order to detect defective work. Any problems of that nature would be considered "latent" and would not be waived by the owner's final acceptance.

CASE STUDY 13-1

Construction contract stated that Owner could retain 10 percent of the contract price until "all work" was completed. Architect certified that Contractor had achieved substantial completion. Architect prepared punch list of items for Contractor to complete.

Owner continued to hold 10 percent retainage, refusing to make further payments until Contractor completed all punch list items. Contractor sued Owner for reduction in retainage.

The Court of Appeal of Louisiana ruled in favor of Contractor, saying the contract term should not be enforced literally and that it was "unconscionable" for Owner to retain 10 percent once substantial completion was achieved. "If corrective work is required, the owner is entitled to deduct the cost of this work from the retainage and withhold it until the work is satisfactory. However, the owner is not entitled to withhold the entire retainage (in this case 10 percent of the contract price) until every minor deficiency is taken care of."

State v. Laconco, Inc.,
430 So.2d 1376 (La.App. 1983).

CASE STUDY 13-2

Owner rejected completed industrial building because the metal siding had an uneven finish when viewed from an angle in strong sunlight. Owner relied on contract clause ·giving its architect the final decision regarding "artistic effect."

In response to Contractor's suit, the U.S. Court of Appeals, Seventh Circuit, ruled that Owner was not entitled to reject the building on these grounds.

The Court said that aesthetic factors must be considered in a reasonable commercial context. The building was intended as a functional, industrial facility, not a thing of beauty. When considered in that context, Owner's rejection due to an uneven finish was unreasonable.

Morin Building Products Co., Inc. v. Baystone Construction, Inc., 717 F.2d 413 (7th Cir. 1983).

Once the final inspection has determined that the punch list is complete, the owner formally accepts the project and pays the contractor the remaining contract balance being held as retainage. At this point, the owner has released any claims against the contractor except for warranty claims, discussed below, and other claims pertaining to latent defects in the work.

Similarly, the contractor loses the right to assert claims for additional compensation against the project owner once the owner has finally accepted the project. If the contractor wants to reserve a claim to be pursued after final acceptance, it must do so in writing. The owner, in turn, may not want to close out the project with the knowledge there is an unresolved claim out there. In other words, final acceptance is the time for each party to "speak now or forever hold its peace."

The courts are not favorably disposed toward contractors who accept final payment and then try to assert a claim for additional compensation. Nor are the courts kindly disposed toward project owners who accept a project and then turn around with a claim against the contractor for a problem the owner

CASE STUDY 13-3

Owner's on-site representative inspected Contractor's installation of a roof. Contractor's work was later accepted and final payment was made.

After final acceptance and payment, Owner sued Contractor for defective workmanship in the roof installation. Contractor responded that Owner's claim had been waived by final acceptance. The California Court of Appeal agreed.

The Court said that Owner's on-site representative knew or should have known of the defects prior to final acceptance. The knowledge of Owner's agent is imputed to Owner. Therefore, Owner accepted the project with the imputed knowledge of patent, or apparent, defects and thereby waived the right to bring a claim against Contractor for those defects.

Renows, Inc. v. Hensel Phelps Construction Co., 201 Cal.Rptr. 242 (Cal.App. 1984).

CASE STUDY 13-4

Contractor completed a project. Owner inspected and accepted the project and made final payment to Contractor.

Contractor then brought a claim against Owner for additional compensation due to unforeseen site conditions encountered during construction. Owner responded that under the terms of the contract, acceptance of final payment operated as a waiver and release by Contractor of any claim relating to the contract.

The Court of Appeals of Ohio agreed with Owner. The contract made it clear that acceptance of final payment precluded Contractor from asserting any new claims. The clause, which is quite standard, is enforceable. Once Contractor accepted final payment, it could not claim any additional compensation.

Mon-Rite Construction Co., Inc. v. Northeast Ohio Regional Sewer District, 485 N.E.2d 799 (Ohio App. 1985).

should have known about prior to final acceptance. There must be closure at some point, and final acceptance is that point.

Final acceptance affects the rights of the construction lender and the surety as well. Once the project is complete, the owner may obtain long-term real estate financing at interest rates far lower than the higher-risk, shorter-term construction loan. Once the project is refinanced, the construction lender is paid off in full.

The effect of final acceptance on the contractor's performance surety is the subject of some debate, however. Traditionally, it was believed that a performance bond served only to guarantee the contractor's successful completion of the project. Once the project had been accepted by the owner, the surety's obligation on the bond ceased.

Many courts have taken the position, however, that the full and faithful performance of the contract includes the avoidance of any latent defects in the work. Therefore, if latent defects are discovered after final acceptance, and the contractor is contractually obligated to correct those defects, the surety still has a contingent obligation on the performance bond. If the contractor fails to come in and correct the latent defects, the owner may bring an action against the performance bond. This is the majority rule in the country today. It is implicitly recognized by the bonding companies who include language in their performance bonds requiring that any suit against the bond be initiated within a certain period of time (usually 1 or 2 years) after final acceptance of the project. These limitation periods stated in performance bonds are enforced against project owners.

WAIVERS AND RELEASES

One of the crucial aspects of project closeout is the furnishing of lien waivers and the exchange of releases. As these documents differ in their nature and effect, they will be discussed separately.

Lien Waivers

Before a project owner releases all retainage to the contractor, that is, makes final payment, the owner wants to be sure its property cannot be subjected to liens asserted by unpaid contractors, suppliers, or laborers.

Waiver of a prime contractor's lien rights is simple. The owner requires that the contractor's duly authorized officer execute an unequivocal full waiver and release of any and all lien rights arising under the applicable statutes. The owner obtains this waiver prior to releasing final payment to the contractor.

The release of subcontractor and supplier lien rights is more difficult. These lien rights cannot be waived by the prime contractor on behalf of the subcontractors or suppliers. The lien rights arise as a matter of law by virtue of furnishing labor or materials to the project. The rights can be waived only by the parties possessing the rights. And the project owner has no contractual relationship with those parties and therefore very little leverage.

The best course for an owner to follow is to require the prime contractor to furnish a complete list of all parties who furnished labor or materials to the project. Before the prime contractor receives its final payment, it must swear, in an affidavit, that the list is complete and that all parties on the list have been paid in full. Furthermore, the prime contractor must furnish executed full lien waivers from every party appearing on the list. Finally, the prime contractor must agree, in its lien waiver form, that it will indemnify and hold the owner harmless from any lien claims which are asserted after final payment and acceptance.

This method is not foolproof. There is always the possibility that an unpaid party far down the contractual chain will surface and assert a lien within the statutory period. As a practical matter, however, the procedure described above will give the owner adequate protection against potential lienors.

The following language is representative of the lien waiver form a project owner might ask a prime contractor to sign.

In consideration of the payment of the sum of $_____ , which sum represents the full amount of retainage and the balance of the contract price owed by the owner to the contractor, the contractor does hereby:

1 Certify to the owner that the firms, persons, corporations, or other entities listed in Attachment A are the only entities which have furnished labor or materials to the project and that each entity has been paid in full for the labor or materials provided.

2 Release, waive, and forever quitclaim unto the owner, its successors and assigns, any and all manner of liens of any nature against the property of the owner which the contractor has or may have by virtue of the labor or materials furnished by the contractor under the contract.

3 Agree to indemnify and hold the owner harmless against any loss, damage, claim, or cost, including reasonable attorney's fees, incurred by the owner due to any lien asserted by a party who alleges to have furnished labor or materials to the project.

IN WITNESS WHEREOF...

Releases

In addition to the owner's obtaining a lien waiver from the prime contractor(s) prior to final payment and acceptance, it is common for the parties to exchange reciprocal releases. As discussed earlier, final acceptance accomplishes, as a matter of law, the release of most claims either party would have against the other. Because so many claims and disputes arise during the course of a typical construction project, however, it is frequently advantageous to have explicit written releases.

These releases are very simple documents. The contractor's release is frequently combined with the lien waiver. The release language includes a blanket release of any claim, demand, or cause of action against the other party. It usually refers to, but is not limited to, any specific claims or disputes that have arisen and makes it clear that these claims are released as part of the final closeout of the project.

If either party wishes to reserve a claim which will survive final acceptance, this is the time and place to do so. Owners usually recite the fact that they are not releasing the contractor from any continuing warranty obligations under the contract.

CONTRACTOR'S CONTINUING OBLIGATIONS

After the owner's final acceptance of the project, the contractor's continuing obligations are in the form of warranties and guarantees.

Warranties

Most construction contracts include an express warranty of the materials and workmanship, usually for a period of 1 year, but sometimes longer. As de-

---

CASE STUDY 13-5

Contractor achieved substantial completion of a project and was given a punch list by Owner. Owner told Contractor, however, that Contractor would only be allowed to complete the punch list if it first signed a waiver of its lien rights.

Contractor refused to sign the lien waiver, saying it had not yet been paid in full. Owner refused to allow Contractor back on the job site and refused to make final payment. Contractor filed suit.

The Supreme Court of Minnesota ruled that Owner breached the construction contract by denying Contractor access to the site to complete the punch list. Owner had no legal right to demand a lien waiver as a precondition to Contractor's completion of its work.

Zobel & Dahl Construction v. Crotty,
356 N.W.2d 42 (Minn. 1984).

CASE STUDY 13-6

Upon completion of a construction project, Owner and Contractor settled a claim Owner had against Contractor for late performance. Owner signed a release pertaining to "all claims and causes of action the undersigned now has or hereafter may have concerning the contract which is attached hereto."

Owner later discovered structural defects in the building and filed suit against Contractor. Contractor responded that Owner's claim was barred by the release.

The Court of Appeals of Indiana ruled that the claim was barred by the release language. The release failed to state that it was limited to the Owner's delay claim. Given the unqualified language of the release, it also pertained to any other claim Owner might have.

Grimm v. F. D. Borkholder Co., Inc., 454 N.E.2d 84 (Ind.App. 1983).

---

scribed earlier, these warranties should apply only to latent defects in the work. If a problem could have been discovered during a reasonable final inspection, and the owner accepted the problem nonetheless, the owner will be deemed to have released any claim against the contractor for that problem, that is, of course, unless the owner expressly reserved the right to make the claim when accepting the project.

The contractor's obligation on the warranty is to come back onto the job site and correct any defective work brought to its attention by the owner within the warranty period. The owner has the burden, however, of showing that the problem can be traced to defective materials or workmanship. The contractor is not the guarantor of a successfully operating facility. It simply warrants that its materials and workmanship are free of defects.

The warranty is not the owner's sole remedy in the event latent problems are discovered. The warranty entitles the owner to bring the contractor back onto the job at no additional charge. The warranty does not preclude the owner from suing the contractor for damages when latent defects are discovered, even if the warranty period has expired.

Guarantees

Guarantees are essentially the same as warranties from a legal standpoint. The term "guarantee" usually refers to a particular aspect of the work where a longer-term commitment is being made by the contractor. Common examples would be the roof or the boiler system.

Items covered by a guarantee are also covered by the general 1-year warranty of materials and workmanship. The guarantee may extend several years beyond the expiration of the 1-year warranty, however. Additionally, guarantees may be covered by a guarantee bond which the contractor is required to purchase in

CASE STUDY 13-7

Construction contract included AIA Document A201, "General Conditions of the Contract for Construction." This document establishes a 1-year warranty period, during which time the contractor must return to the site and correct defective work.

More than a year after completion, Owner sued Contractor for defective work. Contractor argued that Owner should have given Contractor notice of the problem during the warranty period and Contrac-

tor would have taken care of it. Contractor contended that Owner, having failed to give notice, could not now sue for damages for defective work.

The New York Supreme Court, Appellate Division, rejected this argument. The 1-year warranty is not an exclusive remedy for the project owner who discovers defective work. If an owner chooses to ignore the warranty, this does not preclude the owner from pursuing any other legal remedies which may be available, including a suit for damages.

John W. Cowper Co., Inc. v. Buffalo Hotel Development Venture, 496 N.Y.S.2d 127 (N.Y.A.D. 1985).

order to assure the owner of a remedy in the event the contractor is not around to honor its guarantee. This is particularly common on roof guarantees.

PROJECT CLOSEOUT CHECKLIST

It is impossible to provide an exhaustive list of every detail which requires attention upon the closeout of a project. The requirements vary greatly with the nature of the job. It can almost be assumed, however, that the list will be longer than one expects.

CASE STUDY 13-8

A roofing contractor extended a 5-year guaranty on a completed roof. Contractor guaranteed the watertight integrity of the roof "without reference to or consideration of the cause or the nature of the leaks or the defects in the roofing."

The roof later leaked. It was determined that the problem resulted from the faulty design of the roof by Owner's architect. Owner demanded that Contractor

repair the roof. Contractor responded that it did not cause the problem so it was not responsible under the guaranty.

The Court of Appeals of North Carolina ruled that Contractor was responsible because the guaranty expressly pertained to all leaks, regardless of the cause. The guaranty imposed liability on Contractor which was broader than the responsibility a contractor would normally have for the sufficiency of its work.

Burke County Public Schools Board of Education v. Juno Construction Corp., 273 S.E.2d 504 (N.C.App. 1981).

Everyone is eager to close out a project promptly. The owner is eager to switch over to long-term financing at lower interest rates. The contractor wants to receive its retainage. The bonding company wants to take a contingent liability off its books. The construction lender wants to be repaid on its loan. Yet the process can take a long time.

It is necessary to plan in advance if delays are to be avoided. The following list provides some suggestions of the types of matters which must be addressed when closing out a construction project.

> Punch lists for each section of the specifications
> Warranties
> Instructions and manuals for owner
> Record drawings for owner
> Copies of all shop drawings and submittals for owner
> Samples for owner
> Keys and key schedule for owner
> Executed change orders
> Payment affidavits and lien waivers
> Copies of test reports for owner
> Release from construction lender
> Mechanical system records
> Product data and lists of spare parts
> Elevator inspection
> Fire marshall's inspection
> Sprinkler insurance inspection
> Occupancy permit
> Application for final payment
> Architect's certification of final completion
> Owner's final acceptance of project

KEY TERMS AND CONCEPTS

substantial completion   The point at which the project can be occupied by the project owner and put to beneficial use for its intended purpose. Substantial completion is achieved even though not every requirement of the contract has been strictly complied with. Once a contractor has achieved substantial completion, it cannot be held liable for breach of contract. It is entitled to the contract sum less the cost of completing or correcting the remaining work items. A contractor cannot be assessed liquidated damages after it achieves substantial completion, as liquidated damages are intended to compensate the owner for the loss of use of the project.

punch list   The items of incomplete or incorrect work which remain to be done after the contractor reaches substantial completion. The punch list items must be completed prior to final inspection and acceptance.

final inspection   The last inspection of the contractor's work by the project owner or the owner's representative. The inspection must be reasonably complete, but it need not include examination of concealed work or the testing of materials. Any defect in the work which could reasonably be observed during final inspection is considered a "patent defect." Defective work which could not reasonably be observed is considered a "latent defect."

final acceptance The project owner's acknowledgment that the punch list has been completed and the contract has been fully performed. Upon final acceptance, the owner waives the right to recover from the contractor for patent defects, but not for latent defects. The owner also assumes the risk of loss or destruction of the project. During the construction process this risk rested with the contractor, unless assumed by contract by a third-party insurer.

final payment The owner's payment of the contract balance to the contractor. This is usually concurrent with final acceptance of the project. Once the contractor accepts final payment, it waives the right to bring any claim against the owner for additional compensation unless that claim has been expressly reserved in writing as part of the final acceptance and payment process.

lien waivers Documents whereby a party which furnished labor or materials to the project waives any statutory lien rights it may have gained by virtue of its contribution to the project. When a prime contractor signs a final lien waiver, it usually also acknowledges it has been paid in full, swears that it has paid all its subcontractors and suppliers in full, and agrees to indemnify the project owner if any subcontractor or supplier asserts a lien against the owner's project.

warranty A contractor's promise that it will return to the project site and correct any latent defects in the material or workmanship that are discovered within a stipulated period of time (usually 1 year) of final acceptance. The contractor's warranty is not the owner's exclusive remedy in the event latent defects are discovered. The owner may elect to sue for damages arising from latent defects which are not corrected or are discovered after expiration of the warranty period.

INSTRUCTIONS TO BIDDERS

AIA Document A701

THE AMERICAN INSTITUTE OF ARCHITECTS

AIA Document A701

Instructions to Bidders
1978 EDITION

Use only with the 1976 Edition of AIA Document A201, General Conditions of the Contract for Construction

TABLE OF ARTICLES

1. DEFINITIONS

2. BIDDER'S REPRESENTATIONS

3. BIDDING DOCUMENTS

4. BIDDING PROCEDURES

5. CONSIDERATION OF BIDS

6. POST-BID INFORMATION

7. PERFORMANCE BOND AND
   LABOR AND MATERIAL PAYMENT BOND

8. FORM OF AGREEMENT BETWEEN OWNER
   AND CONTRACTOR

9. SUPPLEMENTARY INSTRUCTIONS

AIA DOCUMENT A701 • INSTRUCTIONS TO BIDDERS • THIRD EDITION • MAY 1978 • AIA® • ©1978
THE AMERICAN INSTITUTE OF ARCHITECTS, 1735 NEW YORK AVE., N.W., WASHINGTON, D. C. 20006

A701-1978 1

INSTRUCTIONS TO BIDDERS

ARTICLE 1

DEFINITIONS

1.1 Bidding Documents include the Advertisement or Invitation to Bid, Instructions to Bidders, the bid form, other sample bidding and contract forms and the proposed Contract Documents including any Addenda issued prior to receipt of bids. The Contract Documents proposed for the Work consist of the Owner-Contractor Agreement, the Conditions of the Contract (General, Supplementary and other Conditions), the Drawings, the Specifications and all Addenda issued prior to and all Modifications issued after execution of the Contract.

1.2 All definitions set forth in the General Conditions of the Contract for Construction, AIA Document A201, or in other Contract Documents are applicable to the Bidding Documents.

1.3 Addenda are written or graphic instruments issued by the Architect prior to the execution of the Contract which modify or interpret the Bidding Documents by additions, deletions, clarifications or corrections.

1.4 A Bid is a complete and properly signed proposal to do the Work or designated portion thereof for the sums stipulated therein, submitted in accordance with the Bidding Documents.

1.5 The Base Bid is the sum stated in the Bid for which the Bidder offers to perform the Work described in the Bidding Documents as the base, to which work may be added or from which work may be deleted for sums stated in Alternate Bids.

1.6 An Alternate Bid (or Alternate) is an amount stated in the Bid to be added to or deducted from the amount of the Base Bid if the corresponding change in the Work, as described in the Bidding Documents, is accepted.

1.7 A Unit Price is an amount stated in the Bid as a price per unit of measurement for materials or services as described in the Bidding Documents or in the proposed Contract Documents.

1.8 A Bidder is a person or entity who submits a Bid.

1.9 A Sub-bidder is a person or entity who submits a bid to a Bidder for materials or labor for a portion of the Work.

ARTICLE 2

BIDDER'S REPRESENTATIONS

2.1 Each Bidder by making his Bid represents that:

2.1.1 He has read and understands the Bidding Documents and his Bid is made in accordance therewith.

2.1.2 He has visited the site, has familiarized himself with the local conditions under which the Work is to be performed and has correlated his observations with the requirements of the proposed Contract Documents.

2.1.3 His Bid is based upon the materials, systems and equipment required by the Bidding Documents without exception.

ARTICLE 3

BIDDING DOCUMENTS

3.1   **COPIES**

3.1.1 Bidders may obtain complete sets of the Bidding Documents from the issuing office designated in the Advertisement or Invitation to Bid in the number and for the deposit sum, if any, stated therein. The deposit will be refunded to Bidders who submit a bona fide Bid and return the Bidding Documents in good condition within ten days after receipt of Bids. The cost of replacement of any missing or damaged documents will be deducted from the deposit. A Bidder receiving a Contract award may retain the Bidding Documents and his deposit will be refunded.

3.1.2 Bidding Documents will not be issued directly to Sub-bidders or others unless specifically offered in the Advertisement or Invitation to Bid.

3.1.3 Bidders shall use complete sets of Bidding Documents in preparing Bids; neither the Owner nor the Architect assume any responsibility for errors or misinterpretations resulting from the use of incomplete sets of Bidding Documents.

3.1.4 The Owner or the Architect in making copies of the Bidding Documents available on the above terms do so only for the purpose of obtaining Bids on the Work and do not confer a license or grant for any other use.

3.2   **INTERPRETATION OR CORRECTION OF BIDDING DOCUMENTS**

3.2.1 Bidders and Sub-bidders shall promptly notify the Architect of any ambiguity, inconsistency or error which they may discover upon examination of the Bidding Documents or of the site and local conditions.

3.2.2 Bidders and Sub-bidders requiring clarification or interpretation of the Bidding Documents shall make a written request which shall reach the Architect at least seven days prior to the date for receipt of Bids.

3.2.3 Any interpretation, correction or change of the Bidding Documents will be made by Addendum. Interpretations, corrections or changes of the Bidding Documents made in any other manner will not be binding, and Bidders shall not rely upon such interpretations, corrections and changes.

3.3   **SUBSTITUTIONS**

3.3.1 The materials, products and equipment described in the Bidding Documents establish a standard of required function, dimension, appearance and quality to be met by any proposed substitution.

3.3.2 No substitution will be considered prior to receipt of Bids unless written request for approval has been received by the Architect at least ten days prior to the date for receipt of Bids. Each such request shall include the name of the material or equipment for which it is to be substituted and a complete description of the proposed substitute including drawings, cuts, performance and test data and any other information necessary for an evaluation. A statement setting forth any changes in other materials, equipment or other Work that incorporation of the substitute would require shall be included. The burden of proof of the merit of the proposed substitute is upon the proposer. The Architect's decision of approval or disapproval of a proposed substitution shall be final.

3.3.3 If the Architect approves any proposed substitution prior to receipt of Bids, such approval will be set forth in an Addendum. Bidders shall not rely upon approvals made in any other manner.

3.3.4 No substitutions will be considered after the Contract award unless specifically provided in the Contract Documents.

3.4 ADDENDA

3.4.1 Addenda will be mailed or delivered to all who are known by the Architect to have received a complete set of Bidding Documents.

3.4.2 Copies of Addenda will be made available for inspection wherever Bidding Documents are on file for that purpose.

3.4.3 No Addenda will be issued later than four days prior to the date for receipt of Bids except an Addendum withdrawing the request for Bids or one which includes postponement of the date for receipt of Bids.

3.4.4 Each Bidder shall ascertain prior to submitting his bid that he has received all Addenda issued, and he shall acknowledge their receipt in his Bid.

ARTICLE 4

BIDDING PROCEDURE

4.1 FORM AND STYLE OF BIDS

4.1.1 Bids shall be submitted on forms identical to the form included with the Bidding Documents, in the quantity required by Article 9.

4.1.2 All blanks on the bid form shall be filled in by typewriter or manually in ink.

4.1.3 Where so indicated by the makeup of the bid form, sums shall be expressed in both words and figures, and in case of discrepancy between the two, the amount written in words shall govern.

4.1.4 Any interlineation, alteration or erasure must be initialed by the signer of the Bid.

4.1.5 All requested Alternates shall be bid. If no change in the Base Bid is required, enter "No Change."

4.1.6 Where two or more Bids for designated portions of the Work have been requested, the Bidder may, without forfeiture of his bid security, state his refusal to accept award of less than the combination of Bids he so stipulates. The Bidder shall make no additional stipulations on the bid form nor qualify his Bid in any other manner.

4.1.7 Each copy of the Bid shall include the legal name of the Bidder and a statement that the Bidder is a sole proprietor, a partnership, a corporation, or some other legal entity. Each copy shall be signed by the person or persons legally authorized to bind the Bidder to a contract. A Bid by a corporation shall further give the state of incorporation and have the corporate seal affixed. A Bid submitted by an agent shall have a current power of attorney attached certifying the agent's authority to bind the Bidder.

4.2 BID SECURITY

4.2.1 If so stipulated in the Advertisement or Invitation to Bid, each Bid shall be accompanied by a bid security in the form and amount required by Article 9 pledging that the Bidder will enter into a contract with the Owner on the terms stated in his Bid and will, if required, furnish bonds as described hereunder in Article 7 covering the faithful performance of the Contract and the payment of all obligations arising thereunder. Should the Bidder refuse to enter into such Contract or fail to furnish such bonds if required, the amount of the bid security shall be forfeited to the Owner as liquidated damages, not as a penalty. The amount of the bid security shall not be forfeited to the Owner in the event the Owner fails to comply with subparagraph 6.2.1.

4.2.2 If a surety bond is required it shall be written on AIA Document A310, Bid Bond, and the attorney-in-fact who executes the bond on behalf of the surety shall affix to the bond a certified and current copy of his power of attorney.

4.2.3 The Owner will have the right to retain the bid security of Bidders to whom an award is being considered until either (a) the Contract has been executed and bonds, if required, have been furnished, or (b) the specified time has elapsed so that Bids may be withdrawn, or (c) all Bids have been rejected.

4.3 SUBMISSION OF BIDS

4.3.1 All copies of the Bid, the bid security, if any, and any other documents required to be submitted with the Bid shall be enclosed in a sealed opaque envelope. The envelope shall be addressed to the party receiving the Bids and shall be identified with the Project name, the Bidder's name and address and, if applicable, the designated portion of the Work for which the Bid is submitted. If the Bid is sent by mail the sealed envelope shall be enclosed in a separate mailing envelope with the notation "SEALED BID ENCLOSED" on the face thereof.

4.3.2 Bids shall be deposited at the designated location prior to the time and date for receipt of Bids indicated in the Advertisement or Invitation to Bid, or any extension thereof made by Addendum. Bids received after the time and date for receipt of Bids will be returned unopened.

4.3.3 The Bidder shall assume full responsibility for timely delivery at the location designated for receipt of Bids.

4.3.4 Oral, telephonic or telegraphic Bids are invalid and will not receive consideration.

4.4 MODIFICATION OR WITHDRAWAL OF BID

4.4.1 A Bid may not be modified, withdrawn or canceled by the Bidder during the stipulated time period following the time and date designated for the receipt of Bids, and each Bidder so agrees in submitting his Bid.

AIA DOCUMENT A701 • INSTRUCTIONS TO BIDDERS • THIRD EDITION • MAY 1978 • AIA® • ©1978
THE AMERICAN INSTITUTE OF ARCHITECTS, 1735 NEW YORK AVE., N.W., WASHINGTON, D. C. 20006

4.4.2 Prior to the time and date designated for receipt of Bids, any Bid submitted may be modified or withdrawn by notice to the party receiving Bids at the place designated for receipt of Bids. Such notice shall be in writing over the signature of the Bidder or by telegram; if by telegram, written confirmation over the signature of the Bidder shall be mailed and postmarked on or before the date and time set for receipt of Bids, and it shall be so worded as not to reveal the amount of the original Bid.

4.4.3 Withdrawn Bids may be resubmitted up to the time designated for the receipt of Bids provided that they are then fully in conformance with these Instructions to Bidders.

4.4.4 Bid security, if any is required, shall be in an amount sufficient for the Bid as modified or resubmitted.

ARTICLE 5

CONSIDERATION OF BIDS

5.1 **OPENING OF BIDS**

5.1.1 Unless stated otherwise in the Advertisement or Invitation to Bid, the properly identified Bids received on time will be opened publicly and will be read aloud. An abstract of the Base Bids and Alternate Bids, if any, will be made available to Bidders. When it has been stated that Bids will be opened privately, an abstract of the same information may, at the discretion of the Owner, be made available to the Bidders within a reasonable time.

5.2 **REJECTION OF BIDS**

5.2.1 The Owner shall have the right to reject any or all Bids and to reject a Bid not accompanied by any required bid security or by other data required by the Bidding Documents, or to reject a Bid which is in any way incomplete or irregular.

5.3 **ACCEPTANCE OF BID (AWARD)**

5.3.1 It is the intent of the Owner to award a Contract to the lowest responsible Bidder provided the Bid has been submitted in accordance with the requirements of the Bidding Documents and does not exceed the funds available. The Owner shall have the right to waive any informality or irregularity in any Bid or Bids received and to accept the Bid or Bids which, in his judgment, is in his own best interests.

5.3.2 The Owner shall have the right to accept Alternates in any order or combination, unless otherwise specifically provided in Article 9, and to determine the low Bidder on the basis of the sum of the Base Bid and the Alternates accepted.

ARTICLE 6

POST BID INFORMATION

6.1 **CONTRACTOR'S QUALIFICATION STATEMENT**

6.1.1 Bidders to whom award of a Contract is under consideration shall submit to the Architect, upon request, a properly executed AIA Document A305, Contractor's Qualification Statement, unless such a Statement has been previously required and submitted as a prerequisite to the issuance of Bidding Documents.

6.2 **OWNER'S FINANCIAL CAPABILITY**

6.2.1 The Owner shall, at the request of the Bidder to whom award of a Contract is under consideration and no later than seven days prior to the expiration of the time for withdrawal of Bids, furnish to the Bidder reasonable evidence that the Owner has made financial arrangements to fulfill the Contract obligations. Unless such reasonable evidence is furnished, the Bidder will not be required to execute the Owner-Contractor Agreement.

6.3 **SUBMITTALS**

6.3.1 The Bidder shall, within seven days of notification of selection for the award of a Contract for the Work, submit the following information to the Architect:

.1 a designation of the Work to be performed by the Bidder with his own forces;

.2 the proprietary names and the suppliers of principal items or systems of materials and equipment proposed for the Work;

.3 a list of names of the Subcontractors or other persons or entities (including those who are to furnish materials or equipment fabricated to a special design) proposed for the principal portions of the Work.

6.3.2 The Bidder will be required to establish to the satisfaction of the Architect and the Owner the reliability and responsibility of the persons or entities proposed to furnish and perform the Work described in the Bidding Documents.

6.3.3 Prior to the award of the Contract, the Architect will notify the Bidder in writing if either the Owner or the Architect, after due investigation, has reasonable objection to any such proposed person or entity. If the Owner or Architect has reasonable objection to any such proposed person or entity, the Bidder may, at his option, (1) withdraw his Bid, or (2) submit an acceptable substitute person or entity with an adjustment in his bid price to cover the difference in cost occasioned by such substitution. The Owner may, at his discretion, accept the adjusted bid price or he may disqualify the Bidder. In the event of either withdrawal or disqualification under this Subparagraph, bid security will not be forfeited, notwithstanding the provisions of Paragraph 4.4.1.

6.3.4 Persons and entities proposed by the Bidder and to whom the Owner and the Architect have made no reasonable objection under the provisions of Subparagraph 6.3.3 must be used on the Work for which they were proposed and shall not be changed except with the written consent of the Owner and the Architect.

ARTICLE 7

PERFORMANCE BOND AND LABOR AND MATERIAL PAYMENT BOND

7.1 **BOND REQUIREMENTS**

7.1.1 Prior to execution of the Contract, if required in Article 9 hereinafter, the Bidder shall furnish bonds covering the faithful performance of the Contract and the payment of all obligations arising thereunder in such form and amount as the Owner may prescribe. Bonds may be secured through the Bidder's usual sources. If the furnishing of such bonds is stipulated hereinafter in Article 9, the cost shall be included in the Bid.

7.1.2 If the Owner has reserved the right to require that bonds be furnished subsequent to the execution of the Contract, the cost shall be adjusted as provided in the Contract Documents.

7.1.3 If the Owner requires that bonds be obtained from other than the Bidder's usual source, any change in cost will be adjusted as provided in the Contract Documents.

7.2 **TIME OF DELIVERY AND FORM OF BONDS**

7.2.1 The Bidder shall deliver the required bonds to the Owner not later than the date of execution of the Contract, or if the Work is to be commenced prior thereto in response to a letter of intent, the Bidder shall, prior to commencement of the Work, submit evidence satisfactory to the Owner that such bonds will be furnished.

7.2.2 Unless otherwise required in Article 9, the bonds shall be written on AIA Document A311, Performance Bond and Labor and Material Payment Bond.

7.2.3 The Bidder shall require the attorney-in-fact who executes the required bonds on behalf of the surety to affix thereto a certified and current copy of his power of attorney.

ARTICLE 8

FORM OF AGREEMENT BETWEEN OWNER AND CONTRACTOR

8.1 **FORM TO BE USED**

8.1.1 Unless otherwise required in the Bidding Documents, the Agreement for the Work will be written on AIA Document A101, Standard Form of Agreement Between Owner and Contractor, where the basis of payment is a Stipulated Sum.

ARTICLE 9

SUPPLEMENTARY INSTRUCTIONS

AIA DOCUMENT A701 • INSTRUCTIONS TO BIDDERS • THIRD EDITION • MAY 1978 • AIA® • ©1978
THE AMERICAN INSTITUTE OF ARCHITECTS, 1735 NEW YORK AVE., N.W., WASHINGTON, D. C. 20006

APPENDIX **B**

BID BOND

AIA Document A301

THE AMERICAN INSTITUTE OF ARCHITECTS

AIA Document A310

Bid Bond

KNOW ALL MEN BY THESE PRESENTS, that we

(Here insert full name and address or legal title of Contractor)

as Principal, hereinafter called the Principal, and

(Here insert full name and address or legal title of Surety)

a corporation duly organized under the laws of the State of
as Surety, hereinafter called the Surety, are held and firmly bound unto

(Here insert full name and address or legal title of Owner)

as Obligee, hereinafter called the Obligee, in the sum of

Dollars ($),

for the payment of which sum well and truly to be made, the said Principal and the said Surety, bind ourselves, our heirs, executors, administrators, successors and assigns, jointly and severally, firmly by these presents.

WHEREAS, the Principal has submitted a bid for

(Here insert full name, address and description of project)

NOW, THEREFORE, if the Obligee shall accept the bid of the Principal and the Principal shall enter into a Contract with the Obligee in accordance with the terms of such bid, and give such bond or bonds as may be specified in the bidding or Contract Documents with good and sufficient surety for the faithful performance of such Contract and for the prompt payment of labor and material furnished in the prosecution thereof, or in the event of the failure of the Principal to enter such Contract and give such bond or bonds, if the Principal shall pay to the Obligee the difference not to exceed the penalty hereof between the amount specified in said bid and such larger amount for which the Obligee may in good faith contract with another party to perform the Work covered by said bid, then this obligation shall be null and void, otherwise to remain in full force and effect.

Signed and sealed this   day of   19

_____
(Witness)

_____ (Principal)   (Seal)

_____
(Title)

_____
(Witness)

_____ (Surety)   (Seal)

_____
(Title)

AIA DOCUMENT A310 · BID BOND · AIA ® · FEBRUARY 1970 ED · THE AMERICAN INSTITUTE OF ARCHITECTS, 1735 N.Y. AVE., N.W., WASHINGTON, D. C. 20006

1

STANDARD FORM OF AGREEMENT BETWEEN OWNER AND ARCHITECT

AIA Document B141

THE AMERICAN INSTITUTE OF ARCHITECTS

AIA Document B141

Standard Form of Agreement Between Owner and Architect

1977 EDITION

*THIS DOCUMENT HAS IMPORTANT LEGAL CONSEQUENCES; CONSULTATION WITH
AN ATTORNEY IS ENCOURAGED WITH RESPECT TO ITS COMPLETION OR MODIFICATION*

AGREEMENT

made as of the   day of   in the year of Nineteen
Hundred and

BETWEEN the Owner:

and the Architect:

For the following Project:
(Include detailed description of Project location and scope.)

The Owner and the Architect agree as set forth below.

AIA DOCUMENT B141 • OWNER-ARCHITECT AGREEMENT • THIRTEENTH EDITION • JULY 1977 • AIA® • © 1977
THE AMERICAN INSTITUTE OF ARCHITECTS, 1735 NEW YORK AVENUE, N.W., WASHINGTON, D.C. 20006   **B141-1977 1**

[Page 2 is blank]

TERMS AND CONDITIONS OF AGREEMENT BETWEEN OWNER AND ARCHITECT

ARTICLE 1
ARCHITECT'S SERVICES AND RESPONSIBILITIES

BASIC SERVICES

The Architect's Basic Services consist of the five phases described in Paragraphs 1.1 through 1.5 and include normal structural, mechanical and electrical engineering services and any other services included in Article 15 as part of Basic Services.

1.1   SCHEMATIC DESIGN PHASE

1.1.1   The Architect shall review the program furnished by the Owner to ascertain the requirements of the Project and shall review the understanding of such requirements with the Owner.

1.1.2   The Architect shall provide a preliminary evaluation of the program and the Project budget requirements, each in terms of the other, subject to the limitations set forth in Subparagraph 3.2.1.

1.1.3   The Architect shall review with the Owner alternative approaches to design and construction of the Project.

1.1.4   Based on the mutually agreed upon program and Project budget requirements, the Architect shall prepare, for approval by the Owner, Schematic Design Documents consisting of drawings and other documents illustrating the scale and relationship of Project components.

1.1.5   The Architect shall submit to the Owner a Statement of Probable Construction Cost based on current area, volume or other unit costs.

1.2   DESIGN DEVELOPMENT PHASE

1.2.1   Based on the approved Schematic Design Documents and any adjustments authorized by the Owner in the program or Project budget, the Architect shall prepare, for approval by the Owner, Design Development Documents consisting of drawings and other documents to fix and describe the size and character of the entire Project as to architectural, structural, mechanical and electrical systems, materials and such other elements as may be appropriate.

1.2.2   The Architect shall submit to the Owner a further Statement of Probable Construction Cost.

1.3   CONSTRUCTION DOCUMENTS PHASE

1.3.1   Based on the approved Design Development Documents and any further adjustments in the scope or quality of the Project or in the Project budget authorized by the Owner, the Architect shall prepare, for approval by the Owner, Construction Documents consisting of Drawings and Specifications setting forth in detail the requirements for the construction of the Project.

1.3.2   The Architect shall assist the Owner in the preparation of the necessary bidding information, bidding forms, the Conditions of the Contract, and the form of Agreement between the Owner and the Contractor.

1.3.3   The Architect shall advise the Owner of any adjust-

ments to previous Statements of Probable Construction Cost indicated by changes in requirements or general market conditions.

1.3.4   The Architect shall assist the Owner in connection with the Owner's responsibility for filing documents required for the approval of governmental authorities having jurisdiction over the Project.

1.4   BIDDING OR NEGOTIATION PHASE

1.4.1   The Architect, following the Owner's approval of the Construction Documents and of the latest Statement of Probable Construction Cost, shall assist the Owner in obtaining bids or negotiated proposals, and assist in awarding and preparing contracts for construction.

1.5   CONSTRUCTION PHASE—ADMINISTRATION OF THE CONSTRUCTION CONTRACT

1.5.1   The Construction Phase will commence with the award of the Contract for Construction and, together with the Architect's obligation to provide Basic Services under this Agreement, will terminate when final payment to the Contractor is due, or in the absence of a final Certificate for Payment or of such due date, sixty days after the Date of Substantial Completion of the Work, whichever occurs first.

1.5.2   Unless otherwise provided in this Agreement and incorporated in the Contract Documents, the Architect shall provide administration of the Contract for Construction as set forth below and in the edition of AIA Document A201, General Conditions of the Contract for Construction, current as of the date of this Agreement.

1.5.3   The Architect shall be a representative of the Owner during the Construction Phase, and shall advise and consult with the Owner. Instructions to the Contractor shall be forwarded through the Architect. The Architect shall have authority to act on behalf of the Owner only to the extent provided in the Contract Documents unless otherwise modified by written instrument in accordance with Subparagraph 1.5.16.

1.5.4   The Architect shall visit the site at intervals appropriate to the stage of construction or as otherwise agreed by the Architect in writing to become generally familiar with the progress and quality of the Work and to determine in general if the Work is proceeding in accordance with the Contract Documents. However, the Architect shall not be required to make exhaustive or continuous on-site inspections to check the quality or quantity of the Work. On the basis of such on-site observations as an architect, the Architect shall keep the Owner informed of the progress and quality of the Work, and shall endeavor to guard the Owner against defects and deficiencies in the Work of the Contractor.

1.5.5   The Architect shall not have control or charge of and shall not be responsible for construction means, methods, techniques, sequences or procedures, or for safety precautions and programs in connection with the Work, for the acts or omissions of the Contractor, Subcontractors or any other persons performing any of the Work, or for the failure of any of them to carry out the Work in accordance with the Contract Documents.

1.5.6 The Architect shall at all times have access to the Work wherever it is in preparation or progress.

1.5.7 The Architect shall determine the amounts owing to the Contractor based on observations at the site and on evaluations of the Contractor's Applications for Payment, and shall issue Certificates for Payment in such amounts, as provided in the Contract Documents.

1.5.8 The issuance of a Certificate for Payment shall constitute a representation by the Architect to the Owner, based on the Architect's observations at the site as provided in Subparagraph 1.5.4 and on the data comprising the Contractor's Application for Payment, that the Work has progressed to the point indicated; that, to the best of the Architect's knowledge, information and belief, the quality of the Work is in accordance with the Contract Documents (subject to an evaluation of the Work for conformance with the Contract Documents upon Substantial Completion, to the results of any subsequent tests required by or performed under the Contract Documents, to minor deviations from the Contract Documents correctable prior to completion, and to any specific qualifications stated in the Certificate for Payment), and that the Contractor is entitled to payment in the amount certified. However, the issuance of a Certificate for Payment shall not be a representation that the Architect has made any examination to ascertain how and for what purpose the Contractor has used the moneys paid on account of the Contract Sum.

1.5.9 The Architect shall be the interpreter of the requirements of the Contract Documents and the judge of the performance thereunder by both the Owner and Contractor. The Architect shall render interpretations necessary for the proper execution or progress of the Work with reasonable promptness on written request of either the Owner or the Contractor, and shall render written decisions, within a reasonable time, on all claims, disputes and other matters in question between the Owner and the Contractor relating to the execution or progress of the Work or the interpretation of the Contract Documents.

1.5.10 Interpretations and decisions of the Architect shall be consistent with the intent of and reasonably inferable from the Contract Documents and shall be in written or graphic form. In the capacity of interpreter and judge, the Architect shall endeavor to secure faithful performance by both the Owner and the Contractor, shall not show partiality to either, and shall not be liable for the result of any interpretation or decision rendered in good faith in such capacity.

1.5.11 The Architect's decisions in matters relating to artistic effect shall be final if consistent with the intent of the Contract Documents. The Architect's decisions on any other claims, disputes or other matters, including those in question between the Owner and the Contractor, shall be subject to arbitration as provided in this Agreement and in the Contract Documents.

1.5.12 The Architect shall have authority to reject Work which does not conform to the Contract Documents. Whenever, in the Architect's reasonable opinion, it is

necessary or advisable for the implementation of the intent of the Contract Documents, the Architect will have authority to require special inspection or testing of the Work in accordance with the provisions of the Contract Documents, whether or not such Work be then fabricated, installed or completed.

1.5.13 The Architect shall review and approve or take other appropriate action upon the Contractor's submittals such as Shop Drawings, Product Data and Samples, but only for conformance with the design concept of the Work and with the information given in the Contract Documents. Such action shall be taken with reasonable promptness so as to cause no delay. The Architect's approval of a specific item shall not indicate approval of an assembly of which the item is a component.

1.5.14 The Architect shall prepare Change Orders for the Owner's approval and execution in accordance with the Contract Documents, and shall have authority to order minor changes in the Work not involving an adjustment in the Contract Sum or an extension of the Contract Time which are not inconsistent with the intent of the Contract Documents.

1.5.15 The Architect shall conduct inspections to determine the Dates of Substantial Completion and final completion, shall receive and forward to the Owner for the Owner's review written warranties and related documents required by the Contract Documents and assembled by the Contractor, and shall issue a final Certificate for Payment.

1.5.16 The extent of the duties, responsibilities and limitations of authority of the Architect as the Owner's representative during construction shall not be modified or extended without written consent of the Owner, the Contractor and the Architect.

1.6 PROJECT REPRESENTATION BEYOND BASIC SERVICES

1.6.1 If the Owner and Architect agree that more extensive representation at the site than is described in Paragraph 1.5 shall be provided, the Architect shall provide one or more Project Representatives to assist the Architect in carrying out such responsibilities at the site.

1.6.2 Such Project Representatives shall be selected, employed and directed by the Architect, and the Architect shall be compensated therefor as mutually agreed between the Owner and the Architect as set forth in an exhibit appended to this Agreement, which shall describe the duties, responsibilities and limitations of authority of such Project Representatives.

1.6.3 Through the observations by such Project Representatives, the Architect shall endeavor to provide further protection for the Owner against defects and deficiencies in the Work, but the furnishing of such project representation shall not modify the rights, responsibilities or obligations of the Architect as described in Paragraph 1.5.

1.7 ADDITIONAL SERVICES

The following Services are not included in Basic Services unless so identified in Article 15. They shall be provided if authorized or confirmed in writing by the Owner, and they shall be paid for by the Owner as provided in this Agreement, in addition to the compensation for Basic Services.

AIA DOCUMENT B141 • OWNER-ARCHITECT AGREEMENT • THIRTEENTH EDITION • JULY 1977 • AIA® • © 1977
THE AMERICAN INSTITUTE OF ARCHITECTS, 1735 NEW YORK AVENUE, N.W., WASHINGTON, D.C. 20006

1.7.1 Providing analyses of the Owner's needs, and programming the requirements of the Project.

1.7.2 Providing financial feasibility or other special studies.

1.7.3 Providing planning surveys, site evaluations, environmental studies or comparative studies of prospective sites, and preparing special surveys, studies and submissions required for approvals of governmental authorities or others having jurisdiction over the Project.

1.7.4 Providing services relative to future facilities, systems and equipment which are not intended to be constructed during the Construction Phase.

1.7.5 Providing services to investigate existing conditions or facilities or to make measured drawings thereof, or to verify the accuracy of drawings or other information furnished by the Owner.

1.7.6 Preparing documents of alternate, separate or sequential bids or providing extra services in connection with bidding, negotiation or construction prior to the completion of the Construction Documents Phase, when requested by the Owner.

1.7.7 Providing coordination of Work performed by separate contractors or by the Owner's own forces.

1.7.8 Providing services in connection with the work of a construction manager or separate consultants retained by the Owner.

1.7.9 Providing Detailed Estimates of Construction Cost, analyses of owning and operating costs, or detailed quantity surveys or inventories of material, equipment and labor.

1.7.10 Providing interior design and other similar services required for or in connection with the selection, procurement or installation of furniture, furnishings and related equipment.

1.7.11 Providing services for planning tenant or rental spaces.

1.7.12 Making revisions in Drawings, Specifications or other documents when such revisions are inconsistent with written approvals or instructions previously given, are required by the enactment or revision of codes, laws or regulations subsequent to the preparation of such documents or are due to other causes not solely within the control of the Architect.

1.7.13 Preparing Drawings, Specifications and supporting data and providing other services in connection with Change Orders to the extent that the adjustment in the Basic Compensation resulting from the adjusted Construction Cost is not commensurate with the services required of the Architect, provided such Change Orders are required by causes not solely within the control of the Architect.

1.7.14 Making investigations, surveys, valuations, inventories or detailed appraisals of existing facilities, and services required in connection with construction performed by the Owner.

1.7.15 Providing consultation concerning replacement of any Work damaged by fire or other cause during con-

struction, and furnishing services as may be required in connection with the replacement of such Work.

1.7.16 Providing services made necessary by the default of the Contractor, or by major defects or deficiencies in the Work of the Contractor, or by failure of performance of either the Owner or Contractor under the Contract for Construction.

1.7.17 Preparing a set of reproducible record drawings showing significant changes in the Work made during construction based on marked-up prints, drawings and other data furnished by the Contractor to the Architect.

1.7.18 Providing extensive assistance in the utilization of any equipment or system such as initial start-up or testing, adjusting and balancing, preparation of operation and maintenance manuals, training personnel for operation and maintenance, and consultation during operation.

1.7.19 Providing services after issuance to the Owner of the final Certificate for Payment, or in the absence of a final Certificate for Payment, more than sixty days after the Date of Substantial Completion of the Work.

1.7.20 Preparing to serve or serving as an expert witness in connection with any public hearing, arbitration proceeding or legal proceeding.

1.7.21 Providing services of consultants for other than the normal architectural, structural, mechanical and electrical engineering services for the Project.

1.7.22 Providing any other services not otherwise included in this Agreement or not customarily furnished in accordance with generally accepted architectural practice.

1.8 TIME

1.8.1 The Architect shall perform Basic and Additional Services as expeditiously as is consistent with professional skill and care and the orderly progress of the Work. Upon request of the Owner, the Architect shall submit for the Owner's approval a schedule for the performance of the Architect's services which shall be adjusted as required as the Project proceeds, and shall include allowances for periods of time required for the Owner's review and approval of submissions and for approvals of authorities having jurisdiction over the Project. This schedule, when approved by the Owner, shall not, except for reasonable cause, be exceeded by the Architect.

ARTICLE 2

THE OWNER'S RESPONSIBILITIES

2.1 The Owner shall provide full information regarding requirements for the Project including a program, which shall set forth the Owner's design objectives, constraints and criteria, including space requirements and relationships, flexibility and expandability, special equipment and systems and site requirements.

2.2 If the Owner provides a budget for the Project it shall include contingencies for bidding, changes in the Work during construction, and other costs which are the responsibility of the Owner, including those described in this Article 2 and in Subparagraph 3.1.2. The Owner shall, at the request of the Architect, provide a statement of funds available for the Project, and their source.

2.3 The Owner shall designate, when necessary, a representative authorized to act in the Owner's behalf with respect to the Project. The Owner or such authorized representative shall examine the documents submitted by the Architect and shall render decisions pertaining thereto promptly, to avoid unreasonable delay in the progress of the Architect's services.

2.4 The Owner shall furnish a legal description and a certified land survey of the site, giving, as applicable, grades and lines of streets, alleys, pavements and adjoining property; rights-of-way, restrictions, easements, encroachments, zoning, deed restrictions, boundaries and contours of the site; locations, dimensions and complete data pertaining to existing buildings, other improvements and trees; and full information concerning available service and utility lines both public and private, above and below grade, including inverts and depths.

2.5 The Owner shall furnish the services of soil engineers or other consultants when such services are deemed necessary by the Architect. Such services shall include test borings, test pits, soil bearing values, percolation tests, air and water pollution tests, ground corrosion and resistivity tests, including necessary operations for determining subsoil, air and water conditions, with reports and appropriate professional recommendations.

2.6 The Owner shall furnish structural, mechanical, chemical and other laboratory tests, inspections and reports as required by law or the Contract Documents.

2.7 The Owner shall furnish all legal, accounting and insurance counseling services as may be necessary at any time for the Project, including such auditing services as the Owner may require to verify the Contractor's Applications for Payment or to ascertain how or for what purposes the Contractor uses the moneys paid by or on behalf of the Owner.

2.8 The services, information, surveys and reports required by Paragraphs 2.4 through 2.7 inclusive shall be furnished at the Owner's expense, and the Architect shall be entitled to rely upon the accuracy and completeness thereof.

2.9 If the Owner observes or otherwise becomes aware of any fault or defect in the Project or nonconformance with the Contract Documents, prompt written notice thereof shall be given by the Owner to the Architect.

2.10 The Owner shall furnish required information and services and shall render approvals and decisions as expeditiously as necessary for the orderly progress of the Architect's services and of the Work.

ARTICLE 3

CONSTRUCTION COST

3.1 DEFINITION

3.1.1 The Construction Cost shall be the total cost or estimated cost to the Owner of all elements of the Project designed or specified by the Architect.

3.1.2 The Construction Cost shall include at current market rates, including a reasonable allowance for overhead and profit, the cost of labor and materials furnished by the Owner and any equipment which has been de-

signed, specified, selected or specially provided for by the Architect.

3.1.3 Construction Cost does not include the compensation of the Architect and the Architect's consultants, the cost of the land, rights-of-way, or other costs which are the responsibility of the Owner as provided in Article 2.

3.2 RESPONSIBILITY FOR CONSTRUCTION COST

3.2.1 Evaluations of the Owner's Project budget, Statements of Probable Construction Cost and Detailed Estimates of Construction Cost, if any, prepared by the Architect, represent the Architect's best judgment as a design professional familiar with the construction industry. It is recognized, however, that neither the Architect nor the Owner has control over the cost of labor, materials or equipment, over the Contractor's methods of determining bid prices, or over competitive bidding, market or negotiating conditions. Accordingly, the Architect cannot and does not warrant or represent that bids or negotiated prices will not vary from the Project budget proposed, established or approved by the Owner, if any, or from any Statement of Probable Construction Cost or other cost estimate or evaluation prepared by the Architect.

3.2.2 No fixed limit of Construction Cost shall be established as a condition of this Agreement by the furnishing, proposal or establishment of a Project budget under Subparagraph 1.1.2 or Paragraph 2.2 or otherwise, unless such fixed limit has been agreed upon in writing and signed by the parties hereto. If such a fixed limit has been established, the Architect shall be permitted to include contingencies for design, bidding and price escalation, to determine what materials, equipment, component systems and types of construction are to be included in the Contract Documents, to make reasonable adjustments in the scope of the Project and to include in the Contract Documents alternate bids to adjust the Construction Cost to the fixed limit. Any such fixed limit shall be increased in the amount of any increase in the Contract Sum occurring after execution of the Contract for Construction.

3.2.3 If the Bidding or Negotiation Phase has not commenced within three months after the Architect submits the Construction Documents to the Owner, any Project budget or fixed limit of Construction Cost shall be adjusted to reflect any change in the general level of prices in the construction industry between the date of submission of the Construction Documents to the Owner and the date on which proposals are sought.

3.2.4 If a Project budget or fixed limit of Construction Cost (adjusted as provided in Subparagraph 3.2.3) is exceeded by the lowest bona fide bid or negotiated proposal, the Owner shall (1) give written approval of an increase in such fixed limit, (2) authorize rebidding or renegotiating of the Project within a reasonable time, (3) if the Project is abandoned, terminate in accordance with Paragraph 10.2, or (4) cooperate in revising the Project scope and quality as required to reduce the Construction Cost. In the case of (4), provided a fixed limit of Construction Cost has been established as a condition of this Agreement, the Architect, without additional charge, shall modify the Drawings and Specifications as necessary to comply

AIA DOCUMENT B141 • OWNER-ARCHITECT AGREEMENT • THIRTEENTH EDITION • JULY 1977 • AIA® • © 1977
THE AMERICAN INSTITUTE OF ARCHITECTS, 1735 NEW YORK AVENUE, N.W., WASHINGTON, D.C. 20006

with the fixed limit. The providing of such service shall be the limit of the Architect's responsibility arising from the establishment of such fixed limit, and having done so, the Architect shall be entitled to compensation for all services performed, in accordance with this Agreement, whether or not the Construction Phase is commenced.

ARTICLE 4

DIRECT PERSONNEL EXPENSE

4.1 Direct Personnel Expense is defined as the direct salaries of all the Architect's personnel engaged on the Project, and the portion of the cost of their mandatory and customary contributions and benefits related thereto, such as employment taxes and other statutory employee benefits, insurance, sick leave, holidays, vacations, pensions and similar contributions and benefits.

ARTICLE 5

REIMBURSABLE EXPENSES

5.1 Reimbursable Expenses are in addition to the Compensation for Basic and Additional Services and include actual expenditures made by the Architect and the Architect's employees and consultants in the interest of the Project for the expenses listed in the following subparagraphs:

5.1.1 Expense of transportation in connection with the Project; living expenses in connection with out-of-town travel; long distance communications; and fees paid for securing approval of authorities having jurisdiction over the Project.

5.1.2 Expense of reproductions, postage and handling of Drawings, Specifications and other documents, excluding reproductions for the office use of the Architect and the Architect's consultants.

5.1.3 Expense of data processing and photographic production techniques when used in connection with Additional Services.

5.1.4 If authorized in advance by the Owner, expense of overtime work requiring higher than regular rates.

5.1.5 Expense of renderings, models and mock-ups requested by the Owner.

5.1.6 Expense of any additional insurance coverage or limits, including professional liability insurance, requested by the Owner in excess of that normally carried by the Architect and the Architect's consultants.

ARTICLE 6

PAYMENTS TO THE ARCHITECT

6.1 PAYMENTS ON ACCOUNT OF BASIC SERVICES

6.1.1 An initial payment as set forth in Paragraph 14.1 is the minimum payment under this Agreement.

6.1.2 Subsequent payments for Basic Services shall be made monthly and shall be in proportion to services performed within each Phase of services, on the basis set forth in Article 14.

6.1.3 If and to the extent that the Contract Time initially established in the Contract for Construction is exceeded or extended through no fault of the Architect, compensation for any Basic Services required for such extended period of Administration of the Construction Contract shall be computed as set forth in Paragraph 14.4 for Additional Services.

6.1.4 When compensation is based on a percentage of Construction Cost, and any portions of the Project are deleted or otherwise not constructed, compensation for such portions of the Project shall be payable to the extent services are performed on such portions, in accordance with the schedule set forth in Subparagraph 14.2.2, based on (1) the lowest bona fide bid or negotiated proposal or, (2) if no such bid or proposal is received, the most recent Statement of Probable Construction Cost or Detailed Estimate of Construction Cost for such portions of the Project.

6.2 PAYMENTS ON ACCOUNT OF ADDITIONAL SERVICES

6.2.1 Payments on account of the Architect's Additional Services as defined in Paragraph 1.7 and for Reimbursable Expenses as defined in Article 5 shall be made monthly upon presentation of the Architect's statement of services rendered or expenses incurred.

6.3 PAYMENTS WITHHELD

6.3.1 No deductions shall be made from the Architect's compensation on account of penalty, liquidated damages or other sums withheld from payments to contractors, or on account of the cost of changes in the Work other than those for which the Architect is held legally liable.

6.4 PROJECT SUSPENSION OR TERMINATION

6.4.1 If the Project is suspended or abandoned in whole or in part for more than three months, the Architect shall be compensated for all services performed prior to receipt of written notice from the Owner of such suspension or abandonment, together with Reimbursable Expenses then due and all Termination Expenses as defined in Paragraph 10.4. If the Project is resumed after being suspended for more than three months, the Architect's compensation shall be equitably adjusted.

ARTICLE 7

ARCHITECT'S ACCOUNTING RECORDS

7.1 Records of Reimbursable Expenses and expenses pertaining to Additional Services and services performed on the basis of a Multiple of Direct Personnel Expense shall be kept on the basis of generally accepted accounting principles and shall be available to the Owner or the Owner's authorized representative at mutually convenient times.

ARTICLE 8

OWNERSHIP AND USE OF DOCUMENTS

8.1 Drawings and Specifications as instruments of service are and shall remain the property of the Architect whether the Project for which they are made is executed or not. The Owner shall be permitted to retain copies, including reproducible copies, of Drawings and Specifications for information and reference in connection with the Owner's use and occupancy of the Project. The Drawings and Specifications shall not be used by the Owner on other projects, for additions to this Project, or for completion of this Project by others provided the Architect is not in default under this Agreement, except by agreement in writing and with appropriate compensation to the Architect.

8.2 Submission or distribution to meet official regulatory requirements or for other purposes in connection with the Project is not to be construed as publication in derogation of the Architect's rights.

ARTICLE 9

ARBITRATION

9.1 All claims, disputes and other matters in question between the parties to this Agreement, arising out of or relating to this Agreement or the breach thereof, shall be decided by arbitration in accordance with the Construction Industry Arbitration Rules of the American Arbitration Association then obtaining unless the parties mutually agree otherwise. No arbitration, arising out of or relating to this Agreement, shall include, by consolidation, joinder or in any other manner, any additional person not a party to this Agreement except by written consent containing a specific reference to this Agreement and signed by the Architect, the Owner, and any other person sought to be joined. Any consent to arbitration involving an additional person or persons shall not constitute consent to arbitration of any dispute not described therein or with any person not named or described therein. This Agreement to arbitrate and any agreement to arbitrate with an additional person or persons duly consented to by the parties to this Agreement shall be specifically enforceable under the prevailing arbitration law.

9.2 Notice of the demand for arbitration shall be filed in writing with the other party to this Agreement and with the American Arbitration Association. The demand shall be made within a reasonable time after the claim, dispute or other matter in question has arisen. In no event shall the demand for arbitration be made after the date when institution of legal or equitable proceedings based on such claim, dispute or other matter in question would be barred by the applicable statute of limitations.

9.3 The award rendered by the arbitrators shall be final, and judgment may be entered upon it in accordance with applicable law in any court having jurisdiction thereof.

ARTICLE 10

TERMINATION OF AGREEMENT

10.1 This Agreement may be terminated by either party upon seven days' written notice should the other party fail substantially to perform in accordance with its terms through no fault of the party initiating the termination.

10.2 This Agreement may be terminated by the Owner upon at least seven days' written notice to the Architect in the event that the Project is permanently abandoned.

10.3 In the event of termination not the fault of the Architect, the Architect shall be compensated for all services performed to termination date, together with Reimbursable Expenses then due and all Termination Expenses as defined in Paragraph 10.4.

10.4 Termination Expenses include expenses directly attributable to termination for which the Architect is not otherwise compensated, plus an amount computed as a percentage of the total Basic and Additional Compensation earned to the time of termination, as follows:

- **.1** 20 percent if termination occurs during the Schematic Design Phase; or
- **.2** 10 percent if termination occurs during the Design Development Phase; or
- **.3** 5 percent if termination occurs during any subsequent phase.

ARTICLE 11

MISCELLANEOUS PROVISIONS

11.1 Unless otherwise specified, this Agreement shall be governed by the law of the principal place of business of the Architect.

11.2 Terms in this Agreement shall have the same meaning as those in AIA Document A201, General Conditions of the Contract for Construction, current as of the date of this Agreement.

11.3 As between the parties to this Agreement: as to all acts or failures to act by either party to this Agreement, any applicable statute of limitations shall commence to run and any alleged cause of action shall be deemed to have accrued in any and all events not later than the relevant Date of Substantial Completion of the Work, and as to any acts or failures to act occurring after the relevant Date of Substantial Completion, not later than the date of issuance of the final Certificate for Payment.

11.4 The Owner and the Architect waive all rights against each other and against the contractors, consultants, agents and employees of the other for damages covered by any property insurance during construction as set forth in the edition of AIA Document A201, General Conditions, current as of the date of this Agreement. The Owner and the Architect each shall require appropriate similar waivers from their contractors, consultants and agents.

ARTICLE 12

SUCCESSORS AND ASSIGNS

12.1 The Owner and the Architect, respectively, bind themselves, their partners, successors, assigns and legal representatives to the other party to this Agreement and to the partners, successors, assigns and legal representatives of such other party with respect to all covenants of this Agreement. Neither the Owner nor the Architect shall assign, sublet or transfer any interest in this Agreement without the written consent of the other.

ARTICLE 13

EXTENT OF AGREEMENT

13.1 This Agreement represents the entire and integrated agreement between the Owner and the Architect and supersedes all prior negotiations, representations or agreements, either written or oral. This Agreement may be amended only by written instrument signed by both Owner and Architect.

AIA DOCUMENT B141 • OWNER-ARCHITECT AGREEMENT • THIRTEENTH EDITION • JULY 1977 • AIA® • © 1977
THE AMERICAN INSTITUTE OF ARCHITECTS, 1735 NEW YORK AVENUE, N.W., WASHINGTON, D.C. 20006

ARTICLE 14

BASIS OF COMPENSATION

The Owner shall compensate the Architect for the Scope of Services provided, in accordance with Article 6, Payments to the Architect, and the other Terms and Conditions of this Agreement, as follows:

14.1 AN INITIAL PAYMENT of   dollars ($

shall be made upon execution of this Agreement and credited to the Owner's account as follows:

14.2 BASIC COMPENSATION

14.2.1 FOR BASIC SERVICES, as described in Paragraphs 1.1 through 1.5, and any other services included in Article 15 as part of Basic Services, Basic Compensation shall be computed as follows:

(Here insert basis of compensation, including fixed amounts, multiples or percentages, and identify Phases to which particular methods of compensation apply, if necessary.)

14.2.2 Where compensation is based on a Stipulated Sum or Percentage of Construction Cost, payments for Basic Services shall be made as provided in Subparagraph 6.1.2, so that Basic Compensation for each Phase shall equal the following percentages of the total Basic Compensation payable:

(Include any additional Phases as appropriate.)

Schematic Design Phase:	percent (%)
Design Development Phase:	percent (%)
Construction Documents Phase:	percent (%)
Bidding or Negotiation Phase:	percent (%)
Construction Phase:	percent (%)

14.3 FOR PROJECT REPRESENTATION BEYOND BASIC SERVICES, as described in Paragraph 1.6, Compensation shall be computed separately in accordance with Subparagraph 1.6.2.

14.4 COMPENSATION FOR ADDITIONAL SERVICES

14.4.1 FOR ADDITIONAL SERVICES OF THE ARCHITECT, as described in Paragraph 1.7, and any other services included in Article 15 as part of Additional Services, but excluding Additional Services of consultants, Compensation shall be computed as follows:

(Here insert basis of compensation, including rates and/or multiples of Direct Personnel Expense for Principals and employees, and identify Principals and classify employees, if required. Identify specific services to which particular methods of compensation apply, if necessary.)

14.4.2 FOR ADDITIONAL SERVICES OF CONSULTANTS, including additional structural, mechanical and electrical engineering services and those provided under Subparagraph 1.7.21 or identified in Article 15 as part of Additional Services, a multiple of ( ) times the amounts billed to the Architect for such services.

(Identify specific types of consultants in Article 15, if required.)

14.5 FOR REIMBURSABLE EXPENSES, as described in Article 5, and any other items included in Article 15 as Reimbursable Expenses, a multiple of ( ) times the amounts expended by the Architect, the Architect's employees and consultants in the interest of the Project.

14.6 Payments due the Architect and unpaid under this Agreement shall bear interest from the date payment is due at the rate entered below, or in the absence thereof, at the legal rate prevailing at the principal place of business of the Architect.

(Here insert any rate of interest agreed upon.)

(Usury laws and requirements under the Federal Truth in Lending Act, similar state and local consumer credit laws and other regulations at the Owner's and Architect's principal places of business, the location of the Project and elsewhere may affect the validity of this provision. Specific legal advice should be obtained with respect to deletion, modification, or other requirements such as written disclosures or waivers.)

14.7 The Owner and the Architect agree in accordance with the Terms and Conditions of this Agreement that:

14.7.1 IF THE SCOPE of the Project or of the Architect's Services is changed materially, the amounts of compensation shall be equitably adjusted.

14.7.2 IF THE SERVICES covered by this Agreement have not been completed within

( ) months of the date hereof, through no fault of the Architect, the amounts of compensation, rates and multiples set forth herein shall be equitably adjusted.

ARTICLE 15
OTHER CONDITIONS OR SERVICES

SAMPLE

SAMPLE

This Agreement entered into as of the day and year first written above.

OWNER
ARCHITECT

_____   _____

_____   _____

_____   _____

BY_____   BY_____

AIA DOCUMENT B141 • OWNER-ARCHITECT AGREEMENT • THIRTEENTH EDITION • JULY 1977 • AIA® • © 1977
THE AMERICAN INSTITUTE OF ARCHITECTS, 1735 NEW YORK AVENUE, N.W., WASHINGTON, D.C. 20006

APPENDIX **D**

PERFORMANCE BOND

AIA Document A311

THE AMERICAN INSTITUTE OF ARCHITECTS

AIA Document A311

Performance Bond

SAMPLE

KNOW ALL MEN BY THESE PRESENTS: that

(Here insert full name and address or legal title of Contractor)

as Principal, hereinafter called Contractor, and,

(Here insert full name and address or legal title of Surety)

as Surety, hereinafter called Surety, are held and firmly bound unto

(Here insert full name and address or legal title of Owner)

as Obligee, hereinafter called Owner, in the amount of

Dollars ($),

for the payment whereof Contractor and Surety bind themselves, their heirs, executors, administrators, successors and assigns, jointly and severally, firmly by these presents.

WHEREAS,

Contractor has by written agreement dated   19   , entered into a contract with Owner for
(Here insert full name, address and description of project)

in accordance with Drawings and Specifications prepared by

(Here insert full name and address or legal title of Architect)

which contract is by reference made a part hereof, and is hereinafter referred to as the Contract.

AIA DOCUMENT A311 • PERFORMANCE BOND AND LABOR AND MATERIAL PAYMENT BOND • AIA ®
FEBRUARY 1970 ED. • THE AMERICAN INSTITUTE OF ARCHITECTS, 1735 N.Y. AVE., N.W., WASHINGTON, D. C. 20006

1

PERFORMANCE BOND

NOW, THEREFORE, THE CONDITION OF THIS OBLIGATION is such that, if Contractor shall promptly and faithfully perform said Contract, then this obligation shall be null and void; otherwise it shall remain in full force and effect.

The Surety hereby waives notice of any alteration or extension of time made by the Owner.

Whenever Contractor shall be, and declared by Owner to be in default under the Contract, the Owner having performed Owner's obligations thereunder, the Surety may promptly remedy the default, or shall promptly

1) Complete the Contract in accordance with its terms and conditions, or

2) Obtain a bid or bids for completing the Contract in accordance with its terms and conditions, and upon determination by Surety of the lowest responsible bidder, or, if the Owner elects, upon determination by the Owner and the Surety jointly of the lowest responsible bidder, arrange for a contract between such bidder and Owner, and make available as Work progresses (even though there should be a default or a succession of defaults under the contract or contracts of completion arranged under this paragraph) sufficient funds to pay the cost of completion less the balance of the contract price; but not exceeding, including other costs and damages for which the Surety may be liable hereunder, the amount set forth in the first paragraph hereof. The term "balance of the contract price," as used in this paragraph, shall mean the total amount payable by Owner to Contractor under the Contract and any amendments thereto, less the amount properly paid by Owner to Contractor.

Any suit under this bond must be instituted before the expiration of two (2) years from the date on which final payment under the Contract falls due.

No right of action shall accrue on this bond to or for the use of any person or corporation other than the Owner named herein or the heirs, executors, administrators or successors of the Owner.

AIA trademarked material has been reproduced with permission of The American Institute of Architects under permission number 87008 . Further reproduction is prohibited.

Because AIA Documents are revised from time to time, users should ascertain from the AIA the current edition of the Document reproduced herein.

Copies of the AIA Document may be purchased from The American Institute of Architects or its local distributors.

Signed and sealed this   day of   19

_____   { _____
(Witness)   (Principal)   (Seal)

                                                _____
                                                 (Title)

_____   { _____
(Witness)   (Surety)   (Seal)

                                                _____
                                                 (Title)

AIA DOCUMENT A311 • PERFORMANCE BOND AND LABOR AND MATERIAL PAYMENT BOND • AIA ®
FEBRUARY 1970 ED. • THE AMERICAN INSTITUTE OF ARCHITECTS, 1735 N.Y. AVE., N.W., WASHINGTON, D. C. 20006

2

THE AMERICAN INSTITUTE OF ARCHITECTS

AIA Document A311

Labor and Material Payment Bond

THIS BOND IS ISSUED SIMULTANEOUSLY WITH PERFORMANCE BOND IN FAVOR OF THE OWNER CONDITIONED ON THE FULL AND FAITHFUL PERFORMANCE OF THE CONTRACT

KNOW ALL MEN BY THESE PRESENTS: that

(Here insert full name and address or legal title of Contractor)

as Principal, hereinafter called Principal, and

(Here insert full name and address or legal title of Surety)

as Surety, hereinafter called Surety, are held and firmly bound unto

(Here insert full name and address or legal title of Owner)

as Obligee, hereinafter called Owner, for the use and benefit of claimants as hereinbelow defined, in the

amount of

(Here insert a sum equal to at least one-half of the contract price)   Dollars ($),

for the payment whereof Principal and Surety bind themselves, their heirs, executors, administrators, successors and assigns, jointly and severally, firmly by these presents.

WHEREAS,

Principal has by written agreement dated   19   , entered into a contract with Owner for

(Here insert full name, address and description of project)

in accordance with Drawings and Specifications prepared by

(Here insert full name and address or legal title of Architect)

which contract is by reference made a part hereof, and is hereinafter referred to as the Contract.

LABOR AND MATERIAL PAYMENT BOND

NOW, THEREFORE, THE CONDITION OF THIS OBLIGATION is such that, if Principal shall promptly make payment to all claimants as hereinafter defined, for all labor and material used or reasonably required for use in the performance of the Contract, then this obligation shall be void; otherwise it shall remain in full force and effect, subject, however, to the following conditions:

1. A claimant is defined as one having a direct contract with the Principal or with a Subcontractor of the Principal for labor, material, or both, used or reasonably required for use in the performance of the Contract, labor and material being construed to include that part of water, gas, power, light, heat, oil, gasoline, telephone service or rental of equipment directly applicable to the Contract.

2. The above named Principal and Surety hereby jointly and severally agree with the Owner that every claimant as herein defined, who has not been paid in full before the expiration of a period of ninety (90) days after the date on which the last of such claimant's work or labor was done or performed, or materials were furnished by such claimant, may sue on this bond for the use of such claimant, prosecute the suit to final judgment for such sum or sums as may be justly due claimant, and have execution thereon. The Owner shall not be liable for the payment of any costs or expenses of any such suit.

3. No suit or action shall be commenced hereunder by any claimant:

a) Unless claimant, other than one having a direct contract with the Principal, shall have given written notice to any two of the following: the Principal, the Owner, or the Surety above named, within ninety (90) days after such claimant did or performed the last of the work or labor, or furnished the last of the materials for which said claim is made, stating with substantial

accuracy the amount claimed and the name of the party to whom the materials were furnished, or for whom the work or labor was done or performed. Such notice shall be served by mailing the same by registered mail or certified mail, postage prepaid, in an envelope addressed to the Principal, Owner or Surety, at any place where an office is regularly maintained for the transaction of business, or served in any manner in which legal process may be served in the state in which the aforesaid project is located, save that such service need not be made by a public officer.

b) After the expiration of one (1) year following the date on which Principal ceased Work on said Contract, it being understood, however, that if any limitation embodied in this bond is prohibited by any law controlling the construction hereof such limitation shall be deemed to be amended so as to be equal to the minimum period of limitation permitted by such law.

c) Other than in a state court of competent jurisdiction in and for the county or other political subdivision of the state in which the Project, or any part thereof, is situated, or in the United States District Court for the district in which the Project, or any part thereof, is situated, and not elsewhere.

4. The amount of this bond shall be reduced by and to the extent of any payment or payments made in good faith hereunder, inclusive of the payment by Surety of mechanics' liens which may be filed of record against said improvement, whether or not claim for the amount of such lien be presented under and against this bond.

Signed and sealed this   day of   19

_____   (Principal)   (Seal)

(Witness)

       (Title)

_____   (Surety)   (Seal)

(Witness)

       (Title)

APPENDIX

GENERAL CONDITIONS OF THE CONTRACT FOR CONSTRUCTION

AIA Document A201

THE AMERICAN INSTITUTE OF ARCHITECTS

AIA Document A201

General Conditions of the Contract for Construction

THIS DOCUMENT HAS IMPORTANT LEGAL CONSEQUENCES; CONSULTATION WITH AN ATTORNEY IS ENCOURAGED WITH RESPECT TO ITS MODIFICATION

1976 EDITION
TABLE OF ARTICLES

This document has been approved and endorsed by The Associated General Contractors of America.

INDEX

AIA DOCUMENT A201 • GENERAL CONDITIONS OF THE CONTRACT FOR CONSTRUCTION • THIRTEENTH EDITION • AUGUST 1976
AIA® • © 1976 • THE AMERICAN INSTITUTE OF ARCHITECTS, 1735 NEW YORK AVENUE, N.W., WASHINGTON, D.C. 20006

GENERAL CONDITIONS OF THE CONTRACT FOR CONSTRUCTION

ARTICLE 1

CONTRACT DOCUMENTS

1.1   DEFINITIONS

1.1.1   THE CONTRACT DOCUMENTS

The Contract Documents consist of the Owner-Contractor Agreement, the Conditions of the Contract (General, Supplementary and other Conditions), the Drawings, the Specifications, and all Addenda issued prior to and all Modifications issued after execution of the Contract. A Modification is (1) a written amendment to the Contract signed by both parties, (2) a Change Order, (3) a written interpretation issued by the Architect pursuant to Subparagraph 2.2.8, or (4) a written order for a minor change in the Work issued by the Architect pursuant to Paragraph 12.4. The Contract Documents do not include Bidding Documents such as the Advertisement or Invitation to Bid, the Instructions to Bidders, sample forms, the Contractor's Bid or portions of Addenda relating to any of these, or any other documents, unless specifically enumerated in the Owner-Contractor Agreement.

1.1.2   THE CONTRACT

The Contract Documents form the Contract for Construction. This Contract represents the entire and integrated agreement between the parties hereto and supersedes all prior negotiations, representations, or agreements, either written or oral. The Contract may be amended or modified only by a Modification as defined in Subparagraph 1.1.1. The Contract Documents shall not be construed to create any contractual relationship of any kind between the Architect and the Contractor, but the Architect shall be entitled to performance of obligations intended for his benefit, and to enforcement thereof. Nothing contained in the Contract Documents shall create any contractual relationship between the Owner or the Architect and any Subcontractor or Sub-subcontractor.

1.1.3   THE WORK

The Work comprises the completed construction required by the Contract Documents and includes all labor necessary to produce such construction, and all materials and equipment incorporated or to be incorporated in such construction.

1.1.4   THE PROJECT

The Project is the total construction of which the Work performed under the Contract Documents may be the whole or a part.

1.2   EXECUTION, CORRELATION AND INTENT

1.2.1 The Contract Documents shall be signed in not less than triplicate by the Owner and Contractor. If either Owner or the Contractor or both do not sign the Conditions of the Contract, Drawings, Specifications, or any of the other Contract Documents, the Architect shall identify such Documents.

1.2.2 By executing the Contract, the Contractor represents that he has visited the site, familiarized himself with the local conditions under which the Work is to be performed, and correlated his observations with the requirements of the Contract Documents.

1.2.3 The intent of the Contract Documents is to include all items necessary for the proper execution and completion of the Work. The Contract Documents are complementary, and what is required by any one shall be as binding as if required by all. Work not covered in the Contract Documents will not be required unless it is consistent therewith and is reasonably inferable therefrom as being necessary to produce the intended results. Words and abbreviations which have well-known technical or trade meanings are used in the Contract Documents in accordance with such recognized meanings.

1.2.4 The organization of the Specifications into divisions, sections and articles, and the arrangement of Drawings shall not control the Contractor in dividing the Work among Subcontractors or in establishing the extent of Work to be performed by any trade.

1.3   OWNERSHIP AND USE OF DOCUMENTS

1.3.1 All Drawings, Specifications and copies thereof furnished by the Architect are and shall remain his property. They are to be used only with respect to this Project and are not to be used on any other project. With the exception of one contract set for each party to the Contract, such documents are to be returned or suitably accounted for to the Architect on request at the completion of the Work. Submission or distribution to meet official regulatory requirements or for other purposes in connection with the Project is not to be construed as publication in derogation of the Architect's common law copyright or other reserved rights.

ARTICLE 2

ARCHITECT

2.1   DEFINITION

2.1.1 The Architect is the person lawfully licensed to practice architecture, or an entity lawfully practicing architecture identified as such in the Owner-Contractor Agreement, and is referred to throughout the Contract Documents as if singular in number and masculine in gender. The term Architect means the Architect or his authorized representative.

2.2   ADMINISTRATION OF THE CONTRACT

2.2.1 The Architect will provide administration of the Contract as hereinafter described.

2.2.2 The Architect will be the Owner's representative during construction and until final payment is due. The Architect will advise and consult with the Owner. The Owner's instructions to the Contractor shall be forwarded through the Architect. The Architect will have authority to act on behalf of the Owner only to the extent provided in the Contract Documents, unless otherwise modified by written instrument in accordance with Subparagraph 2.2.18.

2.2.3 The Architect will visit the site at intervals appropriate to the stage of construction to familiarize himself generally with the progress and quality of the Work and to determine in general if the Work is proceeding in accordance with the Contract Documents. However, the Architect will not be required to make exhaustive or continuous on-site inspections to check the quality or quantity of the Work. On the basis of his on-site observations as an architect, he will keep the Owner informed of the progress of the Work, and will endeavor to guard the Owner against defects and deficiencies in the Work of the Contractor.

2.2.4 The Architect will not be responsible for and will not have control or charge of construction means, methods, techniques, sequences or procedures, or for safety precautions and programs in connection with the Work, and he will not be responsible for the Contractor's failure to carry out the Work in accordance with the Contract Documents. The Architect will not be responsible for or have control or charge over the acts or omissions of the Contractor, Subcontractors, or any of their agents or employees, or any other persons performing any of the Work.

2.2.5 The Architect shall at all times have access to the Work wherever it is in preparation and progress. The Contractor shall provide facilities for such access so the Architect may perform his functions under the Contract Documents.

2.2.6 Based on the Architect's observations and an evaluation of the Contractor's Applications for Payment, the Architect will determine the amounts owing to the Contractor and will issue Certificates for Payment in such amounts, as provided in Paragraph 9.4.

2.2.7 The Architect will be the interpreter of the requirements of the Contract Documents and the judge of the performance thereunder by both the Owner and Contractor.

2.2.8 The Architect will render interpretations necessary for the proper execution or progress of the Work, with reasonable promptness and in accordance with any time limit agreed upon. Either party to the Contract may make written request to the Architect for such interpretations.

2.2.9 Claims, disputes and other matters in question between the Contractor and the Owner relating to the execution or progress of the Work or the interpretation of the Contract Documents shall be referred initially to the Architect for decision which he will render in writing within a reasonable time.

2.2.10 All interpretations and decisions of the Architect shall be consistent with the intent of and reasonably inferable from the Contract Documents and will be in writing or in the form of drawings. In his capacity as interpreter and judge, he will endeavor to secure faithful performance by both the Owner and the Contractor, will not

show partiality to either, and will not be liable for the result of any interpretation or decision rendered in good faith in such capacity.

2.2.11 The Architect's decisions in matters relating to artistic effect will be final if consistent with the intent of the Contract Documents.

2.2.12 Any claim, dispute or other matter in question between the Contractor and the Owner referred to the Architect, except those relating to artistic effect as provided in Subparagraph 2.2.11 and except those which have been waived by the making or acceptance of final payment as provided in Subparagraphs 9.9.4 and 9.9.5, shall be subject to arbitration upon the written demand of either party. However, no demand for arbitration of any such claim, dispute or other matter may be made until the earlier of (1) the date on which the Architect has rendered a written decision, or (2) the tenth day after the parties have presented their evidence to the Architect or have been given a reasonable opportunity to do so, if the Architect has not rendered his written decision by that date. When such a written decision of the Architect states (1) that the decision is final but subject to appeal, and (2) that any demand for arbitration of a claim, dispute or other matter covered by such decision must be made within thirty days after the date on which the party making the demand receives the written decision, failure to demand arbitration within said thirty days' period will result in the Architect's decision becoming final and binding upon the Owner and the Contractor. If the Architect renders a decision after arbitration proceedings have been initiated, such decision may be entered as evidence but will not supersede any arbitration proceedings unless the decision is acceptable to all parties concerned.

2.2.13 The Architect will have authority to reject Work which does not conform to the Contract Documents. Whenever, in his opinion, he considers it necessary or advisable for the implementation of the intent of the Contract Documents, he will have authority to require special inspection or testing of the Work in accordance with Subparagraph 7.7.2 whether or not such Work be then fabricated, installed or completed. However, neither the Architect's authority to act under this Subparagraph 2.2.13, nor any decision made by him in good faith either to exercise or not to exercise such authority, shall give rise to any duty or responsibility of the Architect to the Contractor, any Subcontractor, any of their agents or employees, or any other person performing any of the Work.

2.2.14 The Architect will review and approve or take other appropriate action upon Contractor's submittals such as Shop Drawings, Product Data and Samples, but only for conformance with the design concept of the Work and with the information given in the Contract Documents. Such action shall be taken with reasonable promptness so as to cause no delay. The Architect's approval of a specific item shall not indicate approval of an assembly of which the item is a component.

2.2.15 The Architect will prepare Change Orders in accordance with Article 12, and will have authority to order minor changes in the Work as provided in Subparagraph 12.4.1.

2.2.16 The Architect will conduct inspections to determine the dates of Substantial Completion and final completion, will receive and forward to the Owner for the Owner's review written warranties and related documents required by the Contract and assembled by the Contractor, and will issue a final Certificate for Payment upon compliance with the requirements of Paragraph 9.9.

2.2.17 If the Owner and Architect agree, the Architect will provide one or more Project Representatives to assist the Architect in carrying out his responsibilities at the site. The duties, responsibilities and limitations of authority of any such Project Representative shall be as set forth in an exhibit to be incorporated in the Contract Documents.

2.2.18 The duties, responsibilities and limitations of authority of the Architect as the Owner's representative during construction as set forth in the Contract Documents will not be modified or extended without written consent of the Owner, the Contractor and the Architect.

2.2.19 In case of the termination of the employment of the Architect, the Owner shall appoint an architect against whom the Contractor makes no reasonable objection whose status under the Contract Documents shall be that of the former architect. Any dispute in connection with such appointment shall be subject to arbitration.

ARTICLE 3

OWNER

3.1 DEFINITION

3.1.1 The Owner is the person or entity identified as such in the Owner-Contractor Agreement and is referred to throughout the Contract Documents as if singular in number and masculine in gender. The term Owner means the Owner or his authorized representative.

3.2 INFORMATION AND SERVICES REQUIRED OF THE OWNER

3.2.1 The Owner shall, at the request of the Contractor, at the time of execution of the Owner-Contractor Agreement, furnish to the Contractor reasonable evidence that he has made financial arrangements to fulfill his obligations under the Contract. Unless such reasonable evidence is furnished, the Contractor is not required to execute the Owner-Contractor Agreement or to commence the Work.

3.2.2 The Owner shall furnish all surveys describing the physical characteristics, legal limitations and utility locations for the site of the Project, and a legal description of the site.

3.2.3 Except as provided in Subparagraph 4.7.1, the Owner shall secure and pay for necessary approvals, easements, assessments and charges required for the construction, use or occupancy of permanent structures or for permanent changes in existing facilities.

3.2.4 Information or services under the Owner's control shall be furnished by the Owner with reasonable promptness to avoid delay in the orderly progress of the Work.

3.2.5 Unless otherwise provided in the Contract Documents, the Contractor will be furnished, free of charge, all copies of Drawings and Specifications reasonably necessary for the execution of the Work.

3.2.6 The Owner shall forward all instructions to the Contractor through the Architect.

3.2.7 The foregoing are in addition to other duties and responsibilities of the Owner enumerated herein and especially those in respect to Work by Owner or by Separate Contractors, Payments and Completion, and Insurance in Articles 6, 9 and 11 respectively.

3.3 OWNER'S RIGHT TO STOP THE WORK

3.3.1 If the Contractor fails to correct defective Work as required by Paragraph 13.2 or persistently fails to carry out the Work in accordance with the Contract Documents, the Owner, by a written order signed personally or by an agent specifically so empowered by the Owner in writing, may order the Contractor to stop the Work, or any portion thereof, until the cause for such order has been eliminated; however, this right of the Owner to stop the Work shall not give rise to any duty on the part of the Owner to exercise this right for the benefit of the Contractor or any other person or entity, except to the extent required by Subparagraph 6.1.3.

3.4 OWNER'S RIGHT TO CARRY OUT THE WORK

3.4.1 If the Contractor defaults or neglects to carry out the Work in accordance with the Contract Documents and fails within seven days after receipt of written notice from the Owner to commence and continue correction of such default or neglect with diligence and promptness, the Owner may, after seven days following receipt by the Contractor of an additional written notice and without prejudice to any other remedy he may have, make good such deficiencies. In such case an appropriate Change Order shall be issued deducting from the payments then or thereafter due the Contractor the cost of correcting such deficiencies, including compensation for the Architect's additional services made necessary by such default, neglect or failure. Such action by the Owner and the amount charged to the Contractor are both subject to the prior approval of the Architect. If the payments then or thereafter due the Contractor are not sufficient to cover such amount, the Contractor shall pay the difference to the Owner.

ARTICLE 4

CONTRACTOR

4.1 DEFINITION

4.1.1 The Contractor is the person or entity identified as such in the Owner-Contractor Agreement and is referred to throughout the Contract Documents as if singular in number and masculine in gender. The term Contractor means the Contractor or his authorized representative.

4.2 REVIEW OF CONTRACT DOCUMENTS

4.2.1 The Contractor shall carefully study and compare the Contract Documents and shall at once report to the Architect any error, inconsistency or omission he may discover. The Contractor shall not be liable to the Owner or the Architect for any damage resulting from any such errors, inconsistencies or omissions in the Contract Documents. The Contractor shall perform no portion of the Work at any time without Contract Documents or, where required, approved Shop Drawings, Product Data or Samples for such portion of the Work.

4.3 SUPERVISION AND CONSTRUCTION PROCEDURES

4.3.1 The Contractor shall supervise and direct the Work, using his best skill and attention. He shall be solely responsible for all construction means, methods, techniques, sequences and procedures and for coordinating all portions of the Work under the Contract.

4.3.2 The Contractor shall be responsible to the Owner for the acts and omissions of his employees, Subcontractors and their agents and employees, and other persons performing any of the Work under a contract with the Contractor.

4.3.3 The Contractor shall not be relieved from his obligations to perform the Work in accordance with the Contract Documents either by the activities or duties of the Architect in his administration of the Contract, or by inspections, tests or approvals required or performed under Paragraph 7.7 by persons other than the Contractor.

4.4 LABOR AND MATERIALS

4.4.1 Unless otherwise provided in the Contract Documents, the Contractor shall provide and pay for all labor, materials, equipment, tools, construction equipment and machinery, water, heat, utilities, transportation, and other facilities and services necessary for the proper execution and completion of the Work, whether temporary or permanent and whether or not incorporated or to be incorporated in the Work.

4.4.2 The Contractor shall at all times enforce strict discipline and good order among his employees and shall not employ on the Work any unfit person or anyone not skilled in the task assigned to him.

4.5 WARRANTY

4.5.1 The Contractor warrants to the Owner and the Architect that all materials and equipment furnished under this Contract will be new unless otherwise specified, and that all Work will be of good quality, free from faults and defects and in conformance with the Contract Documents. All Work not conforming to these requirements, including substitutions not properly approved and authorized, may be considered defective. If required by the Architect, the Contractor shall furnish satisfactory evidence as to the kind and quality of materials and equipment. This warranty is not limited by the provisions of Paragraph 13.2.

4.6 TAXES

4.6.1 The Contractor shall pay all sales, consumer, use and other similar taxes for the Work or portions thereof provided by the Contractor which are legally enacted at the time bids are received, whether or not yet effective.

4.7 PERMITS, FEES AND NOTICES

4.7.1 Unless otherwise provided in the Contract Documents, the Contractor shall secure and pay for the building permit and for all other permits and governmental fees, licenses and inspections necessary for the proper execution and completion of the Work which are customarily secured after execution of the Contract and which are legally required at the time the bids are received.

4.7.2 The Contractor shall give all notices and comply with all laws, ordinances, rules, regulations and lawful orders of any public authority bearing on the performance of the Work.

4.7.3 It is not the responsibility of the Contractor to make certain that the Contract Documents are in accordance with applicable laws, statutes, building codes and regulations. If the Contractor observes that any of the Contract Documents are at variance therewith in any respect, he shall promptly notify the Architect in writing, and any necessary changes shall be accomplished by appropriate Modification.

4.7.4 If the Contractor performs any Work knowing it to be contrary to such laws, ordinances, rules and regulations, and without such notice to the Architect, he shall assume full responsibility therefor and shall bear all costs attributable thereto.

4.8 ALLOWANCES

4.8.1 The Contractor shall include in the Contract Sum all allowances stated in the Contract Documents. Items covered by these allowances shall be supplied for such amounts and by such persons as the Owner may direct, but the Contractor will not be required to employ persons against whom he makes a reasonable objection.

4.8.2 Unless otherwise provided in the Contract Documents:

.1 these allowances shall cover the cost to the Contractor, less any applicable trade discount, of the materials and equipment required by the allowance delivered at the site, and all applicable taxes;

.2 the Contractor's costs for unloading and handling on the site, labor, installation costs, overhead, profit and other expenses contemplated for the original allowance shall be included in the Contract Sum and not in the allowance;

.3 whenever the cost is more than or less than the allowance, the Contract Sum shall be adjusted accordingly by Change Order, the amount of which will recognize changes, if any, in handling costs on the site, labor, installation costs, overhead, profit and other expenses.

4.9 SUPERINTENDENT

4.9.1 The Contractor shall employ a competent superintendent and necessary assistants who shall be in attendance at the Project site during the progress of the Work. The superintendent shall represent the Contractor and all communications given to the superintendent shall be as binding as if given to the Contractor. Important communications shall be confirmed in writing. Other communications shall be so confirmed on written request in each case.

4.10 PROGRESS SCHEDULE

4.10.1 The Contractor, immediately after being awarded the Contract, shall prepare and submit for the Owner's and Architect's information an estimated progress schedule for the Work. The progress schedule shall be related to the entire Project to the extent required by the Contract Documents, and shall provide for expeditious and practicable execution of the Work.

4.11 DOCUMENTS AND SAMPLES AT THE SITE

4.11.1 The Contractor shall maintain at the site for the Owner one record copy of all Drawings, Specifications, Addenda, Change Orders and other Modifications, in good order and marked currently to record all changes made during construction, and approved Shop Drawings, Product Data and Samples. These shall be available to the Architect and shall be delivered to him for the Owner upon completion of the Work.

4.12 SHOP DRAWINGS, PRODUCT DATA AND SAMPLES

4.12.1 Shop Drawings are drawings, diagrams, schedules and other data specially prepared for the Work by the Contractor or any Subcontractor, manufacturer, supplier or distributor to illustrate some portion of the Work.

4.12.2 Product Data are illustrations, standard schedules, performance charts, instructions, brochures, diagrams and other information furnished by the Contractor to illustrate a material, product or system for some portion of the Work.

4.12.3 Samples are physical examples which illustrate materials, equipment or workmanship and establish standards by which the Work will be judged.

4.12.4 The Contractor shall review, approve and submit, with reasonable promptness and in such sequence as to cause no delay in the Work or in the work of the Owner or any separate contractor, all Shop Drawings, Product Data and Samples required by the Contract Documents.

4.12.5 By approving and submitting Shop Drawings, Product Data and Samples, the Contractor represents that he has determined and verified all materials, field measurements, and field construction criteria related thereto, or will do so, and that he has checked and coordinated the information contained within such submittals with the requirements of the Work and of the Contract Documents.

4.12.6 The Contractor shall not be relieved of responsibility for any deviation from the requirements of the Contract Documents by the Architect's approval of Shop Drawings, Product Data or Samples under Subparagraph 2.2.14 unless the Contractor has specifically informed the Architect in writing of such deviation at the time of submission and the Architect has given written approval to the specific deviation. The Contractor shall not be relieved from responsibility for errors or omissions in the Shop Drawings, Product Data or Samples by the Architect's approval thereof.

4.12.7 The Contractor shall direct specific attention, in writing or on resubmitted Shop Drawings, Product Data or Samples, to revisions other than those requested by the Architect on previous submittals.

4.12.8 No portion of the Work requiring submission of a Shop Drawing, Product Data or Sample shall be commenced until the submittal has been approved by the Architect as provided in Subparagraph 2.2.14. All such

portions of the Work shall be in accordance with approved submittals.

4.13 USE OF SITE

4.13.1 The Contractor shall confine operations at the site to areas permitted by law, ordinances, permits and the Contract Documents and shall not unreasonably encumber the site with any materials or equipment.

4.14 CUTTING AND PATCHING OF WORK

4.14.1 The Contractor shall be responsible for all cutting, fitting or patching that may be required to complete the Work or to make its several parts fit together properly.

4.14.2 The Contractor shall not damage or endanger any portion of the Work or the work of the Owner or any separate contractors by cutting, patching or otherwise altering any work, or by excavation. The Contractor shall not cut or otherwise alter the work of the Owner or any separate contractor except with the written consent of the Owner and of such separate contractor. The Contractor shall not unreasonably withhold from the Owner or any separate contractor his consent to cutting or otherwise altering the Work.

4.15 CLEANING UP

4.15.1 The Contractor at all times shall keep the premises free from accumulation of waste materials or rubbish caused by his operations. At the completion of the Work he shall remove all his waste materials and rubbish from and about the Project as well as all his tools, construction equipment, machinery and surplus materials.

4.15.2 If the Contractor fails to clean up at the completion of the Work, the Owner may do so as provided in Paragraph 3.4 and the cost thereof shall be charged to the Contractor.

4.16 COMMUNICATIONS

4.16.1 The Contractor shall forward all communications to the Owner through the Architect.

4.17 ROYALTIES AND PATENTS

4.17.1 The Contractor shall pay all royalties and license fees. He shall defend all suits or claims for infringement of any patent rights and shall save the Owner harmless from loss on account thereof, except that the Owner shall be responsible for all such loss when a particular design, process or the product of a particular manufacturer or manufacturers is specified, but if the Contractor has reason to believe that the design, process or product specified is an infringement of a patent, he shall be responsible for such loss unless he promptly gives such information to the Architect.

4.18 INDEMNIFICATION

4.18.1 To the fullest extent permitted by law, the Contractor shall indemnify and hold harmless the Owner and the Architect and their agents and employees from and against all claims, damages, losses and expenses, including but not limited to attorneys' fees, arising out of or resulting from the performance of the Work, provided that any such claim, damage, loss or expense (1) is attributable to bodily injury, sickness, disease or death, or to injury to or destruction of tangible property (other than the Work itself) including the loss of use resulting therefrom, and (2) is caused in whole or in part by any negligent act or omission of the Contractor, any Subcontractor, anyone directly or indirectly employed by any of them or anyone for whose acts any of them may be liable, regardless of whether or not it is caused in part by a party indemnified hereunder. Such obligation shall not be construed to negate, abridge, or otherwise reduce any other right or obligation of indemnity which would otherwise exist as to any party or person described in this Paragraph 4.18.

4.18.2 In any and all claims against the Owner or the Architect or any of their agents or employees by any employee of the Contractor, any Subcontractor, anyone directly or indirectly employed by any of them or anyone for whose acts any of them may be liable, the indemnification obligation under this Paragraph 4.18 shall not be limited in any way by any limitation on the amount or type of damages, compensation or benefits payable by or for the Contractor or any Subcontractor under workers' or workmen's compensation acts, disability benefit acts or other employee benefit acts.

4.18.3 The obligations of the Contractor under this Paragraph 4.18 shall not extend to the liability of the Architect, his agents or employees, arising out of (1) the preparation or approval of maps, drawings, opinions, reports, surveys, change orders, designs or specifications, or (2) the giving of or the failure to give directions or instructions by the Architect, his agents or employees provided such giving or failure to give is the primary cause of the injury or damage.

ARTICLE 5

SUBCONTRACTORS

5.1 DEFINITION

5.1.1 A Subcontractor is a person or entity who has a direct contract with the Contractor to perform any of the Work at the site. The term Subcontractor is referred to throughout the Contract Documents as if singular in number and masculine in gender and means a Subcontractor or his authorized representative. The term Subcontractor does not include any separate contractor or his subcontractors.

5.1.2 A Sub-subcontractor is a person or entity who has a direct or indirect contract with a Subcontractor to perform any of the Work at the site. The term Sub-subcontractor is referred to throughout the Contract Documents as if singular in number and masculine in gender and means a Sub-subcontractor or an authorized representative thereof.

5.2 AWARD OF SUBCONTRACTS AND OTHER CONTRACTS FOR PORTIONS OF THE WORK

5.2.1 Unless otherwise required by the Contract Documents or the Bidding Documents, the Contractor, as soon as practicable after the award of the Contract, shall furnish to the Owner and the Architect in writing the names of the persons or entities (including those who are to furnish materials or equipment fabricated to a special design) proposed for each of the principal portions of the Work. The Architect will promptly reply to the Contractor in writing stating whether or not the Owner or the Architect, after due investigation, has reasonable objection to any

such proposed person or entity. Failure of the Owner or Architect to reply promptly shall constitute notice of no reasonable objection.

5.2.2 The Contractor shall not contract with any such proposed person or entity to whom the Owner or the Architect has made reasonable objection under the provisions of Subparagraph 5.2.1. The Contractor shall not be required to contract with anyone to whom he has a reasonable objection.

5.2.3 If the Owner or the Architect has reasonable objection to any such proposed person or entity, the Contractor shall submit a substitute to whom the Owner or the Architect has no reasonable objection, and the Contract Sum shall be increased or decreased by the difference in cost occasioned by such substitution and an appropriate Change Order shall be issued; however, no increase in the Contract Sum shall be allowed for any such substitution unless the Contractor has acted promptly and responsively in submitting names as required by Subparagraph 5.2.1.

5.2.4 The Contractor shall make no substitution for any Subcontractor, person or entity previously selected if the Owner or Architect makes reasonable objection to such substitution.

5.3 SUBCONTRACTUAL RELATIONS

5.3.1 By an appropriate agreement, written where legally required for validity, the Contractor shall require each Subcontractor, to the extent of the Work to be performed by the Subcontractor, to be bound to the Contractor by the terms of the Contract Documents, and to assume toward the Contractor all the obligations and responsibilities which the Contractor, by these Documents, assumes toward the Owner and the Architect. Said agreement shall preserve and protect the rights of the Owner and the Architect under the Contract Documents with respect to the Work to be performed by the Subcontractor so that the subcontracting thereof will not prejudice such rights, and shall allow to the Subcontractor, unless specifically provided otherwise in the Contractor-Subcontractor agreement, the benefit of all rights, remedies and redress against the Contractor that the Contractor, by these Documents, has against the Owner. Where appropriate, the Contractor shall require each Subcontractor to enter into similar agreements with his Sub-subcontractors. The Contractor shall make available to each proposed Subcontractor, prior to the execution of the Subcontract, copies of the Contract Documents to which the Subcontractor will be bound by this Paragraph 5.3, and identify to the Subcontractor any terms and conditions of the proposed Subcontract which may be at variance with the Contract Documents. Each Subcontractor shall similarly make copies of such Documents available to his Sub-subcontractors.

ARTICLE 6

WORK BY OWNER OR BY SEPARATE CONTRACTORS

6.1 OWNER'S RIGHT TO PERFORM WORK AND TO AWARD SEPARATE CONTRACTS

6.1.1 The Owner reserves the right to perform work related to the Project with his own forces, and to award separate contracts in connection with other portions of the Project or other work on the site under these or similar Conditions of the Contract. If the Contractor claims that delay or additional cost is involved because of such action by the Owner, he shall make such claim as provided elsewhere in the Contract Documents.

6.1.2 When separate contracts are awarded for different portions of the Project or other work on the site, the term Contractor in the Contract Documents in each case shall mean the Contractor who executes each separate Owner-Contractor Agreement.

6.1.3 The Owner will provide for the coordination of the work of his own forces and of each separate contractor with the Work of the Contractor, who shall cooperate therewith as provided in Paragraph 6.2.

6.2   MUTUAL RESPONSIBILITY

6.2.1 The Contractor shall afford the Owner and separate contractors reasonable opportunity for the introduction and storage of their materials and equipment and the execution of their work, and shall connect and coordinate his Work with theirs as required by the Contract Documents.

6.2.2 If any part of the Contractor's Work depends for proper execution or results upon the work of the Owner or any separate contractor, the Contractor shall, prior to proceeding with the Work, promptly report to the Architect any apparent discrepancies or defects in such other work that render it unsuitable for such proper execution and results. Failure of the Contractor so to report shall constitute an acceptance of the Owner's or separate contractors' work as fit and proper to receive his Work, except as to defects which may subsequently become apparent in such work by others.

6.2.3 Any costs caused by defective or ill-timed work shall be borne by the party responsible therefor.

6.2.4 Should the Contractor wrongfully cause damage to the work or property of the Owner, or to other work on the site, the Contractor shall promptly remedy such damage as provided in Subparagraph 10.2.5.

6.2.5 Should the Contractor wrongfully cause damage to the work or property of any separate contractor, the Contractor shall upon due notice promptly attempt to settle with such other contractor by agreement, or otherwise to resolve the dispute. If such separate contractor sues or initiates an arbitration proceeding against the Owner on account of any damage alleged to have been caused by the Contractor, the Owner shall notify the Contractor who shall defend such proceedings at the Owner's expense, and if any judgment or award against the Owner arises therefrom the Contractor shall pay or satisfy it and shall reimburse the Owner for all attorneys' fees and court or arbitration costs which the Owner has incurred.

6.3   OWNER'S RIGHT TO CLEAN UP

6.3.1 If a dispute arises between the Contractor and separate contractors as to their responsibility for cleaning up as required by Paragraph 4.15, the Owner may clean up

and charge the cost thereof to the contractors responsible therefor as the Architect shall determine to be just.

ARTICLE 7

MISCELLANEOUS PROVISIONS

7.1   GOVERNING LAW

7.1.1 The Contract shall be governed by the law of the place where the Project is located.

7.2   SUCCESSORS AND ASSIGNS

7.2.1 The Owner and the Contractor each binds himself, his partners, successors, assigns and legal representatives to the other party hereto and to the partners, successors, assigns and legal representatives of such other party with respect to all covenants, agreements and obligations contained in the Contract Documents. Neither party to the Contract shall assign the Contract or sublet it as a whole without the written consent of the other, nor shall the Contractor assign any moneys due or to become due to him hereunder, without the previous written consent of the Owner.

7.3   WRITTEN NOTICE

7.3.1 Written notice shall be deemed to have been duly served if delivered in person to the individual or member of the firm or entity or to an officer of the corporation for whom it was intended, or if delivered at or sent by registered or certified mail to the last business address known to him who gives the notice.

7.4   CLAIMS FOR DAMAGES

7.4.1 Should either party to the Contract suffer injury or damage to person or property because of any act or omission of the other party or of any of his employees, agents or others for whose acts he is legally liable, claim shall be made in writing to such other party within a reasonable time after the first observance of such injury or damage.

**7.5   PERFORMANCE BOND AND LABOR AND
    MATERIAL PAYMENT BOND**

7.5.1 The Owner shall have the right to require the Contractor to furnish bonds covering the faithful performance of the Contract and the payment of all obligations arising thereunder if and as required in the Bidding Documents or in the Contract Documents.

7.6   RIGHTS AND REMEDIES

7.6.1 The duties and obligations imposed by the Contract Documents and the rights and remedies available thereunder shall be in addition to and not a limitation of any duties, obligations, rights and remedies otherwise imposed or available by law.

7.6.2 No action or failure to act by the Owner, Architect or Contractor shall constitute a waiver of any right or duty afforded any of them under the Contract, nor shall any such action or failure to act constitute an approval of or acquiescence in any breach thereunder, except as may be specifically agreed in writing.

7.7 TESTS

7.7.1 If the Contract Documents, laws, ordinances, rules, regulations or orders of any public authority having jurisdiction require any portion of the Work to be inspected, tested or approved, the Contractor shall give the Architect timely notice of its readiness so the Architect may observe such inspection, testing or approval. The Contractor shall bear all costs of such inspections, tests or approvals conducted by public authorities. Unless otherwise provided, the Owner shall bear all costs of other inspections, tests or approvals.

7.7.2 If the Architect determines that any Work requires special inspection, testing, or approval which Subparagraph 7.7.1 does not include, he will, upon written authorization from the Owner, instruct the Contractor to order such special inspection, testing or approval, and the Contractor shall give notice as provided in Subparagraph 7.7.1. If such special inspection or testing reveals a failure of the Work to comply with the requirements of the Contract Documents, the Contractor shall bear all costs thereof, including compensation for the Architect's additional services made necessary by such failure; otherwise the Owner shall bear such costs, and an appropriate Change Order shall be issued.

7.7.3 Required certificates of inspection, testing or approval shall be secured by the Contractor and promptly delivered by him to the Architect.

7.7.4 If the Architect is to observe the inspections, tests or approvals required by the Contract Documents, he will do so promptly and, where practicable, at the source of supply.

7.8 INTEREST

7.8.1 Payments due and unpaid under the Contract Documents shall bear interest from the date payment is due at such rate as the parties may agree upon in writing or, in the absence thereof, at the legal rate prevailing at the place of the Project.

7.9 ARBITRATION

7.9.1 All claims, disputes and other matters in question between the Contractor and the Owner arising out of, or relating to, the Contract Documents or the breach thereof, except as provided in Subparagraph 2.2.11 with respect to the Architect's decisions on matters relating to artistic effect, and except for claims which have been waived by the making or acceptance of final payment as provided by Subparagraphs 9.9.4 and 9.9.5, shall be decided by arbitration in accordance with the Construction Industry Arbitration Rules of the American Arbitration Association then obtaining unless the parties mutually agree otherwise. No arbitration arising out of or relating to the Contract Documents shall include, by consolidation, joinder or in any other manner, the Architect, his employees or consultants except by written consent containing a specific reference to the Owner-Contractor Agreement and signed by the Architect, the Owner, the Contractor and any other person sought to be joined. No arbitration shall include by consolidation, joinder or in any other manner, parties other than the Owner, the Contractor and any other persons substantially involved in a common question of fact or law, whose presence is

required if complete relief is to be accorded in the arbitration. No person other than the Owner or Contractor shall be included as an original third party or additional third party to an arbitration whose interest or responsibility is insubstantial. Any consent to arbitration involving an additional person or persons shall not constitute consent to arbitration of any dispute not described therein or with any person not named or described therein. The foregoing agreement to arbitrate and any other agreement to arbitrate with an additional person or persons duly consented to by the parties to the Owner-Contractor Agreement shall be specifically enforceable under the prevailing arbitration law. The award rendered by the arbitrators shall be final, and judgment may be entered upon it in accordance with applicable law in any court having jurisdiction thereof.

7.9.2 Notice of the demand for arbitration shall be filed in writing with the other party to the Owner-Contractor Agreement and with the American Arbitration Association, and a copy shall be filed with the Architect. The demand for arbitration shall be made within the time limits specified in Subparagraph 2.2.12 where applicable, and in all other cases within a reasonable time after the claim, dispute or other matter in question has arisen, and in no event shall it be made after the date when institution of legal or equitable proceedings based on such claim, dispute or other matter in question would be barred by the applicable statute of limitations.

7.9.3 Unless otherwise agreed in writing, the Contractor shall carry on the Work and maintain its progress during any arbitration proceedings, and the Owner shall continue to make payments to the Contractor in accordance with the Contract Documents.

ARTICLE 8

TIME

8.1 DEFINITIONS

8.1.1 Unless otherwise provided, the Contract Time is the period of time allotted in the Contract Documents for Substantial Completion of the Work as defined in Subparagraph 8.1.3, including authorized adjustments thereto.

8.1.2 The date of commencement of the Work is the date established in a notice to proceed. If there is no notice to proceed, it shall be the date of the Owner-Contractor Agreement or such other date as may be established therein.

8.1.3 The Date of Substantial Completion of the Work or designated portion thereof is the Date certified by the Architect when construction is sufficiently complete, in accordance with the Contract Documents, so the Owner can occupy or utilize the Work or designated portion thereof for the use for which it is intended.

8.1.4 The term day as used in the Contract Documents shall mean calendar day unless otherwise specifically designated.

8.2 PROGRESS AND COMPLETION

8.2.1 All time limits stated in the Contract Documents are of the essence of the Contract.

8.2.2 The Contractor shall begin the Work on the date of commencement as defined in Subparagraph 8.1.2. He shall carry the Work forward expeditiously with adequate forces and shall achieve Substantial Completion within the Contract Time.

8.3 DELAYS AND EXTENSIONS OF TIME

8.3.1 If the Contractor is delayed at any time in the progress of the Work by any act or neglect of the Owner or the Architect, or by any employee of either, or by any separate contractor employed by the Owner, or by changes ordered in the Work, or by labor disputes, fire, unusual delay in transportation, adverse weather conditions not reasonably anticipatable, unavoidable casualties or any causes beyond the Contractor's control, or by delay authorized by the Owner pending arbitration, or by any other cause which the Architect determines may justify the delay, then the Contract Time shall be extended by Change Order for such reasonable time as the Architect may determine.

8.3.2 Any claim for extension of time shall be made in writing to the Architect not more than twenty days after the commencement of the delay; otherwise it shall be waived. In the case of a continuing delay only one claim is necessary. The Contractor shall provide an estimate of the probable effect of such delay on the progress of the Work.

8.3.3 If no agreement is made stating the dates upon which interpretations as provided in Subparagraph 2.2.8 shall be furnished, then no claim for delay shall be allowed on account of failure to furnish such interpretations until fifteen days after written request is made for them, and not then unless such claim is reasonable.

8.3.4 This Paragraph 8.3 does not exclude the recovery of damages for delay by either party under other provisions of the Contract Documents.

ARTICLE 9

PAYMENTS AND COMPLETION

9.1 CONTRACT SUM

9.1.1 The Contract Sum is stated in the Owner-Contractor Agreement and, including authorized adjustments thereto, is the total amount payable by the Owner to the Contractor for the performance of the Work under the Contract Documents.

9.2 SCHEDULE OF VALUES

9.2.1 Before the first Application for Payment, the Contractor shall submit to the Architect a schedule of values allocated to the various portions of the Work, prepared in such form and supported by such data to substantiate its accuracy as the Architect may require. This schedule, unless objected to by the Architect, shall be used only as a basis for the Contractor's Applications for Payment.

9.3 APPLICATIONS FOR PAYMENT

9.3.1 At least ten days before the date for each progress payment established in the Owner-Contractor Agreement, the Contractor shall submit to the Architect an itemized Application for Payment, notarized if required, supported by such data substantiating the Contractor's right to payment as the Owner or the Architect may require, and reflecting retainage, if any, as provided elsewhere in the Contract Documents.

9.3.2 Unless otherwise provided in the Contract Documents, payments will be made on account of materials or equipment not incorporated in the Work but delivered and suitably stored at the site and, if approved in advance by the Owner, payments may similarly be made for materials or equipment suitably stored at some other location agreed upon in writing. Payments for materials or equipment stored on or off the site shall be conditioned upon submission by the Contractor of bills of sale or such other procedures satisfactory to the Owner to establish the Owner's title to such materials or equipment or otherwise protect the Owner's interest, including applicable insurance and transportation to the site for those materials and equipment stored off the site.

9.3.3 The Contractor warrants that title to all Work, materials and equipment covered by an Application for Payment will pass to the Owner either by incorporation in the construction or upon the receipt of payment by the Contractor, whichever occurs first, free and clear of all liens, claims, security interests or encumbrances, hereinafter referred to in this Article 9 as "liens"; and that no Work, materials or equipment covered by an Application for Payment will have been acquired by the Contractor, or by any other person performing Work at the site or furnishing materials and equipment for the Project, subject to an agreement under which an interest therein or an encumbrance thereon is retained by the seller or otherwise imposed by the Contractor or such other person.

9.4 CERTIFICATES FOR PAYMENT

9.4.1 The Architect will, within seven days after the receipt of the Contractor's Application for Payment, either issue a Certificate for Payment to the Owner, with a copy to the Contractor, for such amount as the Architect determines is properly due, or notify the Contractor in writing his reasons for withholding a Certificate as provided in Subparagraph 9.6.1.

9.4.2 The issuance of a Certificate for Payment will constitute a representation by the Architect to the Owner, based on his observations at the site as provided in Subparagraph 2.2.3 and the data comprising the Application for Payment, that the Work has progressed to the point indicated; that, to the best of his knowledge, information and belief, the quality of the Work is in accordance with the Contract Documents (subject to an evaluation of the Work for conformance with the Contract Documents upon Substantial Completion, to the results of any subsequent tests required by or performed under the Contract Documents, to minor deviations from the Contract Documents correctable prior to completion, and to any specific qualifications stated in his Certificate); and that the Contractor is entitled to payment in the amount certified. However, by issuing a Certificate for Payment, the Architect shall not thereby be deemed to represent that he has made exhaustive or continuous on-site inspections to check the quality or quantity of the Work or that he has reviewed the construction means, methods, techniques, sequences or procedures, or that he has made any examination to ascertain how or for what purpose the Contractor has used the moneys previously paid on account of the Contract Sum.

9.5 PROGRESS PAYMENTS

9.5.1 After the Architect has issued a Certificate for Payment, the Owner shall make payment in the manner and within the time provided in the Contract Documents.

9.5.2 The Contractor shall promptly pay each Subcontractor, upon receipt of payment from the Owner, out of the amount paid to the Contractor on account of such Subcontractor's Work, the amount to which said Subcontractor is entitled, reflecting the percentage actually retained, if any, from payments to the Contractor on account of such Subcontractor's Work. The Contractor shall, by an appropriate agreement with each Subcontractor, require each Subcontractor to make payments to his Subsubcontractors in similar manner.

9.5.3 The Architect may, on request and at his discretion, furnish to any Subcontractor, if practicable, information regarding the percentages of completion or the amounts applied for by the Contractor and the action taken thereon by the Architect on account of Work done by such Subcontractor.

9.5.4 Neither the Owner nor the Architect shall have any obligation to pay or to see to the payment of any moneys to any Subcontractor except as may otherwise be required by law.

9.5.5 No Certificate for a progress payment, nor any progress payment, nor any partial or entire use or occupancy of the Project by the Owner, shall constitute an acceptance of any Work not in accordance with the Contract Documents.

9.6 PAYMENTS WITHHELD

9.6.1 The Architect may decline to certify payment and may withhold his Certificate in whole or in part, to the extent necessary reasonably to protect the Owner, if in his opinion he is unable to make representations to the Owner as provided in Subparagraph 9.4.2. If the Architect is unable to make representations to the Owner as provided in Subparagraph 9.4.2 and to certify payment in the amount of the Application, he will notify the Contractor as provided in Subparagraph 9.4.1. If the Contractor and the Architect cannot agree on a revised amount, the Architect will promptly issue a Certificate for Payment for the amount for which he is able to make such representations to the Owner. The Architect may also decline to certify payment or, because of subsequently discovered evidence or subsequent observations, he may nullify the whole or any part of any Certificate for Payment previously issued, to such extent as may be necessary in his opinion to protect the Owner from loss because of:

.1 defective Work not remedied,

.2 third party claims filed or reasonable evidence indicating probable filing of such claims,

.3 failure of the Contractor to make payments properly to Subcontractors or for labor, materials or equipment,

.4 reasonable evidence that the Work cannot be completed for the unpaid balance of the Contract Sum,

.5 damage to the Owner or another contractor,

.6 reasonable evidence that the Work will not be completed within the Contract Time, or

.7 persistent failure to carry out the Work in accordance with the Contract Documents.

9.6.2 When the above grounds in Subparagraph 9.6.1 are removed, payment shall be made for amounts withheld because of them.

9.7 FAILURE OF PAYMENT

9.7.1 If the Architect does not issue a Certificate for Payment, through no fault of the Contractor, within seven days after receipt of the Contractor's Application for Payment, or if the Owner does not pay the Contractor within seven days after the date established in the Contract Documents any amount certified by the Architect or awarded by arbitration, then the Contractor may, upon seven additional days' written notice to the Owner and the Architect, stop the Work until payment of the amount owing has been received. The Contract Sum shall be increased by the amount of the Contractor's reasonable costs of shut-down, delay and start-up, which shall be effected by appropriate Change Order in accordance with Paragraph 12.3.

9.8 SUBSTANTIAL COMPLETION

9.8.1 When the Contractor considers that the Work, or a designated portion thereof which is acceptable to the Owner, is substantially complete as defined in Subparagraph 8.1.3, the Contractor shall prepare for submission to the Architect a list of items to be completed or corrected. The failure to include any items on such list does not alter the responsibility of the Contractor to complete all Work in accordance with the Contract Documents. When the Architect on the basis of an inspection determines that the Work or designated portion thereof is substantially complete, he will then prepare a Certificate of Substantial Completion which shall establish the Date of Substantial Completion, shall state the responsibilities of the Owner and the Contractor for security, maintenance, heat, utilities, damage to the Work, and insurance, and shall fix the time within which the Contractor shall complete the items listed therein. Warranties required by the Contract Documents shall commence on the Date of Substantial Completion of the Work or designated portion thereof unless otherwise provided in the Certificate of Substantial Completion. The Certificate of Substantial Completion shall be submitted to the Owner and the Contractor for their written acceptance of the responsibilities assigned to them in such Certificate.

9.8.2 Upon Substantial Completion of the Work or designated portion thereof and upon application by the Contractor and certification by the Architect, the Owner shall make payment, reflecting adjustment in retainage, if any, for such Work or portion thereof, as provided in the Contract Documents.

9.9 FINAL COMPLETION AND FINAL PAYMENT

9.9.1 Upon receipt of written notice that the Work is ready for final inspection and acceptance and upon receipt of a final Application for Payment, the Architect will

AIA DOCUMENT A201 • GENERAL CONDITIONS OF THE CONTRACT FOR CONSTRUCTION • THIRTEENTH EDITION • AUGUST 1976
AIA® • © 1976 • THE AMERICAN INSTITUTE OF ARCHITECTS, 1735 NEW YORK AVENUE, N.W., WASHINGTON, D.C. 20006

promptly make such inspection and, when he finds the Work acceptable under the Contract Documents and the Contract fully performed, he will promptly issue a final Certificate for Payment stating that to the best of his knowledge, information and belief, and on the basis of his observations and inspections, the Work has been completed in accordance with the terms and conditions of the Contract Documents and that the entire balance found to be due the Contractor and noted in said final Certificate, is due and payable. The Architect's final Certificate for Payment will constitute a further representation that the conditions precedent to the Contractor's being entitled to final payment as set forth in Subparagraph 9.9.2 have been fulfilled.

9.9.2 Neither the final payment nor the remaining retained percentage shall become due until the Contractor submits to the Architect (1) an affidavit that all payrolls, bills for materials and equipment, and other indebtedness connected with the Work for which the Owner or his property might in any way be responsible, have been paid or otherwise satisfied, (2) consent of surety, if any, to final payment and (3), if required by the Owner, other data establishing payment or satisfaction of all such obligations, such as receipts, releases and waivers of liens arising out of the Contract, to the extent and in such form as may be designated by the Owner. If any Subcontractor refuses to furnish a release or waiver required by the Owner, the Contractor may furnish a bond satisfactory to the Owner to indemnify him against any such lien. If any such lien remains unsatisfied after all payments are made, the Contractor shall refund to the Owner all moneys that the latter may be compelled to pay in discharging such lien, including all costs and reasonable attorneys' fees.

9.9.3 If, after Substantial Completion of the Work, final completion thereof is materially delayed through no fault of the Contractor or by the issuance of Change Orders affecting final completion, and the Architect so confirms, the Owner shall, upon application by the Contractor and certification by the Architect, and without terminating the Contract, make payment of the balance due for that portion of the Work fully completed and accepted. If the remaining balance for Work not fully completed or corrected is less than the retainage stipulated in the Contract Documents, and if bonds have been furnished as provided in Paragraph 7.5, the written consent of the surety to the payment of the balance due for that portion of the Work fully completed and accepted shall be submitted by the Contractor to the Architect prior to certification of such payment. Such payment shall be made under the terms and conditions governing final payment, except that it shall not constitute a waiver of claims.

9.9.4 The making of final payment shall constitute a waiver of all claims by the Owner except those arising from:

.1 unsettled liens,

.2 faulty or defective Work appearing after Substantial Completion,

.3 failure of the Work to comply with the requirements of the Contract Documents, or

.4 terms of any special warranties required by the Contract Documents.

9.9.5 The acceptance of final payment shall constitute a waiver of all claims by the Contractor except those previously made in writing and identified by the Contractor as unsettled at the time of the final Application for Payment.

ARTICLE 10
PROTECTION OF PERSONS AND PROPERTY

10.1   SAFETY PRECAUTIONS AND PROGRAMS

10.1.1 The Contractor shall be responsible for initiating, maintaining and supervising all safety precautions and programs in connection with the Work.

10.2   SAFETY OF PERSONS AND PROPERTY

10.2.1 The Contractor shall take all reasonable precautions for the safety of, and shall provide all reasonable protection to prevent damage, injury or loss to:

.1 all employees on the Work and all other persons who may be affected thereby;

.2 all the Work and all materials and equipment to be incorporated therein, whether in storage on or off the site, under the care, custody or control of the Contractor or any of his Subcontractors or Sub-subcontractors; and

.3 other property at the site or adjacent thereto, including trees, shrubs, lawns, walks, pavements, roadways, structures and utilities not designated for removal, relocation or replacement in the course of construction.

10.2.2 The Contractor shall give all notices and comply with all applicable laws, ordinances, rules, regulations and lawful orders of any public authority bearing on the safety of persons or property or their protection from damage, injury or loss.

10.2.3 The Contractor shall erect and maintain, as required by existing conditions and progress of the Work, all reasonable safeguards for safety and protection, including posting danger signs and other warnings against hazards, promulgating safety regulations and notifying owners and users of adjacent utilities.

10.2.4 When the use or storage of explosives or other hazardous materials or equipment is necessary for the execution of the Work, the Contractor shall exercise the utmost care and shall carry on such activities under the supervision of properly qualified personnel.

10.2.5 The Contractor shall promptly remedy all damage or loss (other than damage or loss insured under Paragraph 11.3) to any property referred to in Clauses 10.2.1.2 and 10.2.1.3 caused in whole or in part by the Contractor, any Subcontractor, any Sub-subcontractor, or anyone directly or indirectly employed by any of them, or by anyone for whose acts any of them may be liable and for which the Contractor is responsible under Clauses 10.2.1.2 and 10.2.1.3, except damage or loss attributable to the acts or omissions of the Owner or Architect or anyone directly or indirectly employed by either of them, or by anyone for whose acts either of them may be liable, and not attributable to the fault or negligence of the Contractor. The foregoing obligations of the Contractor are in addition to his obligations under Paragraph 4.18.

10.2.6 The Contractor shall designate a responsible member of his organization at the site whose duty shall be the prevention of accidents. This person shall be the Contractor's superintendent unless otherwise designated by the Contractor in writing to the Owner and the Architect.

10.2.7 The Contractor shall not load or permit any part of the Work to be loaded so as to endanger its safety.

10.3 EMERGENCIES

10.3.1 In any emergency affecting the safety of persons or property, the Contractor shall act, at his discretion, to prevent threatened damage, injury or loss. Any additional compensation or extension of time claimed by the Contractor on account of emergency work shall be determined as provided in Article 12 for Changes in the Work.

ARTICLE 11

INSURANCE

11.1 CONTRACTOR'S LIABILITY INSURANCE

11.1.1 The Contractor shall purchase and maintain such insurance as will protect him from claims set forth below which may arise out of or result from the Contractor's operations under the Contract, whether such operations be by himself or by any Subcontractor or by anyone directly or indirectly employed by any of them, or by anyone for whose acts any of them may be liable:

.1 claims under workers' or workmen's compensation, disability benefit and other similar employee benefit acts;

.2 claims for damages because of bodily injury, occupational sickness or disease, or death of his employees;

.3 claims for damages because of bodily injury, sickness or disease, or death of any person other than his employees;

.4 claims for damages insured by usual personal injury liability coverage which are sustained (1) by any person as a result of an offense directly or indirectly related to the employment of such person by the Contractor, or (2) by any other person;

.5 claims for damages, other than to the Work itself, because of injury to or destruction of tangible property, including loss of use resulting therefrom; and

.6 claims for damages because of bodily injury or death of any person or property damage arising out of the ownership, maintenance or use of any motor vehicle.

11.1.2 The insurance required by Subparagraph 11.1.1 shall be written for not less than any limits of liability specified in the Contract Documents, or required by law, whichever is greater.

11.1.3 The insurance required by Subparagraph 11.1.1 shall include contractual liability insurance applicable to the Contractor's obligations under Paragraph 4.18.

11.1.4 Certificates of Insurance acceptable to the Owner shall be filed with the Owner prior to commencement of the Work. These Certificates shall contain a provision that coverages afforded under the policies will not be cancelled until at least thirty days' prior written notice has been given to the Owner.

11.2 OWNER'S LIABILITY INSURANCE

11.2.1 The Owner shall be responsible for purchasing and maintaining his own liability insurance and, at his option, may purchase and maintain such insurance as will protect him against claims which may arise from operations under the Contract.

11.3 PROPERTY INSURANCE

11.3.1 Unless otherwise provided, the Owner shall purchase and maintain property insurance upon the entire Work at the site to the full insurable value thereof. This insurance shall include the interests of the Owner, the Contractor, Subcontractors and Sub-subcontractors in the Work and shall insure against the perils of fire and extended coverage and shall include "all risk" insurance for physical loss or damage including, without duplication of coverage, theft, vandalism and malicious mischief. If the Owner does not intend to purchase such insurance for the full insurable value of the entire Work, he shall inform the Contractor in writing prior to commencement of the Work. The Contractor may then effect insurance which will protect the interests of himself, his Subcontractors and the Sub-subcontractors in the Work, and by appropriate Change Order the cost thereof shall be charged to the Owner. If the Contractor is damaged by failure of the Owner to purchase or maintain such insurance and to so notify the Contractor, then the Owner shall bear all reasonable costs properly attributable thereto. If not covered under the all risk insurance or otherwise provided in the Contract Documents, the Contractor shall effect and maintain similar property insurance on portions of the Work stored off the site or in transit when such portions of the Work are to be included in an Application for Payment under Subparagraph 9.3.2.

11.3.2 The Owner shall purchase and maintain such boiler and machinery insurance as may be required by the Contract Documents or by law. This insurance shall include the interests of the Owner, the Contractor, Subcontractors and Sub-subcontractors in the Work.

11.3.3 Any loss insured under Subparagraph 11.3.1 is to be adjusted with the Owner and made payable to the Owner as trustee for the insureds, as their interests may appear, subject to the requirements of any applicable mortgagee clause and of Subparagraph 11.3.8. The Contractor shall pay each Subcontractor a just share of any insurance moneys received by the Contractor, and by appropriate agreement, written where legally required for validity, shall require each Subcontractor to make payments to his Sub-subcontractors in similar manner.

11.3.4 The Owner shall file a copy of all policies with the Contractor before an exposure to loss may occur.

11.3.5 If the Contractor requests in writing that insurance for risks other than those described in Subparagraphs 11.3.1 and 11.3.2 or other special hazards be included in the property insurance policy, the Owner shall, if possible, include such insurance, and the cost thereof shall be charged to the Contractor by appropriate Change Order.

11.3.6 The Owner and Contractor waive all rights against (1) each other and the Subcontractors, Sub-subcontractors, agents and employees each of the other, and (2) the Architect and separate contractors, if any, and their sub-contractors, sub-subcontractors, agents and employees, for damages caused by fire or other perils to the extent covered by insurance obtained pursuant to this Paragraph 11.3 or any other property insurance applicable to the Work, except such rights as they may have to the pro-ceeds of such insurance held by the Owner as trustee. The foregoing waiver afforded the Architect, his agents and employees shall not extend to the liability imposed by Subparagraph 4.18.3. The Owner or the Contractor, as appropriate, shall require of the Architect, separate con-tractors, Subcontractors and Sub-subcontractors by ap-propriate agreements, written where legally required for validity, similar waivers each in favor of all other parties enumerated in this Subparagraph 11.3.6.

11.3.7 If required in writing by any party in interest, the Owner as trustee shall, upon the occurrence of an insured loss, give bond for the proper performance of his duties. He shall deposit in a separate account any money so re-ceived, and he shall distribute it in accordance with such agreement as the parties in interest may reach, or in ac-cordance with an award by arbitration in which case the procedure shall be as provided in Paragraph 7.9. If after such loss no other special agreement is made, replace-ment of damaged work shall be covered by an appropri-ate Change Order.

11.3.8 The Owner as trustee shall have power to adjust and settle any loss with the insurers unless one of the parties in interest shall object in writing within five days after the occurrence of loss to the Owner's exercise of this power, and if such objection be made, arbitrators shall be chosen as provided in Paragraph 7.9. The Owner as trustee shall, in that case, make settlement with the insurers in accordance with the directions of such arbitrators. If dis-tribution of the insurance proceeds by arbitration is re-quired, the arbitrators will direct such distribution.

11.3.9 If the Owner finds it necessary to occupy or use a portion or portions of the Work prior to Substantial Com-pletion thereof, such occupancy or use shall not com-mence prior to a time mutually agreed to by the Owner and Contractor and to which the insurance company or companies providing the property insurance have con-sented by endorsement to the policy or policies. This in-surance shall not be cancelled or lapsed on account of such partial occupancy or use. Consent of the Contractor and of the insurance company or companies to such occupancy or use shall not be unreasonably withheld.

11.4   LOSS OF USE INSURANCE

11.4.1 The Owner, at his option, may purchase and main-tain such insurance as will insure him against loss of use of his property due to fire or other hazards, however caused. The Owner waives all rights of action against the Contractor for loss of use of his property, including con-sequential losses due to fire or other hazards however caused, to the extent covered by insurance under this Paragraph 11.4.

ARTICLE 12

CHANGES IN THE WORK

12.1   CHANGE ORDERS

12.1.1 A Change Order is a written order to the Contrac-tor signed by the Owner and the Architect, issued after execution of the Contract, authorizing a change in the Work or an adjustment in the Contract Sum or the Con-tract Time. The Contract Sum and the Contract Time may be changed only by Change Order. A Change Order signed by the Contractor indicates his agreement there-with, including the adjustment in the Contract Sum or the Contract Time.

12.1.2 The Owner, without invalidating the Contract, may order changes in the Work within the general scope of the Contract consisting of additions, deletions or other revisions, the Contract Sum and the Contract Time being adjusted accordingly. All such changes in the Work shall be authorized by Change Order, and shall be performed under the applicable conditions of the Contract Docu-ments.

12.1.3 The cost or credit to the Owner resulting from a change in the Work shall be determined in one or more of the following ways:

.1 by mutual acceptance of a lump sum properly itemized and supported by sufficient substantiating data to permit evaluation;

.2 by unit prices stated in the Contract Documents or subsequently agreed upon;

.3 by cost to be determined in a manner agreed upon by the parties and a mutually acceptable fixed or percentage fee; or

.4 by the method provided in Subparagraph 12.1.4.

12.1.4 If none of the methods set forth in Clauses 12.1.3.1, 12.1.3.2 or 12.1.3.3 is agreed upon, the Contrac-tor, provided he receives a written order signed by the Owner, shall promptly proceed with the Work involved. The cost of such Work shall then be determined by the Architect on the basis of the reasonable expenditures and savings of those performing the Work attributable to the change, including, in the case of an increase in the Con-tract Sum, a reasonable allowance for overhead and profit. In such case, and also under Clauses 12.1.3.3 and 12.1.3.4 above, the Contractor shall keep and present, in such form as the Architect may prescribe, an itemized account-ing together with appropriate supporting data for inclu-sion in a Change Order. Unless otherwise provided in the Contract Documents, cost shall be limited to the fol-lowing: cost of materials, including sales tax and cost of delivery; cost of labor, including social security, old age and unemployment insurance, and fringe benefits re-quired by agreement or custom; workers' or workmen's compensation insurance; bond premiums; rental value of equipment and machinery; and the additional costs of supervision and field office personnel directly attributable to the change. Pending final determination of cost to the Owner, payments on account shall be made on the Archi-tect's Certificate for Payment. The amount of credit to be allowed by the Contractor to the Owner for any deletion or change which results in a net decrease in the Contract Sum will be the amount of the actual net cost as confirmed by the Architect. When both additions and credits covering related Work or substitutions are involved in any one change, the allowance for overhead and profit shall be figured on the basis of the net increase, if any, with respect to that change.

12.1.5 If unit prices are stated in the Contract Documents or subsequently agreed upon, and if the quantities originally contemplated are so changed in a proposed Change Order that application of the agreed unit prices to the quantities of Work proposed will cause substantial inequity to the Owner or the Contractor, the applicable unit prices shall be equitably adjusted.

12.2   CONCEALED CONDITIONS

12.2.1 Should concealed conditions encountered in the performance of the Work below the surface of the ground or should concealed or unknown conditions in an existing structure be at variance with the conditions indicated by the Contract Documents, or should unknown physical conditions below the surface of the ground or should concealed or unknown conditions in an existing structure of an unusual nature, differing materially from those ordinarily encountered and generally recognized as inherent in work of the character provided for in this Contract, be encountered, the Contract Sum shall be equitably adjusted by Change Order upon claim by either party made within twenty days after the first observance of the conditions.

12.3   CLAIMS FOR ADDITIONAL COST

12.3.1 If the Contractor wishes to make a claim for an increase in the Contract Sum, he shall give the Architect written notice thereof within twenty days after the occurrence of the event giving rise to such claim. This notice shall be given by the Contractor before proceeding to execute the Work, except in an emergency endangering life or property in which case the Contractor shall proceed in accordance with Paragraph 10.3. No such claim shall be valid unless so made. If the Owner and the Contractor cannot agree on the amount of the adjustment in the Contract Sum, it shall be determined by the Architect. Any change in the Contract Sum resulting from such claim shall be authorized by Change Order.

12.3.2 If the Contractor claims that additional cost is involved because of, but not limited to, (1) any written interpretation pursuant to Subparagraph 2.2.8, (2) any order by the Owner to stop the Work pursuant to Paragraph 3.3 where the Contractor was not at fault, (3) any written order for a minor change in the Work issued pursuant to Paragraph 12.4, or (4) failure of payment by the Owner pursuant to Paragraph 9.7, the Contractor shall make such claim as provided in Subparagraph 12.3.1.

12.4   MINOR CHANGES IN THE WORK

12.4.1 The Architect will have authority to order minor changes in the Work not involving an adjustment in the Contract Sum or an extension of the Contract Time and not inconsistent with the intent of the Contract Documents. Such changes shall be effected by written order, and shall be binding on the Owner and the Contractor.

The Contractor shall carry out such written orders promptly.

ARTICLE 13

UNCOVERING AND CORRECTION OF WORK

13.1   UNCOVERING OF WORK

13.1.1 If any portion of the Work should be covered contrary to the request of the Architect or to requirements specifically expressed in the Contract Documents, it must, if required in writing by the Architect, be uncovered for his observation and shall be replaced at the Contractor's expense.

13.1.2 If any other portion of the Work has been covered which the Architect has not specifically requested to observe prior to being covered, the Architect may request to see such Work and it shall be uncovered by the Contractor. If such Work be found in accordance with the Contract Documents, the cost of uncovering and replacement shall, by appropriate Change Order, be charged to the Owner. If such Work be found not in accordance with the Contract Documents, the Contractor shall pay such costs unless it be found that this condition was caused by the Owner or a separate contractor as provided in Article 6, in which event the Owner shall be responsible for the payment of such costs.

13.2   CORRECTION OF WORK

13.2.1 The Contractor shall promptly correct all Work rejected by the Architect as defective or as failing to conform to the Contract Documents whether observed before or after Substantial Completion and whether or not fabricated, installed or completed. The Contractor shall bear all costs of correcting such rejected Work, including compensation for the Architect's additional services made necessary thereby.

13.2.2 If, within one year after the Date of Substantial Completion of the Work or designated portion thereof or within one year after acceptance by the Owner of designated equipment or within such longer period of time as may be prescribed by law or by the terms of any applicable special warranty required by the Contract Documents, any of the Work is found to be defective or not in accordance with the Contract Documents, the Contractor shall correct it promptly after receipt of a written notice from the Owner to do so unless the Owner has previously given the Contractor a written acceptance of such condition. This obligation shall survive termination of the Contract. The Owner shall give such notice promptly after discovery of the condition.

13.2.3 The Contractor shall remove from the site all portions of the Work which are defective or non-conforming and which have not been corrected under Subparagraphs 4.5.1, 13.2.1 and 13.2.2, unless removal is waived by the Owner.

13.2.4 If the Contractor fails to correct defective or non-conforming Work as provided in Subparagraphs 4.5.1, 13.2.1 and 13.2.2, the Owner may correct it in accordance with Paragraph 3.4.

13.2.5 If the Contractor does not proceed with the correction of such defective or non-conforming Work within a reasonable time fixed by written notice from the Architect, the Owner may remove it and may store the materials or equipment at the expense of the Contractor. If the Contractor does not pay the cost of such removal and storage within ten days thereafter, the Owner may upon ten additional days' written notice sell such Work at auction or at private sale and shall account for the net proceeds thereof, after deducting all the costs that should have been borne by the Contractor, including compensation for the Architect's additional services made necessary thereby. If such proceeds of sale do not cover all costs which the Contractor should have borne, the difference shall be charged to the Contractor and an appropriate Change Order shall be issued. If the payments then or thereafter due the Contractor are not sufficient to cover such amount, the Contractor shall pay the difference to the Owner.

13.2.6 The Contractor shall bear the cost of making good all work of the Owner or separate contractors destroyed or damaged by such correction or removal.

13.2.7 Nothing contained in this Paragraph 13.2 shall be construed to establish a period of limitation with respect to any other obligation which the Contractor might have under the Contract Documents, including Paragraph 4.5 hereof. The establishment of the time period of one year after the Date of Substantial Completion or such longer period of time as may be prescribed by law or by the terms of any warranty required by the Contract Documents relates only to the specific obligation of the Contractor to correct the Work, and has no relationship to the time within which his obligation to comply with the Contract Documents may be sought to be enforced, nor to the time within which proceedings may be commenced to establish the Contractor's liability with respect to his obligations other than specifically to correct the Work.

13.3   ACCEPTANCE OF DEFECTIVE OR NON-CONFORMING WORK

13.3.1 If the Owner prefers to accept defective or non-conforming Work, he may do so instead of requiring its removal and correction, in which case a Change Order will be issued to reflect a reduction in the Contract Sum where appropriate and equitable. Such adjustment shall be effected whether or not final payment has been made.

ARTICLE 14

TERMINATION OF THE CONTRACT

14.1   TERMINATION BY THE CONTRACTOR

14.1.1 If the Work is stopped for a period of thirty days under an order of any court or other public authority having jurisdiction, or as a result of an act of government, such as a declaration of a national emergency making materials unavailable, through no act or fault of the Contractor or a Subcontractor or their agents or employees or any other persons performing any of the Work under a contract with the Contractor, or if the Work should be stopped for a period of thirty days by the Contractor because the Architect has not issued a Certificate for Payment as provided in Paragraph 9.7 or because the Owner has not made payment thereon as provided in Paragraph 9.7, then the Contractor may, upon seven additional days' written notice to the Owner and the Architect, terminate the Contract and recover from the Owner payment for all Work executed and for any proven loss sustained upon any materials, equipment, tools, construction equipment and machinery, including reasonable profit and damages.

14.2   TERMINATION BY THE OWNER

14.2.1 If the Contractor is adjudged a bankrupt, or if he makes a general assignment for the benefit of his creditors, or if a receiver is appointed on account of his insolvency, or if he persistently or repeatedly refuses or fails, except in cases for which extension of time is provided, to supply enough properly skilled workmen or proper materials, or if he fails to make prompt payment to Subcontractors or for materials or labor, or persistently disregards laws, ordinances, rules, regulations or orders of any public authority having jurisdiction, or otherwise is guilty of a substantial violation of a provision of the Contract Documents, then the Owner, upon certification by the Architect that sufficient cause exists to justify such action, may, without prejudice to any right or remedy and after giving the Contractor and his surety, if any, seven days' written notice, terminate the employment of the Contractor and take possession of the site and of all materials, equipment, tools, construction equipment and machinery thereon owned by the Contractor and may finish the Work by whatever method he may deem expedient. In such case the Contractor shall not be entitled to receive any further payment until the Work is finished.

14.2.2 If the unpaid balance of the Contract Sum exceeds the costs of finishing the Work, including compensation for the Architect's additional services made necessary thereby, such excess shall be paid to the Contractor. If such costs exceed the unpaid balance, the Contractor shall pay the difference to the Owner. The amount to be paid to the Contractor or to the Owner, as the case may be, shall be certified by the Architect, upon application, in the manner provided in Paragraph 9.4, and this obligation for payment shall survive the termination of the Contract.

STANDARD FORM OF AGREEMENT BETWEEN OWNER AND CONTRACTOR

AIA Document A101

THE AMERICAN INSTITUTE OF ARCHITECTS

AIA Document A101

Standard Form of Agreement Between Owner and Contractor

where the basis of payment is a

STIPULATED SUM

1977 EDITION

THIS DOCUMENT HAS IMPORTANT LEGAL CONSEQUENCES; CONSULTATION WITH AN ATTORNEY IS ENCOURAGED WITH RESPECT TO ITS COMPLETION OR MODIFICATION

Use only with the 1976 Edition of AIA Document A201, General Conditions of the Contract for Construction.

This document has been approved and endorsed by The Associated General Contractors of America.

AGREEMENT

made as of the   day of   in the year of Nineteen
Hundred and

BETWEEN the Owner:

and the Contractor:

The Project:

The Architect:

The Owner and the Contractor agree as set forth below.

ARTICLE 1

THE CONTRACT DOCUMENTS

The Contract Documents consist of this Agreement, the Conditions of the Contract (General, Supplementary and other Conditions), the Drawings, the Specifications, all Addenda issued prior to and all Modifications issued after execution of this Agreement. These form the Contract, and all are as fully a part of the Contract as if attached to this Agreement or repeated herein. An enumeration of the Contract Documents appears in Article 7.

ARTICLE 2

THE WORK

The Contractor shall perform all the Work required by the Contract Documents for

(Here insert the caption descriptive of the Work as used on other Contract Documents.)

ARTICLE 3

TIME OF COMMENCEMENT AND SUBSTANTIAL COMPLETION

The Work to be performed under this Contract shall be commenced

and, subject to authorized adjustments, Substantial Completion shall be achieved not later than

(Here insert any special provisions for liquidated damages relating to failure to complete on time.)

ARTICLE 4
CONTRACT SUM

The Owner shall pay the Contractor in current funds for the performance of the Work, subject to additions and deductions by Change Order as provided in the Contract Documents, the Contract Sum of

The Contract Sum is determined as follows:
(State here the base bid or other lump sum amount, accepted alternates, and unit prices, as applicable.)

ARTICLE 5
PROGRESS PAYMENTS

Based upon Applications for Payment submitted to the Architect by the Contractor and Certificates for Payment issued by the Architect, the Owner shall make progress payments on account of the Contract Sum to the Contractor as provided in the Contract Documents for the period ending the   day of the month as follows:

Not later than   days following the end of the period covered by the Application for Payment   percent (%) of the portion of the Contract Sum properly allocable to labor, materials and equipment incorporated in the Work and   percent (%) of the portion of the Contract Sum properly allocable to materials and equipment suitably stored at the site or at some other location agreed upon in writing, for the period covered by the Application for Payment, less the aggregate of previous payments made by the Owner; and upon Substantial Completion of the entire Work, a sum sufficient to increase the total payments to   percent (%) of the Contract Sum, less such amounts as the Architect shall determine for all incomplete Work and unsettled claims as provided in the Contract Documents.

(If not covered elsewhere in the Contract Documents, here insert any provision for limiting or reducing the amount retained after the Work reaches a certain stage of completion.)

Payments due and unpaid under the Contract Documents shall bear interest from the date payment is due at the rate entered below, or in the absence thereof, at the legal rate prevailing at the place of the Project.
(Here insert any rate of interest agreed upon.)

(Usury laws and requirements under the Federal Truth in Lending Act, similar state and local consumer credit laws and other regulations at the Owner's and Contractor's principal places of business, the location of the Project and elsewhere may affect the validity of this provision. Specific legal advice should be obtained with respect to deletion, modification, or other requirements such as written disclosures or waivers.)

ARTICLE 6

FINAL PAYMENT

Final payment, constituting the entire unpaid balance of the Contract Sum, shall be paid by the Owner to the Contractor when the Work has been completed, the Contract fully performed, and a final Certificate for Payment has been issued by the Architect.

ARTICLE 7

MISCELLANEOUS PROVISIONS

7.1 Terms used in this Agreement which are defined in the Conditions of the Contract shall have the meanings designated in those Conditions.

7.2 The Contract Documents, which constitute the entire agreement between the Owner and the Contractor, are listed in Article 1 and, except for Modifications issued after execution of this Agreement, are enumerated as follows:

(List below the Agreement, the Conditions of the Contract (General, Supplementary, and other Conditions), the Drawings, the Specifications, and any Addenda and accepted alternates, showing page or sheet numbers in all cases and dates where applicable.)

This Agreement entered into as of the day and year first written above.

OWNER   CONTRACTOR

_____   _____

_____   _____

_____   _____

STANDARD FORM OF AGREEMENT BETWEEN CONTRACTOR AND SUBCONTRACTOR

AIA Document A401

THE AMERICAN INSTITUTE OF ARCHITECTS

AIA Document A401

SUBCONTRACT

Standard Form of Agreement Between Contractor and Subcontractor

1978 EDITION

Use with the latest edition of the appropriate AIA Documents as follows:

A101, Owner-Contractor Agreement — Stipulated Sum
A107, Abbreviated Owner-Contractor Agreement with General Conditions
A111, Owner-Contractor Agreement — Cost Plus Fee
A201, General Conditions of the Contract for Construction.

THIS DOCUMENT HAS IMPORTANT LEGAL CONSEQUENCES; CONSULTATION WITH AN ATTORNEY IS ENCOURAGED WITH RESPECT TO ITS COMPLETION OR MODIFICATION

This document has been approved and endorsed by the American Subcontractors Association and the Associated Specialty Contractors, Inc.

AGREEMENT

made as of the day of in the year Nineteen Hundred and

BETWEEN the Contractor:

and the Subcontractor:

The Project:

The Owner:

The Architect:

The Contractor and Subcontractor agree as set forth below.

ARTICLE 1
THE CONTRACT DOCUMENTS

1.1 The Contract Documents for this Subcontract consist of this Agreement and any Exhibits attached hereto, the Agreement between the Owner and Contractor dated as of , the Conditions of the Contract between the Owner and Contractor (General, Supplementary and other Conditions), the Drawings, the Specifications, all Addenda issued prior to and all Modifications issued after execution of the Agreement between the Owner and Contractor and agreed upon by the parties to this Subcontract. These form the Subcontract, and are as fully a part of the Subcontract as if attached to this Agreement or repeated herein.

1.2 Copies of the above documents which are applicable to the Work under this Subcontract shall be furnished to the Subcontractor upon his request. An enumeration of the applicable Contract Documents appears in Article 15.

ARTICLE 2
THE WORK

2.1 The Subcontractor shall perform all the Work required by the Contract Documents for

(Here insert a precise description of the Work covered by this Subcontract and refer to numbers of Drawings and pages of Specifications including Addenda, Modifications and accepted Alternates.)

ARTICLE 3
TIME OF COMMENCEMENT AND SUBSTANTIAL COMPLETION

3.1 The Work to be performed under this Subcontract shall be commenced and, subject to authorized adjustments, shall be substantially completed not later than

(Here insert the specific provisions that are applicable to this Subcontract including any information pertaining to notice to proceed or other method of modification for commencement of Work, starting and completion dates, or duration, and any provisions for liquidated damages relating to failure to complete on time.)

3.2 Time is of the essence of this Subcontract.

3.3 No extension of time will be valid without the Contractor's written consent after claim made by the Subcontractor in accordance with Paragraph 11.10.

ARTICLE 4
THE CONTRACT SUM

4.1 The Contractor shall pay the Subcontractor in current funds for the performance of the Work, subject to additions and deductions authorized pursuant to Paragraph 11.9, the Contract Sum of

dollars ($).

The Contract Sum is determined as follows:

(State here the base bid or other lump sum amount, accepted alternates, and unit prices, as applicable.)

ARTICLE 5
PROGRESS PAYMENTS

5.1 The Contractor shall pay the Subcontractor monthly progress payments in accordance with Paragraph 12.4 of this Subcontract.

5.2 Applications for monthly progress payments shall be in writing and in accordance with Paragraph 11.8, shall state the estimated percentage of the Work in this Subcontract that has been satisfactorily completed and shall be submitted to the Contractor on or before the   day of each month.

(Here insert details on (1) payment procedures and date of monthly applications, or other procedure if on other than a monthly basis, (2) the basis on which payment will be made on account of materials and equipment suitably stored at the site or other location agreed upon in writing, and (3) any provisions consistent with the Contract Documents for limiting or reducing the amount retained after the Work reaches a certain stage of completion.)

5.3 When the Subcontractor's Work or a designated portion thereof is substantially complete and in accordance with the Contract Documents, the Contractor shall, upon application by the Subcontractor, make prompt application for payment of such Work. Within thirty days following issuance by the Architect of the Certificate for Payment covering such substantially completed Work, the Contractor shall, to the full extent provided in the Contract Documents, make payment to the Subcontractor of the entire unpaid balance of the Contract Sum or of that portion of the Contract Sum attributable to the substantially completed Work, less any portion of the funds for the Subcontractor's Work withheld in accordance with the Certificate to cover costs of items to be completed or corrected by the Subcontractor.

(Delete the above Paragraph if the Contract Documents do not provide for, and the Subcontractor agrees to forego, release of retainage for the Subcontractor's Work prior to completion of the entire Project.)

5.4 Progress payments or final payment due and unpaid under this Subcontract shall bear interest from the date payment is due at the rate entered below or, in the absence thereof, at the legal rate prevailing at the place of the Project.

(Here insert any rate of interest agreed upon.)

(Usury laws and requirements under the Federal Truth in Lending Act, similar state and local consumer credit laws and other regulations at the Owner's, Contractor's and Subcontractor's principal places of business, the location of the Project and elsewhere may affect the validity of this provision. Specific legal advice should be obtained with respect to deletion, modification, or other requirements such as written disclosures or waivers.)

ARTICLE 6
FINAL PAYMENT

6.1 Final payment, constituting the entire unpaid balance of the Contract Sum, shall be due when the Work described in this Subcontract is fully completed and performed in accordance with the Contract Documents and is satisfactory to the Architect, and shall be payable as follows, in accordance with Article 5 and with Paragraph 12.4 of this Subcontract:

(Here insert the relevant conditions under which, or time in which, final payment will become payable.)

6.2 Before issuance of the final payment, the Subcontractor, if required, shall submit evidence satisfactory to the Contractor that all payrolls, bills for materials and equipment, and all known indebtedness connected with the Subcontractor's Work have been satisfied.

ARTICLE 7
PERFORMANCE BOND AND LABOR AND MATERIAL PAYMENT BOND

(Here insert any requirement for the furnishing of bonds by the Subcontractor.)

ARTICLE 8
TEMPORARY FACILITIES AND SERVICES

8.1 Unless otherwise provided in this Subcontract, the Contractor shall furnish and make available at no cost to the Subcontractor the following temporary facilities and services:

ARTICLE 9
INSURANCE

9.1 Prior to starting work, the Subcontractor shall obtain the required insurance from a responsible insurer, and shall furnish satisfactory evidence to the Contractor that the Subcontractor has complied with the requirements of this Article 9. Similarly, the Contractor shall furnish to the Subcontractor satisfactory evidence of insurance required of the Contractor by the Contract Documents.

9.2 The Contractor and Subcontractor waive all rights against each other and against the Owner, the Architect, separate contractors and all other subcontractors for damages caused by fire or other perils to the extent covered by property insurance provided under the General Conditions, except such rights as they may have to the proceeds of such insurance.

(Here insert any insurance requirements and Subcontractor's responsibility for obtaining, maintaining and paying for necessary insurance with limits equaling or exceeding those specified in the Contract Documents and inserted below, or required by law. If applicable, this shall include fire insurance and extended coverage, public liability, property damage, employer's liability, and workers' or workmen's compensation insurance for the Subcontractor and his employees. The insertion should cover provisions for notice of cancellation, allocation of insurance proceeds, and other aspects of insurance.)

ARTICLE 10
WORKING CONDITIONS

(Here insert any applicable arrangements concerning working conditions and labor matters for the Project.)

GENERAL CONDITIONS

ARTICLE 11
SUBCONTRACTOR

11.1 RIGHTS AND RESPONSIBILITIES

11.1.1 The Subcontractor shall be bound to the Contractor by the terms of this Agreement and, to the extent that provisions of the Contract Documents between the Owner and Contractor apply to the Work of the Subcontractor as defined in this Agreement, the Subcontractor shall assume toward the Contractor all the obligations and responsibilities which the Contractor, by those Documents, assumes toward the Owner and the Architect, and shall have the benefit of all rights, remedies and redress against the Contractor which the Contractor, by those Documents, has against the Owner, insofar as applicable to this Subcontract, provided that where any provision of the Contract Documents between the Owner and Contractor is inconsistent with any provision of this Agreement, this Agreement shall govern.

11.1.2 The Subcontractor shall not assign this subcontract without the written consent of the Contractor, nor subcontract the whole of this Subcontract without the written consent of the Contractor, nor further subcontract portions of this Subcontract without written notification to the Contractor when such notification is requested by the Contractor. The Subcontractor shall not assign any amounts due or to become due under this Subcontract without written notice to the Contractor.

11.2 EXECUTION AND PROGRESS OF THE WORK

11.2.1 The Subcontractor agrees that the Contractor's equipment will be available to the Subcontractor only at the Contractor's discretion and on mutually satisfactory terms.

11.2.2 The Subcontractor shall cooperate with the Contractor in scheduling and performing his Work to avoid conflict or interference with the work of others.

11.2.3 The Subcontractor shall promptly submit shop drawings and samples required in order to perform his Work efficiently, expeditiously and in a manner that will not cause delay in the progress of the Work of the Contractor or other subcontractors.

11.2.4 The Subcontractor shall furnish periodic progress reports on the Work as mutually agreed, including information on the status of materials and equipment under this Subcontract which may be in the course of preparation or manufacture.

11.2.5 The Subcontractor agrees that all Work shall be done subject to the final approval of the Architect. The Architect's decisions in matters relating to artistic effect shall be final if consistent with the intent of the Contract Documents.

11.2.6 The Subcontractor shall pay for all materials, equipment and labor used in, or in connection with, the performance of this Subcontract through the period covered by previous payments received from the Contractor, and shall furnish satisfactory evidence, when requested by the Contractor, to verify compliance with the above requirements.

11.3 LAWS, PERMITS, FEES AND NOTICES

11.3.1 The Subcontractor shall give all notices and comply with all laws, ordinances, rules, regulations and orders of any public authority bearing on the performance of the Work under this Subcontract. The Subcontractor shall secure and pay for all permits and governmental fees, licenses and inspections necessary for the proper execution and completion of the Subcontractor's Work, the furnishing of which is required of the Contractor by the Contract Documents.

11.3.2 The Subcontractor shall comply with Federal, State and local tax laws, social security acts, unemployment compensation acts and workers' or workmen's compensation acts insofar as applicable to the performance of this Subcontract.

11.4 WORK OF OTHERS

11.4.1 In carrying out his Work, the Subcontractor shall take necessary precautions to protect properly the finished work of other trades from damage caused by his operations.

11.4.2 The Subcontractor shall cooperate with the Contractor and other subcontractors whose work might interfere with the Subcontractor's Work, and shall participate in the preparation of coordinated drawings in areas of congestion as required by the Contract Documents, specifically noting and advising the Contractor of any such interference.

11.5 SAFETY PRECAUTIONS AND PROCEDURES

11.5.1 The Subcontractor shall take all reasonable safety precautions with respect to his Work, shall comply with all safety measures initiated by the Contractor and with all applicable laws, ordinances, rules, regulations and orders of any public authority for the safety of persons or property in accordance with the requirements of the Contract Documents. The Subcontractor shall report within three days to the Contractor any injury to any of the Subcontractor's employees at the site.

11.6 CLEANING UP

11.6.1 The Subcontractor shall at all times keep the premises free from accumulation of waste materials or rubbish arising out of the operations of this Subcontract. Unless otherwise provided, the Subcontractor shall not be held responsible for unclean conditions caused by other contractors or subcontractors.

11.7 WARRANTY

11.7.1 The Subcontractor warrants to the Owner, the Architect and the Contractor that all materials and equipment furnished shall be new unless otherwise specified, and that all Work under this Subcontract shall be of good quality, free from faults and defects and in conformance with the Contract Documents. All Work not conforming to these requirements, including substitutions not properly approved and authorized, may be considered defec-

AIA DOCUMENT A401 · CONTRACTOR-SUBCONTRACTOR AGREEMENT · ELEVENTH EDITION · APRIL 1978 · AIA®
©1978 · THE AMERICAN INSTITUTE OF ARCHITECTS, 1735 NEW YORK AVE., N.W., WASHINGTON, D.C. 20006

tive. The warranty provided in this Paragraph 11.7 shall be in addition to and not in limitation of any other warranty or remedy required by law or by the Contract Documents.

11.8 APPLICATIONS FOR PAYMENT

11.8.1 The Subcontractor shall submit to the Contractor applications for payment at such times as stipulated in Article 5 to enable the Contractor to apply for payment.

11.8.2 If payments are made on the valuation of Work done, the Subcontractor shall, before the first application, submit to the Contractor a schedule of values of the various parts of the Work aggregating the total sum of this Subcontract, made out in such detail as the Subcontractor and Contractor may agree upon or as required by the Owner, and supported by such evidence as to its correctness as the Contractor may direct. This schedule, when approved by the Contractor, shall be used only as a basis for Applications for Payment, unless it be found to be in error. In applying for payment, the Subcontractor shall submit a statement based upon this schedule.

11.8.3 If payments are made on account of materials or equipment not incorporated in the Work but delivered and suitably stored at the site or at some other location agreed upon in writing, such payments shall be in accordance with the Terms and Conditions of the Contract Documents.

11.9 CHANGES IN THE WORK

11.9.1 The Subcontractor may be ordered in writing by the Contractor, without invalidating this Subcontract, to make changes in the Work within the general scope of this Subcontract consisting of additions, deletions or other revisions, the Contract Sum and the Contract Time being adjusted accordingly. The Subcontractor, prior to the commencement of such changed or revised Work, shall submit promptly to the Contractor written copies of any claim for adjustment to the Contract Sum and Contract Time for such revised Work in a manner consistent with the Contract Documents.

11.10 CLAIMS OF THE SUBCONTRACTOR

11.10.1 The Subcontractor shall make all claims promptly to the Contractor for additional cost, extensions of time, and damages for delays or other causes in accordance with the Contract Documents. Any such claim which will affect or become part of a claim which the Contractor is required to make under the Contract Documents within a specified time period or in a specified manner shall be made in sufficient time to permit the Contractor to satisfy the requirements of the Contract Documents. Such claims shall be received by the Contractor not less than two working days preceding the time by which the Contractor's claim must be made. Failure of the Subcontractor to make such a timely claim shall bind the Subcontractor to the same consequences as those to which the Contractor is bound.

11.11 INDEMNIFICATION

11.11.1 To the fullest extent permitted by law, the Subcontractor shall indemnify and hold harmless the Owner, the Architect and the Contractor and all of their agents and employees from and against all claims, damages, losses and expenses, including but not limited to attorney's fees, arising out of or resulting from the performance of the Subcontractor's Work under this Subcontract, provided that any such claim, damage, loss, or expense is attributable to bodily injury, sickness, disease, or death, or to injury to or destruction of tangible property (other than the Work itself) including the loss of use resulting therefrom, to the extent caused in whole or in part by any negligent act or omission of the Subcontractor or anyone directly or indirectly employed by him or anyone for whose acts he may be liable, regardless of whether it is caused in part by a party indemnified hereunder. Such obligation shall not be construed to negate, or abridge, or otherwise reduce any other right or obligation of indemnity which would otherwise exist as to any party or person described in this Paragraph 11.11.

11.11.2 In any and all claims against the Owner, the Architect, or the Contractor or any of their agents or employees by any employee of the Subcontractor, anyone directly or indirectly employed by him or anyone for whose acts he may be liable, the indemnification obligation under this Paragraph 11.11 shall not be limited in any way by any limitation on the amount or type of damages, compensation or benefits payable by or for the Subcontractor under workers' or workmen's compensation acts, disability benefit acts or other employee benefit acts.

11.11.3 The obligations of the Subcontractor under this Paragraph 11.11 shall not extend to the liability of the Architect, his agents or employees arising out of (1) the preparation or approval of maps, drawings, opinions, reports, surveys, Change Orders, designs or specifications, or (2) the giving of or the failure to give directions or instructions by the Architect, his agents or employees provided such giving or failure to give is the primary cause of the injury or damage.

11.12 SUBCONTRACTOR'S REMEDIES

11.12.1 If the Contractor does not pay the Subcontractor through no fault of the Subcontractor, within seven days from the time payment should be made as provided in Paragraph 12.4, the Subcontractor may, without prejudice to any other remedy he may have, upon seven additional days' written notice to the Contractor, stop his Work until payment of the amount owing has been received. The Contract Sum shall, by appropriate adjustment, be increased by the amount of the Subcontractor's reasonable costs of shutdown, delay and start-up.

ARTICLE 12
CONTRACTOR

12.1 RIGHTS AND RESPONSIBILITIES

12.1.1 The Contractor shall be bound to the Subcontractor by the terms of this Agreement, and to the extent that provisions of the Contract Documents between the Owner and the Contractor apply to the Work of the Subcontractor as defined in this Agreement, the Contractor shall assume toward the Subcontractor all the obligations and responsibilities that the Owner, by those Documents, assumes toward the Contractor, and shall have the benefit of all rights, remedies and redress against the Subcontractor which the Owner, by those Documents, has against the Contractor. Where any provision of the

AIA DOCUMENT A401 • CONTRACTOR-SUBCONTRACTOR AGREEMENT • ELEVENTH EDITION • APRIL 1978 • AIA®
©1978 • THE AMERICAN INSTITUTE OF ARCHITECTS, 1735 NEW YORK AVE., N.W., WASHINGTON, D.C. 20006

INDEX

INDEX